SOPHOCLES

SELECTED FRAGMENTARY PLAYS

VOLUME I

ARIS & PHILLIPS CLASSICAL TEXTS

SOPHOCLES

Selected Fragmentary Plays

with Introductions, Translations and Commentaries by

Alan H. Sommerstein, David Fitzpatrick
and Thomas Talboy

Volume I

Hermione, Polyxene, The Diners, Tereus, Troilus, Phaedra

Aris & Phillips Classical Texts
are published by
Oxbow Books, Park End Place, Oxford OX1 1HN

ISBN 978 0 85668 765 5   0 85668 765 0 cloth
ISBN 978 0 85668 766 2   0 85668 766 9 paper

A CIP record for this book is available from the British Library.

Cover illustration: Procne/Aedon in the act of killing Itys.
After a fragment of a red-figure kylix, perhaps by Onesimos:
Basel (H. Cahn) HC599.

Printed and bound by Short Run Press, Exeter

To the memory

of

MALCOLM WILLCOCK

CONTENTS

PREFACE

This edition was inspired by the edition of selected fragmentary plays of Euripides by Christopher Collard, Martin Cropp and the late Kevin Lee, published in this series in 1995 and recently (2004) followed by a second volume edited by Collard, Cropp and John Gibert. In 1998 Alan Sommerstein, then director of the newly-founded Centre for Ancient Drama and its Reception (CADRE) at the University of Nottingham, established there a project for the study of the fragmentary tragedies of Sophocles, which has had two main outcomes. The first was an international conference, held in Nottingham in July 2000, twenty papers from which (including one by each of the editors of the present volume) were later published as *Shards from Kolonos: Studies in Sophoclean Fragments* (Bari, 2003); the second is the edition of which the present volume is the initial instalment.

The original plan was for an edition comprising some nine or ten plays, with contributions by Alan Sommerstein, David Fitzpatrick, Thomas Talboy and Amy Clark (who was likewise a participant in the 2000 conference and a contributor to *Shards from Kolonos*). There were various subsequent changes to the plan, the most important, and most regretted, occurring when Amy Clark found she would be unable to complete her contribution – comprising the two *Tyro* plays and *Niobe* – within the time scale envisaged, owing to health and other problems. As a result of this the team have decided to bring out a second volume, to which all four members will contribute, and which will contain the three plays just mentioned together with (probably) *Ajax the Locrian, The Epigonoi,* the two *Nauplius* plays, *Oenomaus, The Shepherds* and *Triptolemus*. It is envisaged that this volume will be published in 2010.

We were able to plan the format and norms of the edition at the 2000 conference and at a subsequent meeting in Nottingham; for the most part, however, our collaboration has been by email. It has felt none the less close for that: in the cyberworld there has been no distance between the banks of the Trent and the shores of the Pacific.

Alan Sommerstein has acted as general editor of the volume. The *Tereus* and *Phaedra* sections were drafted by David Fitzpatrick and Thomas Talboy respectively, and revised in close consultation between them and Alan Sommerstein; in the Table of Contents each therefore bears the initials of two editors, and uses of the first person plural in the introductions and commentaries to these plays refer to these two editors unless the context requires a broader interpretation.

Alan Sommerstein gratefully acknowledges the assistance of the Arts and Humanities Research Board (as it then was), which awarded him a semester of research leave in the latter part of 2003, additional to a semester granted by the

University of Nottingham, and thus enabled him to complete in good time his own contribution to this volume. By allowing the Department of Classics to provide replacement teaching during this period, the AHRB also indirectly caused Eleanor OKell to come to Nottingham where her stimulating, questioning presence provided valuable input.

All the editors express their gratitude to the many scholars and students whose comments on various occasions when their ideas have been formally or informally presented have helped to improve the final product offered here, among others to Mary Bachvarova, David Carter, Chris Collard, Michael Halleran, André Lardinois, Nick Lowe, José Maria Lucas de Dios, Jenny March, and Anthony Podlecki. We are particularly grateful to Prof. Peter Parsons and Dr Dirk Obbink for making available to us, in advance of publication, the *editio princeps* of a new Oxyrhynchus papyrus of Sophocles' *Epigonoi*; and above all to Malcolm Willcock, who read the whole volume in proof, made many valuable suggestions, and has greatly improved the accuracy and user-friendliness of the final product.

One of us paid tribute, in a preface to an earlier volume in this series, to Adrian Phillips' long and illustrious stewardship of it. We are very happy now to express our gratitude to David Brown, the proprietor of Oxbow Books, who is worthily maintaining and extending the tradition established by the late John Aris a quarter of a century ago, and to his editors Clare Litt and Tara Evans for their unvarying helpfulness.

* * *

While this book was still in proof, we received the sad news of the death of Malcolm Willcock on 2 May 2006. We are grieved that he was not spared to see the publication of a volume to which he contributed so much, and can only now express our recognition of all he did for it, as well as for the series in which it appears and for many, many aspects of classical scholarship and education, by humbly dedicating the volume to his memory.

May 2006

A.H. Sommerstein
D.G. Fitzpatrick
T.H. Talboy

GENERAL INTRODUCTION

Sophocles' career and oeuvre

Sophocles, son of Sophillus,[1] was a member, and probably a native,[2] of the Athenian deme of Colonus Hippios, a mile or two to the north of (now deep inside) the city. He was born in or close to 496 BC.[3] The first firm date in his dramatic career is 468, when he gained his first victory,[4] probably with a production that included *Triptolemus*;[5] Plutarch[6] claims that this was his first production and that Aeschylus (till then, since the death of Phrynichus, the undisputed master of the tragic scene) was one of the unsuccessful competitors, but another source[7] puts Sophocles' first production in 470, and Plutarch, or the author on whom he is relying, is under considerable suspicion of having improved the story.[8] Over a period of two-thirds of a century he gained a total of eighteen victories according to one source,[9] or twenty-four according to another;[10] probably this means that he won eighteen times at the City Dionysia and six times at the Lenaea, at which there is other evidence that he sometimes competed.[11] His main ancient biographer,[12] on the authority of the great Hellenistic scholar Aristophanes of Byzantium, gives his total output as 130 plays "of

---

[1]This spelling (not "Sophilus") is found in an inscription of 264/3 BC (the *Marmor Parium, FGrH* 239 A 56) and is guaranteed by metre in an epigram of about the same date (*AP* 7.21, by Simias of Rhodes).

[2]His father must have been resident in the deme at the time when the first deme register was compiled in, or soon after, 508/7.

[3]The *Life of Sophocles* (§2) puts his birth in 495/4; D.S. 13.103.4 says he died in 406/5 aged ninety; the *Marmor Parium* (*FGrH* 239 A 56) says he was twenty-eight when he won his first victory in 469/8.

[4]*Marm.Par.* (*FGrH* 239 A 56); Plut. *Cim.* 8.8–9.

[5]Pliny the Elder (*NH* 18.65) says that *Triptolemus* was produced "about 145 years" before the death of Alexander the Great, i.e. about 468 BC.

[6]*Cim.* 8.8–9.

[7]Two versions of the chronicle of Eusebius (Jerome's and the Armenian text) say he brought his work before the public in 471/0; they also say that he "was famous" two or three years later, no doubt referring to his victory in 468.

[8]See S. Scullion, *CQ* 52 (2002) 87–90.

[9]D.S. 13.103.4.

[10]*Suda* σ815. A third source, Carystius reported in *Life of Sophocles* §8, gives the number as 20 (κ΄), but this may just be a scribal error for 24 (κδ΄). The *Life* adds that Sophocles often took second place in the competition, but never third.

[11]*IG* ii² 2319.77–79; see p. 215 below.

[12]*Life of Sophocles* §18.

which 17 are regarded as spurious"; the *Suda* lexicon[13] says he produced 123 plays "or, according to some, many more". These two statements are most easily reconciled by supposing the figure of 17 spurious plays to be an error for 7, which would leave the two sources agreeing on a total of 123 genuine plays. These cannot be put into exact correspondence with the play-titles recorded in ancient sources: sometimes the same title was given to more than one play,[14] sometimes a single play was known by alternative names,[15] and we may not always know when this was the case. Some plays, too, may never have happened to be cited by ancient writers at all: *Eurypylus* is known to us *only* from a set of papyrus fragments,[16] and another papyrus gives us several fragments of a satyr-play about Oeneus[17] whose style strongly suggests it is by Sophocles but for which no suitable Sophoclean title is recorded. However, a figure of 123 genuine plays seems not unreasonable; one might have expected an even number,[18] but possibly Sophocles did not complete the four plays that should have made up his last, posthumous production.[19]

---

[13]*Suda* σ815.

[14]We can only know this when ancient sources actually refer to a "first" and/or a "second" play of the same name, as they do in the case of *Athamas*, *Thyestes* (three plays), *The Lemnian Women*, *Tyro* (see vol. ii) and *Phineus*. There may be other instances of which we happen not to be informed; our knowledge of the existence of the third *Thyestes*, and of two plays called *The Lemnian Women*, depends in each case on a single source.

[15]It is argued in the present volume that *The Gathering of the Achaeans* is identical with *The Diners*, and *The Women of Phthia* with *Hermione*; both identifications are controversial. The only double-titled Sophoclean plays directly attested in ancient sources (just one source each) are *Atreus or The Women of Mycenae* and *Pandora or The Hammerers*.

[16]Strictly speaking, we do not know the title of the play from which these fragments come; but from their content, from the extremely close similarity between the papyrus (*POxy* 1175) containing them and that containing the satyr-play *The Trackers* (*POxy* 1174), and from the apparent coincidence of one partly preserved line (fr. 210.9) with a line quoted by Plutarch (*Mor.* 458d) from a description by Sophocles of "the arming of Neoptolemus and Eurypylus", we can be virtually certain that they are from a play by Sophocles centring on the duel between these two heroes at Troy in which Eurypylus was killed (cf. *Little Iliad* Arg. §3 and fr. 7 West). No known Sophoclean title fits such a play (*Mysians* is excluded, since that play had a chorus of men, whereas the chorus that laments with Eurypylus' mother in fr. 210.30–46 appears to consist of women).

[17]Soph. frr. dub. 1130–3.

[18]Tragic productions at the City Dionysia consisted of four plays, at the Lenaea apparently of two (inferred from *IG* ii² 2319.78–81).

[19]It is also conceivable that Sophocles, though (unlike most leading poets of his time) he never accepted invitations from foreign rulers to visit their courts (*Life of Sophocles* §10),

In his early days Sophocles seems to have benefited from the patronage of a leading political figure, Cimon; whether or not it is true that Cimon was one of the judges responsible for giving Sophocles his first victory in 468,[20] it is certainly significant that it was Sophocles, not the then far more distinguished Aeschylus, who was represented playing a lyre in one of the paintings of the Stoa Poikile in the Agora,[21] a building inspired and largely financed by Cimon and originally named after his brother-in-law.[22] Even after Cimon's death, a first-hand anecdote by Ion of Chios[23] indicates that political relations between Sophocles and Cimon's former rival, Pericles, remained somewhat cool. In his fifties and later, Sophocles was a significant figure in public life; he does not appear to have been prominent as a speaker in the Assembly or the courts,[24] but he was chairman of the Hellenotamiae (the treasurers of the funds of the Athenian Alliance) in 443/2,[25] was elected a year or two later as one of the ten generals[26] and on at least one occasion as an ambassador,[27] and in his mid-eighties was elected again as one of the ten *probouloi* who served as a sort of supervisory board for about eighteen months after the Sicilian disaster (413–411) in which capacity he concurred – though only, he afterwards claimed, *faute de mieux* – in recommending the suspension of sanctions against unconstitutional proposals which made possible the establishment of the oligarchy of the Four Hundred in 411.[28] This episode does not appear to have dented his popularity (he won first prize, with *Philoctetes*,

---

may on some occasion have sent abroad for production a play that he never produced in Athens.

[20]Plut. *Cim.* 8.8–9.

[21]*Life of Sophocles* §3.

[22]It was called the Stoa of Peisianax (Plut. *Cim.* 4.6; D.L. 7.5.5); Peisianax appears to have been a brother of Cimon's wife Isodice (see J.K. Davies, *Athenian Propertied Families 600–300 BC* [Oxford, 1971] 377–9 ["Peisianax II"]).

[23]*FGrH* 392 F 6 (cited by Athenaeus 13.604d): "Pericles said I knew how to write poetry but knew nothing about strategy."

[24]Though he is once found giving a speech in a public prosecution (Arist. *Rhet.* 1374b36–1375a2), and demanding the death penalty for a man who had inflicted such humiliation (*hybris*) on another that the victim had committed suicide. "I will not," Sophocles is reported to have said, "propose a lesser penalty than that which the victim proposed for himself."

[25]*IG* i 3 269.36.

[26]Ion of Chios, *FGrH* 392 F 6; Androtion, *FGrH* 324 F 38; Strabo 14.1.18.

[27]*Life of Sophocles* §1 (end).

[28]Arist. *Rhet.* 1419a26–30.

at the City Dionysia of 409, the first held after the restoration of full democracy).

Sophocles had some connection with the cult of the god (formerly hero) Asclepius, which was introduced to Athens in 421/0, and wrote a paean in his honour;[29] he gave prominence to Asclepius in at least two plays.[30]

Sophocles died, aged about ninety, in the winter of 406/5;[31] the script of Aristophanes' *Frogs*, then nearing production, had to be revised to take account of his death.[32] Among his children[33] were a legitimate son, Iophon, also a tragic dramatist, who apparently did not long survive him,[34] and an illegitimate son Ariston,[35] whose own son, Sophocles the younger, produced his grandfather's last plays, including *Oedipus at Colonus*, in 401,[36] and went on to become himself the leading tragic dramatist of the early fourth century (though not a word of any of his plays survives today).

Only two of Sophocles' seven surviving plays are firmly dated (*Philoctetes* and *Oedipus at Colonus*, mentioned above); in addition, the lost play *Triptolemus* is reported to have been produced about 468[37] and may therefore have been one of the plays with which Sophocles won his

---

[29]For surviving fragments of the paean see *PMG* 737; for references to other discussions of Sophocles' connection with Asclepius, see pp. 285–6 with n.132.

[30]In *Philoctetes* (1333–4, 1437–8), in one of his two *Phineus* plays (fr. 710), and perhaps also in *Phaedra* (see pp. 285–6).

[31]He died after Euripides (*Suda* σ815; *Life of Euripides* §2; *Gnomologium Vaticanum* 517 Sternbach), in the Athenian year 406/5 (*Marm.Par.* [*FGrH* 239 A 64]; D.S. 13.103.4; Hypothesis to *OC*), before the Lenaea when two comic dramatists referred to his death, Aristophanes in *Frogs* and Phrynichus in *Muses* (fr. 32).

[32]The relevant passages, which were probably inserted into a completed script at a late stage, are *Frogs* 71–88, 786–795, and 1515–9; see A.H. Sommerstein, *Aristophanes: Frogs* (Warminster, 1996) 20–21. Some scholars, notably C.F. Russo (*G&R* 13 [1966] 1–13; *Aristophanes: An Author for the Stage* [London, 1994] 198–202), have argued that much more substantial modifications were made to *Frogs* after Sophocles' death.

[33]*Suda* σ815 names three further sons, in a sequence that suggests that one (Leosthenes) was legitimate and two (Stephanus and Menecleides) illegitimate; cf. A. von Blumenthal, *RE* iii.a (1929) 1042.

[34]He was alive in 405 (Ar. *Frogs* 73–79), but probably dead by 401 when the posthumous production of *Oedipus at Colonus* and other plays was put on not by him but by his inexperienced nephew.

[35]Ariston's mother was Theoris of Sicyon (*Life of Sophocles* §13; schol. Ar. *Frogs* 78; *Suda* ι451).

[36]Hypothesis to *Oedipus at Colonus*.

[37]See n.4 above.

first victory.[38] There is general agreement, on grounds of style and technique, that *Electra* is fairly late,[39] and that the other four surviving plays are earlier, with *Oedipus Tyrannus* probably later than *Ajax, Antigone* and *The Women of Trachis*; but there is not sufficient evidence to reach firm conclusions about the absolute or relative dating of the three last-mentioned plays.[40]

The dating of Sophocles' fragmentary plays is even harder. Many of those of Euripides can be dated with fair confidence by reference to their metrical practice, especially the frequency and nature of "resolution" (substitution of two short syllables for a long one) in his spoken iambics,[41] against the background of a corpus of seventeen extant tragedies[42] of which seven or eight,[43] spanning more than thirty years, are firmly dated; it has thus been possible for Collard and his colleagues, in the volumes of fragmentary Euripidean plays in this series, to present their selected plays in what is at least a close approximation to a chronological sequence. The metrical practice of Sophocles changed much more slowly, and the stylistic features that provide approximate chronological indications for the extant plays (e.g. choral anapaests suggest an early date, actor lyrics independent of the chorus a late one) are generally not available for fragmentary plays. We are thus driven, as will be seen from the introductions to individual plays in this volume, to other kinds of (sometimes equivocal) evidence, principally the following:

---

[38]There is also good reason to believe that Sophocles produced one of his two *Tyro* plays, and another play which may have been *Troilus*, at the Lenaea of 418; see pp. 215–6, discussing *IG* ii² 2319.77–79.

[39]See J.R. March, *Sophocles: Electra* (Warminster, 2000) 20–22.

[40]Though *The Women of Trachis* may well be the earliest and belong to the 450s; see p. 93 n.22. The date of 442 often assigned to *Antigone* is based only on the statement in one of the Hypotheses to that play that Sophocles' election to a generalship (for 441/0) was due to the success he achieved with *Antigone* – which is no more reliable than the statement of some of his early biographers (*Life of Sophocles* §14) that he died of joy when *Antigone* was proclaimed victorious. (441 is excluded because that was the year of Euripides' first victory [*Marm.Par., FGrH* 239 A 60]).

[41]For details see Cropp & Fick.

[42]Excluding *Cyclops* (which is a satyr-play) and *Rhesus* (which is probably not by Euripides).

[43]*Alcestis* (438), *Medea* (431), *The Trojan Women* (415), *Helen* (412), *Orestes* (408), *Bacchae* and *Iphigeneia at Aulis* (produced posthumously). We know that a *Hippolytus* by Euripides was produced successfully in 428, but it is disputed whether this was the play (*Hippolytos Stephanephoros*) that has survived; see pp. 266–271, where references are given to earlier discussions.

(i) *References in comedy.* If a comic dramatist quotes, parodies, or unmistakably refers to, a specific tragedy (as Aristophanes in *Birds* does, on a large scale, to *Tereus*), that is decisive evidence that the exploited tragedy is earlier than the exploiting comedy. The tragedy, however, will not necessarily have been very recent: of the four Euripidean plays that feature most prominently in Aristophanes' *Thesmophoriazusae* one, *Telephus*, was then twenty-seven years old.

(ii) *Relationships to surviving plays (or datable lost plays) on the same theme.* Several of the plays in this volume dramatize a story that was also used by Euripides (*Hermione* ~ *Andromache*, *Polyxene* ~ *Hecuba*, *Phaedra* ~ two *Hippolytus* plays) or share strong common themes with a play of his (*Tereus* ~ *Medea*); and sometimes, but by no means always, it is possible to argue, with greater or lesser cogency, that one of a pair of such plays appears to have been produced with (or without) knowledge of the other and therefore is likely (or, as the case may be, unlikely) to be the later of the two. Attempts are made to develop arguments of this kind, where it seems appropriate, in the introductions to the Sophoclean plays mentioned.

(iii) *Artistic evidence.* If a work of art, datable by its style or otherwise, is clearly based not just on a particular myth but on a particular dramatic version of that myth, the drama in question must evidently be earlier than the artwork; but it is rarely possible to come to such a conclusion with any confidence when we know so little for sure of a play as we do of most fragmentary Sophoclean plays.

(iv) *Relationships to the contemporary world.* Tragedy, unlike comedy, does not normally refer directly to contemporary events,[44] and the game of detecting "allusions" to such events in tragic texts has been played so often, and with such conflicting results, that it has come to be widely viewed with great scepticism.[45] It is possible that Sophocles' transfer of the Tereus-Procne story from Phocis to Thrace was stimulated in part by Athenian political and military interest in Thrace in the early years of the

---

[44]At least after the early period when the action of a tragedy was sometimes taken directly from the (near-)contemporary world (Aeschylus' *Persians*, produced in 472, is the last such tragedy we know of). However, there are several transparent references to contemporary political events and issues in Aeschylus' *Eumenides*; see A.H. Sommerstein, *Aeschylus: Eumenides* (Cambridge, 1989) 30–31.

[45]The sceptical reaction was initiated by Günther Zuntz; see his *The Political Plays of Euripides* (Manchester, 1955) 63–79.

Peloponnesian War,[46] but then Athenian interest in Thrace went back much further than this.[47] Sometimes, however, a tragic passage may presuppose a state of affairs in the contemporary world which existed only in particular time periods. When in *The Women of Trachis* (303–5) the sympathetic character Deianeira is made to pray that no offspring of hers may ever become a captive, it is reasonable to doubt whether Sophocles would have put these words in her mouth at a time when Athens was actively at war with Sparta (459–451, 446, or 431–421[48]) and when most Athenians would have been delighted to take prisoner one of the Spartan kings, descendants of Deianeira's son Hyllus; and if (which is by no means certain) *Phaedra* contained a reference to, or prediction of, the raising of Hippolytus from the dead by Asclepius, it strongly suggests that *Phaedra* was produced at a time when Athenians still regarded Asclepius as a (dead) hero rather than a (living) god (i.e. no later than 421, if even as late), since Asclepius as a living god never raised up the dead.[49]

Thus, except in the rare cases where we have evidence directly specifying a date of production, it is impossible to establish the dates of fragmentary Sophoclean plays with even approximate precision, and impossible in general to place them in anything approaching a chronological order. The plays in this volume are therefore presented in (Greek) alphabetical order, as has long been customary in most editions of dramatic fragments.[50]

---

[46]Thucydides (2.29.3), discussing the Athenian alliance with the Thracian king Sitalces made in 431, feels it necessary to argue in a lengthy excursus that there was no connection between Sitalces' father Teres and the Tereus of the myth – which implies that some Athenians at the time did suppose there was such a connection.

[47]Indeed it went back to before the beginning of Sophocles' career, when Cimon, probably in 476, had captured Eion at the mouth of the Strymon (Hdt. 7.107; Thuc. 1.98.1) in an expedition that marked the beginning of the long, and usually disastrous, Athenian obsession with Amphipolis, then called Nine Ways (schol. Aeschines 2.31).

[48]On stylistic grounds, dates later than 421 hardly come into consideration in any case.

[49]See p. 286 n.136.

[50]Including the Sophoclean editions of Nauck, Pearson, Radt, Lucas de Dios, and Lloyd-Jones.

Evidence for the fragmentary plays

From what sources can we acquire information about the plots and scripts of dramas of which no complete text has come down to us? The main ones are as follows.[50a]

(i) *Ancient fragments of play-texts*, commonly called papyri,[51] almost always recovered from the soil of what had been Greek-speaking Egypt, and written between the third century BC and the sixth or seventh century AD. There are far fewer of these for Sophocles (or Aeschylus) than there are for Euripides,[52] and with the exception of the famous Oxyrhynchus papyrus of the satyr-drama *The Trackers (Ichneutae)*,[53] most of them are in a very tattered condition, often with only a few letters of each line surviving. No papyrus fragments survive of actual scripts of any of the six plays in this volume,[54] though a few words of *Tereus* are cited in a papyrus commentary on Eupolis' comedy *The Taxiarchs*.[55]

(ii) *Plot-summaries*, usually referred to by the Greek term *hypothese(i)s*. In medieval manuscripts the text of a play is often preceded by one or more hypotheses, and it has been conventional likewise to print them before the text in modern editions. Surviving ancient hypotheses, however, are mostly separate from the play-text, sometimes forming part of, or seemingly excerpted from, a collection of hypotheses of a particular author's plays.[56] Often, though not always, what is summarized in a hypothesis is not so much the play itself, but the story as presented in the

---

[50a]On all matters discussed in this section and the next, see now the masterly introduction to the study of "lost" tragedies by M.J. Cropp in J. Gregory (ed.) *A Companion to Greek Tragedy* (Oxford, 2005) 271–292.

[51]Many "papyrus" texts, especially in later antiquity, are in fact written on parchment; see I. Gallo, *Greek and Latin Papyrology* tr. M.R. Falivene and J.R. March [London, 1986] 11–16, and L.D. Reynolds and N.G. Wilson, *Scribes and Scholars 3* (Oxford, 1991) 3, 34–35.

[52]The Mertens-Pack[3] database of literary papyri (http://promethee.philo.ulg.ac.be/cedopal/index.htm) contains, as of July 2005, well over twice as many entries for Euripides (text, hypotheses, scholia) as for Aeschylus and Sophocles combined; there are more entries for Euripides' *Phoenician Maidens* alone (27) than for all the extant plays of Aeschylus (6) and Sophocles (15) put together.

[53]*POxy* 1174 = Soph. fr. 314.

[54]Though there are significant papyrus fragments of three of the plays expected to appear in vol. ii (*Ajax the Locrian, The Epigonoi, Niobe*).

[55]*Tereus* fr. R (595b).

[56]Three examples of such collections are *POxy* 2455 and 2457 (from alphabetical collections of Euripidean hypotheses) and 3653 (from an alphabetical collection of Sophoclean hypotheses).

play; in other words, the hypothesis includes many events which are mentioned retrospectively in the play and are not themselves part of its action. This is true both of the papyrus hypothesis to *Tereus* (which we print before the fragments of the text) and of that to Euripides' *Hippolytos Kalyptomenos*, discussed in connection with *Phaedra*.[57]

(iii) *Ancient quotations*, or "fragments" traditionally so called (now often referred to as "book-fragments" to distinguish them from papyrus fragments): passages, ranging in length from a single word to a maximum (so far as Sophocles is concerned[58]) of seventeen lines (fr. 941), cited by ancient authors of all kinds for all sorts of reasons − except that they are virtually never cited for the purpose of giving the reader information about the Sophoclean play. If we look at the number of times that fragments of the six plays included in this volume are cited by authors of different types,[59] we find that by far the largest number of citations (57)[60] − though most of these fragments are very short − are from *grammarians and lexicographers* who are interested in exemplifying a peculiarity of vocabulary, word meaning, inflection, or syntax; next come *anthologists* (23) − or rather, almost exclusively, one anthologist, Stobaeus (fifth century AD)[61] − who are interested in passages that give memorable expression to an (often commonplace) idea, and ancient commentators or *scholiasts* on other poetic and prose texts (11) who are interested in passages that throw some light on the text they are annotating. Other *specialist writers* of various kinds[62] cite these plays (8 times) to illustrate some point arising in their specialist field − geography, poetic technique, zoology, theology, or the language and customs of the symposium; and *miscellaneous writers* (5), such as Plutarch,[63] cite them to illustrate any point to which they are or can be made relevant, on the principle that any statement is more likely to carry conviction if it can be shown that a

---

[57]See pp. 255–266.

[58]The longest of all tragic book-fragments is one from Euripides' *Erechtheus* (fr. 360) cited by the orator Lycurgus (*Against Leocrates* 100) and running to fifty-five lines.

[59]Some fragments are cited, in whole or in part, by more than one author, so that the total number of citations (105) is greater than the total number of actual fragments (88).

[60]Of these, 26 are by the lexicographer Hesychius; Photius comes next with five; about twenty authors of this category are represented in all.

[61]There is a solitary citation in the anthology of Orion.

[62]Aristotle (in the *Historia Animalium* and the *Poetics*), Apollodorus (*FGrH* 244), Strabo, Clement of Alexandria, and Athenaeus.

[63]The others are Aulus Gellius and Favorinus.

respected poet has said it. Lastly, one textual fragment of *Phaedra*[64] is not, at least not avowedly, a quotation at all; it comes to us embedded in the text of another Sophoclean play, *Electra* (1050–4), but Stobaeus cites part of it as from *Phaedra*, and it can be shown that the whole passage makes better sense if the speakers are Phaedra and her nurse than if they are Electra and her sister. Some of the quoting authors – though not usually the grammarians, lexicographers or anthologists – may give additional information about the context of a passage, for example identifying the speaker, the addressee or the occasion.

(iv) *Other ancient statements about a play.* An ancient author may give a great deal of information about a lost play without citing a word of its text. Our most important sources of information about *Hermione*, for example, are an ancient and a medieval commentary on the *Odyssey* which mention key features of the plot and antecedents of Sophocles' play to contrast them with the *Odyssey*'s own account of Hermione's marriage,[65] and one of the most serious problems in the reconstruction of *Polyxene* is how to reconcile the evidence of a quoted fragment[66] for an on-stage appearance of Achilles' ghost in the prologue of the play with the praise of "Longinus" for what, as the context shows, must have been a description of an *off-stage* epiphany of the ghost in the *middle* of the play.[67]

(v) *Other ancient statements about the myth, including literary and dramatic treatments of it by other authors.* These can be of great value, but it must be constantly borne in mind, firstly that a Greek myth was not a fixed, canonized story but was always capable of modification and development, and secondly that any creative author presenting such a myth will be *likely* to modify it in order to extract from it new ideas, new emotional or rhetorical effects. This is particularly true of dramatists, who were forced to present at least one episode of a myth in greater detail than was necessary in any other genre, and who were, moreover, almost always presenting their plays as entries in a competition; and it is a working hypothesis in the present edition that where two or more top-class tragedians have dramatized the same story, *their versions are more likely to differ than to coincide* except on matters essential to the identity of the story or to its crucial links with other parts of the corpus of myth. On the other hand, passing allusions to one myth in a play based on another can

---

[64]*Phaedra* fr. C (693a Lloyd-Jones); see pp. 276, 303–5.
[65]See pp. 3–4, 26–27.
[66]*Polyxene* fr. A (523).
[67]"Longinus" *On the Sublime* 15.7; see pp. 52–57.

be assumed, in the absence of evidence to the contrary, to be to a version of that myth that was familiar to the audience (since otherwise there would be too much risk of their misunderstanding the allusion); in general, the sketchier the reference to a myth, the less likely the author is to be innovating. Those writers, on the other hand, often called mythographers,[68] who see their role as being to collect, digest and narrate the corpus of myth (or parts of it) as such without aspiring to do so creatively, are likely, if they choose to tell a story in detail, to follow an existing version, and very often that version may be a tragic one, since for many myths this would be much the best known treatment. Even when no tragic source is explicitly cited, there may be features of a mythographer's story that betray a tragic model (such as the concentration of many twists and changes of fortune within a short span of time).

(vi) *Artistic evidence.* This can be divided into evidence for the myth and evidence for the play. One would have thought that when an art object (a vase painting, for example), displaying an identifiable mythical scene, shows clear signs of being based on a theatrical model (such as a stage-like setting or mask-like facial features), it would amount virtually to an "illustration" of a play and could be viewed as providing almost direct evidence for it; but although this is sometimes true,[69] it cannot be taken for granted, and often it is demonstrably false – sometimes, for example, a painter may show characters present together in his composition who could not possibly have been present together on stage.[70] Often more valuable is artistic evidence showing how a myth was commonly perceived *before* it came into the hands of the tragic dramatists, especially if (as is

---

[68]Such as the author of the *Bibliotheca* ascribed to Apollodorus (first/second century AD?). Another mythographer, Hyginus (writing in Latin; second century AD?), whose range is wide though his learning is sketchy, provides information of some value relating to four of the six plays in this volume. For discussion of the evidence provided by these and other mythographic texts, see the Introductions to the several plays.

[69]A very striking example is the so-called Würzburg Telephus krater (Martin-von-Wagner-Museum H5697), which illustrates precisely lines 753–6 of Aristophanes' *Thesmophoriazusae.* See E.G. Csapo, *Phoenix* 40 (1986) 379–392; O.P. Taplin, *PCPS* 33 (1987) 96–101; id., *Comic Angels* (Oxford, 1993) 36–40.

[70]See H.A. Shapiro, *Myth into Art* (London, 1994) 7–9 and A.M. Snodgrass, *Homer and the Artists* (Cambridge, 1998) 55–66 on the "synoptic" technique employed by many ancient Greek artists, involving the "combination of several different moments or episodes from a story into a single picture ... [which] corresponds to an impossible moment that no photograph could capture" (Shapiro *op. cit.* 8). For a highly sceptical view of the value of artistic evidence for the study of tragedy, see J.P. Small in J. Gregory (ed.) *A Companion to Greek Tragedy* (Oxford 2005) 103–118.

very often the case) there is little detailed evidence from archaic poetry. Almost all our direct knowledge of the early state of the story out of which Sophocles created *Troilus* comes from archaic and early classical art;[71] pictorial representations provide vital, if sometimes enigmatic, evidence for the prehistory of what became the Tereus-Procne myth;[72] and recent discoveries have shown that the idea that Achilles' ghost demanded the sacrifice of Polyxene because Achilles had been in love with her and now desired her as a posthumous bride, far from being a romantic invention of the Hellenistic age, was familiar in the archaic period.[73]

The editor's task is to determine, as far as can be done on the basis of all the evidence available, what can be said, with what degree of assurance, about the structure of the lost play, its relationship to other treatments of the story, and the placement within it of such fragments as survive. "The evidence available" includes not only that discussed above, bearing on a particular myth or play, but also what is known or reasonably inferred about what was possible, and what it was or was not the practice to do, in Athenian tragedy generally. For example, even if it had not been possible to infer from the context in "Longinus" that the epiphany of Achilles' ghost "to those putting to sea" in *Polyxene* was narrated in a messenger-speech (or equivalent) rather than enacted on stage, it would still have been necessary to conclude that this was so, because there was no way in which the audience of an Athenian tragedy could have been made to witness in performance a fleet putting to sea.[74]

Why study fragments?

What this volume presents is, necessarily, no more than the scattered remnants of six dramas. Of the "best" preserved of them, *Tereus,* only 294 words of text survive out of (probably) seven to ten thousand,[75] and of *Hermione* (even if, as here argued, it is the same play as *The Women of Phthia*) just thirty. Why should these deserve the careful study which we have tried to give them, which great scholars before us have bestowed on

---

[71]See pp. 196–7.
[72]See pp. 143–9.
[73]See pp. 46–47.
[74]Cf. p. 54 n.58.
[75]The *Thesaurus Linguae Graecae* database (http://www.tlg.uci.edu) gives a word count of 7,723 for the shortest of Sophocles' extant plays, *The Women of Trachis*, and 11,234 for the exceptionally long *Oedipus at Colonus*.

them,[76] and in which, by producing this volume, we are inviting our readers to join?

At one level, a simple answer to this question is that *all* study of the past is a study of surviving fragments. The past itself is gone. Crichton and Spielberg[77] notwithstanding, we cannot go back to the Jurassic period; we can only recreate it in imagination (or, now, in computer simulation) from the evidence of what has survived from that period – its rocks, its fossils, and so on – together with our other physical, chemical and biological knowledge. No more can we go back to ancient Athens, smell its odours,[78] sample its food, interview its people. All we are left with is some of their environment and some of their products – among them, a small part of their writings. Some of these writings – the dialogues of Plato, for example – can be regarded as being complete, at least in the sense that we possess (allowing for some textual corruption) the whole of what Plato chose to make available for his public to read (though even in such a case we can never possess the whole of the cultural background against which they read and tried to understand it). But in the case of drama – all drama – we possess, at most, no more than the words, together with some information, of varying quantity and reliability but always very incomplete, about delivery, acting, costume, music, dance, the stage setting, and the hundred and one other features that went to make up the Athenian's experience of a theatrical production. Much of that other information is relevant not just to a particular play but to all drama (or all tragedy) alike, and therefore is available to the student of a fragmentary play as much as to the student of an extant one. Even if we are left with, say, only two per cent of the words, that does not necessarily mean that we have only two per cent as much data to work with.

What, though, can we learn from studying these data?

Our seven complete Sophoclean plays form a very small sample of his complete output, and not a random sample: they are the plays of his that

---

[76]On the history of the study of tragic fragments, see the chapters by R. Kassel and F.D. Harvey in F. McHardy et al. ed. *Lost Dramas of Classical Athens* (Exeter, 2005) 7–48; and on all matters discussed in this and the preceding section, see now the masterly introduction to the study of "lost" tragedies by M.J. Cropp in J. Gregory (ed.), *A Companion to Greek Tragedy* (Oxford, 2005), 103–118.

[77]M. Crichton, *Jurassic Park* (New York, 1990); Steven Spielberg (director), *Jurassic Park* (Universal Pictures, 1992).

[78]But we can nevertheless learn much about the smells its inhabitants thought worthy of note; see P. Thiercy in A.H. Sommerstein et al. ed. *Tragedy, Comedy and the Polis* (Bari, 1993) 505–526.

were most read, especially in schools, in Roman times and later. Hence they are not necessarily representative of the range of plot and theme, style and mood, that we would have seen as "Sophoclean" if we could survey his work in its entirety. To assess this as best we can – and even to do the best we can in assessing and interpreting the extant plays themselves – we must seek to learn as much as we can about the "lost" plays.

A prominent notion in twentieth-century Sophoclean criticism[79] was that of the "Sophoclean hero", the figure of unshakable determination who, as Sophocles himself once put it, stood unmoved as a rock in the storm[80] and could not be persuaded by any argument, promise or threat to deviate from what he or she saw as the proper course of action. Every one of Sophocles' seven extant plays contains such a figure – Heracles, Ajax, Antigone, Oedipus twice, Electra, Philoctetes. There has been a great deal of debate over whether the audience are expected to sympathize automatically with such figures[81] or to maintain a critical distance from them,[82] and no consensus has been reached.

Now four of the six plays in this volume are concerned, in one way or another, with a figure outstanding both for heroic valour and for stubborn self-will – Achilles – or his son Neoptolemus, or both. Neoptolemus is a major character in *Philoctetes*; we are constantly encouraged to ask ourselves whether he is being a worthy son to his father, who appears to be regarded as flawless, and in the end, for all his immaturity and inexperience, he proves that he is. In these four fragmentary plays the father and the son seem to have been presented in a very different light. In *The Diners*, admittedly under grave provocation, Achilles nearly wrecks the expedition against Troy before it has properly begun with an act of childish insult which, to make it seem even worse, is described in words taken verbatim from a play of Aeschylus in which the perpetrator of the act was one of that despicable band, the suitors of Penelope.[83] In *Troilus*,

---

[79]Most influentially described in B.M.W. Knox, *The Heroic Temper* (Berkeley, 1964); see also (among many other studies) R.P. Winnington-Ingram, *Sophocles: An Interpretation* (Cambridge, 1980) 304–329, and the admirable thumbnail sketch by H. Lloyd-Jones, *Sophocles I* (Cambridge MA, 1994) 1–5.

[80]*OC* 1239–48. Oedipus' next action will be to reject his son's repentant supplication and curse him afresh.

[81]A striking example of this tendency is A.F. Garvie, *Sophocles: Ajax* (Warminster, 1998) 11–17.

[82]As for example do Winnington-Ingram *loc.cit.* and M. Whitlock Blundell, *Helping Friends and Harming Enemies* (Cambridge, 1989).

[83]*Syndeipnoi* fr. G (565), echoing Aesch. fr. 180.

where he seems to have been an important offstage presence even though not himself a character in the drama, he commits a treacherous and sacrilegious murder and then savagely mutilates the corpse – and if we ask why, the likeliest reason is that his victim, Troilus, had angrily rejected improper overtures by Achilles towards his sister.[84] In *Polyxene* the ghost of the dead Achilles demands that sister as his bride in the next world, having failed to acquire her in this one, and it is probably Neoptolemus (fresh from a sacrilegious killing of his own, that of her father Priam) who first argues for, and then physically carries out, the slaughter of this innocent maiden.[85] And in *Hermione* Neoptolemus apparently attempts to take vengeance on Apollo for his father's death by sacking the sanctuary of Delphi,[86] and meets his death as a result. These treatments of Achilles, and of his son's actions carried out in his name, tell strongly against the view that for Sophocles an exceptional endowment of one or another virtue (courage, wisdom, endurance, familial devotion) could serve as a free pass to commit any indignity or atrocity.

Another important feature of our selected plays is the light that many of them throw upon, or have thrown upon them by, dramas by other authors based on the same stories. Three of the six, as mentioned above, run parallel to surviving plays of Euripides, and a fourth, *Tereus*, shares important themes with Euripides' *Medea* – despite having a central character, Procne, who must initially differ as much from the barbarian sorceress, and past eloper and serial killer, Medea as the Sophoclean Deianeira does from the character against whom we are clearly meant to measure her, the Aeschylean Clytaemestra.[87] In addition, *Polyxene* and *Phaedra* are paralleled, half a millennium later, by tragedies of Seneca, and in both cases (though more in that of *Phaedra*) there is reason to believe that Seneca incorporated Sophoclean as well as Euripidean features

---

[84]See pp. 203–8.

[85]On Neoptolemus' role, see pp. 42, 49, 60.

[86]See pp. 3–15 (esp. 12) and 20.

[87]Both Clytaemestra and Deianeira kill a husband who has brought home a younger woman as his mistress; in both cases a robe plays a fatal role, and in both cases it is called a "woven net of the Erinyes" (*Trach.* 1051–2 ~ Aesch. *Ag.* 1382, 1580); Clytaemestra is killed by her son, Deianeira is cursed by hers (*Trach.* 807–820). Deianeira, however, had no intention of killing or even harming Heracles, and no ill will towards her rival Iole. See T.B.L. Webster in *Greek Poetry and Life: Essays Presented to Gilbert Murray* (Oxford, 1936) 164–180.

into his composition,[88] as the earlier Roman dramatist, Pacuvius, certainly did in his *Hermiona*.[89]

Study of these plays can also provide valuable evidence about a range of aspects of Sophoclean – and in general of tragic – technique and thought. On technique one may note: (*Hermione*) the motifs of the warner figure[90] and of the vain efforts of the old to rein in the impetuous young, anticipating Euripides' *Bacchae*;[91] (*Polyxene*) the appearances of ghosts[92] and the reporting of a spectacular scene in narrative *after* a somewhat similar scene has been presented on stage;[93] (*The Diners*) a play whose action covers a night rather than a day,[94] an indoor quarrel narrated, and continued, out of doors by the contending parties themselves,[95] and the hasty intervention of a *dea ex machina* to bring about what appears to be a happy ending; (*Tereus*) an important character who cannot speak,[96] (*Troilus*) an important character (Achilles) who does not even appear,[97] strong barbarian colouring in language and otherwise,[98] and probably the return to the stage of a mutilated corpse[99] – again anticipating *Bacchae*; (*Phaedra*) a disastrous *peripeteia* caused, paradoxically, by what is in effect a resurrection from the dead – with another resurrection perhaps announced at the end.[100]

On thought one may note: (*Polyxene*) the dilemma of a leader whose decisions cannot satisfy everyone,[101] (*The Diners*) how a petty quarrel can escalate disastrously; (*Tereus*) the Greek/barbarian and male/female oppositions; (*Phaedra*) the question whether one who is pressed hard by a

---

[88]See pp. 51, 273–4, 283.

[89]See pp. 22–25.

[90]*Hermione* fr. B (694).

[91]Cf. Eur. *Ba.* 210–369 (Teiresias and Cadmus trying to restrain Pentheus); just before that scene, Euripides actually quotes from *Hermione* (*Ba.* 193 ~ *Hermione* fr. D [695]).

[92]See pp. 52–59.

[93]See p. 54.

[94]See pp. 89, 116.

[95]See p. 95.

[96]See pp. 149–151, 183–4.

[97]Achilles may also have been an important "absent character" in Sophocles' *Shepherds* (see vol. ii), and Neoptolemus in his *Eurypylus*. There is no exact parallel in extant tragedy; the nearest approaches are perhaps Aeschylus' *Seven against Thebes* and Euripides' *Andromache*, where Polyneices and Neoptolemus, respectively, appear only as corpses.

[98]See pp. 204–5.

[99]See pp. 205–6, 240–1.

[100]See pp. 280–1, 285–6.

[101]*Polyxene* fr. C (524).

superhuman force (such as Eros) is thereby excused if she does what she knows to be disgraceful.[102]

But after all is said and done, for many, as for ourselves, the most powerful motive for studying these "shards from Colonus" is the simple desire to know – to know, in particular, so far as we can, how a skilful and sensitive poet and dramatist interpreted, adapted and presented these famous, much-told and often gruesome tales in a manner, always novel, that would win the approval of a panel of élite judges strongly influenced by the feelings of a large popular audience.

Content and form of this edition

This edition follows basically the same pattern as the editions of fragmentary Euripidean plays in this series by C. Collard et al. (vol. I, 1995; vol. II, 2004). For each play we present:

(i) A bibliography comprising: editions of the *text and testimonia*; ancient evidence for, and modern discussions of the *myth* on which the play is based; discussions of the *artistic evidence* for this myth; and the *main discussions* of the play itself.

(ii) An introduction usually divided into two main sections, on the myth and the play. The discussion of the myth examines the evidence (whether early or late) for the state of the myth *before* Sophocles' time, and also other ancient dramatizations of it whether near-contemporary or later; the recent publication of a second papyrus containing part of a hypothesis to Euripides' *Hippolytos Kalyptomenos*, which has heightened the controversy over the relationship between this play, Sophocles' *Phaedra*, and Euripides' surviving *Hippolytos Stephanephoros*, has necessitated a particularly detailed study of *HippK* in the introduction to *Phaedra* (pp. 255–272). The discussion of the play seeks to establish its structure, plot and characters, and to situate the fragments within it, so far as this can reasonably be done. A further section discusses the evidence bearing on the date of the play; in the case of *The Diners*, where such evidence is entirely lacking, there is instead a section on the question whether the play was a tragedy, a satyr-drama, or (like Euripides' *Alcestis*) of an intermediate type.

(iii) The Greek text, with a critical apparatus,[103] and a facing translation with brief notes indicating, where possible, what is known or can be

---

[102]*Phaedra* frr. B, C, D, E (680, 693a, 679, 684).

reasonably inferred about the speaker, addressee, and/or context of each fragment. The fragments are presented in the sequence in which we believe them to have occurred in the play (those which cannot be located in the play with any confidence at all are placed at the end); they are designated by letters of the alphabet in sequence, and also by the numbers they bear in *TrGF*.[104] For most of the plays we have also included a small selection of key testimonia, normally those which refer explicitly to the play, or are highly likely to be based on it, or are discussed in detail in the introduction.

(iv) A commentary keyed to the translation.

Speaker names are given in the Greek text only where the quoting author explicitly identifies the speaker, or where there is change of speaker within a fragment and the identities of the speakers are certain or almost certain; in the latter case the speaker names are given within angled brackets < >. With these exceptions, speakers are identified only in the notes and commentary. Angled brackets are also used, as is conventional, to denote conjectural supplements of a text judged to be defective as a result of omissions in copying, and (sometimes with [?] added) to denote, in translation, tentative conjectural corrections of a text judged incurably corrupt. Other critical signs are used as follows:

† ... †   the text between these marks is judged incurably corrupt
[...]   (in papyrus texts) there is a gap in the papyrus, and any bracketed letters are a conjectural restoration[105] (single square brackets may be similarly used at the beginning or end of a line or passage)

---

[103]This aims to record all significant documentary evidence relevant to the establishing of the text. Information on the readings of manuscripts has been drawn from published sources. As regards conjectural emendations the apparatus is selective, recording, in general, only those which we have adopted or which we consider have a reasonable chance of being, or of pointing the way to, the truth. Readers unfamiliar with critical apparatuses should consult M.L. West, *Textual Criticism and Editorial Technique* (Stuttgart, 1973), esp. 86–94, or L.D. Reynolds and N.G. Wilson, *Scribes and Scholars*³ (Oxford, 1991) 207–241, esp. 237–9.

[104]One or two fragments that we print were not included in *TrGF*; for these we give references to another standard collection.

[105]Where a word of the text is partly preserved and partly lost, the corresponding word in the translation is bracketed in such a way as to indicate the approximate proportions of preserved and lost material; such bracketing in the translation should not be taken (except in the case of proper names) as giving any indication of *which* letters have survived and which have not.

A dot under a letter, in a papyrus text, indicates that the letter is not securely identifiable (the visible traces are compatible with that letter but would also be compatible with one or more others). A dot below the line with no letter above it indicates that there are traces of a letter but that the letter cannot be even tentatively identified.

References by author's name alone, or by abbreviations, are elucidated in the list of References and Abbreviations which follows this introduction. References by author's name *and date* in the introduction to, or the commentary on, a play are to books or articles listed in the bibliography for that play.

Greek names of persons, places or texts have usually been latinized, but a closer transliteration has been used where thought desirable in the interest of communicative efficiency.

REFERENCES AND ABBREVIATIONS

Collections of Fragments

All citations of fragments of Greek authors made in this volume either are from one of the collections in the following list or else are accompanied by the abbreviated title of the edition cited or by the name(s) or initial(s) of the editor(s); fuller particulars will be found on pp. xxxiii–xxxvi below if there might otherwise be difficulty in identifying the edition.

Aeschylus	S.L. Radt, *TrGF* iii (1985)
Alcaeus	D.A. Campbell, *Greek Lyric* i (Cambridge MA, 1982)
Alexis	*PCG* ii (1991)
Anaxandrides	*PCG* ii (1991)
Antiphanes	*PCG* ii (1991)
Archilochus	M.L. West, *Iambi et Elegi Graeci* i^2 (Oxford, 1989)
Aristophanes	*PCG* iii.2 (1984)
Bacchylides	B. Snell and H. Maehler, *Bacchylidis Carmina cum Fragmentis* (Leipzig, 1970)
Callimachus	R.H. Pfeiffer, *Callimachus* (Oxford, 1949–53)
Cantharus	*PCG* iv (1983)
Carcinus junior	B. Snell, *TrGF* i (1971)
Cratinus	*PCG* iv (1983)
Epicharmus	*PCG* i (2001)
Epicrates	*PCG* v (1986)
Eupolis	*PCG* v (1986)
Euripides	R. Kannicht, *TrGF* v (2004)
Hesiod	R. Merkelbach and M.L. West, *Fragmenta Hesiodea* (Oxford, 1967)
Hipponax	M.L. West, *Iambi et Elegi Graeci* i^2 (Oxford, 1989)
Hypereides	F.G. Kenyon, *Hyperidis Orationes et Fragmenta* (Oxford, 1906)
Menander	*PCG* vi.2 (1998)
Pherecrates	*PCG* vii (1989)
Philetaerus	*PCG* vii (1989)
Philocles	B. Snell, *TrGF* i (1971)
Pindar	H. Maehler, *Pindari Carmina cum Fragmentis* ii (Leipzig, 1989)
Phrynichus (com.)	*PCG* vii (1989)

Phrynichus (trag.)	B. Snell, *TrGF* i (1971)
Sappho	D.A. Campbell, *Greek Lyric* i (Cambridge MA, 1982)
Semonides, Solon	M.L. West, *Iambi et Elegi Graeci* ii^2 (Oxford, 1992)
Sophocles	S.L. Radt, *TrGF* iv^2 (1999)
Sositheus (trag.)	B. Snell, *TrGF* i (1971)
Strattis	*PCG* vii (1989)
Theognis (trag.)	B. Snell, *TrGF* i (1971)
Theopompus (com.)	*PCG* vii (1989)

Abbreviations: Ancient Authors and Works

Ach.	*Acharnians* (Aristophanes)
Aen.	*Aeneid* (Virgil)
Aesch.	Aeschylus
Ag.	*Agamemnon* (Aeschylus)
Aj.	*Ajax* (Sophocles)
Alc.	Alcaeus
Alc.	*Alcestis* (Euripides)
Alex.	*Alexandra* (Lycophron)
Alex.Aph.	Alexander of Aphrodisias
An.	*Anabasis* (Xenophon)
Andr.	*Andromache* (Euripides)
Anecd.Bachm.	*Anecdota Graeca e codd. manuscriptis bibliothecae regiae Parisinae* ed. L. Bachmann (Leipzig, 1828–9)
Anecd.Bekk.	*Anecdota Graeca* ed. I. Bekker (Berlin, 1814–21)
Ant.	*Antigone* (Sophocles)
Ant.Rom.	*Antiquitates Romanae* (Dionysius of Halicarnassus)
AP	*Anthologia Palatina*
Apol.	*Apology* (Plato or Xenophon)
Apoll.	Apollodorus[*]
App.Plan.	Planudean appendix to the *Anthology*
Ap.Rh.	Apollonius Rhodius
Ar.	Aristophanes
Arg.	Argument (synopsis of one of the cyclic epics)
Arist.	Aristotle

---

[*]"[Apoll.]", without further specification, refers to the mythological compendium (*Bibliotheca*) ascribed to Apollodorus.

Att.	*Epistulae ad Atticum* (Cicero)
Ba.	*Bacchae* (Euripides)
Bibl.	*Bibliotheca* ([Apollodorus])
Catast.	*Catasterismi* (ascribed to Eratosthenes).
Char.	*Characters* (Theophrastus)
Cho.	*Choephoroi* (Aeschylus)
Cic.	Cicero
Cim.	*Cimon* (Plutarch)
Clem.Alex.	Clement of Alexandria
com. adesp.	*comica adespota* (anonymous fragments of comedy, cited from *PCG* viii [1995])
Cycl.	*Cyclops* (Euripides)
Cyr.	*Cyropaedia* (Xenophon)
Decl.	*Declamationes* (Libanius)
Dem.	Demosthenes
Dio Chrys.	Dio Chrysostom
D.L.	Diogenes Laertius
D.S.	Diodorus Siculus
Dysk.	*Dyskolos* (Menander)
Eccl.	*Ecclesiazusae* (Aristophanes)
El.	*Electra* (Sophocles or Euripides)
EN	*Nicomachean Ethics* (Aristotle)
Epit.	*Epitome* ([Apollodorus] or Athenaeus)
Epitr.	*Epitrepontes* (Menander)
Et.Gen.	*Etymologicum Genuinum*
Et.Gud.	*Etymologicum Gudianum*
Et.Mag.	*Etymologicum Magnum*
Etym.	*Etymologicum* (Orion)
Eum.	*Eumenides* (Aeschylus)
Eur.	Euripides
Fab.	*Fabulae* (Hyginus)
Fab. Inc.	*Fabula Incerta* (Menander)
Fam.	*Epistulae ad Familiares* (Cicero)
GA	*De Generatione Animalium* (Aristotle)
HA	*Historia Animalium* (Aristotle)
Hcld.	*Heracleidae (Children of Heracles)* (Euripides)
Hdt.	Herodotus
Hec.	*Hecuba* (Euripides)
Hel.	*Helen* (Euripides)
Hell.	*Hellenica* (Xenophon)

Her.	*Heroides* (Ovid)
Hes.	Hesiod
HF	*Heracles Furens (The Madness of Heracles)* (Euripides)
h.Hom.Aph.	*Homeric Hymn to Aphrodite*
Hipp. or *HippS*	*Hippolytus (Hippolytos Stephanephoros)* (Euripides)
HippK	*Hippolytos Kalyptomenos* (Euripides)
Hyp.	Hypereides
IA	*Iphigeneia at Aulis* (Euripides)
Inst.Div.	*Institutiones Divinae* (Lactantius)
Isoc.	Isocrates
Isthm.	*Isthmian Odes* (Pindar)
IT	*Iphigeneia in Tauris* (Euripides)
Jul.	*Divus Iulius* (Suetonius)
Leocr.	*Against Leocrates* (Lycurgus)
Lex.Haem.	*Lexicon Αἱμωδεῖν* ed. F.W. Sturz (with *Et.Gud.*) (Leipzig, 1818)
Luc.	Lucian
LXX	Septuagint (Greek translation of the Old Testament)
Lyc.	Lycurgus
Lys.	Lysias
Lys.	*Lysistrata* (Aristophanes) or *Lysis* (Plato)
Marm.Par.	*Marmor Parium* (= *FGrH* 239)
M.Aur.	Marcus Aurelius
Mem.	*Memorabilia* (Xenophon)
Men.	Menander
Met.	*Metamorphoses* (Ovid, Apuleius or Antoninus Liberalis)
Mis.	*Misoumenos* (Menander)
Mor.	*Moralia* (Plutarch)
Mythogr.Vat.	*Mythographi Vaticani*
NA	*De Natura Animalium* (Aelian)
Nem.	*Nemean Odes* (Pindar)
NH	*Naturalis Historia* (Pliny the Elder)
Nic.	Nicander
OC	*Oedipus at Colonus* (Sophocles)
Od.	*Odyssey* (Homer)
Off.	*De Officiis* (Cicero)
Olymp.	*Olympian Odes* (Pindar)
Or.	*Orestes* (Euripides) or *Orationes* (Aelius Aristides, Dio Chrysostom or Libanius)
OT	*Oedipus Tyrannus* (Sophocles)

Sophocles

Paus.	Pausanias, *Description of Greece*
Paus. Att.	Pausanias the Atticist
Perik.	*Perikeiromene* (Menander)
Pers.	*Persians* (Aeschylus)
Ph.	*Phaedra* (Seneca)
Phd.	*Phaedo* (Plato)
Phdr.	*Phaedrus* (Plato)
Phil.	*Philoctetes* (Sophocles) or *Philippics* (Cicero)
Phoen.	*Phoenician Maidens* (Euripides)
Pind.	Pindar
Pl.	Plato
Plin.	Pliny the Elder
Plut.	Plutarch
Poet.	*Poetics* (Aristotle)
Pol.	*Politics* (Aristotle)
Praep.Ev.	*Praeparatio Evangelica* (Eusebius)
Probl.	*Problemata* (Alexander of Aphrodisias)
Prom.	*Prometheus Bound* ([Aeschylus])
Prot.	*Protagoras* (Plato)
PS	*Praeparatio Sophistica* (Phrynichus the Atticist)
Pyth.	*Pythian Odes* (Pindar)
QF	*Epistulae ad Quintum fratrem* (Cicero)
Q.S.	Quintus of Smyrna
Rep.	*Republic* (Plato)
Rhes.	*Rhesus* ([Euripides])
Rhet.	*Rhetoric* (Aristotle)
Sam.	*Samia* (Menander)
schol. or Σ	scholium or scholia (ancient and medieval commentaries)
Sen.	Seneca (the younger)
Strat.	*De Strategematibus* (Heron the Byzantine)
Strom.	*Stromateis* (Clement of Alexandria)
Suet.	Suetonius
Supp.	*Suppliants* (Aeschylus or Euripides)
Symp.	*Symposium* (Plato or Xenophon)
Theocr.	Theocritus
Ther.	*Theriaca* (Nicander)
Thes.	*Theseus* (Plutarch)
Thesm.	*Thesmophoriazusae* (Aristophanes)
Thg.	*Theogony* (Hesiod)

Thphr.	Theophrastus
Thuc.	Thucydides
Thy.	*Thyestes* (Seneca)
Trach.	*Women of Trachis* (Sophocles)
trag.adesp.	*tragica adespota* (anonymous fragments of tragedy, cited from *TrGF* ii [1981])
Tro.	*Trojan Women* (Euripides) or *Troades* (Seneca)
Val. Max.	Valerius Maximus
VH	*Varia Historia* (Aelian)
Virg.	Virgil
Xen.	Xenophon

Abbreviations: Modern Authors and Publications

AA	*Archäologischer Anzeiger*
AC	*L'Antiquité Classique*
AJA	*American Journal of Archaeology*
AJP	*American Journal of Philology*
Arnott	W.G. Arnott, *Menander* (Cambridge MA, 1979–2000)
BICS	*Bulletin of the Institute of Classical Studies, University of* London
BKT	*Berliner Klassikertexte* (Berlin, 1904–39/Mainz, 1996–)
BMCR	*Bryn Mawr Classical Review*
CA	*Classical Antiquity*
CAG	*Commentaria in Aristotelem Graeca* (Berlin, 1882–1909)
Carden	R. Carden, *The Papyrus Fragments of Sophocles* (Berlin, 1974)
C&M	*Classica et Mediaevalia*
CQ	*Classical Quarterly*
CR	*Classical Review*
Cropp & Fick	M.J. Cropp and G. Fick, *Resolutions and Chronology in Euripides: The Fragmentary Tragedies* = *BICS* Suppl. 43 (1985)
CW	*Classical World*
Davies	M. Davies, *Epicorum Graecorum Fragmenta* (Göttingen, 1988)
Diggle	J. Diggle, *Euripides: Phaethon* (Cambridge, 1970)
D-K	H. Diels, *Die Fragmente der Vorsokratiker* (rev. W. Kranz) (Berlin, 1951–2)

EH	*Entretiens sur l'antiquité classique* (Fondation Hardt, Geneva)
FGrH	F. Jacoby et al., *Die Fragmente der griechischen Historiker* (Berlin/Leiden, 1923–)
Fowler	R.L. Fowler, *Early Greek Mythography* i (Oxford, 2000)
Gantz	T.R. Gantz, *Early Greek Myth: A Guide to Literary and Artistic Sources* (Baltimore, 1993)
GG	*Grammatici Graeci* (Leipzig, 1867–1910)
GL	D.A. Campbell, *Greek Lyric* (Cambridge MA, 1982–93)
G&R	*Greece and Rome*
Gramm.Lat.	H. Keil, *Grammatici Latini* (Leipzig, 1855–80)
GRBS	*Greek, Roman and Byzantine Studies*
Hilgard	A. Hilgard, *Scholia in Dionysii Thracis Artem Grammaticam* (= *GG* I.iii) (Leipzig, 1901)
HSCP	*Harvard Studies in Classical Philology*
IG	*Inscriptiones Graecae*
JHS	*Journal of Hellenic Studies*
K-A	= *PCG (q.v.)*
Kannicht	R. Kannicht, *TrGF* v (2004)
Kiso	A. Kiso, *The Lost Sophocles* (New York, 1984)
Kovacs	P.D. Kovacs, *Euripidea* (Leiden, 1994).
KS	U. von Wilamowitz-Moellendorff, *Kleine Schriften* (Berlin, 1935–72)
Kühner-Blass	R. Kühner (rev. F. Blass), *Ausführliche Grammatik der griechischen Sprache³. Erster Teil: Elementar- und Formenlehre* (Hannover, 1890–92)
LCM	*Liverpool Classical Monthly*
LGM	K. Latte and H. Erbse, *Lexica Graeca Minora* (Hildesheim, 1965)
LIMC	*Lexicon Iconographicum Mythologiae Classicae* (Zürich, 1981–97)
Lloyd-Jones	H. Lloyd-Jones, *Sophocles iii: Fragments* (Cambridge MA, 1996)
Lucas de Dios	J.M. Lucas de Dios, *Sófocles: Fragmentos* (Madrid, 1983)
MDAI(A)	*Mitteilungen des Deutschen Archäologischen Instituts (Athenische Abteilung)*
Moorhouse	A.C. Moorhouse, *The Syntax of Sophocles* (Leiden, 1982)

Müller	C. Müller, *Fragmenta Historicorum Graecorum* (Paris, 1841–70)
Nauck	A. Nauck, *Tragicorum Graecorum Fragmenta*² (Leipzig, 1889; reissued, with a supplement by B. Snell, Hildesheim, 1964)
Nickau	K. Nickau, *Ammonii qui dicitur liber de adfinium vocabulorum differentia* (Leipzig, 1966)
NJbb	*Neue Jahrbücher für das klassische Altertum*
*OED*², *OED*³	*Oxford English Dictionary* (2nd and 3rd editions),* online at http://dictionary.oed.com/entrance.dtl
PBerol	Berlin papyri, cited by inventory number
PCG	R. Kassel and C. Austin, *Poetae Comici Graeci* (Berlin, 1983–)
PCPS	*Proceedings of the Cambridge Philological Society*
Pearson	A.C. Pearson, *The Fragments of Sophocles* (Cambridge, 1917)
PMG	D.L. Page, *Poetae Melici Graeci* (Oxford, 1962)
PMich	*Michigan Papyri,* cited by inventory number
POxy	*The Oxyrhynchus Papyri* (London, 1898–); Arabic numerals in *POxy* citations, unless preceded by a date, denote papyri, not pages
PTebt	*The Tebtunis Papyri* (London, 1902–76)
Radt	S.L. Radt, *TrGF iv*² (Göttingen, 1999)
RE	*Paulys Realencyclopädie der klassischen Altertumswissenschaft*
REG	*Revue des Études Grecques*
RhM	*Rheinisches Museum für Philologie*
Sandbach	F.H. Sandbach, *Menandri Reliquiae Selectae*² (Oxford, 1990)
Satyrspiel	R. Krumeich et al., *Das griechische Satyrspiel* (Darmstadt, 1999)
Shards	A.H. Sommerstein ed. *Shards from Kolonos* (Bari, 2003)
SIFC	*Studi Italiani di Filologia Classica*
SLG	D.L. Page, *Supplementum Lyricis Graecis* (Oxford, 1974)
Sutton	D.F. Sutton, *The Lost Sophocles* (Lanham MD, 1984)

---

*The online *OED* is based on the 2nd printed edition (1989) and is being progressively updated with material which will eventually appear in print in the 3rd edition (in preparation).

Theodoridis	Ch. Theodoridis, *Photii Patriarchae Lexicon* (Berlin, 1982–)
Threatte	L. Threatte, *The Grammar of Attic Inscriptions* (Berlin, 1980–96)
TrGF	*Tragicorum Graecorum Fragmenta* (Göttingen, 1971–2004)[*]
von Arnim	J. [H.F.A.] von Arnim, *Stoicorum Veterum Fragmenta* (Leipzig, 1903–24)
Warmington	E.H. Warmington, *Remains of Old Latin* (Cambridge MA, 1935–40)
Wescher	C. Wescher, *Poliorcétique des Grecs* (Paris, 1867)
West	M.L. West, *Greek Epic Fragments* (Cambridge MA, 2003)
WSt	*Wiener Studien*
ZPE	*Zeitschrift für Papyrologie und Epigraphik*

Metrical Symbols

–	a heavy (long) syllable
∪	a light (short) syllable
×	a position that may be occupied by a syllable of either kind ("anceps")

Symbols used in critical apparatus

It is not possible here to list and explain all the symbols used for individual manuscripts (normally capital letters, or sequences of a capital and a lower-case letter, e.g. Xr) or families of manuscripts (normally lower-case letters in bold, e.g. **x**) in the various authors who quote fragments of these plays; the following listing is of abbreviations and symbols which may be used regardless of who is the quoting author. (For critical symbols used in the text itself, see p. xxviii–xxix above.)

| cett. | *ceteri* (the mss. not cited for a different reading) |
| cod. | *codex* (the only, or the only independent, ms. of a text) |

---

[*]When no volume number is given, the reference is to *TrGF* iv^2 (1999).

codd.	*codices* (all mss. of independent value)
om.	*omittit* (omitted by)
pap.	the papyrus
perh.	introduces a tentative suggestion by the present editor(s)
suppl.	*supplevit* (added as a supplement by)
tent.	*tentavit* (tentatively suggested by)
transp.	*transposuit* (transposed by)
vel sim.	*vel similia* (or the like; with variations of little or no significance)
A^{ac}	A *ante correctionem* (before correction)
A^{mg}	A in the margin
A^{pc}	A *post correctionem* (after correction, normally by the original or an unknown hand)
A^s	A *supra lineam* (above the line)
A^2	a second hand in A
Σ	scholium or scholia
Σ^A	the superscript indicates the ms(s). in which the scholium is found
λ	lemma (quotation from text serving as heading to scholium)
Stobaeus^M	the ms. M of Stobaeus

HERMIONE *or* THE WOMEN OF PHTHIA

Texts and Testimonia: Pearson i 141–4, ii 305–7; Lucas de Dios 98–99, 349–350; *TrGF* 192–3, 481–2; Lloyd-Jones 80–81, 330–3.

Myth: Odyssey 4.3–9, with scholia and Eustathius ad loc.; Pindar, *Paean* 6.100–120 and *Nemean* 7, with scholia on both; Pherecydes *FGrH* 3 F 63– 64 = frr. 135A and 64 Fowler; Euripides, *Andromache*; id., *Orestes* 1653– 7 with scholia; Philocles fr. 2; Theognis trag. fr. 2; Asclepiades *FGrH* 12 F 15; Aristodemus ap. schol. Pind. *Nemean* 7.150; Pacuvius, *Hermiona*; Strabo 9.3.9; Virgil, *Aeneid* 3.294–336; Ovid, *Heroides* 8; Velleius Paterculus 1.1.3; [Apollodorus], *Epitome* 6.14; Hyginus, *Fabulae* 123; Pausanias 1.13.9, 10.24.4–6; Servius on *Aeneid* 3.330; Justin 17.3.6. K. Ziegler, *RE* xvi (1935) 2450–9; J. Pouilloux, *Fouilles de Delphes II: La région nord du sanctuaire* (Paris, 1960) 49–60; J. Fontenrose, *The Cult and Myth of Pyrros at Delphi* (Berkeley, 1960); J. Pouilloux and G. Roux, *Énigmes de Delphes* (Paris, 1963) 102–122; M. Delcourt, *Pyrrhos et Pyrrha* (Paris, 1965) 37–53; L. Woodbury, *Phoenix* 33 (1979) 95–133; L. Kahil, *LIMC* v.1 (1990) 388; O. Touchefeu-Meynier, *LIMC* vi.1 (1992) 774–5; Gantz 690–4; M. Lloyd, *Euripides: Andromache* (Warminster, 1994) 1–3.

Artistic evidence: O. Touchefeu-Meynier, *LIMC* vi.1 (1992) 777–9.

Main discussions: R. Wagner, *Epitoma Vaticana ex Apollodori Bibliotheca* (Leipzig, 1891) 274–8; C.R. Post, *HSCP* 33 (1922) 27–28, 38– 39; T. Zieliński, *Tragodumenon libri tres* (Cracow, 1925) 43–45, 114–7; id., *Eos* 31 (1928) 9–33; P.T. Stevens, *Euripides: Andromache* (Oxford, 1971) 3–5; Sutton 57–61, 110–1.

The myth and the play

Neoptolemus,[1] son of Achilles, was from very early times a major figure in accounts of the later stages of the Trojan War. His role in the war was

---

[1] In a minority of Greek texts, and in the great majority of Latin ones, Neoptolemus is given the name Pyrrhus; I shall refer to him consistently as Neoptolemus, except when actually discussing a Latin text or texts.

familiar to the audiences of the *Iliad* and *Odyssey*,[2] and the cyclic epics –
the *Little Iliad,* the *Sack of Troy,* and the *Returns* – had a great deal to say
about him, much of it decidedly negative,[3] though they certainly presented
him as an outstanding warrior and seem to have known the story that made
him the saviour of his grandfather Peleus.[4] Neoptolemus is also prominent
in archaic art (though even more strongly associated with acts of brutal
violence),[5] but little is heard of him in lyric poetry before Pindar and
Bacchylides.

   Aeschylus, so far as we can tell, took no interest in Neoptolemus at all;
he is never mentioned in any of that dramatist's surviving plays or
fragments, and none of Aeschylus' lost plays appears to have dealt with
any episode in which he was involved. Sophocles, in contrast, wrote half a
dozen plays in which Neoptolemus was an important figure. In the
surviving *Philoctetes*, one of Sophocles' latest plays, he is portrayed as the
heir to everything that was best in Achilles, and is ready, despite his
isolation and extreme youth, to defy Odysseus and, if necessary, the whole
Greek army, in order to keep faith with Philoctetes. In *Peleus*, a very
popular play to judge by the frequency of quotations from it in
contemporary comedy,[6] he apparently rescued his grandfather from

---

[2]*Iliad* 19.326–333 (which would gain in ironic point if the story of Peleus' banishment,
and his restoration by Neoptolemus' aid, was already known – cf. 24.488–9, *Odyssey*
11.494–503), 24.467; *Odyssey* 3.188–9, 11.505–540.

[3]Notably his killing of Priam at the altar of Zeus Herkeios (in the *Sack of Troy* [Arg. §2
West]; slightly, but only slightly, mitigated in the *Little Iliad* [fr. 25 West]) and his barbaric
murder of Astyanax (in the *Little Iliad* [frr. 18, 29 West] – which emphasized that this was
his personal act, not a decision by the army; the *Sack of Troy*, on the other hand, made
Odysseus the perpetrator [Arg. §4 West]). Speaking to the ghost of Achilles in the *Odyssey*,
Odysseus makes no mention of either of these crimes, speaking only of Neoptolemus'
excellence in council and battle alike (*Odyssey* 11.510–6), his killing of Eurypylus, the last
external ally to come to the Trojans' aid (11.519–522), and his courage during the hours of
waiting in the Wooden Horse (11.523–532).

[4]Proclus' summary of the *Returns* (Arg. §4 West) mentions that Neoptolemus (who
returned overland from Troy, through Thrace) "comes to the land of the Molossians, where
he is recognized by Peleus"; that implies that Peleus was in exile from Phthia.

[5]The great majority of archaic images of Neoptolemus present the killing of Priam
and/or Astyanax; the next most prominent subject is the sacrifice of Polyxene (see
Introduction to *Polyxene*). See *LIMC s.v.* Astyanax, Ilioupersis, Neoptolemos, Polyxene,
Priamos.

[6]Ar. *Knights* 1099, *Clouds* 1154–5 (unless this is from Euripides' play of the same
name), *Birds* 851, 857, *Thesm.* 870; *com. adesp.* 740 K-A.

oppression and danger.[7] Two other plays presented him as the dedicated and successful "young warrior" (the literal meaning of his name). *The Scyrians* showed him accepting the invitation to join the campaign at Troy – against, it has been suggested, the well-meaning opposition of his family;[8] in *Eurypylus*, which was set in Troy, he was probably an offstage presence,[9] but a very important one, as the slayer of Eurypylus and thus the destroyer of "the last and greatest saviour of the Phrygians' hopes" (fr. 210.76–77).

Two other plays of Sophocles presented a darker side to Neoptolemus. In *Polyxene* (*q.v.*) it is likely that he both argued for, and personally performed, the sacrifice of Priam's daughter; and in *Hermione* Sophocles combined the stories of his marriage to the daughter of Menelaus and Helen, and of his death at Delphi. As we shall see, it was not the first time this combination of the two stories had been made, but perhaps no one, before or after Sophocles, moulded them into a form so discreditable to their central figure.

We know the basic outline of Sophocles' *Hermione* from the scholia, and the commentary of Eustathius, on *Odyssey* 4.3–4. This is the passage in which Telemachus arrives in Sparta and finds Menelaus celebrating a

---

[7]We know from fr. 487 that Peleus in this play was an old man, at one stage cared for only by a single female servant. The remaining fragments reveal little about the plot, but Dictys 6.7–9 is almost certainly based on a tragedy and very probably on that of Sophocles. Neoptolemus, having learned of Peleus' expulsion from his realm by Acastus, is coming to his aid when he is shipwrecked, with his crew, on the Sepiades islands. He finds Peleus in a cave on the shore. By chance the sons of Acastus come there to hunt, and Neoptolemus joins them, disguising himself and telling them a false tale of his own death. During the hunt Neoptolemus kills both the youths. When told that Acastus is on his way, Neoptolemus disguises himself again – this time as his own captive Mestor, son of Priam – meets Acastus and tells him that Neoptolemus is asleep in the cave. Eager to destroy his enemy, Acastus rushes to the cave and is intercepted by Thetis, who has come there in search of Peleus. She taxes him with all his crimes, but persuades Neoptolemus to pardon him; Acastus in gratitude hands over his kingdom to Neoptolemus, who returns to Phthia accompanied by Peleus and Thetis.

[8]Though our evidence for the plot of the play is very limited; see Carden 94–109.

[9]Wilamowitz (*NJbb* 29 [1912] 452 = *KS* i 351–2) suggested that Neoptolemus might be a speaker in one of the papyrus fragments (fr. 206.12–25), in which his home island of Scyros is mentioned; but since the play also included a report of Eurypylus' death followed by lamentations in which his mother took part (fr. 210) it could hardly have had Neoptolemus as an onstage character unless we assume a change of scene (as Wilamowitz admitted), and Neoptolemus could easily have been the subject of conversation between (e.g.) Priam and the newly-arrived Eurypylus (cf. A.S. Hunt in *POxy* ix [1912] 88; Carden 5).

double wedding, of Hermione to Neoptolemus (in fulfilment of a promise
he had made at Troy) and of his illegitimate son Megapenthes to a Spartan
bride. The scholia state:

> Sophocles in *Hermione* says that while Menelaus was still at Troy,
> Hermione had been given in marriage[10] by Tyndareos[11] to Orestes, but
> when Neoptolemus came home, according to [Menelaus'] promise,
> she was taken away from Orestes; later Orestes lived with her again,
> after Neoptolemus had been killed at Pytho by †Tyndareos†, and then
> Tisamenus was born.

Eustathius is clearer on some points, and has considerably more
information about Neoptolemus' death – which, as we shall see, tallies
with what we can gather from other sources:

> Sophocles, they say, in *Hermione* narrates that while Menelaus was
> still at Troy, Hermione had been given in marriage by Tyndareos to
> Orestes, then later taken away from him and given to Neoptolemus
> according to the promise [made by Menelaus] at Troy. But when he
> [Neoptolemus] had been killed at Pytho by Machaereus, when he was
> trying to avenge the slaying of his father by punishing Apollo, she
> was restored[12] again to Orestes; from which union was born
> Tisamenus, meaningfully so named after the "vengeance (*tisis*) with
> power (*menos*)", because his father Orestes had taken vengeance on
> the murderers of Agamemnon.[12a]

The combination of these two episodes is familiar to us from Euripides'
Andromache, and we shall later need to consider the question of priority
between these two plays. For the moment we may simply note four
differences. In the first place, the Sophoclean Neoptolemus is killed "when
… trying to avenge the slaying of his father"; his Euripidean counterpart
did likewise go to Delphi to "demand from Phoebus satisfaction for having
killed his father" (Eur. *Andr.* 53, 1107–8; at 1095 it is implied, admittedly
by Neoptolemus' enemies, that he had "wanted to sack Phoebus' temple"),

---

[10]Greek *ekdothēnai*, which could refer to an actual marriage or to a mere betrothal
(below, pp. 5–7).

[11]Tyndareos, formerly king of Sparta, was the father of Clytaemestra and the foster-
father of Helen (whom he had given in marriage to Menelaus); a marriage between
Hermione and Orestes would eventually unite Sparta and Mycenae under the rule of
Tyndareos' grandson.

[12]This expression (Greek *apokatastēnai*) does not necessarily imply the agency of a
third party such as Menelaus; see n. 71 below.

[12a]For the Greek text of Eustathius' account, see p. 26.

but he was not killed on that occasion – he is killed when making a *second* visit to make atonement for his act of "madness" (Eur. *Andr.* 51–55, 1002–4, 1106–8, 1163). Secondly, whereas in Sophocles Neoptolemus is killed by one Machaereus ("Knife-man"),[13] in Euripides he is killed by the Delphians in a plot masterminded by Orestes (Eur. *Andr.* 993–1008, 1075, 1114–6, 1124) and actively supported by Apollo (*Andr.* 1147–9, cf. 1005, 1161–5, 1211–3). Thirdly, in Sophocles' treatment Hermione was given to Orestes by Tyndareos, while Menelaus was away at the war; in Euripides it was Menelaus himself who had made the betrothal before the war began (*Andr.* 968–9). And lastly, both the scholiast's and Eustathius' words *prima facie* imply that in Sophocles, Hermione remained in Neoptolemus' house until after he was known to be dead; in Euripides, certain that when Neoptolemus returns from Delphi he will punish her for her attempt to murder Andromache and her child, she departs with Orestes knowing that he is plotting Neoptolemus' assassination.

The marriage of Neoptolemus and Hermione, as we have seen, goes back to Homer at least, but it can only contain the seed of tragic conflict if it is combined *either* with the tradition that Neoptolemus was awarded Andromache as a prize of war *or* with that of a marriage or betrothal of Hermione to Orestes. The former combination may have been first made by Euripides; even after his time there was an alternative version according to which Andromache lived out her days in Molossia – at first with Neoptolemus and after his death with Helenus – without ever getting near Phthia[14], and this version was apparently already well enough established in the fifth century to force Euripides to send Andromache off to Molossia at the end of his play (*Andr.* 1244–9) to marry a Helenus of whom he had made no previous mention. There is no indication that Andromache had any role in Sophocles' play.

Side by side with the story of Hermione's marriage to Neoptolemus there existed, by the fifth century, a well-known account, probably of Spartan origin, according to which she had been the wife of Orestes and

---

[13]Regarding this odd name for Neoptolemus' killer, and its connections with alternative versions of the story, see below, pp. 8–11.

[14]Paus. 1.11.1; [Apoll.] *Epit.* 6.12–13 (where however it is Neoptolemus' *mother*, Deidameia, who is married to Helenus). In Virg. *Aen.* 3.294–336 (cf. Justin 17.3.6) Andromache is apparently sent away to Helenus in Chaonia (*transmisit* 329) when Pyrrhus decides to marry Hermione; Servius on *Aen.* 3.297 reports a different version according to which Pyrrhus gave instructions for Andromache's marriage as he lay dying at Delphi.

mother by him of Tisamenus.[15] Tisamenus was a key figure in the story of
the Return of the Heracleidae,[16] a charter-myth for the Spartans' two royal
houses and for their domination of the Peloponnese, and the Spartans
regarded him as one of their heroes.[17] It is therefore highly likely that the
story of the Orestes-Hermione marriage goes back to the seventh or sixth
century;[18] when we first meet it, in the mythographer Pherecydes of
Athens,[19] it is already combined in a single narrative with the story of a
marriage to Neoptolemus, but we do not know whether Pherecydes was the
first to make the combination, and for any certainty about details[20] we have
to wait for the tragedians.

In Sophocles' treatment, as we have seen, Hermione was "given" to
Orestes by Tyndareos, then "taken away" from him by Menelaus and
given to Neoptolemus. This phraseology might be taken to imply that she

---

[15][Apoll.] *Epit.* 6.28, which names the mother of Tisamenus as "Hermione or, according
to some, Erigone", is merely a garbling of the account now found in schol. Lycophron
Alex. 1374 which states that Orestes "married Hermione, by whom he begot Tisamenus, or,
according to some, married Aegisthus' daughter Erigone and begot Penthilus" (cf. note 18
below).

[16]Polybius 2.41.4, 4.1.5; Strabo 8.7.1, 8.8.5; [Apoll.] 2.8.2–3 and *Epit.* 6.28; Paus.
2.18.6–8, 2.38.1, 3.1.5, 4.3.3, 7.1.7–8, 7.6.2. A son of Orestes is mentioned in *POxy* 2455
fr. 11 lines 140–1, a headnote (Hypothesis) to a play of Euripides, probably *Temenidae*
(named for the sons of Temenus, the leader of the Return).

[17]They brought his bones from Helice and reburied them at Sparta (Paus. 7.1.8).

[18]It may well have been told by the Spartan epic poet Cinaethon; he is known to have
mentioned Orestes' liaison with Erigone, daughter of Aegisthus and Clytaemestra, and their
illegitimate son Penthilus (Paus. 2.18.6 = Cinaethon fr. 4 West).

[19]*FGrH* 3 F 63 (Pherecydes fr. 135A Fowler) = schol. Eur. *Or.* 1654. The passage cited
from Pherecydes is lacunose, but a reference to the birth of Tisamenus survives, and as is
pointed out by R.L. Fowler, *Early Greek Mythography* i (Oxford, 2000) 347, Pherecydes
must also have referred to the Orestes-Hermione marriage: the scholiast says that the
content of Eur. *Or.* 1653–7 (where Apollo says [i] that Orestes will marry Hermione, and
[ii] that Neoptolemus never will) is taken from Pherecydes – but then he cites Pherecydes
to the effect that Neoptolemus *did* marry Hermione, adding that Euripides has altered this;
hence the only thing that *can* have been taken from Pherecydes is the marriage to Orestes!
For the full text of the Pherecydes passage, and also of *FgrH* 3 F 64 = schol. Eur. *Or.* 1655,
see p. 26–29.

[20]Except that (i) the first sentence of the quotation, "then he [n.b. not 'Menelaus']
married her [n.b. not 'Hermione'] to Neoptolemus", strongly suggests that Pherecydes had
just previously mentioned an earlier betrothal of Hermione to Orestes effected (before the
war, presumably) by Menelaus (as in Euripides' *Andromache*), and (ii) in Pherecydes it
was only after Neoptolemus' death that Hermione returned to Orestes.

was already living with Orestes when Menelaus intervened,[21] and this was certainly the line taken by two other fifth-century tragic dramatists, Philocles (fr. 2) and Theognis (fr. 2), who had Menelaus give Hermione to Neoptolemus when she was already pregnant by Orestes; but the words of our sources can also be taken as referring to a mere betrothal (cf. *Men. Fab. Inc.* 51–52). In Euripides' account (*Andr.* 966–981) it is fairly clear that we are meant to understand that Hermione, though "given" to Orestes before the war, has never actually lived with him: neither Orestes nor Hermione makes any mention of a forcible removal of Hermione from his home, and his language[22] strongly suggests that he had no means of preventing or even resisting her marriage to Neoptolemus except by persuading Neoptolemus himself to withdraw his suit. Both Sophocles and Euripides no doubt took it for granted that their audiences would assume that at the time Hermione was "given" to him Orestes was a mere child, and that subsequent events, above all the murder of Agamemnon and the exile of Orestes, made any actual wedding impossible until after Menelaus' long-delayed return from Troy – where he had undertaken to give his daughter to Neoptolemus. At any rate, our evidence indicates that in all the fifth-century treatments of the story in which Hermione was married to Neoptolemus, the union was effected by Menelaus; the idea of a direct seizure of Hermione by Neoptolemus appears only in later sources.[23]

We know of one fifth-century treatment in which Hermione was explicitly *not* married to Neoptolemus. At the end of Euripides' *Orestes* (1653–7) Apollo as *deus ex machina* tells Orestes that he is destined to marry Hermione, and that "Neoptolemus, who thinks he is going to marry her, never will", for his fate is to perish at Delphi. This appears to be an *ad hoc* variation to spare Hermione[24] the future trauma that her usual story

---

[21]Cf. Hyginus *Fab.* 123; this also seems to be the scenario presupposed in Ovid, *Heroides* 8 (cf. especially 35, 115–6). See Zieliński (1925) 115.

[22]"When the son of Achilles came back here [to Phthia], I forgave your father, but begged him [Neoptolemus] to give up the marriage with you ... [and, failing to persuade him,] reluctantly went off, robbed of you as my wife" (*Andr.* 971–3, 981).

[23][Apoll.] *Epit.* 6.14; Servius on Virg. *Aen.* 3.330 (where Pyrrhus is said to have acted "trusting in the support of Menelaus"); and probably also Ovid *Her.* 8, which seems to envisage Hermione, already married to Orestes (cf. last note but one), being seized by Pyrrhus in her husband's absence (*ibid.* 81–82), again with the known approval of Menelaus (*ibid.* 33).

[24]Who has suffered quite enough already: in the last half hour or so she has been seized as a hostage, heard of the supposed death of her mother, and been threatened herself with

entailed: *all* the characters whom Apollo is addressing are to live happily ever after.

The story of Neoptolemus' death in Delphi first appears in our evidence in three texts of the early fifth century. Probably the earliest of these was Pindar's *Sixth Paean*, written for performance at Delphi itself. Neoptolemus is the subject of lines 100–120 of this poem. Neoptolemus, we hear, was fetched from Scyros and "sacked the city of Ilium"; but he never returned to either his mother's or his father's homeland, for Apollo had sworn that he who had killed Priam at the altar of Zeus Herkeios should never come home nor see old age, and "he killed him[25] in his own precinct, by the broad navel of the earth, when he was quarrelling with [the god's] servants about perquisites".[26]

Pindar does not explain why Neoptolemus had come to Delphi; no doubt he assumes his audience already know this from earlier poetry. There is evidently some connection between the version he presupposes and that of Pherecydes (*FGrH* 3 F 64), whose account, while corrupt at a crucial point, also involves a quarrel with those in charge of the temple in which Neoptolemus accuses them of taking what they are not entitled to; but they cannot have an immediate common source, since Pherecydes' account includes the marriage with Hermione as a crucial element, while Pindar's effectively rules it out by saying Neoptolemus never returned to his father's home. This is the story as Pherecydes gives it:

> Then Neoptolemus married Hermione, daughter of Menelaus; and he went to Delphi to inquire about [how he could have] children, for he

---

imminent death by fire or sword or both (Orestes' blade is still at her throat even as Apollo speaks).

[25]It is not clear to us – and we cannot tell whether it was clear to Pindar's original audience – whether this means that Apollo struck Neoptolemus down miraculously, or that he caused him to die at human hands (presumably those of one of the "servants", i.e. priests).

[26]Some words are damaged in the (papyrus) text, but the general sense is not in doubt. The "perquisites" are doubtless to be identified with the sacrificial meats mentioned in this connection in other early accounts (see below); the Delphians were apparently claiming the right to seize for themselves a portion of meat from every sacrifice offered at the sanctuary (like the sons of Eli at Shiloh: 1 Samuel 2.12–17; see n.34 below. Aristodemus (cited by schol. Pind. *Nem.* 7.150) says that the Aeginetans (see below) thought that Pindar in the *Sixth Paean* had accused Neoptolemus of having come to Delphi to plunder the temple; the text of the *Paean*, however, cannot be brought to bear that meaning, and Aristodemus must be importing into it an idea he found expressed in other versions of the story – very likely in that of Sophocles.

had had none by Hermione.[27] And when he saw the Delphians at the oracle pilfering [sacrificial] meat, he took the meat away from them, and killed himself with a knife; and their priest buried him under the threshold of the temple.[28]

The statement that Neoptolemus "killed himself with a knife (*makhaira*)" makes no sense in the context; one would expect the knife to be wielded by one of the Delphians, angry at Neoptolemus' interference with their depredations, probably by the very priest mentioned in (what is transmitted as) the next sentence (since the *makhaira* was the priest's instrument for performing sacrificial slaughter). The text can be fairly simply emended to make the priest the killer (see pp. 26–27); it is more doubtful whether we should convert the *makhaira* into a personal name Machaereus (as in Sophocles), since, as we shall see in a moment, the *makhaira* figures in another of the early accounts and the name Machaereus does not.

Pindar returns to the story in the *Seventh Nemean*, composed for a victor from Aegina, the birthplace of Aeacus the great-grandfather of Neoptolemus. This ode is marked by a number of remarks by the poet indicating that he had been criticized by the Aeginetans for his treatment of Neoptolemus in the *Sixth Paean*.[29] He wants to tell the truth about Neoptolemus and do justice to his name (48–49). No Molossian[30] who may be present will criticize him (64–65); the future will show whether he has said anything improper, but he swears he has not (67–73). He will never admit to having "mauled Neoptolemus with harsh words" – but he is getting bored with having to repeat this so often (102–5 – the end of the ode). All these self-exculpatory remarks follow a modified version of the story of Neoptolemus' death (33–47) which Pindar has carefully purged of any possible aspersions on him. He begins by saying that it was a blessing

---

[27]This motive for Neoptolemus' visit to Delphi also appears, as one of three alternative explanations, in schol. Pind. *Nem.* 7.58.

[28]Cf. Asclepiades *FGrH* 12 F 15, who adds that Menelaus later reburied Neoptolemus "in the *temenos*", i.e. in the plot regarded in historical times as the site of his tomb and the centre of his cult.

[29]Presumably because he had described Neoptolemus' death as Apollo's punishment for his sacrilegious slaying of Priam (an idea that later became proverbial, "Neoptolemean revenge" meaning much the same as the modern phrase "poetic justice", cf. Paus. 4.17.4), and perhaps also because of the impiety implicit in the story of his having quarrelled with Apollo's "servants".

[30]The rulers of Molossia, in north-west Greece, were descended from Molossus, son of Neoptolemus and Andromache.

to Delphi that Neoptolemus came there (33–34).[31] Once again he gives him sole credit for the sacking of Troy, and then brings him to Molossia (mentioning, this time, that his descendants still rule that land). Once again he takes him directly from there to Delphi, but this time he specifies the reason, and it is a pious one – to bring to the god the first-fruits of his Trojan spoils (41). At Delphi, "in a quarrel over meat, he confronted a man who stabbed him with a knife (*makhaira*)". The man was apparently not a Delphian,[32] since the "hospitable" Delphians were extremely grieved (43); but, says Pindar, Neoptolemus "had paid what fate decreed" – not, however, as punishment for any crime, but because it was destined that one of the descendants of Aeacus should remain permanently in Apollo's precinct "to watch over the propriety of hero-processions with many sacrifices" (44–47).[33]

From these three accounts[34] one can gather that when the tale came into the hands of the tragic poets some, though by no means all, of its crucial elements were firmly established. Neoptolemus went to Delphi for some legitimate reason, though there was no agreement on what that reason was; at any rate none of the early accounts suggest an illegitimate one. He became involved in a quarrel over the alleged pilfering of sacrificial meats by the Delphians, and was killed with a *makhaira*, probably by one of the priests;[35] and he was buried "under the threshold of the temple", though if,

---

[31]Lit. "As a bringer of aid, I tell you, Neoptolemus came to the great navel of the broad-bosomed earth." This interpretation of a difficult passage fits the context best: Neoptolemus "brought aid" to Delphi by enriching it with his tomb and cult.

[32]And presumably therefore the *makhaira* was not a *sacrificial* knife – but apparently the tradition that Neoptolemus had been killed by a *makhaira* was too firmly fixed for Pindar to use a different word.

[33]This seems to mean that Neoptolemus, in his tomb, will be a spectator of processions and sacrifices in honour of himself as a hero (another, though less plausible, interpretation is that he will make sure they follow the proper rituals in their cults of *other* heroes).

[34]Cf. also schol. Pind. *Nem.* 7.62: "they say that when Neoptolemus was sacrificing, the Delphians grabbed the sacrifices, as was their custom; that Neoptolemus was annoyed and tried to stop them; and that they put paid to him with swords." This reflects a version of the story which comes, as it were, from the same stable as the three we have been considering, but which is not identical with any of them. The first of the two alternative accounts in schol. Pind. *Paean* 6.118 (see *POxy* v 47) is in substance the same except that it does not specify the murder-weapon(s).

[35]So the *Sixth Paean*, and probably Pherecydes too; in the *Seventh Nemean* Pindar has obvious reasons for wanting to avoid the suggestion of hostility between Neoptolemus and the Delphian authorities. Cf. too Paus. 10.24.4 (Paus. 1.13.9, where "the Delphians" kill

as is likely, his *temenos* was already in existence at Delphi,[36] the tale was probably also already in existence that his body had been transferred to it by Menelaus.

What do we know about Sophocles' treatment of the story? For the moment we shall consider only evidence that is known to relate specifically to *Hermione*, leaving aside for the moment the question whether *Hermione* is or is not the same play as *Phthiotides (The Women of Phthia)*.

Sophocles gives Neoptolemus a motive for going to Delphi quite different from anything known to have been suggested before: he is seeking to avenge his father's death by punishing Apollo. This makes his action clearly impious and even hybristic,[37] and makes him unequivocally responsible for his own death – whereas even in Pindar's *Sixth Paean* some of the blame must be taken to lie elsewhere, and in the other two pre-Sophoclean accounts virtually all of it does. At the same time the idea had precedents or at least close analogies. In a play of Aeschylus[38] (fr. 350) Thetis condemned Apollo as a liar, for having promised her "splendid offspring whose lives would be long and free of sickness" and then having himself killed her son; and in the *Iliad* Achilles himself, furious with Apollo for having decoyed him away from pursuing the Trojans and enabled them to make good their escape into the city, says to him: "You have taken great glory away from me and saved them easily, because you feared no retribution to follow; I tell you I *would* punish you, if I only had the power!" (*Iliad* 22.18–20). Since Neoptolemus has a far deeper grievance against Apollo than his father did, it is quite credible that he

---

Neoptolemus – there called Pyrrhus – on the orders of the Pythia, is not necessarily inconsistent with this).

[36]This *temenos* was about 45 metres north-east of the temple entrance. See Paus. 10.24.6; Pouilloux (1960) 49–60; Fontenrose (1960); Pouilloux & Roux (1963) 102–122.

[37]A quite different, though equally or even more discreditable, motive appears in one of the three accounts in schol. Pind. *Nem.* 7.58: Neoptolemus was aiming at domination of the Peloponnese, and began by attempting to plunder the temple at Delphi. This reading of the story in terms of power politics seems influenced by Thuc. 1.121.3, 143.1, and/or by the Sacred War of 355–346, and must surely be later than Sophocles. References to Neoptolemus "attacking the sanctuary" also appear in Strabo 9.3.9 (where this version is *contrasted* with that in which he was seeking justice for his father's death) and Paus. 10.7.1; and in Pacuvius' *Hermiona* (174–5 Warmington; see Appendix) Orestes seems to accuse him of scheming (in this case by means of his marriage) to take control of "someone else's kingdom" (i.e. Sparta, to which Orestes would otherwise have been the heir).

[38]Possibly *The Phrygian Women* (see A.H. Sommerstein, *Aeschylean Tragedy* [Bari, 1996] 374–5). The passage incurred the severe condemnation of Plato (*Rep.* 383a-c).

might go one step further than Achilles and actually try to take revenge instead of merely wishing he could.

At this point we must bring into the discussion a passage from the epitome of the lost end of pseudo-Apollodorus' *Bibliotheca* (6.14):

> And when Orestes went mad, he [Neoptolemus] seized his wife Hermione, who had previously been betrothed[39] to him at Troy; and for this reason he was killed at Delphi by Orestes. But some say that when he came to Delphi he demanded satisfaction from Apollo for [the death of] his father,[40] plundered the dedications and set fire to the temple,[41] and that because of this he was killed by Machaereus the Phocian.

Of the two accounts we are given here of Neoptolemus' death, the first is either a brief and rather inaccurate summary of the version in Euripides' *Andromache*, or else it is based on some later version.[42] The second agrees with Sophocles in two important particulars: it has Neoptolemus attempting to punish Apollo for his father's death, and it converts the *makhaira*, in earlier accounts the weapon with which he was killed, into a person named Machaereus. It is, to say the least, very tempting also to ascribe to Sophocles the two further particulars found here and not in Eustathius' report. The first of these heightens Neoptolemus' guilt and *hybris* even further by making him attempt to sack and burn the temple[43] (cf. Eur. *Andr.* 1095). The second specifies that Machaereus was a Phocian – whereas the only other source to give him an ethnic, Strabo (9.3.9),[44] calls him a Delphian. This too is in keeping with what appears to have been Sophocles' policy in his treatment of Neoptolemus' death: on the one hand he piles guilt on Neoptolemus himself, on the other hand he exonerates Apollo and the Delphians. Even though Neoptolemus is attempting to commit an appalling sacrilege at the holiest site in Greece,

---

[39]sc. in her absence.

[40]Cf. Strabo 9.3.9 and the third explanation in schol. Pind. *Nem.* 7.58.

[41]Cf. the second explanation in schol. Pind. *Paean* 6.118 ("he was killed on account of the <temple> property that he was plundering in order to avenge his father").

[42]It is very similar to the second of the two accounts given by Servius on Virg. *Aen.* 3.330 (cf. Velleius Paterculus 1.1.3), which also has a direct seizure of Hermione by Neoptolemus(-Pyrrhus) followed without further explanation by the murder of the latter by Orestes.

[43]As the Persian invaders were believed to have tried to do (Hdt. 8.35).

[44]Strabo is also the only source, other than the Apollodorean epitome and Eustathius, to mention *both* Machaereus *and* the demand that Apollo give satisfaction for Achilles' death.

and it would have been no crime for a Delphian to kill him, Sophocles apparently does not want it to be a Delphian that kills him, perhaps because that would stir up recollections of the older accounts in which the Delphians were defending not so much the sanctity of the temple as their own right to fleece pilgrims; instead he makes the killer a Phocian, against whom there can be no suspicion of any self-interested motive.

We have three other significant pieces of evidence about Sophocles' *Hermione*. One is the title of the play; whether this is due to Sophocles or to a later editor (or bookseller),[45] it shows that *someone* thought – and expected others to think – that Hermione was the most important or at least the most interesting character in the play, more so than Neoptolemus. The fact that she was a character at all, in a play written around the death of Neoptolemus at Delphi, suggests that the action of the play itself was set not at Delphi but at Phthia[46] (as in Euripides' *Andromache*) and therefore that Neoptolemus can have been present only in its earlier stages; that Phthia rather than Delphi was the scene of the action is confirmed by fr. A (202), which shows (see below) that the action was set in the "fatherland" of at least one of the major characters. It is a reasonable inference from the title that once Neoptolemus had departed, much of the audience's interest was centred on Hermione, and the evidence of Eustathius and the Homeric scholiast suggests that (again as in Euripides) this was done, at least in part, by bringing on to the scene her former fiancé Orestes and showing her deciding to leave Phthia with him.

Another, though a very obscure, item of evidence is a scholium on Euripides' *Orestes* (1655) which quotes Pherecydes' account of Neoptolemus' marriage and death (*FGrH* 3 F 64) and then adds "Sophocles also gives this genealogy". What makes the evidence obscure is that the Pherecydes quotation as transmitted neither is, nor contains, a genealogy: it does not mention the birth of any child to anyone. It does, however, say that Neoptolemus had no children by Hermione, and the scholiast may be saying that Sophocles likewise makes them childless.[47]

---

[45]I have argued in *Seminari Romani* 5 (2002) 1–16 that from the early 440s the titles of tragedies were chosen by the dramatists and publicly announced at the *proagon* a few days before the performance; but we cannot be certain whether Sophocles' play was written before or after this practice began.

[46]In all versions of the story in which Neoptolemus takes Hermione to his home, that home, if it is identified at all, is always identified as Phthia (so already *Odyssey* 4.8–9).

[47]In contrast with several later writers, who did credit them with a son to whom hardly any two of them gave the same name (details in schol. Eur. *Andr.* 32).

Alternatively, as was suggested by R. Wagner,[48] the quotation may have been truncated in the course of transmission and may originally have included a reference to Hermione's reunion with Orestes and the birth of Tisamenus.[49]

Last, and almost least, come the actual fragments ascribed to *Hermione*. There are only two of these, and only one (fr. A [202]) tells us anything of significance. In this, someone apostrophizes "the earth of the streets[50] of my fatherland", having evidently just returned from foreign parts. As we have seen, this, together with the title of the play, shows that the action was set in Phthia, and that in turn virtually determines the identity of the speaker of this fragment. It cannot be Orestes, whose fatherland was Argos or Mycenae.[51] It cannot be Peleus, whose fatherland was Aegina. It cannot be Phoenix (if he had a role in the play – which, as we shall see, he is very likely to have done), for he had come to Phthia as an exile (*Iliad* 9.478–480). Of named characters who are known or likely to have had significant roles in the play, only Neoptolemus remains: he was born in his mother's land, Scyros, but his father's land was Phthia. Thus we can infer that Neoptolemus, who *departs* from Phthia for the last time well before the end of the play, had earlier in the action *arrived* there from abroad; and the importance of Hermione in the play, as attested both by its title and by Eustathius' summary, makes it highly likely that the journey from which he had returned was a journey to Sparta to bring home Hermione as his bride.

That the action of *Hermione* was set at Phthia inevitably raises the question of its possible identification with Sophocles' play *Phthiotides (The Women of Phthia)*, given that tragedies with a chorus of women from a given locality almost invariably[52] have that locality as the scene of their

---

[48]Wagner (1891) 276 n.2.

[49]Though as is noted by Fowler (n.19 above) 347, the mention of Tisamenus in Pherecydes *FGrH* 3 F 63 (= fr. 135A Fowler) is likely to come from an entirely different context (cf. already Jacoby, *FGrH* i 410).

[50]That "of the streets" (and not "of Apollo Agyieus") is the meaning of Greek *aguiaios* is shown in the Commentary on fr. A (202).

[51]Equally impossible is the suggestion of Paul Maas (reported by Radt on the authority of Bruno Snell) that the speaker might be Pylades (whose fatherland was Phocis).

[52]Among plays *named* after their choruses, the only known exception is Euripides' *Phoenician Maidens*, set at Thebes. F. Vater (*Archiv für Philologie und Pädagogik* 17 [1851] 181) suggested, apparently in a spirit of devil's advocacy, that the chorus of *Phthiotides* might have consisted of female servants of Peleus' wife, who would have

action. Of *Phthiotides* we know that it contained a middle-aged or elderly person who admonished a foolish or headstrong young man (fr. B [694]); that in one scene there were two old men on stage together, one of whom undertook to "lead [the other] like a child" (fr. D [695]); that one of the characters was a son (or, just possibly, daughter) about whom, at one stage of the action, uncertainty was expressed (fr. C [696]) as to whether (s)he had already taken action to gain justice for the killing of his/her father – or, assigning a different reference to one pronoun, as to whether such action had been taken against *him* for the killing of his father; and that the play was regarded by Aristotle (*Poet.* 1456a1) as one in which the presentation of character was a more important feature than it was in the average classical tragedy.

That these data are consistent with what we know of *Hermione* is evident:[53] both the young men mentioned can be identified with Neoptolemus[54] (whom Sophocles certainly made foolish and headstrong in *Hermione*), the old men could be Peleus and Phoenix,[55] and the personalities of Neoptolemus and Hermione at least could easily have been made crucial to the development of the action. This is in itself nowhere near demonstrating that our information about *Phthiotides* fits the Neoptolemus-Hermione-Delphi story and no other: we must first consider the possible alternatives.

An early suggestion (Matthiae, Welcker) was that *Phthiotides* was the same play as *Peleus*; but even if Dictys' narrative[56] derives from some other Peleus-tragedy than that of Sophocles, the fragments of *Phthiotides* hardly fit a play about the rescue and restoration of the exiled Peleus. In particular, it is very unlikely that the title character of *Peleus* had a second old man to befriend him (fr. D [695]): we know that at the start of the play he was entirely dependent on the care of a woman (fr. 487), and we know that his eventual rescuer was Neoptolemus. Nor has the son or daughter who has committed, or who may be avenging, the killing of a father, been convincingly identified.

---

accompanied her wherever she might go; but the slaves of a Phthian princess would not have been called "women of Phthia".

[53] As was first seen by Vater (*op. cit.* 180–1, 189).

[54] Not Orestes; see Commentary on fr. C (696).

[55] In the cyclic epic *The Returns* Phoenix had died while accompanying Neoptolemus homewards from Troy (*Returns* Arg. §4 West), and no source is *known* to have brought him back to Phthia; but this is the kind of detail that a dramatist could easily modify.

[56] See n.7 above.

E.A.J. Ahrens in his edition of Sophocles' fragments,[57] and C.R. Post[58] much later, inclined to the view that *Phthiotides* may have dealt with the fortunes of Peleus[59] when he first came to Phthia as a young man, exiled from Aegina for the murder of his brother Phocus. He was purified by the local king, Eurytion, and was given a share of the kingdom and the hand of Eurytion's daughter Antigone, by whom he had a daughter Polydora; but going with Eurytion to help hunt the Calydonian Boar, he accidentally killed him and had to go into exile again, to Acastus in Iolcus. If *Phthiotides* dramatized this story, then in view of fr. C [696] the action would have to have followed, or included, the arrival at Phthia of news of the death of Eurytion, and it is hardly credible that Sophocles could have imagined Peleus returning to Phthia directly after killing its king, his father-in-law and benefactor, at Calydon.[60] This suggestion also, then, must be rejected.

No other alternative having been suggested, I conclude that it should be regarded as established that *Phthiotides* was the same play as *Hermione*, which in that case we know to have included among its characters two old men. It is not formally certain that one of them is the person who admonishes Neoptolemus in fr. B (694), but it is the most economical hypothesis. One of the two old men is doubtless Peleus, and it is plausible to accept Pearson's identification of the other as Phoenix, acting as *paidagōgos* in one sense to Neoptolemus and in another to Peleus just as he had once done to Achilles. We may note also that fr. D (695) suggests that at some point the two old men go, or at least prepare to go, on some kind of expedition together. The only journey (relevant to the plot) that one can readily envisage them making is to Delphi, either as a last attempt

---

[57]E.A.J. Ahrens, *Sophoclis Fragmenta* (Paris, 1844) 287–8.

[58]Post (1922) 38–39.

[59]Narrated by [Apoll.] 3.13.1–2; cf. Pind. fr. 48, Pherecydes *FGrH* 3 F 1 and 61; Polydora is mentioned in the *Iliad* (16.175).

[60]He did, of course, return to Phthia in the end, which suggests that Eurytion left no son to avenge his death. Antigone, who might have been a danger to Peleus, had hanged herself ([Apoll.] 3.13.3; Tzetzes on Lycophron *Alex.* 175, citing Pherecydes *FGrH* 3 F 1) on receiving false news from the wife of Acastus (who was in love with Peleus) that Peleus was about to make a new marriage, and Tzetzes' paraphrase of Pherecydes implies that this was what made it safe for Peleus to return, later on, to Phthia. The deception and death of Antigone might make a plausible subject for a tragedy, but it is no easier to fit the surviving fragments of *Phthiotides* into such a play than into the others that we have considered; Peleus, for example, the obvious candidate for the role of headstrong young man in fr. B (694), would not be available, since at this stage he was in Iolcus, not Phthia.

to save Neoptolemus from the consequences of his folly or in order to bring home his body; the latter is more convenient dramatically, for reasons explained in the Commentary on this fragment.[61]

Apart from the two known fragments of *Hermione* and the three of *Phthiotides*, several other Sophoclean fragments (frr. 646, 795, 871, 872, 1110) have at various times been assigned to one play or the other; none of these suggestions is at all likely.[62] Two South Italian vase-paintings,[63] showing a woman apparently on a journey with a man and another woman, have been tentatively associated by Margot Schmidt[64] with the journeys of Hermione to Phthia (with Neoptolemus) and back to Sparta (with Orestes), but they throw very little light on the story. Neoptolemus' death is not found in art before the fourth century.

Our evidence for *Hermione-Phthiotides*, then, suggests a play with, as characters, Neoptolemus, Hermione, Peleus, Phoenix, Orestes, one or more minor figures, probably a *deus ex machina* or equivalent, and a chorus of women of Phthia, and with an action including *inter alia:*

Return of Neoptolemus to Phthia with Hermione as his bride (very likely a reluctant bride, in view of her previous betrothal to Orestes and of Neoptolemus' hybristic character): fr. A (202)
Advice and warnings to Neoptolemus by Phoenix (or Peleus): fr. B (694)
Neoptolemus departs for Delphi to demand from Apollo satisfaction for the death of his father
Uncertainty at Phthia as to whether he has yet put his plans into action: fr. C (696)

---

[61]See pp. 36–38.

[62]Fr. 646 was for long the only fragment ascribed to *Tyndareos*, and it was doubted whether such a play had ever existed; but the discovery of the Berlin Photius yielded another citation (fr. 647) which removed doubts about the correctness of the attribution. Fr. 795 is tenuously linked to Neoptolemus by its mention of Molossia, but it could just as well refer to Helenus. Fr. 871 is spoken by Menelaus, for whose appearance as a character on stage in *Hermione* there is no evidence. Fr. 872, though it mentions Hermione, cannot possibly come from the play bearing her name, since Plutarch (*Comparison of Lycurgus and Numa* 3.8) cites it with reference to the dress of Spartan *virgins*. Fr. 1110 is a statement by Strabo (9.5.8) that Sophocles called the city or district of Trachis "Phthiotic", which he is more likely to have done in a play that was *not* set in Phthia than in one that was.

[63]A. Cambitoglou and A.D. Trendall, *Apulian Red-figure Vase-painters of the Plain Style* (Cambridge MA, 1961) pl. 2 no. 8 and pl. 10 no. 45 (though in the latter I can see no indication of a journey).

[64]*Gnomon* 42 (1970) 821.

Report of Neoptolemus' death: he attempted to sack and burn the
    sanctuary at Delphi, and was killed by Machaereus the Phocian
Peleus and Phoenix decide to go to Delphi: fr. D (695)
Orestes arrives and takes Hermione away with him
Neoptolemus' body is brought back
Prophecy of the birth of Tisamenus[65]

Remembering that Hermione was the title character, the theme of her
marriage must have been at least as prominent in the early scenes as the
movement leading to the death of Neoptolemus – though the disproportion
can hardly have been so great as it is in Euripides' *Andromache*, where
Neoptolemus' visit to Delphi is never mentioned between lines 76 and
926. One possible reconstruction might be as follows:

Prologue: Peleus and Phoenix. The audience will have been informed
of the current situation and of relevant earlier events, including
Hermione's betrothal to Orestes during the war and Menelaus' decision to
give her to Neoptolemus instead. Peleus may have praised Neoptolemus
for restoring him to his homeland, while also expressing uncertainty about
the wisdom of the marriage he has gone to make; emphasis may well have
been laid on acts of violence in his past (e.g. the killing of Priam,
Astyanax, and the sons of Acastus) by way of preparation for what is to
come.

Parodos: chorus of women of Phthia.

First Episode: return of Neoptolemus (fr. A [202]) and Hermione, the
latter under guard; Neoptolemus declares his determination to avenge
Achilles' death, enters his palace, and orders Hermione taken inside.

First Stasimon.

Second Episode: Hermione comes out and bewails her lot to the chorus,
and to Phoenix[66] when he appears; he promises to help her, and presently
tries unsuccessfully to persuade Neoptolemos (fr. B [694]) to release her;
Neoptolemos brushes him aside and prepares to depart for Delphi.[67]

Second Stasimon.

---

[65]This is likely to have been mentioned in the play, since Eustathius includes it in his
summary even though it is quite irrelevant to the passage of the *Odyssey* on which he is
theoretically commenting.

[66]Slightly more likely than Peleus; see Commentary on fr. B (694).

[67]Might a desperate Hermione now have formed a plan, with the womanly connivance
of the chorus, to murder Neoptolemus when he returned from Delphi?

Third Episode: As Peleus and Phoenix are discussing the grave situation created by Neoptolemus' impious plans (fr. C [696]), a messenger enters and reports his death at the hands of Machaereus the Phocian when he tried to pillage and burn the Delphic sanctuary; as a temple-robber he is being refused burial on Delphian territory.[68] Peleus and Phoenix decide to go together to Delphi and bring Neoptolemus' body home (695).

Third Stasimon.

Fourth Episode: Hermione is gratified that her abductor (as she sees him) has perished, but now she is alone among enemies – or will be, when Peleus returns. Orestes arrives. Perhaps in response to messages from Hermione,[69] he had been on his way to confront Neoptolemus and reclaim her, when at Delphi[70] he learned of Neoptolemus' death. A delighted Hermione accepts his offer to take her back to Argos/Mycenae.[71]

Fourth Stasimon.

Exodos: Peleus[72] returns with Neoptolemus' body; he and the chorus lament. News of Hermione's departure perhaps angers Peleus, but a god (most likely Apollo) appears to vindicate her and Orestes, justify the death of Neoptolemus and probably also that of Achilles, promise some kind of recompense to the blameless Peleus,[73] and predict the birth of Tisamenus

---

[68]The idea that Neoptolemus was initially denied burial is found in Euripides (*Andr.* 1156–7), where it is very poorly motivated, and he probably took it from Sophocles (see below, pp. 20–21).

[69]See below, p. 21.

[70]Where, perhaps, he had gone to seek Apollo's approval for what he intended to do.

[71]In Euripides he takes her to Sparta, so that she can be properly given in marriage by her father (*Andr.* 984–8); but there both she and Orestes know that Menelaus is now at enmity with Neoptolemus and his family, and will therefore be ready to overlook Orestes' presumption in taking Hermione with him first and seeking her father's consent later, all the more so because he will be conscious of having wronged Orestes previously by revoking his own decision to betroth Hermione to him. In Sophocles there is no sign of any hostility between Menelaus and Neoptolemus, and the original betrothal had been made by Tyndareos without Menelaus' knowledge. It is perhaps therefore best to suppose that in Sophocles' play Orestes, considering himself to have always been Hermione's rightful husband, simply took her home without seeking anyone else's consent.

[72]Phoenix would be superfluous in this scene and may well have been dispensed with.

[73]Perhaps the recompense takes the form of allowing Neoptolemus to be buried at Delphi after all (see n.28 above, and cf. Strabo 9.3.9 who says that Neoptolemus was buried in what became his *temenos* "according to an oracle"). His tomb there was so well known that even Euripides cannot abolish it; he implausibly makes Thetis order Peleus to bury Neoptolemus close to Apollo's temple "as a reproach to the Delphians" (*Andr.* 1240–1), ignoring the obvious difficulty that it would also be a reproach to Apollo and that such an action would be impossible without his or the Delphians' permission.

(named after the vengeance Orestes took for his father with Apollo's aid – a nice contrast with the vengeance Neoptolemus tried to take for his father *upon* Apollo), who will rule both Argos/Mycenae and Sparta until his death at the hands of the returning Heracleidae.

If such was the structure of *Hermione-Phthiotides*, it will have been a play of two themes, linked by the figure of the hybristic, headstrong Neoptolemus. On the one hand, he seeks vengeance on Apollo as if Apollo were a human enemy, sacking Delphi to punish his father's divine slayer as he had sacked Troy to punish (the family and compatriots of) his father's human slayer. On the other hand, like his counterpart in Euripides' *Andromache*, he acts foolishly in the matter of marriage. The Euripidean Neoptolemus takes a wife while still keeping in his house the concubine who, though she no longer shares his bed (*Andr.* 36–37), remains the mother of his child; this leads to trouble when the wife proves barren. The Sophoclean Neoptolemus marries a woman who had been promised in good faith to another; it may well be that she was portrayed as having been married very much against her will, and as being treated like a slave. This too was bound to lead to trouble sooner or later, and I have suggested (n.67 above) that Neoptolemus' death at Delphi may have forestalled only by a few days his death at the hands of the ill-used Hermione.

There is obviously a close relationship between this play and Euripides' *Andromache*, and there can be little doubt that Sophocles' play is the earlier of the two.

(1) In Sophocles, Neoptolemus goes to Delphi to gain satisfaction for the death of his father, attempts to sack and burn the temple, and is killed while doing so. In Euripides too he goes to Delphi to gain satisfaction for the death of his father, but it is left quite unclear what exactly he does there. At one point (*Andr.* 1094–5) it is strongly implied, though not stated in terms, that "what he came for previously" was "to sack the temple"; but that only makes it even more obscure how he survived the attempt, only to be killed on a *second* visit when he came to make humble atonement for the first. It is hard to see how Euripides could have thought up this complicated and illogical scenario, or expected his audience to understand its inexplicit presentation, unless he and they were already familiar with Sophocles' clear and simple, if shocking, story.

(2) Euripides says that the corpse of Neoptolemus was thrown out of the temple at Delphi and left lying unburied (*Andr.* 1156–7) without giving any reason why it should thus be treated in a manner that one would have thought highly offensive to the god of purity. In Sophocles' play the

Delphians would have had an excellent reason: Neoptolemus had attempted to plunder the temple, and temple-robbers, like traitors, at least at Athens, were regularly denied burial in the territory of the community in which their crime had been committed.[74] Once again Euripides is trading on his audience's knowledge of Sophocles' play: because Sophocles had made the Delphians leave Neoptolemus unburied, Euripides risks letting them do the same (thus enabling Neoptolemus' body to be brought back and lamented on stage[75]) even though he has abolished their motivation for it.

(3) Euripides makes Orestes say to Hermione that he has come to Phthia "not out of respect for your messages" (*Andr.* 964). We have previously heard no word of any such messages, and the simplest explanation is that the Sophoclean Hermione *had* sent messages to Orestes begging him to rescue her from Neoptolemus,[76] and that Euripides is emphasizing to his audience that in *his* treatment this is *not* the explanation of Orestes' opportune arrival.[77]

Euripides' *Andromache* was produced in the middle 420s, or perhaps a little later.[78] We cannot tell how much earlier Sophocles' play is to be dated.

In addition to the fifth-century plays by Theognis and Philocles already mentioned, the Hellenistic dramatist Theodorus also wrote a *Hermione* (of

---

[74]Thuc. 1.138.6; Xen. *Hell.* 1.7.22; Lyc. *Leocr.* 113; [Plut.] *Lives of the Ten Orators* 834b.

[75]This is particularly important for Euripides, because Neoptolemus – whose unwise actions have been the cause of everything that has happened in the play, and whose death is their only irremediable consequence – has not previously appeared on stage at all.

[76]See Zieliński (1925) 114–7.

[77]Orestes (who had initially claimed to be merely passing through Phthia on his way to Dodona, *Andr.* 885–8) now feels sure enough of his position to admit that he has been hanging round Phthia for some time, hoping that the quarrel between Hermione and Andromache would result in Hermione wishing, or needing, to leave Neoptolemus (*Andr.* 959–966).

[78]See Cropp & Fick 5, 27–65 (esp. 60). By all their criteria *Andromache* forms a group with *Hecuba* (not later than 424) and *Suppliants*, with metrical patterns substantially freer than those of the early "severe-style" plays (438–428) and substantially less free than *Electra* (not before 418, since Ar. *Clouds* 534–6, written for the revised version of the play, assumes that the only tragic Electra is the Aeschylean one) or *Trojan Women* (415); and the bitterly anti-Spartan tone of several passages makes it likely that the play was written and produced when Athens and Sparta were at war and expected to remain so, i.e. no later than 422.

which only the title survives).[79] The *Hermiona* of the Roman dramatist Pacuvius is discussed in the Appendix.

Appendix: Pacuvius' Hermiona

Pacuvius' *Hermiona* is of obvious relevance to the study of Sophocles' *Hermione* as being the only dramatic treatment of the story, after the fifth century, of which we have more than minimal knowledge,[80] and also because in one important respect it adopted a version of the story not known to have been used by any earlier author except Sophocles: namely that the original betrothal of Hermiona[81] to Orestes was made by Tyndareus (181–2, 184).[82] I would argue, however, that we can learn little else about Sophocles' play from the information we have on Pacuvius'.

Discussion of Pacuvius' play has long been dominated by the assumption that its setting was Delphi,[83] but the following three considerations, taken together, make it far more likely that the play was set at Phthia:

(i) As Mette points out,[84] it is *prima facie* unlikely that Hermiona (the speaker of 172 and probably of 183) would accompany her husband to Delphi. This argument might not necessarily apply, however, in the case of an inquiry about childlessness (cf. below): in Euripides' *Ion* Xuthus, consulting the oracle for this reason, takes his wife Creusa with him.[85]

(ii) Verse 190 ("He left his chariot, and cleverly shielded his arm by folding up his cloak") indicates that Pyrrhus was ambushed on the road,

---

[79]One of these three tragedians may well have been responsible for a unique version of the story, reported in schol. Eur. *Andr.* 53, in which Menelaus decides after all that his daughter should be (or should remain) the wife of Orestes, and then himself plots and/or carries out the murder of Neoptolemus.

[80]Of the *Hermiona* of the earlier Roman dramatist Livius Andronicus we know only that Andromache was a character, as was her son by Pyrrhus, and that at some stage she feared that the boy might (be induced to) turn against her (Livius 23 Warmington).

[81]All characters present, or referred to, in Pacuvius' play are given, in this Appendix, the Latin names that he appears on our evidence to have used.

[82]Throughout this Appendix I use the line-numbering of E.H. Warmington, *Remains of Old Latin* (London/Cambridge MA, 1936) 224–235. The most important subsequent discussions of *Hermiona* have been by H.J. Mette, *Lustrum* 9 (1964) 85–87 and in the edition of Pacuvius by G. D'Anna (Rome, 1967).

[83]Originated by O. Ribbeck, *Die römische Tragödie im Zeitalter der Republik* (Leipzig, 1875) 261.

[84]*Lustrum* 9 (1964) 86.

[85]Cf. Wagner (1891) 275.

and is irreconcilable with the usual story of his being attacked in (or even just outside) the sanctuary at Delphi.[86] It does, admittedly, leave open the possibility that an ambush might have been set for him on his *homeward journey.*[87]

(iii) Two references to hospitality in the surviving fragments (191, 193–4) strongly suggest that the action was set at the home of one or more of the characters, and that one or more other characters were his (their) guest(s): this does not suit Delphi at all, whereas at Phthia the hosts would be Peleus and Pyrrhus, the guests Menelaus and perhaps Orestes.[88]

Pyrrhus says early on that he has been forced to take a certain course of action because of the age and childlessness of Peleus and because of *penuriam stirpis* (either the poverty of the family, or its lack of offspring). Ribbeck[89] associated this with Pherecydes' account of Neoptolemus going to Delphi to inquire how he could have children, having had none by Hermione; but the emphasis here is placed not on Pyrrhus' childlessness but on the childlessness of his grandfather, and it is more likely that what he was forced to do was take Hermiona as his wife – which suggests that he was represented as marrying her rather reluctantly, aware of the likely opposition of Orestes and/or of the wrong he was doing to his concubine and her child. At any rate, Orestes and Menelaus arrive at Phthia – independently, one presumes – and there is a direct confrontation between Hermiona's rival husbands (174–6, 184–5) in front of her father (186) and perhaps also of herself.[90] We cannot say for sure how the action then developed, but 189 shows that someone overheard, or was thought to have overheard, a private conversation between two other characters. This may

---

[86]This also makes it virtually certain that in Pacuvius it was Orestes, not the priests of Apollo, that was responsible for Pyrrhus' death (so D'Anna *op. cit.* 101; G. Manuwald, *Pacuvius, summus tragicus poeta* [Munich, 2003] 70).

[87]As apparently in Dictys 6.12–13 – though this typically eccentric account is unfathomably obscure in parts, and it is impossible to say where or by whom, according to the author, Neoptolemus was actually killed.

[88]"Perhaps", because one would expect that Pyrrhus would refuse to admit Orestes into his home; their onstage confrontation must of course be *outside* the house. It has often been suggested that the hospitality-relationship referred to is one between Argos and Delphi; but neither the Greek term *xenia* nor the Roman term *hospitium* was applied to a relationship between one whole community and another. Manuwald *op. cit.* 75 states as a fact that "in der *Hermiona* ... kommt es ... zu Gastfreundschaft und Eintracht zwischen Völkern", citing 193–4 as her sole evidence; it furnishes none.

[89]Ribbeck *loc.cit.*

[90]On the Roman stage, in contrast with the Greek, the number of speaking actors was not limited to three.

have been Orestes eavesdropping on Menelaus and Pyrrhus, but a more interesting possibility[91] is that the secret conversation was between Orestes and Hermiona, the sundered couple who the audience know are destined to be reunited, and that it was Pyrrhus who overheard them. It would be understandable if Orestes then departed in something of a hurry (cf. 196); presently Pyrrhus also departed, most likely in pursuit of him, only to run into his ambush[92] and be killed.

Peleus will have been enraged on hearing this news; Menelaus may have been so likewise, but it is more likely that he came to understand the distress of his daughter (cf. 172, 173, 183, possibly 171) and repented of having handed her over to Pyrrhus. There is certainly some indication that Peleus and Menelaus fell out with one another. In 193–4 two or more persons are urged to "preserve in good faith the concord that is eternally joined to hospitality": that is not worth saying unless they have been linked by hospitality and have quarrelled. Since Orestes, as we have seen, is not likely to have formally become Peleus' and Pyrrhus' guest, one party to the quarrel and the ensuing reconciliation must be Menelaus; the talk of preservation and eternity suggests that we are looking to the future beyond the end of the play, so Pyrrhus is likely to be already dead and the other person concerned will be Peleus. The moral adjuration might well then come from a god – or more probably a goddess, for in 192 some female being describes herself as having "held all Greeks under judgement". The only goddess who could be said to have judged all the Greeks was Athena-Minerva, who punished them for their failure to prevent or avenge the desecration of her temple at Troy by the lesser Ajax, and thereby caused *inter alia* the long wanderings of Menelaus; previously she had been a firm ally of the Greek cause and especially of Achilles (*Iliad* 1.194–222, 19.341–354, 22.177–277), and she is an appropriate person to reconcile Menelaus with Achilles' father. Peleus will have to accept the restoration of Hermiona to Orestes, from whom she should never have been taken away; he will also have to accept the extinction of his own legitimate descent line, but Minerva, like Thetis in Euripides' play, may perhaps have consoled him with the promise of immortality. Menelaus, alone or together with Peleus, may be required to bury Pyrrhus at Delphi.[93]

---

[91]Ribbeck *op. cit.* 266.

[92]Preconcerted, presumably, with his accomplices.

[93]Menelaus does so in schol. Pind. *Nem.* 7.62. In the plot as tentatively reconstructed above there is no place for Delphi – and if Pyrrhus is to be killed in an ambush on the road, it is hard to see how there can be: so within the play Minerva's injunction will be

Except for the basic datum of the prior betrothal by Tyndareus, scarcely any of this matches anything we know or can infer about Sophocles' play. Rather we are dealing here with a novel version of the old story, one that could have been conceived only for the Roman, not the Greek, stage, its key features being (i) the direct confrontation of Pyrrhus and Orestes, (ii) the abandonment of the consistent Greek assumption that Achilles' son perished at Delphi, and less certainly (iii) the clandestine meeting of Orestes and Hermiona while Pyrrhus is not merely still alive but still at home and (iv) the winning over of Menelaus by the daughter he had sacrificed[94] to a marriage of political convenience.

---

unmotivated – but no more so than Thetis' injunction in Eur. *Andr.* 1243–5 that Andromache is to become the wife of Helenus in Molossia, likewise an outcome well established in tradition but totally unprepared for within the play.

[94]I use this expression to hint at a possible link with Euripides' *Iphigeneia at Aulis* (302–505) where Menelaus, having been determined that Iphigeneia shall be sacrificed and having himself intercepted the letter by which Agamemnon had attempted at the last minute to keep her away from Aulis, is won over (too late) by his brother's distress and agrees that Iphigeneia shall be spared and the expedition against Troy abandoned.

ΕΡΜΙΟΝΗ ἢ ΦΘΙΩΤΙΔΕΣ

Selected Testimonia

Eustathius on *Odyssey* 4.3: Σοφοκλῆς δέ φασιν ἐν Ἑρμιόνῃ ἱστορεῖ, ἐν Τροίᾳ ὄντος ἔτι Μενελάου, ἐκδοθῆναι τὴν Ἑρμιόνην ὑπὸ τοῦ Τυνδάρεω τῷ Ὀρέστῃ. εἶτα ὕστερον ἀφαιρεθεῖσαν αὐτοῦ, ἐκδοθῆναι τῷ Νεοπτολέμῳ κατὰ τὴν ἐν Τροίᾳ ὑπόσχεσιν. αὐτοῦ δὲ Πυθοῖ ἀναιρεθέντος ὑπὸ Μαχαιρέως ὅτε τὸν Ἀπόλλω τινύμενος τὸν τοῦ πατρὸς ἐξεδίκει φόνον, ἀποκαταστῆναι αὖθις αὐτὴν τῷ Ὀρέστῃ. ἐξ ὧν γενέσθαι τὸν Τισαμενόν, φερωνύμως οὕτω κληθέντα, παρὰ τὴν μετὰ μένους τίσιν. ἐπεὶ ὁ πατὴρ Ὀρέστης ἐτίσατο τοὺς φονεῖς τοῦ Ἀγαμέμνονος.

Pherecydes, *FGrH* 3 F 64 = fr. 64 Fowler (from schol. Eur. *Or.* 1655): ἔπειτα Νεοπτόλεμος Ἑρμιόνην γαμεῖ τὴν Μενέλεω καὶ ἔρχεται εἰς Δελφοὺς περὶ παίδων χρησόμενος· οὐ γὰρ αὐτῷ ἐγένοντο ἐς Ἑρμιόνης. καὶ ὡς ὁρᾷ κατὰ τὸ χρηστήριον κρέα διαρπάζοντας τοὺς Δελφοὺς ἀφαιρεῖται τὰ κρέα αὐτούς, ἑαυτὸν δὲ κτείνει μαχαίρᾳ. ὁ δὲ τούτων ἱερεὺς αὐτὸν κατορύσσει ὑπὸ τὸν οὐδὸν τοῦ νεώ. (The scholiast adds: ταῦτα γενεαλογεῖ καὶ Σοφοκλῆς.)

ἔπειτα Wilamowitz: ἐπεὶ codd. ‖ ἑαυτὸν ... αὐτὸν κατορύσσει codd. (κτεῖναι Β, κατορύσσει αὐτὸν Β): αὐτὸν δὲ κτείνει Μαχαιρεὺς (perh. rather μαχαίρᾳ) ὁ τούτων ἱερεὺς καὶ αὐτὸν (αὐτὸν del. Wilamowitz) κατορύσσει Leopardus ‖ after νεώ Wagner posited a lacuna containing mention of the marriage of Hermione to Orestes and the birth of Tisamenus

HERMIONE *or* THE WOMEN OF PHTHIA

Selected Testimonia

Eustathius on *Odyssey* 4.3: Sophocles, they say, in *Hermione* narrates that while Menelaus was still at Troy, Hermione had been given in marriage by Tyndareos to Orestes, then later taken away from him and given to Neoptolemus according to the promise [made by Menelaus] at Troy. But when he [Neoptolemus] had been killed at Pytho by Machaereus, when he was trying to avenge the slaying of his father by punishing Apollo, she was restored again to Orestes; from which union was born Tisamenus, meaningfully so named after the "vengeance (*tisis*) with power (*menos*)", because his father Orestes had taken vengeance on the murderers of Agamemnon.

Pherecydes, *FGrH* 3 F 64 = fr. 64 Fowler (from schol. Eur. *Or.* 1655): Then Neoptolemus married Hermione, daughter of Menelaus; and he went to Delphi to inquire about [how he could have] children, for he had had none by Hermione. And when he saw the Delphians at the oracle pilfering [sacrificial] meat, he took the meat away from them, and killed himself with a knife; and their priest buried him under the threshold of the temple. (*The scholiast adds:* Sophocles also gives this genealogy.)

Possible emended versions of second sentence:
… and Machaereus, their priest, killed him and buried him … (Leopardus)
… and their priest killed him with a knife and buried him … (suggested by present editor)

The "genealogical" information ascribed to Sophocles may be either that Neoptolemus and Hermione had no children, or (if Wagner's proposal of a lacuna is correct, see opposite) that Orestes had a son, Tisamenus, by Hermione; see Introduction, pp.13–14. Pherecydes' account of Neoptolemus' death cannot be Sophoclean, since it contradicts the account given by Eustathius (and the Odyssey scholia) which is explicitly attributed to Sophocles.

Pherecydes, *FGrH* **3 F 63 = fr. 135A Fowler (from schol. Eur.** *Or.*
1654): ἐπεὶ Νεοπτολέμῳ αὐτὴν συνῴκισε, καὶ ἀπέθανεν <
> τῶν δὲ γίνεται Τεισαμενός.
γίνεται Schwartz: γαρ M: γὰρ A: om. T.

[Apollodorus], *Epitome* **6.13-14:** Νεοπτόλεμος ... μανέντος Ὀρέστου
ἁρπάζει τὴν ἐκείνου γυναῖκα Ἑρμιόνην κατηγγυημένην αὐτῷ πρότερον ἐν
Τροίᾳ, καὶ διὰ τοῦτο ἐν Δελφοῖς ὑπὸ Ὀρέστου κτείνεται. ἔνιοι δὲ αὐτόν
φασι παραγενόμενον εἰς Δελφοὺς ἀπαιτεῖν ὑπὲρ τοῦ πατρὸς τὸν Ἀπόλλωνα
δίκας καὶ συλᾶν τὰ ἀναθήματα καὶ τὸν νεὼν ἐμπιμπράναι, καὶ διὰ τοῦτο
ὑπὸ Μαχαιρέως τοῦ Φωκέως ἀναιρεθῆναι.
Μαχαιρέως S: βαχαιρέως E.

A (202)

ἀλλ', ὦ πατρῴας γῆς ἀγυιαῖον πέδον

A (202) Herodian *GG* iii.1.131.16–17, iii.2.889.32; Stephanus of
Byzantium, *Ethnica* 23.4–5 Meineke; *Etymologicum Symeonis* 1.52.26
(Σοφοκλῆς Ἑρμιόνῃ) | ἀγυιαῖον Bothe: ἀγυιαίου Steph., Herodian, *Et.
Sym.*

B (694)

νέος πέφυκας· πολλὰ καὶ μαθεῖν σε δεῖ

καὶ πόλλ' ἀκοῦσαι καὶ διδάσκεσθαι μακρά

B (694) Stobaeus 2.31.16 (Σοφοκλῆς φοιωτδ [Φθιωτίδων Gaisford])

Pherecydes, *FGrH* **3 F 63 = fr. 135A Fowler (from schol. Eur.** *Or.* **1654):** After he [Menelaus?] gave her [Hermione] in marriage to Neoptolemus, and he [Neoptolemus] died <   > and to them was born Teisamenus.

The lacuna must have contained mention of the marriage of Hermione to Orestes, but we cannot tell how Pherecydes said it came about.

[Apollodorus], *Epitome* **6.13-14:** When Orestes went mad, Neoptolemus seized his wife Hermione, who had previously been betrothed to him [Neoptolemus] at Troy; and for this reason he was killed at Delphi by Orestes. But some say that when he came to Delphi he demanded satisfaction from Apollo for [the death of] his father, plundered the dedications and set fire to the temple, and that because of this he was killed by Machaereus the Phocian.

A (202)

But, O earth of the streets of my fatherland …

Probably Neoptolemus, on his return to Phthia with Hermione.

B (694)

You are young: you need to learn a lot, be told a lot, and be

taught a great deal.

An older man (Phoenix or Peleus) advising Neoptolemus.

C (696)

ἡ πατροκτόνος δίκη

κεκλῆτ' ἂν αὐτῷ

C (696) Anonymous, *On Syntax*, in Bekker, *Anecdota* 128.1–8 (Σοφοκλῆς Φθιωτίσιν) | 1 πατροκτόνος cod.: πατρόκτονος Vater || 2 κεκλῆτ' Schneider: κεκλῆτ' cod.: κέκλητ' Radt

D (695)

γέρων γέροντα παιδαγωγήσω σ' ἐγώ

D (695) Aulus Gellius, *Attic Nights* 13.19.3 (*in tragoedia Sophocli ... cui titulus est Φιλοτιδες* [corr. Casaubon])

E (203)

γνωστός (= γνώριμος)

E (203) Antiatticist in Bekker, *Anecdota* 87.25 (Σοφοκλῆς Ἑρμιόνη)

C (696)

The case against him [Apollo] for the murder of his
[Neoptolemus'] father may have been called on.

After Neoptolemus' departure for Delphi, someone (Phoenix or Peleus?)
fears he may already have taken an irrevocable step.

D (695)

I shall lead you like a child, although we are both old men.

Phoenix to Peleus (or vice versa) as they prepare to go to Delphi, either in
the hope of saving Neoptolemus or to bring back his body.

The following fragment cannot be assigned to a context:

E (203)

well-known

HERMIONE *or* THE WOMEN OF PHTHIA

A (202)

It is common in tragedy for a person returning to his homeland, or arriving in a place with which he has past associations or to which he has yearned to come, to apostrophize the land, the city, etc.; he usually does this at the beginning of his entrance-speech (Aesch. *Pers.* 249–250, *Ag.* 810; Eur. *Alc.* 1, *HF* 523, *Or.* 356, fr. 558, 696; Ar. *Ach.* 729, *Wealth* 771–3; Men. *Aspis* 491). Here *all(a)* "but", a particle of transition, shows that we are already some way into the speech, but there are also parallels for this (Eur. *Tro.* 45–46; Men. *Sam.* 101); the Herald in Aeschylus' *Agamemnon* ("overcome with emotion" – O.P. Taplin, *The Stagecraft of Aeschylus* [Oxford, 1977] 298) greets the land of Argos *twice* (503, 509). For another possible interpretation of the line see below.

That the speaker here is Neoptolemus has been shown in the Introduction (p. 14). Eustathius' synopsis makes it highly likely that the journey from which he has returned was one to Sparta, whence he has brought Hermione home as his bride – very possibly a reluctant bride, given her previous betrothal to Orestes. It is possible, then, that he is not so much greeting the land as inviting it to greet its new princess; cf. Aesch. *Ag.* 518–528, Ar. *Birds* 1706–19 (both spoken by heralds proclaiming the return of a king – who in both cases is bringing a noble female home with him).

of the streets of my fatherland: this rendering is based on Bothe's emendation, which seems inevitable in view of the statement of the three quoting authors (Herodian, Stephanus of Byzantium and the *Etymologicum Symeonis*) that *aguiaios* is an adjective of location (*topikon*), derived from the noun *aguia* "street", i.e. that it specifies that the thing described belongs to a particular place, viz. the street(s), just as *arouraios*, which two of the quoting authors cite as a parallel formation, specifies that the thing described belongs to a particular place, viz. the fields; this interpretation of *aguiaios* is confirmed by the only other text in which it occurs (schol. Ar. *Knights* 1320). The manuscripts of both authors give the adjective in the genitive case (*aguiaiou*), agreeing with *patrōiās gēs* "fatherland"; Bothe suggested that it should be accusative (*aguiaion*), agreeing with *pedon* "earth, soil" – for whereas soil may be the soil of an (unpaved) street, one's fatherland cannot be the land of a street or streets. There is no evidence that *aguiaios* could mean "of Apollo (Agyieus)"; the word for that is *aguiātēs* (fem. *aguiātis*), cf. Eur. *Ion* 186. Since one of the appurtenances of the theatre was a pillar and altar of Apollo Agyieus in front of the *skēnē* (Aesch. *Ag.* 1081; Eur. *Phoen.* 631; Ar. *Wasps* 875ff, *Thesm.* 748; Pherecrates fr. 92; Men. *Dysk.* 659, *Mis.* 314 Sandbach = 715 Arnott, *Sam.* 309, 444, fr. 884; it is to this Apollo that Clytaemestra prays in *El.* 634–659), it is nevertheless possible in principle that Neoptolemus might accompany his words with a gesture towards this shrine; but it is not likely that he would go out of his way to show courtesy to a god whom he regards as his father's murderer. What *is* likely is that Sophocles has chosen to use the word here because of its indirect Apolline associations, on the lips of a character who will later defy Apollo and be destroyed by him.

B (694)

An older man tells a younger man that he has a lot to learn. If we are right to identify *Phthiotides* with *Hermione* (see Introduction), the young man is certainly Neoptolemus, who has evidently not yet departed for Delphi. It is possible that Neoptolemus has just uttered some dangerously headstrong words about his intentions there, but it is also possible that the older man's warning is concerned with another rash action by Neoptolemus, his determination to retain Hermione as his wife against her will and thereby make a mortal enemy of Orestes.

The prolixity of the older man's language (in one sentence he manages to say the same thing three times) perhaps suggests that he may be Phoenix, who in the *Iliad* makes the longest speech of the entire poem (9.434–605, twenty-four lines longer than Nestor's at 11.656–803) – that, too, a speech of advice to a young man embarking on a rash course of action – rather than Peleus; but we cannot be certain.

In Stobaeus another line follows ("Always desire to learn something new and useful") as if part of the same quotation; but A. Nauck, *Philologus* 4 (1849) 541, recognized that it did not fit. The first two lines characterize the addressee as having much to learn because he is young and inexperienced; the supposed third line presupposes an addressee who might plausibly (though, the speaker believes, wrongly) imagine that he already had all the knowledge he needed, and tells him he should always be open to the possibility of acquiring more. This third line is therefore now regarded as a separate quotation (*trag. adesp.* 516a).

C (696)

Despite uncertainties about the syntax, meaning and reference of some words in this fragment (see below), it is at any rate clear that it refers to an accusation against someone of being responsible, directly or indirectly, for the killing either of his own father or of the accuser's father; furthermore, since the verb *keklēit(o)* is in the perfect optative (the fragment's preservation, indeed, is due to its being chosen as an illustration of the use of the perfect optative with the particle *an*), it is being said that it is *possible* (but not certain) that this accusation has *already* been openly put forward. It is shown in the Introduction (pp.15–16) that such a statement does not fit into any known episode in the story of the house of Peleus except that of the events leading to the death of Neoptolemus. Two of the characters figuring in these events, Neoptolemus and Orestes, had had occasion to seek satisfaction for the killing of their fathers. Orestes, however, on any scenario, must already have taken his revenge well before Neoptolemus' final and fatal visit to Delphi: in all accounts he slew his father's murderers before Menelaus returned home (*Odyssey* 3.306–312, cf. ib. 249–261, Eur. *El.* 1278–80, *Or.* 53–56), in most it was Menelaus who took the initiative in transferring Hermione from him to Neoptolemus, and even those who speak of Neoptolemus himself seizing her by force (e.g. [Apoll.] *Epit.* 6.14 and one of the two versions reported by Servius on Virg. *Aen.* 3.330) make it clear in one way or another that this happened after Orestes' revenge and/or after Menelaus' return. Hence our fragment must refer to an accusation by Neoptolemus against Apollo in connection with the latter's role in bringing about the death of Achilles – an accusation such as he is known to have made in Sophocles' *Hermione* – and thus it provides crucial evidence for the identification of *Phthiotides* with that play.

For it to be "*possible* (but not certain) that this accusation has *already* been openly put forward", the sentence must have been uttered after Neoptolemus' departure for Delphi but before word has reached Phthia as to what befell him there. Since the act of trying to hold a god to account for his actions is a dangerous one, the speaker of the sentence and its addressee must either be both of them friendly to Neoptolemus (in which case one of them is probably urging the other to help save Neoptolemus from the consequences of his rashness) or both of them his enemies (in which case one of them is probably encouraging the other by suggesting that he is likely to have divine assistance in any action he takes against Neoptolemus): there is nothing that one of Neoptolemus' friends could hope to achieve by drawing the possibility of such an action to the attention of one of his enemies (or vice versa).

If speaker and addressee are both enemies of Neoptolemus, they would almost certainly be Hermione and Orestes respectively; but in Sophocles' play Orestes probably did not arrive in Phthia until *after* Neoptolemus was known to be dead (see Introduction, pp. 5, 19), and by then his demand for satisfaction from Apollo was no longer a possibility but a known fact. It follows that the speaker and addressee were probably both friends of Neoptolemus, i.e. Phoenix and Peleus; if my tentative suggestion is correct that fr. B (694) was spoken by Phoenix, then Phoenix, having conversed with Neoptolemus since his return from Sparta, will know more than Peleus about Neoptolemus' current state of mind, and it is therefore more likely that he will be telling Peleus what he fears Neoptolemus may have said or done than that Peleus will be telling him.

the case ... may have been called on: the magistrate presiding over an Athenian lawcourt was said to "call" (*kalein*) a case when he began the trial by ordering the clerk of the court to read out the statement submitted by the plaintiff/prosecutor identifying himself, the defendant, the charge, and the penalty demanded (if the penalty was not fixed by law); cf. Ar. *Clouds* 780, *Wasps* 824–5, 894–7, 1441, [Dem.] 58.43. By this announcement he was deemed to have called (summoned) the parties to appear before him immediately (cf. Ar. *Wasps* 899–903). In our passage the language is metaphorical, for no source suggests that the issue between Neoptolemus and Apollo was ever submitted to any third party for judgement; similarly in Aeschylus' *Agamemnon* (41, 534–7, 812–7, 1412–21) the language of judicial proceedings is repeatedly used in reference to unilateral, violent acts of revenge. Once a case had been called on, the trial was under way and it was too late for either side to offer a compromise (except sometimes on the question of the penalty): the only possibilities, for each, were victory and defeat. Hence to say of Neoptolemus' claim "the case may have been called on" is to say "the die may have been cast", "he may have committed himself irrevocably". And if he has, considering who his opponent is, the outcome can hardly be in doubt.

against him (i.e. Apollo): this rendering assumes that Greek *autōi* is dative of disadvantage; "by him [i.e. Neoptolemus]" (dative of agent) is also possible, particularly since the verb is perfect passive (cf. *Trach.* 664, *Aj.* 1129, *OT* 1373; see Moorhouse 85–86).

for the murder of his father: lit. "slaying a father", the epithet being transferred from the person to the contest in which he is involved; cf. Aesch. *Ag.* 1592 *kreourgon ēmar* "day that prepares meat" (i.e. day on which a meat meal is prepared), *Cho.* 584 *xiphēphorous agōnas* "sword-carrying contests" (i.e. contests in which a sword is carried), Garvie on *Cho.* 260–3. It is theoretically possible that Soph. meant the word to be accented not as *patroktónos* "slaying a father" but as *patróktonos* "relating to the slaying of a father"; that accentuation, however, is nowhere reliably attested.

D (695)

This line is quoted by Aulus Gellius because it was found in identical form both in Sophocles' *Phthiotides* and in Euripides' *Bacchae* (193).[1] The Euripidean line is punctuated as a question by most modern editors; we cannot tell whether the Sophoclean line was also a question ("shall I ...?") or whether it was a statement of undertaking ("I shall ..."). In Euripides the line is spoken by Cadmus to Teiresias – who, though not quite as aged as Cadmus is (cf. 175), is as usual blind and is apparently (cf. 198, 363–5) without the young attendant-guide who normally accompanies him in other tragedies (e.g. *Ant.* 989–990, 1087; *OT* 444; in Eur. *Phoen.* 834–840, 953–4 his own daughter acts as attendant). The pair are going to Mount Cithaeron to take part in the worship of Dionysus; when Cadmus eventually returns to the scene (Teiresias is by then forgotten) it will be with the dismembered corpse of his grandson Pentheus. In *Phthiotides*, if it is identical with *Hermione* (see Introduction), the two old men are likely to be Peleus and Phoenix. If both of them, at their age, are going on a difficult journey, there must be an important reason for it, and the only plausible reason we know of would be one connected with Neoptolemus' disastrous expedition to Delphi. If so, when Peleus returns (whether or not accompanied by Phoenix) he too will be bringing with him the body of his grandson (which, as explained in the Introduction, pp. 20–21, will have been refused burial by the Delphians).

Regarding the placing of the proposed journey of Peleus and Phoenix in the plot of the play, there are four main possibilities:

---

[1] I have therefore adopted the translation of it by Richard Seaford, *Euripides: Bacchae* (Warminster, 1996) 79, only removing the question-mark and the interrogative word-order.

(a) Fearing what may befall Neoptolemus if he carries out his intention of demanding satisfaction from Apollo for his father's death, Peleus and Phoenix decide to go to Delphi to stop him; but they arrive too late, and can do no more than bring home his body for burial.

(b) Learning from a messenger that Neoptolemus has been killed and that the Delphians are refusing him burial, they decide to go to Delphi to bring his body home, and do so.

(c) A combination of the above: Peleus and Phoenix decide to go to Delphi in the hope of preventing Neoptolemus from carrying out his designs, but before they can leave a messenger brings news of his death, and when they eventually do go it is for the purpose of bringing back his corpse.

(d) As a variant on any of the above three scenarios, the two old men may be about to set out for Delphi when they are forestalled by the arrival of another party (perhaps of Neoptolemus' soldiers or servants) bringing his body home.

Of these options, (d) is the least likely, because it is essentially what happens in Euripides' *Andromache*. In that play Peleus (who had earlier rescued Andromache and her son from the murderous plans of Menelaus and Hermione, and taken them to his own home) returns to Neoptolemus' house (*Andr.* 1047ff) because he has heard a rumour that Hermione had left home. On learning that she has eloped with Orestes, who was plotting to have Neoptolemus killed at Delphi, Peleus immediately orders a messenger to go to Delphi to warn his grandson (1066–9) – but before his orders can be carried out, a servant of Neoptolemus arrives *from* Delphi to announce that his master is dead and (1158–60) that his body is already being brought home (it arrives immediately afterwards, at 1166). Not only is it in principle more likely that Euripides is varying Sophocles' treatment than that he is repeating it; we can also see reasons why Sophocles would want there to be an interval between the news of Neoptolemus' death and the return of his body, and why Euripides would not. Sophocles needs an interval because this will provide the opportunity for Hermione to let herself be taken away by Orestes (see Introduction, pp. 5, 19) at a time when, however improperly she is acting, she is at any rate not violating her duties as a wife, since she no longer *is* a wife. In Euripides, Hermione has already departed, and if Peleus or anyone else went to Delphi there would be nothing to fill up the time till they return except a choral song; the play has already had five of these, and Euripides prefers to bring back the body immediately and have a *kommos* (1173–1225) dominated by the solo voice of Peleus.

Of the other options above, (a) requires Peleus to be, in effect, his own messenger reporting Neoptolemus' death as well as being his chief mourner, a combination found in no extant tragedy (the nearest approach is in *Trach.*, where Hyllus reports Heracles' torments [734–812] – but neither Hyllus nor anyone else mourns for Heracles in that play, since at its end he is still alive); which leaves (b) and (c) as the most plausible options. Of these (c) has two advantages: (i) it provides an unexpected change of direction, as the two old men's original plan is frustrated, and thereby increases the complexity of the action; (ii) it provides them with a stronger and more urgent motive for their initial decision to go to Delphi.

It is even harder in the case of this fragment that in those of frr. B (694) and C (696) to decide whether Peleus or Phoenix is the speaker. In the *Iliad*, though Phoenix is an old man (9.432, 446, 607), he is significantly younger than Peleus (cf. 9.481–2), and the promise by the speaker here to "lead [the addressee] like a child" (literally, to be his *paidagōgos*) would be appropriate to a person of inferior (though not servile) status who had actually performed the function of *paidagōgos* to Achilles (*Iliad* 9.485–495). On the other hand, if Phoenix was blind, as he was in the Euripidean play that bore his name (Ar. *Ach.* 421), Peleus might offer to guide him, as Cadmus offers to guide his younger fellow-traveller Teiresias in *Bacchae*; but a blind Phoenix could hardly have made an efficient personal attendant for Achilles, and the story in [Apoll.] 3.13.8 that Peleus took Phoenix to Cheiron, who restored his sight, may well have been derived from the predictions of a *deus ex machina* in Euripides' play. Yet again, then, we may tentatively name Phoenix as the most likely speaker of this fragment.

Since *Hermione-Phthiotides* was written before the middle 420s (see Introduction, p. 21), whereas *Bacchae* was written close to the end of Euripides' life and produced posthumously, it was Euripides who repeated word for word a line from a play of his rival's. It is too much to ask of coincidence that the two poets should independently have hit on the same line in two scenes which also independently share two other highly distinctive features – that the two old men concerned are about to attempt to dissuade the grandson of one of them from an impious course of action, and that the grandfather will next be seen when he returns with that grandson's dead body. Euripides must have quoted the Sophoclean line deliberately, perhaps precisely in order to remind (some) spectators of the Sophoclean scene and put them on the alert to notice parallels (or differences) between the two plays: similarly in the last spoken line of his *Hecuba* (1292), by making Agamemnon echo (much less precisely) the first line of Aeschylus' *Agamemnon*, Euripides has ironically drawn attention to Agamemnon's complete failure to credit the very accurate prophecies by Polymestor (1275–81) of Agamemnon's fate as Aeschylus had depicted it (see W.G. Thalmann, *CA* 12 [1993] 126–159, esp. 154–5; C.W. Marshall, *CW* 95 [2001] 61).

lead you like a child: lit. "be your *paidagōgos*" (for this term see on *Troilus* fr. A [620]). The passage may echo, or may be echoed by, fr. 487 (from *Peleus*), where a woman caring for the aged and probably, in that play, exiled Peleus, says "I am Peleus' guide in his old age (*gerontagōgō*) and I educate him afresh" (i.e. I combine, in what is Peleus' second childhood, the functions of *paidagōgos* and schoolteacher), an expression that evidently stuck in the popular mind and was imitated by two comic dramatists (Ar. *Knights* 1099, *com. adesp.* 740), both of whom cast the personified Athenian *demos* as the "old man" to be cared for.

E (203)

There are two adjectives formed with the suffix *–tos* from the root of the verb *gignōskein* "know", *gnōtos* and *gnōstos*. Some adjectives formed with this suffix are semantically equivalent to perfect passive participles, while others have the sense of "capable of being X-ed"; so *gnōtos* and *gnōstos* might both, in principle, mean either "known" or "knowable". In fact their meaning depends very largely on who is using them. In archaic and classical Greek *gnōtos* is found only in poetry; in Homer (*Iliad* 7.401, *Odyssey* 24.182) it means "knowable" (it is also found as a noun meaning "kinsman"), in later poetry (*OT* 58, 396, Theognis 267, Pind. *Nem.* 10.31) usually "known"; Eur. *Hel.* 41 is close to the not entirely sharp boundary between the two senses, and in Soph. fr. 282 we do not have sufficient context to decide between them. *Gnōstos*, on the other hand, is very common in philosophical texts concerned with knowledge (e.g. Plato's *Theaetetus* and the logical works of Aristotle), and in these it regularly means "knowable". Before the Hellenistic age *gnōstos* is rare in texts of other kinds, and when it does occur (*OT* 361, Aesch. *Cho.* 702, Aeneas Tacticus 16.19, 18.20, and *IG* ii 2 1632.185 where *Gnōstē* is the name of a ship) it means "known"; in our passage, too, the Antiatticist gives its meaning as *gnōrimos* "(well) known".

Now in the development of Attic Greek through and beyond the classical age, there was a strong tendency for -*s*- to be inserted after verbal roots ending in vowels before certain suffixes or endings, notably those of the perfect mediopassive, aorist passive, nouns in -*ma* and -*mos*, and adjectives in -*tos* and -*teos*; see Kühner-Blass ii 131–3, Threatte ii 558– 561, 584–5. And since *gnōtos* is the usual form in early poetry while *gnōstos* is far commoner in later usage, it is possible in principle that *gnōt*- should be restored for *gnōst*- in Aeschylus and Sophocles. However, different verbs succumbed to the tendency at different times, and given that the intrusive -*s*- appears in forms of *gignōskein* as early as the 450s (*IG* i^3 14.29, 30) it would be arbitrary to deny that Aeschylus and Sophocles could have used it (cf. too *eugnōst*- in *Aj.* 704, and *agnōst*- in Eur. *IT* 94, *Hel.* 504).

POLYXENE

Texts and Testimonia: Pearson ii 161–8; Lucas de Dios 261–7; *TrGF* 403–7; Lloyd-Jones 262–7.

Myth: Odyssey 3.130–185; *Cypria* fr. 27 Davies [not in West]; *Sack of Troy* Arg. §4 West; *Nostoi* Arg. §3 West; Stesichorus *PMG* 135; Ibycus *PMG* 307; Simonides *PMG* 557; Euripides, *Hecuba* and *Trojan Women*; Lycophron 323–4 with scholia; Ennius, *Hecuba* and *Andromacha*; Accius, *Troades*; Strabo 10.3.14; Virgil, *Aeneid* 3.321–4; Ovid, *Metamorphoses* 13.439–535; *AP* 9.117; Seneca, *Troades* (and *Agamemnon* 640); "Longinus", *On the Sublime* 15.7; Dictys Cretensis 3.2–3, 4.10–11; Dares Phrygius 27; Hyginus *Fab.* 110; schol. Eur. *Tro.* 16; Dio Chrysostom 6.18; Servius on Virgil, *Aeneid* 3.321; Quintus of Smyrna 14.179–330. W.H. Friedrich, *Hermes* 70 (1935) 98–100; C. Fontinoy, *AC* 19 (1950) 383–396; E. Wüst, *RE* xxi.2 (1952) 1840–6; D.J. Conacher, *Euripidean Drama* (Toronto, 1967) 146–150; D.M. Robertson, *BICS* 17 (1970) 13–15; E. Fantham, *Seneca: Troades* (Princeton, 1982) 50–77; M. Davies, *The Epic Cycle* (Bristol, 1989) 76, 80–82; Gantz 658–9; O. Touchefeu-Meynier, *LIMC* vii.1 (1994) 431; J. Gregory, *Euripides: Hecuba* (Atlanta, 1999) xvii–xxiii; P. Michelakis, *Achilles in Greek Tragedy* (Cambridge, 2002) 58–61, 77–80.

Artistic evidence: Pausanias 1.22.6; *App.Plan.* 150; A.J.N.W. Prag, *The Oresteia: Iconographic and Narrative Sources* (Warminster, 1985) 61–66; O. Touchefeu-Meynier, *LIMC* vii.1 (1994) 431–5; J.M. Mossman, *Wild Justice: A Study of Euripides' Hecuba* (Oxford, 1995) 256–263; N. Sevinç, *Studia Troica* 6 (1996) 251–264; G. Schwarz, *MDAI(A)* 116 (2001) 35–50.

Main discussions: T. Zieliński, *Tragodumenon libri tres* (Cracow, 1925) 18–24; id., *Eos* 31 (1928) 1–7; W.H. Friedrich, *Untersuchungen zu Senecas dramatischer Technik* (Borna/Leipzig, 1933) 102–7; W.M. Calder III, *GRBS* 7 (1966) 31–56; Sutton 113–5; E. Fantham, *Seneca: Troades* (Princeton, 1982) 57–60; K.C. King, *Achilles: Paradigms of the War Hero from Homer to the Middle Ages* (Berkeley, 1987) 184–201; J.M. Mossman, *Wild Justice: A Study of Euripides' Hecuba* (Oxford, 1995) 42–47; R. Bardel in F. McHardy et al. ed. *Lost Dramas of Classical Athens: Greek Tragic Fragments* (Exeter, 2005) 92–100.

The myth: literary and artistic evidence

Polyxene, daughter of Priam, is never mentioned in the Homeric epics, but from archaic times onwards she regularly has a prominent role in two episodes of the Trojan War saga.

One of these is the story of her death at the end of the war. The cyclic epics offer two quite different accounts of her end. In the *Cypria* (fr. 27 Davies = Glaucus of Rhegium fr. 6a Müller) she was said to have been fatally wounded by Odysseus and Diomedes at the time of the capture of the city, and afterwards to have been buried by Neoptolemus. Since the *Cypria* ended at the point where the *Iliad* begins, this must have been a forward reference; it could, for example, have occurred in a catalogue of the children of Priam, or in a narrative of the killing of Troilus (see below) such as we know the *Cypria* to have contained.[1] In the *Sack of Troy*, however,[2] we meet for the first time the version, thenceforward canonical, in which Polyxene is sacrificed at the tomb of Achilles; in the sixth century, Ibycus (*PMG* 307) names Neoptolemus as her slayer, and this becomes the regular, though not the invariable, assumption in later texts.[3]

There are half a dozen representations in archaic and early classical art either of the sacrifice itself, or of Polyxene being led or dragged towards the tomb.[4] Where the person leading, dragging or slaying her is named, it is usually Neoptolemus, but on one image (a red-figure cup by the Brygos Painter, Louvre G152 = *LIMC* Akamas & Demophon 11) his place is taken by Acamas, one of the sons of Theseus. In this painting Polyxene has apparently untied her belt and is holding it in her hand; in two others[5] Neoptolemus, leading her towards the tomb, has his hand on her wrist. Since the untying of the belt, from Homer (*Odyssey* 11.245) onwards, can symbolize the loss of virginity, and the "hand-on-wrist" gesture in art regularly symbolizes the appropriation of a woman by a man,[6] this is

---

[1] *Cypria* Arg. §11 West.

[2] *Sack of Troy* Arg. §4 West.

[3] Polyxene was probably mentioned by Ibycus' older contemporary, Stesichorus, in a poem about the sack of Troy (*PMG* 135), but we do not know what was said about her.

[4] See *LIMC* s.v. Polyxene; Prag (1985) 61–66; Mossman (1995) 256–263.

[5] A fragmentary red-figure cup by Hieron and Macron, Louvre G153 = *LIMC* Akamas & Demophon 12; a black-figure hydria from the Leagros Group, Berlin F1902 = *LIMC* Polyxene 22. See Prag (1985) 61–62, Mossman (1995) 257–9.

[6] See I. Jenkins, *BICS* 30 (1983) 139–141, who refers *inter alia* to Berlin F1902 (see previous note).

prima facie evidence that the sacrifice was this early being viewed as the giving to Achilles of a posthumous bride[7] – a notion which for the next half-millennium appears in our sources only in dubious and contested allusions in Euripides and Lycophron,[8] but which is taken for granted in an epigram of the time of Augustus or Tiberius,[9] and is a major theme in Seneca's treatment of the story (see below, pp. 50–51).

For fifth-century Athenians the most famous and familiar portrayal of the sacrifice of Polyxene would have been the painting by Polygnotus that eventually found a home in one of the buildings of the Propylaea. Pausanias (1.22.6) merely says this showed Polyxene "about to be slain" near Achilles' tomb, but we have an epigram by Pollianus (*App.Plan.* 150) on "the Polyxena of Polycleitus [sic]" which may in fact be a description of it.[10] Two features of the description contrast strikingly with the account of the sacrifice given by Talthybius in Euripides' *Hecuba*. There, Polyxene is defiant and courageous; in the epigram she is beseeching to be spared. And, though both in the epigram and in Euripides Polyxene's garments are torn and she covers with her hand "what ought to be hidden from the eyes of males",[11] there is again a difference. In Euripides she has torn her robe *herself* (Eur. *Hec.* 558–565), displaying her breasts and in effect

---

[7] See Fontinoy (1950). The whole Trojan war thus comes to be bracketed between the sacrifice of one virgin "bride of Achilles", Iphigeneia, to enable the fleet to sail *to* Troy, and the sacrifice of another to enable the fleet to sail *home from* Troy; on the links between these two sacrifices cf. Friedrich (1935).

[8] Eur. *Hec.* 612 "a bride who is no bride, a virgin who is no virgin"; Lycophron 323–4. Both could in principle be otherwise understood (cf. King [1987] 185–8; N. Loraux, *Tragic Ways of Killing a Woman* [Cambridge MA, 1987] 39–41), especially in view of the frequently found idea that a girl who dies unmarried becomes the bride of Hades (see R.A.S. Seaford, *JHS* 107 [1987] 106–8; R. Rehm, *Marriage to Death* [Princeton, 1994]); but *if* the notion of Polyxene as Achilles' "bride" was already in being, it would have informed audience/reader responses to these passages.

[9] *AP* 9.117, by Statilius Flaccus, one of whose other poems was translated into Latin by Germanicus; see A.S.F. Gow and D.L. Page, *The Greek Anthology: The Garland of Philip and Some Contemporary Epigrams* ii (Cambridge, 1968) 451.

[10] Mossman (1995) 260–1, however, suggests the epigram is merely a "conflation of literary sources and scraps of art historical knowledge or half-knowledge". If she is right, then, given that the epigram's version of the sacrifice is inconsistent with that in Euripides' very well-known *Hecuba*, there is a strong possibility that Sophocles was the author's main (direct or indirect) literary source.

[11] Eur. *Hec.* 570 – where Polyxene has the presence of mind to do this *as she falls dying*. In the epigram, more credibly, she is attempting thus to preserve her modesty *before* receiving the fatal stroke.

challenging Neoptolemus, as Helen had recently challenged Menelaus,[12] to defile such beauty with blood if he dared; the epigram merely states that the robe "has been torn", suggesting that Polyxene has been physically resisting her sacrificers and has had to be subdued by main force. If this is what Polygnotus painted, it appears that Euripides drastically altered his treatment; Sophocles, who had himself been included in one of Polygnotus' most celebrated public paintings,[13] may well have followed him more closely – unless indeed it was Polygnotus that was following Sophocles.

The other early story in which Polyxene regularly figures is that of the killing of Troilus.[14] Homer mentions Troilus only once (*Iliad* 24.257), as a son of Priam "who delighted in horses" and who, like Hector and Mestor[15] and all Priam's other sons of any manly worth,[16] have been "destroyed by Ares"; this gives the impression of a young warrior who met a valiant martial death. To judge by everything we learn from later sources, Homer is here sanitizing the story as he often does. Already in the *Cypria* the incident seems to have been described in terms which led Proclus in his summary to speak of the killing as murder,[17] and a host of representations of the event in archaic and early classical art[18] tell a consistent story involving not only murder but sacrilege and outrage to a corpse – and generally with Polyxene present.[19]

In this story, Troilus (usually shown as little more than a boy) goes with Polyxene to a spring, only to find Achilles lying in ambush there. Troilus has brought (usually) two horses with him, and he flees on one of them, while Polyxene escapes on foot; "swift-footed" Achilles pursues and

---

[12] Eur. *Andr.* 627–631; Ar. *Lys.* 155–6, where the scholia cite the *Little Iliad* (fr. 28 West).

[13] *Life of* Sophocles §5 (in the Stoa Poikile).

[14] On this, see more fully the Introduction to *Troilus* in this volume.

[15] Not otherwise heard of until much later; according to [Apoll.] *Epit.* 3.32 (cf. Dio Chrys. 11.77) he was killed by Achilles during a cattle-raid on Mount Ida.

[16] Or so Priam here says, embittered as he is by the loss of Hector and of several other sons who have fallen in the *Iliad*'s various battles.

[17] *Cypria* Arg. §11 West.

[18] See A. Kossatz-Deissmann in *LIMC* i.1 72–95; Gantz 597–602.

[19] Polyxene appears on more than half of the surviving archaic representations of the ambush or pursuit of Troilus (though not on those showing the actual killing or its aftermath, presumably because by that stage she is taken to have got clear away). The last known such representation featuring her is Vatican 16557 = *LIMC* Achilleus 347, which probably belongs to the 440s.

overtakes the mounted Troilus, kills him in the sanctuary of Apollo Thymbraios, and cuts off his head; when Hector and other Trojans attempt to avenge Troilus' death, Achilles (still in the sanctuary, sometimes actually standing on the altar) brandishes the head at them, almost as if about to throw it.[20] The importance of Polyxene's role is confirmed by the scanty papyrus fragments of the text of, and commentary on, a poem by Ibycus about the Troilus story (*SLG* 224 = *GL* 282B fr. 12) which contain two or three references to a sister.[21]

It is with Polyxene that we are at present concerned. Why is her presence so crucial? The episode appears at first sight to have had no fundamental effect on her life: she returns to Troy unscathed, though she has lost a brother in terrible circumstances. To be sure, she has performed a useful plot function in bringing back to Troy the news that Troilus is in danger, so that a Trojan force can sally forth to protect him (or, as it turns out, to attempt to avenge him); but for that purpose it was not necessary for tellers of the story to have a daughter of Priam come out of the city so inadequately escorted – the message could have been brought by a servant of Troilus.[22] One other event has happened this day, however, whose effect upon Polyxene will be literally vital. She has been seen by Achilles.[23]

Several late sources[24] speak of Achilles as having been in love with Polyxene, and often say that his ghost demanded her sacrifice (see below) for that reason. Until recently there was no direct evidence at all for this story before the second century AD; some of the incidents included in its surviving versions were radically inconsistent with central features of the Trojan War saga as generally accepted in the archaic and classical periods,[25] and several of the writers concerned invented occasions for

---

[20] Cf. *Iliad* 13.197–205 (Ajax son of Oileus beheads the corpse of Imbrius and throws the head at Hector); 14.496–507 (Peneleos displays to the Trojans the severed head of Ilioneus on the end of his spear, and they panic and flee); 18.334–5 (Achilles vows not to bury Patroclus till he has brought him the armour and the head of Hector).

[21] Cf. E.A.B. Jenner, *Prudentia* 30.2 (1998) 3.

[22] As indeed it apparently was in Sophocles' *Troilus* (fr. E [619]).

[23] Cf. R. Förster, *Hermes* 18 (1883) 475–8; Zieliński (1925) 21; M. Robertson in J.P. Descoeudres ed. *Eumousia: Ceramic and Iconographic Studies in Honour of Alexander Cambitoglou* (Sydney, 1990) 65; Schwartz (2001) 44.

[24] Dictys 3.2–3, 4.10–11; Hyginus *Fab.* 110; schol. Eur. *Tro.* 16; schol. Lycophron 323; Dio Chrys. 6.18; Servius on Virg. *Aen.* 3.321.

[25] Notably the story, found in most of the above sources, that Achilles was killed (according to several accounts, in the sanctuary of Apollo Thymbraios) after being lured to

Achilles to see Polyxene and fall in love with her,[26] apparently unaware of their having briefly encountered one another at the time of Troilus' death. And yet the evident importance of that encounter in archaic tellings of the Troilus story, and the slimmer but not negligible early evidence of a nuptial aspect to Polyxene's ultimate sacrifice, always made it unlikely that the idea of Achilles being in love with Polyxene was, as has often been claimed,[27] wholly a romantic invention of the Hellenistic age or later.[28] Moreover, the postdating by late authors of Achilles' first sight of Polyxene would not in fact prove that they were unaware of a tradition that he had seen and desired her much earlier: some of the same authors, for example, also postdate the killing of Troilus, placing it after the death of Hector and shortly before that of Achilles, in defiance of a clear statement in the *Iliad* itself.[29] It was therefore always wrong to exclude *a priori* the possibility that Sophocles in *Polyxene* assumed that Achilles during his lifetime had been enamoured of Polyxene. Still more was it wrong to exclude the possibility that in the Sophoclean play Achilles' ghost might have explicitly demanded her as a posthumous bride; it need hardly be said that given ancient Greek assumptions about marriage, and the past career of Achilles himself,[30] such a demand would not in itself imply (though it also would not exclude) any previous erotic interest in the maiden on his part.

In recent years, at any rate, much stronger evidence has emerged that the story that Achilles had loved Polyxene, and had wished to marry her, was indeed known in archaic times. In 1990, Martin Robertson drew

---

a meeting with members of Priam's family to negotiate a marriage between himself and Polyxene.

[26] He saw her standing on the ramparts of the city (Servius), or when she visited Hector's tomb (Dares 27); or she came with her father when he visited Achilles to ransom Hector's body (Servius, Dictys – though this last, as we shall see, has now proved not to be a late invention at all).

[27] So still in C. Collard, *Euripides: Hecuba* (Warminster, 1991) *ad* 41; Gantz 659; J.R. March, *Dictionary of Classical Mythology* (London, 1998) 330.

[28] The notice of Polyxene's death and burial in the *Cypria* might well also be relevant; it may well have been mentioned there in connection with the killing of Troilus (see above, p. 42), and the fact of Polyxene's being buried by Neoptolemus implies a connection of some kind between her and Achilles. See Robertson *op.cit.* 65, Schwarz (2001) 38.

[29] Dares 33, Dictys 4.9 = *FGrH* 49 F 7a (contrast *Iliad* 24.257).

[30] Above all the quarrel over Briseis in the *Iliad* – recalled in Euripides' *Hecuba* by the description of Polyxene as a "prize of honour" (*geras, Hec.* 41), a word often applied to Briseis, and by Achilles' question "Where are you going, Danaans, leaving my tomb prizeless (*ageraston*)?" (*Hec.* 113–5, cf. *Iliad* 1.119).

attention to an Etruscan vase of the mid-sixth century[31] which pairs the killing of Troilus with a scene in which a woman seeks refuge at an altar from two armed men, and argued that the latter scene could well represent the slaying of Polyxene by Odysseus and Diomedes as narrated in the *Cypria*, which would imply that there existed at the time an awareness of a connection between these two events. Then in 1998 Y. Tuna-Nörling[32] published an Attic vase, datable to the second quarter of the fifth century, showing the familiar scene of the Ransoming of Hector, but with one unusual feature: Hermes was shown leading a maiden "hand-on-wrist", as though he were bringing her as a bride to Achilles. This idea, or anything resembling it, does not appear in any literary source before Dictys,[33] and when it does appear, the maiden is Polyxene.

As Gerda Schwarz has since argued,[34] this evidence, added to what we previously knew, makes the conclusion all but irresistible that the idea of Achilles having been in love with Polyxene was well known in the archaic period; more likely than not, indeed, it was already present in the *Cypria*. That does not in itself necessarily entail that Sophocles used this theme, but it is more than ever inadmissible to take it for granted that he did not.

In Euripides' *Hecuba* (37–41, 93–95, 107–115) the demand for Polyxene's sacrifice is made when the ghost of Achilles appears suddenly above his tomb just as the Achaean fleet is putting to sea to sail home. The appearance of the ghost at the moment of departure featured in Sophocles' play and apparently also in a poem by Simonides ("Longinus" *On the Sublime* 15.7), but we cannot automatically conclude that in both or either of these texts the purpose of this epiphany was to demand the sacrifice. This is because in our earliest reference to such an epiphany, in the cyclic epic *The Returns*,[35] the ghost of Achilles does something quite different: he tries to stop "those with Agamemnon" from sailing by "foretelling what was to happen to them" – and we know that in Sophocles' play someone (though not necessarily Achilles, as we shall see) prophesied the murder of

---

[31] Paris, Louvre E 703 = *LIMC* Achle 17; see Robertson *op.cit.* 64–65.

[32] *Proceedings of the Fifteenth International Congress of Classical Archaeology, Amsterdam 1998* (Amsterdam, 1999) 418–420 and Pl. 35b-c; see also *AA* 2001(1) 27–44. In view of the date of the vase, is there a possibility that it may have been influenced by Aeschylus' *Phrygians*, and that Polyxene was part of the extravagant ransom (it included Hector's weight in gold: schol. *Iliad* 22.351) offered by Priam in that play?

[33] See n.26 above.

[34] Schwarz (2001) (discussing also a range of other artistic evidence, notably a late sixth-century sarcophagus from the eastern Troad published by Sevinç [1996]).

[35] *Returns* Arg. §3 West.

Agamemnon (fr. E [526]) and possibly also the storm at sea in which much of the Achaean fleet was wrecked (fr. D [525]). On one vase-painting (*LIMC* Polyxene 22, mentioned above) showing Polyxene being dragged towards Achilles' tomb, a little winged *eidolon* is shown hovering above the tomb; this may allude to the appearance of the ghost, or may merely help to confirm for the viewer that the tomb is a tomb.

The sacrifice of Polyxene is a major part of the action of Euripides' tragedy *Hecuba*, which metrical and other evidence suggests was produced in the mid 420s.[36] The play opens with the appearance of the ghost of her young brother Polydorus,[37] treacherously killed by the Thracian king Polymestor to whom he had been sent for safe keeping.[38] Among other things he mentions how Achilles appeared above his tomb ("in golden armour", we hear later), stopped the Achaean fleet from sailing[39] and demanded to receive Polyxene as a sacrifice (37–41). His mother Hecuba, who appears next, has had a dream to similar though vaguer effect (92–97), in which Achilles demanded "one of the wretched maidens of Troy"; presently the chorus of Trojan women bring the accurate and terrible news (104–115). They report (116–140) that there has been a debate in the army, Agamemnon opposing the sacrifice for the sake of his concubine Cassandra (Polyxene's sister), the sons of Theseus supporting it; views were evenly divided, but Odysseus (spoken of in terms appropriate to a fifth-century Athenian demagogue) persuaded the army that they must show due honour and gratitude to Achilles. Hecuba then calls Polyxene out of the captives' hut and breaks the news to her; very shortly Odysseus comes to collect the sacrificial victim. Hecuba pleads with him in vain, and then urges Polyxene to supplicate him also; but when Polyxene sees that

---

[36] On the metrical evidence see p. 21 n.78 above. One passage of *Hecuba* (171–4) is quoted with slight modification in Aristophanes' *Clouds* (1165–6), originally produced in 423.

[37] Who, as is noted by Robertson *op.cit.* 68, substitutes for Troilus (never mentioned in Euripides' play) as the youngest son of Priam and Hecuba (whereas the Homeric Polydorus, killed by Achilles at *Iliad* 20.407–418, is not Hecuba's son, cf. *Iliad* 22.46–48).

[38] The plot of the play requires that Polymestor be within easy reach of the camp; accordingly the setting is not the coast of the Troad (as it doubtless was in Sophocles' play; cf. Sutton 113) but that of the Thracian Chersonese (33) on the European side of the Hellespont, despite the well-established location of Achilles' tomb near Sigeum on the Asian side.

[39] Neoptolemus' prayer to his father's spirit to "be gracious to us, and let us cast off the stern-cables of our ships and all return safely to our homeland" (538–541) implies that Achilles has said the fleet will not be able to sail unless the sacrifice takes place.

Odysseus is determined not even to let her perform the ritual acts of supplication, she declares herself ready to accept death in preference to slavery, dissuades her mother who tries to insist on dying with her, and allows herself to be taken on her last journey. Presently the herald Talthybius brings Hecuba news of the sacrifice, at which Polyxene behaved with outstanding courage and Neoptolemus could hardly bring himself to slay her; so much did the army admire her that they have themselves been making preparations for her funeral, including the building of a pyre, but it is now for Hecuba to take charge of the last rites. The play then takes a different direction with the discovery of Polydorus' body on the seashore and Hecuba's plot against his murderer Polymestor, who is blinded and his sons killed by the Trojan women; it ends with her going to see to what will now be a double funeral.

The sacrifice features more briefly in Euripides' later play *The Trojan Women*. It has in fact taken place before the play begins, but Hecuba is unaware of it (39–40). She is informed, as gently as possible, by Talthybius (260–270) – so gently, in fact, that she does not understand what he means, until Andromache tells her plainly (622–9). Andromache argues that Polyxene dead is better off than she herself is alive (630–683), but both women are almost immediately afterwards shattered anew by the arrival of orders for the death of Hector's young son Astyanax, and Polyxene, her death eclipsed by this even greater atrocity, is not mentioned again. In this play, in contrast with *Hecuba*, Polyxene seems to receive no proper burial; we hear only of Andromache throwing a garment over her corpse (627). It is striking that Neoptolemus – the actual sacrificer of Polyxene, and the new master of Andromache – though he has a significant offstage role in both Euripidean plays, does not actually appear in either.

Several Roman tragedians included, or may have included, the sacrifice of Polyxena[40] in their plots, and are thus (particularly where they diverge from Euripides) potential witnesses to the content of Sophocles' play.[41] The *Hecuba* of Ennius (239–169 BC) appears to have been virtually a

---

[40] In discussion of Latin tragedies, characters will be referred to by their Latin names (Odysseus as Ulysses; Neoptolemus as Pyrrhus).

[41] Ovid's treatment (*Met.* 13.399–575) is unhelpful: he has Polyxena seized and taken to Achilles' tomb for sacrifice immediately the ghost has spoken (449–452).

translation of Euripides' play of the same name,[42] but he seems to have dealt with some of the same story material in another play, *Andromacha.* Two fragments apparently from that play, speaking of a man "who resolutely aided and upheld the common weal, stood together with the Achaeans ... [who] in perilous situations did not hesitate to stake his life and did not spare himself" (Ennius *trag.* 74–77 Jocelyn), quoted by Cicero in his speech *pro Sestio* (120), have been ascribed[43] to a speech (by Ulysses, cf. Eur. *Hec.* 309–316?) praising Achilles and arguing for acceptance of his demand for Polyxena to be sacrificed.[44] A fragment of the *Troades* of Accius (170–ca.86 BC) in which, "amid thunders and whirlwinds", the speaker wonders if he has heard the noise of an earthquake or "the sound of hell" (Accius 659–660 Warmington) closely resembles a passage of Seneca's *Troades* (172–3) describing the portents preceding the appearance of Achilles' ghost, and both may derive from a messenger-speech in Sophocles' play (cf. *OC* 1456–71).

Lucius Annaeus Seneca (ca. 3 BC – AD 65) made Polyxena (though she never speaks) the focus of his tragedy *Troades.*[45] The play begins with Hecuba and the Trojan women awaiting their fate after the capture of the city. Talthybius tells them that the sailing of the fleet has been delayed by the appearance of Achilles' ghost demanding that Polyxena be sacrificed by the hand of Pyrrhus as "the bride of our ashes" (195, cf. 202, 287–9, 362–5, 944, 1001–2, 1132–6).[46] Pyrrhus demands immediate compliance; Agamemnon, on moral grounds, refuses. A fierce quarrel, in which Pyrrhus is at one moment on the point of killing Agamemnon (307–310), ends when Agamemnon suddenly suggests referring the issue to the seer Calchas. Calchas confirms that the sacrifice is necessary; he adds that Polyxena must go to her death dressed as a Greek bride – and also that before the fleet sails Astyanax too must be killed. The middle third of the

---

[42] It is, in fact, called a translation by A. Gellius (11.4.3), who cites Ennius' rendering of Eur. *Hec.* 293–5 (Ennius *trag.* 172–4 Jocelyn); cf. also Ennius *trag.* 181 (~ Eur. *Hec.* 824ff) and 183–4 (Eur. *Hec.* 497–8).

[43] H.D. Jocelyn, *The Tragedies of Ennius* (Cambridge, 1967) 238–242.

[44] In addition, Fantham (1982) 64 suggests that Ennius *trag.* 98 ("Greeting, region of Acheron, deep infernal realms of Orcus!") may come from "a messenger-narrative quoting [the] last words [of Polyxena]".

[45] See the editions of E. Fantham (Princeton, 1982), A.J. Boyle (Leeds, 1994) and A.J. Keulen (Leiden, 2001). Fantham (50–77) has an excellent survey of the development of the mythical material used by Seneca; Sophocles' play is discussed on pp.57–60.

[46] The same notion appears when the sacrifice is referred to in Seneca's *Agamemnon* (640).

play is taken up with Andromacha's unavailing attempts to save her son, ending with his being led away by Ulysses.

We then return to Polyxena. Helen, who has been sent to bring the unsuspecting maiden to Pyrrhus, tells her that Pyrrhus has chosen her as his bride. Andromacha is scathing about the idea, and presently Helen's human feelings get the better of her: she breaks down and tells Polyxena the truth. Polyxena takes pride in an honourable death,[47] and begins to prepare for it as if for her wedding,[48] Hecuba faints. Helen reports the result of the lottery for captives: Andromacha will go to Pyrrhus, Cassandra to Agamemnon, Hecuba to Ulysses. Pyrrhus takes Polyxena away. Presently a messenger reports to Andromacha and Hecuba that both Polyxena and Astyanax are dead, but both died nobly – Astyanax by his own act; and the play ends, as do both the *Hecuba* and *Trojan Women* of Euripides, with orders for the Trojan women to go to the ships.

Much of this can be traced to the two Euripidean plays (some of it perhaps by way of the *Astyanax* of Accius). Certain elements, and in particular the quarrel between Agamemnon and Pyrrhus, have no Euripidean source and may derive from Sophocles; but some of them could equally well be invented by Ennius, Accius, or other Roman tragedians who may have created new dramatic versions of the story – or indeed by Seneca himself.[49]

The play

Our direct evidence for Sophocles' play is fairly scanty; in particular, we know nothing at all for sure about how the title character was presented, how she faced the prospect of death, what attempts (if any) were made to save her, or how she and her slayer bore themselves at the climax. Our evidence centres rather on Agamemnon, Menelaus and the ghost of Achilles.

---

[47] This is communicated through Andromacha's description of her bearing and actions; Polyxena herself remains mute.

[48] "She thought of that [marriage to Pyrrhus] as death; she thinks of this as marriage" (948).

[49] Fantham (1982) 68–75 does well to remind us that while Seneca was familiar with earlier dramatic treatments of the myths he used, and could at any time adopt or adapt a motif from any of them, it is absurd to suppose that he was incapable of making innovations of his own.

The appearance, or appearances, of Achilles' ghost were the most celebrated feature of the play. We have two, possibly three, significant relevant pieces of information.

(1) Fr. A (523) is spoken by the ghost of Achilles, just come from the underworld. Since Apollodorus[50] (*FGrH* 244 F 102a.2) says that "Sophocles *brings on* (*eisagei*) the ghost of Achilles saying [these words]", we can be sure that these three lines are not merely reported by another character (e.g. a messenger) but that the ghost itself is one of the actual *dramatis personae*. At what point in the play the ghost came on stage is a question that will be dealt with presently.

(2) "Longinus" (*On the Sublime* 15.7), discussing the ability of dramatists by vivid description to make their audiences feel they are witnessing events which are in fact only being narrated to them, praises Sophocles' narrative of the death and (as he calls it) self-burial of Oedipus (*OC* 1579–1666) and says he did excellently also "at the time when the Greeks sailed away [from Troy], in connection with the appearance of Achilles over his tomb to those putting to sea – a sight which perhaps no one has presented more vividly to the imagination than Simonides".[51] As W.H. Friedrich pointed out,[52] the context requires us to suppose that this refers to a passage in which the ghost was *not* actually visible to the audience, in other words to a *narrative* of its appearance by some eyewitness (whether a major named character or an anonymous messenger). It follows that there must have been at least two appearances by the ghost of Achilles in the course of the play, one enacted and one narrated. It also follows that the location of the dramatic action was *not* at

---

[50] This Apollodorus is the Athenian-Alexandrian scholar of the second century BC, not the mythographer (who probably lived early in the Imperial period). His quotation and exegesis of the fragment is preserved by Stobaeus (1.49.50), who cites a passage from Porphyry's work *On the Styx* which had in turn cited Apollodorus.

[51] The jump from Sophocles to Simonides is very abrupt. W. Bühler, *Beiträge zur Erklärung der Schrift vom Erhabenen* [Göttingen, 1964] 111–2, posits a substantial lacuna; if he is right, it would follow that the "sight which [Simonides] presented ... vividly to the imagination" was *not* the appearance of Achilles' ghost. It is also possible, however, I suggest, that all that has dropped out of the text is the single word *plēn* "except", giving the meaning "a sight which perhaps no one has presented more vividly ... except Simonides". For the Greek text of the passage, see p. 69.

[52] Friedrich (1933) 104–7; cf. also Gregory (1999) xxi n.25. This chapter of "Longinus" contains in all ten tragic citations or references, and every one of the other nine relates to a being or an event which is not presented visibly to the audience but only described in words – a fact which Bardel (2005), despite some detailed exegesis of "the very language that pseudo-Longinus deploys" (p.99), manages not to notice.

Achilles' tomb; since we know Agamemnon had an important role, and since in the *Iliad* other leaders normally come to visit him rather than vice versa,[53] the scene is most likely to have been in front of his hut in the Achaean camp.

(3) In one fragment for certain (fr. E [526]), and not improbably in another also (fr. D [525]), future events are foretold that will be disastrous for some of those about to depart from Troy – the devastating storm in the Aegean, and the murder of Agamemnon. In view of the statement in Proclus' summary of the *Returns* (Arg. §3 West) that the wraith of Achilles "appeared as those with Agamemnon were sailing off, and tried to prevent them by foretelling what was to happen", it is *prima facie* reasonable[54] to suppose that it is the ghost who makes these prophecies. The prophecy of Agamemnon's murder is addressed to Agamemnon himself.

We can be virtually certain that on at least one of the occasions on which Achilles appeared, he demanded that Polyxene be sacrificed at his tomb.[55]

If we can determine how many times the ghost of Achilles appeared, place these appearances (at least approximately) within the structure of the play, and infer the gist of what the ghost said on each occasion, then – bearing in mind that we also know of two other events the play contained, a quarrel between Agamemnon and Menelaus about whether to depart immediately (fr. B [522]) and the sacrifice of Polyxene – we will have gone far to reconstruct its broad outlines.

It has sometimes been argued[56] that the parallels with the opening of Euripides' *Hecuba* (spoken by the ghost of Polydorus) and of Seneca's *Agamemnon* (spoken by the ghost of Thyestes) in themselves make it highly likely that the ghost of Achilles also appeared on stage at the beginning of our play. This is not so: Seneca may be imitating Euripides, and Euripides might have wished to move the ghost-scene from the middle

---

[53] *Iliad* 9.65–90, 669, 10.25–35, 23.35–56, 24.653–5. In 10.72–79 Agamemnon has no alternative but to visit Nestor, since Nestor is asleep and Agamemnon does not want to involve subordinates in what is to be a secret consultation.

[54] Though, as we shall see, probably wrong.

[55] Hyginus (*Fab.* 110), in a very brief notice, makes Achilles ask only for a share of the booty, without specifying what it is to be; but it is unimaginable that a dramatist could have presented the Achaeans interpreting such a demand, which could have been fulfilled in many ways, as a requirement to perform a human sacrifice.

[56] For example by Friedrich (1933) 106 and Calder (1966) 43–45.

of the play to the beginning because it suited him better to have it there. However, there are other compelling reasons to assign fr. A (523) to the prologue. The fragment contains no indication that this is not the first time that Achilles has come up from the underworld; it is therefore likely that the enacted appearance of the ghost came earlier in the play than its narrated appearance. This is a sequencing that involves considerable danger of anticlimax; contrast the treatment of the Erinyes in Aeschylus' *Oresteia*, who initially are seen only by the half-maddened Orestes (*Cho.* 1048–62), then beheld and described fairly fully by the sane though very frightened Pythia at Delphi (*Eum.* 34–59), after which a few of them are seen by the audience, huddled on chairs asleep (*Eum.* 67–68, cf. 47) until the ghost of Clytaemestra succeeds in goading them into wakefulness (*Eum.* 140–2) after which, at last, the' whole twelve begin to sing and dance as a regular chorus and the audience see the full horror of their appearance.[57] Sophocles must have been aware of the risk, and will have done all he could to diminish it.[58] One obvious way to do this would be so to arrange things that when the ghost appears in person on stage, it is *not seen by any of the other dramatis personae* but only by the audience, so that when it later appears "to those putting to sea", even though we the audience are not ourselves amazed by the epiphany (having already seen something similar for ourselves), we can experience vicariously the amazement of those who did see it and of those to whom it is being reported. And normally[59] the only way in which an event taking place on stage in a Greek tragedy can remain unknown to all the other *dramatis personae* is if it occurs in the prologue, before the entrance of the chorus. It is likely, therefore, that the ghost of Achilles, like the ghost of Polydorus in *Hecuba*, opened the play.

---

[57] See A.L. Brown, *JHS* 103 (1983) 13–24, and A.H. Sommerstein, *Aeschylus: Eumenides* (Cambridge, 1989) 89, 92–93, 108–9.

[58] Why should he have devised so troublesome an arrangement in the first place? Probably because he wanted to have the audience see Achilles' ghost, but (given the resources of the Athenian theatre) could not put on stage the appearance of the ghost at the moment of the fleet's departure.

[59] The exceptions are (i) where the chorus have left the scene during the play and will return later, (ii) where they have been sworn to secrecy: (i) is rare, and as for (ii), it is hard to see why Achilles' ghost should want the chorus to keep secret his demand for the sacrifice of Polyxene, his prophecies of the future, or anything else.

If this is so, Achilles cannot at this stage have demanded the sacrifice of Polyxene,[60] since he has no one to whom to address the demand; and while he might have made prophecies of future disasters[61] he cannot have made the only such prophecy which we know for sure the play contained, that of Agamemnon's death of which fr. E (526) formed part, since that was addressed to Agamemnon. What he could have done was to make clear to the audience the point of the Trojan saga at which the action is set, to tell *them* that he is *going* to demand the sacrifice of Polyxene (a fact of which the Achaeans and Trojans will for the time being remain ignorant), and perhaps also to tell them *why* he is going to do so (this may have prompted a retrospective narrative of the story of Troilus). [62]

The actual demand for the sacrifice will have been made, as in Euripides and as in Seneca, just as the fleet (not necessarily the whole of it – see below) is about to put to sea. As we have seen, this appearance by the ghost must have been reported, not enacted on stage; the reporter may have been one of the leaders who were on board the ships or an anonymous messenger.

What of the prophecy or prophecies? They can hardly have been given at the time of the epiphany to the fleet: they would not combine at all well with the demand for Polyxene to be sacrificed. It is one thing to say "don't go until you have sacrificed Polyxene to me", and quite another thing to say "don't go, or you'll be shipwrecked and your leader will be murdered on his arrival home"; any ghost who tried to present both injunctions at once would have found that each interfered with the other (Achilles could hardly expect the army to sacrifice Polyxene in order to facilitate their

---

[60] Thus the problem that baffled Calder (1966) 46 n.89 – how could Menelaus have insisted on departing, as he evidently did, if Achilles had demanded Polyxene's sacrifice as the price of departure? – is solved, or rather it dissolves. Mossman (1995) 43 also gets into deep water through assuming that Achilles had demanded the sacrifice at the start of the play: knowing that in that case the demand would have to have been discussed during the ensuing quarrel between Agamemnon and Menelaus, she suggests that "Agamemnon's reluctance to leave was prompted by his unwillingness to kill [Polyxena]" even though this involves rejecting the plain statement of Strabo 10.3.14, fully supported by his quotation of the Sophoclean text (fr. B [522]), that Agamemnon wanted to stay (briefly) at Troy in order to make (animal) sacrifices in the hope of averting the wrath of Athena.

[61] Cf. Eur. *Tro.* 65–94 where Athena and Poseidon agree to create a storm and wreck the Achaean fleet; throughout the play Achaeans and Trojans alike remain totally unaware of this.

[62] The reference to the mutilation of Troilus' corpse (fr. G [528]) may have come in this context, but other contexts are equally possible, e.g. Polyxene reflecting on the miseries and sufferings of her life.

departure, if they accepted his warning that they had better not depart). Do we, then, have to assume yet a third appearance by the ghost, perhaps to wind up the play?

No, we do not. One thing that we can say for certain about the prophecy of Agamemnon's death in fr. E (526) is that Agamemnon himself heard it. Another thing we can say for certain is that *he did not believe it*. If he had, he would have been on his guard when he arrived home, would probably not have allowed his wife to bathe him, would certainly not have allowed her to dress him in a new robe – and the prophecy would not have been fulfilled. A *vague* prediction of his murder, not specifying the killer or the method, might well have secured its own fulfilment by causing Agamemnon to take precautions against imaginary sources of danger[63] while ignoring the real one; but this *precise* prophecy, if believed, would be almost bound to secure its own *non*-fulfilment. And Agamemnon could hardly have failed to believe a prophecy by Achilles' ghost, when he has just obeyed its injunction to the extent of taking an innocent life. Rather we must have here a prophecy delivered by a person, or under circumstances, which more or less guarantee that Agamemnon will ignore it. This device is used twice by Euripides. At the end of *Hecuba* (1275–81) Agamemnon is told that he will be killed by his wife, in the bath, with an axe; he disregards the prophecy because it comes from the evil Polymestor, merely ordering him to be abandoned on a desert island (1284–6). In *Trojan Women* (356–364, 445–461) a similar prophecy is made in the presence of Agamemnon's herald Talthybius; admittedly much of it is enigmatically expressed, but it is clear enough that to bring Cassandra to his home will be fatal for Agamemnon (357–360, 457, 460–1). But the prophecy is uttered by Cassandra herself, whom Talthybius believes to be mad; and he takes no notice of it and, we may presume, says nothing of it to his master. In Sophocles' play the prophecy might likewise come from Cassandra,[64] doubtless under different circumstances (e.g. with Agamemnon present); but we have no other evidence for Cassandra (or

---

[63] As he is advised to do, and announces his intention of doing, in Aeschylus' *Agamemnon* (respectively 788–798 + 807–9, and 830–850). The most famous example of a prophecy that thus puts the addressee off his guard against the real danger threatening him is the Delphic oracle given to Oedipus in *OT* (779–793): if Apollo had answered the question actually put to him (which must have been "Who is my father?" or maybe "Am I the son of Polybus?"), Oedipus would never have turned his back on Corinth (794–7) and therefore would never have killed Laius or married Iocaste.

[64] So Friedrich (1935) 99 n.2.

any other Trojan, besides Polyxene) as a character in the play,[65] and another possibility is that the foreteller may have been Polyxene herself.

We have now inferred enough about the structure of the play to be able to look at its sections successively, though about some there may be little that we can say.

(a) Prologue, spoken by the ghost of Achilles (already discussed).

(b) Interval of ignorance during which no one (except the audience) knows that the Achaeans will shortly be required to sacrifice Polyxene. This interval must include, and may well be largely filled by, the dispute between Agamemnon and Menelaus attested by fr. B (522). This episode is based ultimately on Nestor's narrative in the *Odyssey* (3.130–185) and on the early part of the *Nostoi* (Arg. §1 West). In the *Odyssey* version, Menelaus and Agamemnon debate before a tumultuous, drunken assembly whether or not to sail home, Agamemnon being anxious to remain and sacrifice to Athene in the hope of appeasing her anger (presumably over the seizure of Cassandra from her temple by the lesser Ajax, though Nestor mentions no particulars). No decision is reached; Diomedes, Nestor, Odysseus and others (though not, initially, Menelaus) depart the next morning; Odysseus goes only as far as Tenedos and then returns; Nestor and Diomedes sail on to Lesbos, where they are joined by Menelaus; Agamemnon and the rest presumably leave Troy soon afterwards, and most of them are caught up in a storm (4.499–516) which Odysseus apparently escapes by sailing independently (9.39). The account in the *Nostoi*, in the summary form in which we have it, is almost entirely consistent with this. It is puzzling, and unexplained, that in both versions, though it is Menelaus who initially argues for immediate departure, he is not among those who actually do depart immediately.

We know that in Sophocles' play, as in both the epic accounts, "Menelaus was eager to depart from Troy, while Agamemnon wished to delay a little in order to propitiate Athena" (Strabo 10.3.14, before quoting fr. B [522]). In the fragment Menelaus tells Agamemnon he can stay and sacrifice as many sheep as he likes – having evidently just affirmed that *he*, Menelaus, is going to depart. For dramatic purposes it

---

[65] Fantham (1982) 59–60 thinks that "it would be extraordinary if this play of sacrifice represented the victim in isolation without illustrating the grief of her family or countrymen [sic]" and therefore posits the presence of Hecuba as a character and of a chorus of Trojan women; but to isolate a victim can intensify the pathos of her situation (cf. Aesch. *Ag.* 224–247). Mossman (1995) 46 n.65 is justly sceptical of Fantham's argument.

would be inconvenient to reproduce the elaborately staggered departures of the epic tradition; there are unlikely to have been more than two separate departures (or attempts at departure) in the play.[66] The later one, we know, included Agamemnon. What of the earlier one? Did Menelaus and Agamemnon eventually agree to leave together, or did Menelaus, and those who agreed with him, attempt to sail on their own?

The latter alternative is much the more likely. If the whole fleet had attempted to put to sea, the chorus of the play, whether it consisted of Achaean soldiers/sailors or of captive Trojan women (see below), would have been on board ship, together with all the principals, and there would have been no one in the camp to keep the play going![67] We should therefore assume that, as in the epics, the quarrel was unresolved, and a large part of the army (perhaps even the whole of it bar Agamemnon's own contingent) decided unilaterally to leave Troy without waiting for Agamemnon.

(c) The chorus. Some[68] have held that the chorus of this play consisted of captive Trojan women; others prefer a chorus of members of the Achaean army.[69] The latter is more plausible: in particular, it is hard to envisage Sophocles making Agamemnon and Menelaus engage in a verbal battle in front of a chorus of enemy prisoners.[70] If the action is set before Agamemnon's hut, the chorus might well comprise members of his contingent, Argives or Mycenaeans.

---

[66] In Euripides' *Trojan Women* the whole fleet apparently sails together, except for Neoptolemus (1126–33), who leaves early in order to bring aid to his persecuted grandfather Peleus (with the result of preventing his new concubine, Andromache, from taking final leave of her mother-in-law and from burying her son).

[67] This difficulty was perceived by Friedrich (1933) 107, but he wrongly supposed that it ruled out the possibility that the ghost's appearance to the fleet was narrated in a messenger-speech. His own suggestion that the epiphany occurred before the beginning of the action, and was vividly narrated in a choral song, runs up against the difficulties pointed out in note 59 above, which Friedrich does not discuss.

[68] Notably Fantham (1982) 59–60.

[69] This proposal, first made by Welcker, has been supported in recent decades by Calder (1966) 37–38 and by Lucas de Dios. However, fr. 887, which these writers all cite, should never have been brought into the discussion: including as it does a prayer for victory in the war, it cannot come from a play whose action takes place after the victory has been won.

[70] In Euripides, especially in his later plays (though even here *Bacchae* is an exception), the presence of the chorus can sometimes be almost totally forgotten; this never (to our knowledge) happens in Sophocles, not even in the late *Phil.* or *OC*.

(d) The abortive attempt at departure. The quarrel between Agamemnon and Menelaus perhaps filled the "first episode", with Menelaus leaving at the end of it, declaring that he and those who thought like him would now sail immediately, while Agamemnon went back into his hut and the chorus sang the "first stasimon". Then news will have come of the stunning apparition of Achilles' ghost, demanding the sacrifice of Polyxene to him or in his honour, which prevented the fleet from sailing. This creates a new situation, effectively superseding the Agamemnon-Menelaus dispute and making it irrelevant. Both in Euripides (*Hec.* 111–2,[71] 538–541) and in Seneca (*Tro.* 164–7, 193, 199–201, 365–6, 370) it is assumed, rather than stated, that Achilles told the Achaeans that their fleet would be detained at Troy, by calm or adverse winds, until his demand was satisfied: it may well be that Euripides and Seneca were able to take this as known because it had been made explicit by Sophocles.

(e) Towards the sacrifice. We can be sure that in the end Polyxene was indeed sacrificed. We can also be sure that the path leading from Achilles' demand to its fulfilment was not a simple and direct one; one would expect this phase of the action to be treated more elaborately than in Euripides' *Hecuba* (where it leads up, not to the culminating climax of the play, but to a secondary, intermediate climax) though probably not as elaborately as in his *Iphigeneia at Aulis* (where the issue of Iphigeneia's sacrifice is central to the action from beginning to end). We can be virtually certain, too, that Polyxene herself played a major role on stage in this phase; there is no known case of a tragedy being named after a person who does not have a substantial speaking part.[72] Can we infer anything more about this scene or scenes? The two main surviving later treatments of the story, and one fragment of Sophocles' play, may give us some help.

---

[71] D. Kovacs, *The Heroic Muse* (Baltimore, 1987) 145 n.58, W.G. Thalmann, *CA* 12 (1993) 155, and J. Gregory, *Euripides: Hecuba* (Atlanta, 1999) xxix-xxxi, are wrong to treat this passage as showing that Achilles is not envisaged in Euripides' play as controlling the winds. To say that he "stopped" the ships when they had the wind full in their sails (112) is to say that he stopped or reversed the wind: as every spectator will have known, a sailing ship with a steady wind behind it cannot be pulled up like a horse.

[72] The smallest speaking part of any title character in a surviving tragedy, in proportion to the length of the play, is that of the Aeschylean Agamemnon, who speaks 82 lines (4.9% of the text). Fantham (1982) 72 suggests that Polyxene may have been silent in Sophocles' play as she is in Seneca's, but this seems inconsistent with her criticism of Calder for taking precisely this view (pp.59–60).

(i) Neoptolemus. We have seen that both in art and in literature it is normally Neoptolemus who actually performs the sacrifice; and in Seneca it is he who quarrels with Agamemnon over whether it should be performed. It is thus remarkable that in Euripides' *Hecuba* Neoptolemus does not appear on stage, and that in the chorus's report of the debate in the army over whether to accede to Achilles' demand (116–140) he is not mentioned as having taken any part, when one would have expected him, rather than Odysseus (131–140) or the sons of Theseus (122–9), to be foremost in supporting his father's claim to be honoured. This surprising absence of any involvement by Neoptolemus in the run-up to the sacrifice is most easily explained as due to Euripides' desire to avoid following too closely the model of an earlier drama – and Sophocles' play is the only relevant drama we know of that could have been earlier. It is thus likely that Neoptolemus was a character in Sophocles' play and was eager, perhaps (as in Seneca) even going to the brink of violence, for the sacrifice to be carried out.

(ii) The attitude of Polyxene. In Euripides, Polyxene is at first distressed (*Hec.* 191–210),[73] but when she sees that Odysseus is adamant she accepts her fate with spirit and courage. In Seneca her "mighty spirit rejoices" (*Tro.* 945) from the moment she hears the news, and she goes to her death with pride, without hesitation – and without a word, on or off stage. This behaviour, which is highly appropriate for a Senecan heroine,[74] cannot, as we have seen, derive from Sophocles, and it is also reasonable to assume that Sophocles and Euripides differed from each other in their characterization of Polyxene. Probably then, at least at first, the Sophoclean Polyxene pleaded for her life as Iphigeneia does in Eur. *IA* 1211–1342.

(iii) The role of Agamemnon. The longest surviving fragment of *Polyxene*, fr. C (524), is spoken by a king (v.3), the leader of an army (v.1), who laments that it is not possible for a person in his

---

[73] Lines 211–5, in which Polyxene says she is lamenting only for her mother and that for herself death is a better lot than life, break the symmetry of the lyrics and ruin the surprise effect of what Polyxene will later say to Odysseus. They were rightly deleted by Wilamowitz (*Hermes* 44 [1909] 449–450 = *Kleine Schriften* iv [Berlin, 1962] 228), though recent editors are divided: J. Diggle (Oxford, 1984) and C. Collard (Warminster, 1994) accept the deletion (so too Mossman, *Wild Justice* 53–54), while S.G. Daitz (Leipzig, 1990), D. Kovacs (Cambridge MA, 1995), and J. Gregory (Atlanta, 1999) retain the lines.

[74] Cf. Fantham, *Seneca: Troades* 17, 90–91.

position to please everyone by acceding to their wishes: even Zeus, he says, always displeases someone or other, whether he makes the weather wet or dry (vv.3–4). This speaker can only be Agamemnon: in this play there is no other "mortal born of a mortal woman" (v.6) who could speak of his position as a monarchical one carrying sole responsibility for major decisions. Evidently he has been asked to make a decision between two opposing positions, both strongly held, and is certain that whatever he decides, it will cause grave offence or distress to one party or the other. This does not fit the quarrel with Menelaus, in which both epic sources make Agamemnon himself one of the contending parties, and fr. B (522) strongly suggests that Sophocles did likewise; it is therefore likely to refer to the play's other major dispute, over the proposed sacrifice of Polyxene.

Putting these indications together, we can tentatively posit a debate between Neoptolemus[75] and Polyxene, with Agamemnon in the position of judge, having to decide whether to dishonour Neoptolemus as once he had dishonoured Neoptolemus' father, or to condemn the innocent Polyxene to death as once he had condemned his own daughter. Though one contender is a male warrior and the other a maiden, there is little between them in age, and Polyxene, like Hecuba in Euripides' play, can exploit in support of her case Agamemnon's relationship with her sister Cassandra. Neoptolemus, for his part, can point to his father's enormous services to the Achaean cause and his own contribution to the final victory, but his strongest argument of all will be the same argument that had once prevailed at Aulis. Here, as there, if the sacrifice is not performed, the fleet will not be able to sail; and this time there is not even the alternative of disbanding the army and sending it home[76] – for if it cannot sail, it cannot get home.

---

[75] Calder (1966) 35–37 prefers to identify the speaker arguing in favour of the sacrifice as Odysseus. He claims that schol. Eur. *Hec.* 41 implies that in Sophocles' play Polyxene was not slain by Neoptolemus; this scholium does not in fact mention Sophocles' play at all, and since such omissions in scholia can easily be due to compression or to scribal carelessness, it is dangerous to draw inferences from them where there is no corroboration. A debate between Neoptolemus and Agamemnon himself, as in Seneca, can be ruled out, since if Agamemnon is the arbiter he cannot also be one of the disputants; cf. F. Corsaro, *Siculorum Gymnasium* 44 (1991) 15–16.

[76] Cf. Eur. *IA* 95, 352–3, 495, 515; the existence of this alternative is also implied at Aesch. *Ag.* 212–3 (though Agamemnon calls it by the emotive and misleading name

What can Agamemnon do? In Euripides he has no decision to take; he is merely one of the speakers in the debate, arguing against the sacrifice (*Hec.* 120–2) and acquiescing in the verdict when it goes against him. In Seneca he is also opposed to the sacrifice, but resolves a deadlocked and dangerous argument with Pyrrhus by referring the decision to Calchas. In Sophocles his evident reluctance to give a verdict (fr. C [524]) may point to a similar outcome,[77] and Calder[78] may be right to suppose that in Sophocles too the decision was referred to Calchas. If so, the number of speaking actors being limited to three, it would be necessary for at least one of the participants in the debate scene to be got off stage before Calchas arrived; perhaps all three withdrew into Agamemnon's hut to await him, a choral song followed, and when the three came out again on Calchas' arrival the mask and costume of one of them had been taken over by a mute performer.[79] Calchas must have confirmed that it was necessary to obey Achilles and perform the sacrifice, after which Polyxene will have been led off by Neoptolemus; Agamemnon may have gone with or after them, but it is also possible that he may have deliberately stayed away from the sacrifice, as if still trying to disclaim responsibility for it.

(f) *The prophecies.* We have seen that the prophecies of disaster from which come fr. E (526) and probably fr. D (525) must have been delivered by someone whom Agamemnon can reasonably, or at least understandably, disbelieve. One obvious possibility is Cassandra, perhaps bursting out of Agamemnon's hut (cf. Eur. *Tro.* 308) to confront him after Polyxene has been led off. Another is Polyxene

---

"desertion"; see my *Aeschylean Tragedy* [Bari, 1996] 362–5). Electra says at Soph. *El.* 573–4 that the army would have been unable to go home, but she offers no evidence in support of this claim.

[77] There is an analogous evasion of responsibility by Agamemnon in Euripides' *Hecuba*, though not in relation to Polyxene. When Hecuba appeals to him to punish Polymestor for the murder of her son Polydorus, he is reluctant to agree, because the army regards Polymestor as a friend and will accuse him of having been indulgent to Hecuba on account of his passion for Cassandra (*Hec.* 850–863); he tacitly consents, however, to see that if Hecuba tries to take her own revenge on Polymestor she is neither prevented nor punished (864–904).

[78] Calder (1966) 48; cf. Fantham (1982) 59.

[79] Similarly in *Oedipus at Colonus* Ismene, who has been a speaking participant in her first scene (324–509), is silent when Theseus brings her and Antigone back (1096–1555), but has a speaking (or rather singing) part again in the *exodos* (1689–1736). Polyxene may in this, her final scene, have been arrayed as a bride (cf. Comm. on fr. F [527]), if Achilles' ghost had demanded her as such.

herself, either just before her final exit[80] or even during the debate with Neoptolemus, warning Agamemnon of what will happen if he allows her to be sacrificed. Polyxene, unlike her sister Cassandra and her brother Helenus, is never spoken of as herself having prophetic powers, but she might (for example) say she was repeating what Cassandra had told her.

(g) The sacrifice will have been reported by a messenger to the chorus (and to Agamemnon, if he had not gone to attend it). So far as we can tell, nothing of the narrative survives. Both Euripides and Seneca emphasize the nobility of Polyxene's demeanour, and in both accounts Neoptolemus proves in the end reluctant to slay the victim (Eur. *Hec.* 566, Sen. *Tro.* 1154); we cannot be sure that Sophocles presented the event in the same light. Indeed, the evidence of *App.Plan.* 150 (see pp. 43–44 above) suggests that his treatment may have been drastically different, with Polyxene begging for her life till the last moment and putting up physical resistance that had to be suppressed by force.[81]

(h) The end of the play. Since *Polyxene* began with a dispute over whether the Achaeans should depart from Troy forthwith, and continued with their departure being delayed by the demand made by Achilles' ghost, it is reasonable to suppose that it ended, like Euripides' *Hecuba* and *Trojan Women* (and like Seneca's *Troades*), with the actual sailing of the fleet, or at least with final preparations for it. Agamemnon might well go off, accompanied by his followers (i.e. the chorus), to make the sacrifices to Athena which earlier in the play he had been intending to make, with departure from Troy to follow. As in the two Euripidean plays, we have heard dire prophecies which we, but not the Achaeans, know are certain to be fulfilled. Achilles' anger has been appeased, but not that of Athena, nor the anger which an earlier sacrifice of another maiden had aroused in the victim's mother.

---

[80] In which case it would have to be Neoptolemus that remained mute during the Calchas scene.

[81] Cf. Aesch. *Ag.* 224–247 where Iphigeneia pleads with her father (228) but is lifted up over the altar "like a yearling goat" at his orders (231–4) and her mouth gagged to prevent any ill-omened utterance (235–8) so that she can only beg for mercy with her eyes (240–3). So in the Polyxene painting described by Pollianus "the whole of the Trojan War lies in the eyes of the maiden" (*App.Plan.* 150.5–6). Did the narrative of the Sophoclean messenger include echoes of Aeschylus' description of the sacrifice of Iphigeneia, as the prophecy of Agamemnon's murder included echoes of Aeschylus' descriptions of that event?

We can thus tentatively posit for Sophocles' play the following list of *dramatis personae*:

> *Ghost of Achilles*
> *Agamemnon*
> *Menelaus*
> *Chorus of Argive Soldiers*
> *First Messenger*[82] (reporting appearance of Achilles' ghost)
> *Neoptolemus*
> *Polyxene*
> *Calchas*
> *Second Messenger* (reporting the sacrifice)

There may have been one or two other characters, particularly if the plot was more complex than appears from our scanty evidence, but the above total of eight (excluding the chorus) is already high for Sophocles.[83] The structure of the play, as provisionally reconstructed above, may be summarized as follows:

Prologue (Ghost of Achilles)
Parodos
First Episode (quarrel of Agamemnon and Menelaus; Menelaus leaves, intending to sail for home)
First Stasimon
Second Episode (First Messenger narrating apparition of Ghost preventing fleet from sailing)
Second Stasimon
Third Episode (debate between Neoptolemus and Polyxene; Agamemnon refers issue to Calchas)
Third Stasimon
Fourth Episode (Calchas declares sacrifice necessary; Polyxene predicts future disasters [?]; Polyxene led off)
Fourth Stasimon

---

[82] The function of First Messenger, or Second Messenger, or both, may have been discharged by the herald Talthybius.

[83] Of the seven extant Sophoclean plays, *Antigone* and the two *Oedipus* plays each have eight individual speaking parts; none has more (whereas five extant Euripidean plays have between 9 and 11 individual parts).

Exodos (Second Messenger reports sacrifice; Agamemnon and chorus depart, intending to make offerings to Athena and then sail for home)

Our main clue to the date of the play is provided by its relationship with Euripides' *Hecuba*, which was probably produced between 426 and 424 BC (see p. 48 above). Three considerations tend to indicate that Sophocles' play was the earlier of the two.[84]

(i) In *Polyxene* the ghost of Achilles appeared on stage, probably at the beginning of the play, and there was also a vivid report of an epiphany of the same ghost which was not seen by the audience. In *Hecuba* there are three vivid retrospective references to this epiphany (37–41, 93–95, 109–115), and the prologue-speaker is also a ghost – but a different ghost, that of Polydorus. Since an onstage appearance by the ghost of Achilles was an obvious move in theatrical terms, and had mythical precedent going back as far as the *Nostoi*, one would have expected this idea to be used by the first author to dramatize the story, leaving the second to find a variant.[85]

(ii) Euripides' decision to give Neoptolemus no role in the events leading up to the sacrifice is best explained (see above) on the assumption that he wanted to avoid repeating a previous dramatic treatment.

---

[84] It has further been argued (Zieliński [1925] 18–22; cf. Fantham [1982] 60–61) that the case for Sophocles' priority is supported by an apparent inconsistency in Euripides' play as to whether the ghost of Achilles demanded an unspecified Trojan maiden (thus Hecuba's dream in 93–97, and the chorus's report of the ghost's words in 113–5) or Polyxene and no other (this is stated by Polydorus in 40–41, by Odysseus at 305 and 389–390, and is presupposed by the Greeks' debate reported in 116–140) – the latter, argues Zieliński, being an idea carried over from Sophocles' treatment and inappropriate to Euripides'. It is, however, doubtful whether there is any real inconsistency. Once the audience know from 40–41 that the ghost's demand was for Polyxene, they will understand later passages in the light of this, assuming that Hecuba's dream is a true but not fully detailed premonition and that the chorus in 113–5 are reporting only part of what the ghost said. As for Hecuba's argument in 251–270, which has also been brought into this debate, far from implying (as Zieliński and Fantham claim) that Achilles has not made a specific demand for Polyxene, this passage actually presupposes that he has, and argues that his demand is unjust (262–3).

[85] Cf. Mossman (1995) 45: "The terrifying appearance of the ghost was just the sort of Grand Guignol horror that Euripides delights to describe: only the fact that it had already been done, and by all accounts done extremely well, can explain why he did not let himself go here." Similarly Bardel (2005) 95.

(iii) Euripides seems to assume (see above) that his audience already
know that Achilles is not only *forbidding* the fleet to sail until they
have sacrificed Polyxene, but making it *physically impossible* for
them to do so; he never makes this explicit, and his failure to do so
is best explained if, again, the idea was already familiar from a
previous dramatic treatment.

It can therefore safely be assumed that Sophocles' play was produced no
later than 425 (or 430, if Eur. *Hcld.* 855 imitates fr. D [525] – see
Commentary). We cannot be more precise than this. Calder (1966) 56
argued for a considerably earlier date on the basis of some Aeschylean
vocabulary features. However, his evidence is weak: the "Aeschylean"
parallel for one of the items in question (*melambatheis* "black ... deep
below" fr. A [523].1) occurs in the probably spurious *Prometheus Bound*
(219) which may have been produced as late as 431;[86] two others, both
echoes of the *Oresteia*,[87] appear in the prophecy of Agamemnon's murder,
and that is enough to account for them regardless of date;[88] there remains
only the verb *thuēpolein* "make sacrifices" (fr. B [522].2), which occurs
only once in Aeschylus (*Ag.* 262) and four times in Euripides.[89] Arguments
from putative structural weaknesses in the play are even more hazardous,
given the state of our knowledge; we should remember that Euripides
assumed his audience would be familiar with the play, that he thrice
stimulated their recollection of the appearances (enacted and narrated) of
Achilles' ghost, and that "Longinus" thought that the narrative of the
ghost's second appearance was one of Sophocles' two greatest triumphs of
visualization.

---

[86] See R. Bees, *Zur Datierung des Prometheus Desmotes* (Stuttgart, 1993), and my
Aeschylean Tragedy (Bari, 1996) 326 n.14.

[87] *apeiros* "endless" and *endutērion* "garment specially donned", both applied to the
robe (with no holes for head or arms) in which Clytaemestra trapped her husband; cf.
respectively Aesch. *Ag.* 1382 and *Cho.* 998 (*podenduton*), both referring to the same
garment.

[88] So rightly Mossman (1995) 45. Cf. *El.* 1413, 1415; Eur. *Hec.* 1277 (*oikouros*
"housekeeper" referring to Clytaemestra, with sinister implications, cf. Aesch. *Ag.* 155,
809, 1225), 1293 (~ Aesch. *Ag.* 1).

[89] *Hcld.* 401; *El.* 665, 1134; fr. 781.56. It also appears in a fragment of Sophocles'
Andromeda (fr. 126.3).

ΠΟΛΥΞΕΝΗ

Selected Testimonia

"Longinus", *On the Sublime* 15.7: ἄκρως δὲ καὶ ὁ Σοφοκλῆς ...
πεφάνтασται ... κατὰ τὸν ἀπόπλουν τῶν Ἑλλήνων ἐπὶ τἀχιλλέως
προφαινομένου τοῖς ἀναγομένοις ὑπὲρ τοῦ τάφου, ἣν οὐκ οἶδ' εἴ τις ὄψιν
ἐναργέστερον εἰδωλοποίησε Σιμωνίδου.

ἐπὶ τἀχιλλέως Vahlen: ἔπειτ' Ἀχιλλέως cod. ‖ Bühler posited a substantial lacuna
after τάφου ‖ perh. <πλὴν> Σιμωνίδου

Strabo 10.3.14: ὁ δ' οὖν Σοφοκλῆς ποιήσας τὸν Μενέλαον ἐκ τῆς Τροίας
ἀπαίρειν σπεύδοντα ἐν τῇ Πολυξένῃ, τὸν δ' Ἀγαμέμνονα μικρὸν
ὑπολειφθῆναι βουλόμενον τοῦ ἐξιλάσασθαι τὴν Ἀθηνᾶν χάριν, εἰσάγει
λέγοντα τὸν Μενέλαον [fr. B (522) follows].

POLYXENE

Selected Testimonia

"Longinus", *On the Sublime* **15.7**: Sophocles too has used his imagination excellently … at the time when the Greeks sailed away [from Troy], in connection with the appearance of Achilles at his tomb to those putting to sea – a sight which perhaps no one has presented more vividly to the imagination than Simonides [*or, with the present editor's suggested emendation*, which perhaps no one but Simonides has presented more vividly to the imagination].

Strabo 10.3.14: Sophocles, at any rate, presenting Menelaus as being eager to depart from Troy in *Polyxene*, while Agamemnon wished to delay a little in order to propitiate Athena, brings on Menelaus saying [*fr. B (522) follows*]

A (523)

ΨΥΧΗ ΑΧΙΛΛΕΩΣ

ἀκτὰς ἀπαίωνάς τε καὶ μελαμβαθεῖς
λιποῦσα λίμνης ἦλθον, ἄρσενας †χοὰς†
Ἀχέροντος ὀξυπλῆγας ἠχούσας γόους.

A (523) Apollodorus, *On the Gods* 20 (*FGrH* 244 F 102a) | 1 ἀκτὰς Jacobs: ὦ τὰς codd. | ἀπαίωνάς Canter: ἀπ' αἰῶνας codd. | μελαμβαθεῖς F: μελαμβαφεῖς P ‖ 2 ἦλθον ἄρσενας χοὰς (see below) appears in codd. after v.3: transp. Jacobs | χοὰς codd.: ῥοὰς Meineke: γύας Wecklein: βοὰς Blaydes: perh. πέτρας: Apollodorus (ἄρσενας ... τὰς οὐδὲν ἐκτρεφούσας) had a feminine noun in his text ‖ 3 ὀξυπλῆγας codd.: ὀξυπλῆγος Grotius | ἠχούσας Grotius: ἠχοῦσα codd.: ἠχούσης Heyne

B (522)

ΜΕΝΕΛΑΟΣ

σὺ δ' αὖθι μίμνων που κατ' Ἰδαίαν χθόνα
ποίμνας Ὀλύμπου συναγαγὼν θυηπόλει.

B (522) Strabo 10.3.14 | 1 σὺ **nxyq**: σοῦ BCD | που κατ' Xylander: τοῦ κατ' BCD: τὴν κατ' **nq**: κατ' **xy**

A (523)

I have come here leaving the black lake-shores deep below,

unvisited by Apollo, the barren <cliffs[?]> of Acheron which

echo the sound of mourning blows and piercing wails.

The ghost of Achilles, probably in the prologue (though not its very first words).

B (522)

You stay right here, somewhere in the land of Ida, and collect

all the flocks of Olympus to make sacrifices!

Menelaus telling Agamemnon that he refuses to stay at Troy and make sacrifices, as Agamemnon wishes to do, in the hope of propitiating Athena.

C (524)

οὐ γάρ τις ἂν δύναιτο πρωράτης στρατοῦ
τοῖς πᾶσιν εἶξαι καὶ προσαρκέσαι χάριν·
ἐπεὶ οὐδ' ὁ κρείσσων Ζεὺς ἐμοῦ τυραννίδι
οὔτ' ἐξεπομβρῶν οὔτ' ἐπαυχμήσας φίλος·
βροτοῖς δ' ἂν ἐλθὼν ἐς λόγον δίκην ὄφλοι.   5
πῶς δῆτ' ἔγωγ' ἂν θνητὸς ἐκ θνητῆς τε φὺς
Διὸς γενοίμην εὖ φρονεῖν σοφώτερος;

C (524) Stobaeus 4.8.13 | 2 πᾶσιν εἶξαι Wecklein: πᾶσι δεῖξαι codd. ‖ 4 ἐξεπομβρῶν Grotius: ἐξ ἐπομβρῶν Aᵖᶜ: ἐξεπόμβρων M: ἐξ ἐπόμβρων SAᵃᶜ ‖ 5 δ' ἂν ἐλθὼν Dobree: ἀνελθὼν codd. | ἐς λόγον δίκην Dobree: ἐς δίκην λόγων codd.: ἐς δίκην ψόγους Degani | ὄφλοι Heath: ὄφλαι codd. ‖ 6 ἔγωγ' ἂν θνητὸς Hense: ἐγὼ θνητός γ' ἂν (γὰν M, γ' ὢν A) codd. ‖ 7 εὖ φρονεῖν vel sim. codd.: εὖ φρονῶν Pearson

D (525)

ἀπ' αἰθέρος τε κἀπὸ λυγαίου νέφους

D (525) Σ Apollonius Rhodius 2.1120 | νέφους L: σκότους P: κνέφους Meineke

C (524)

For no one whose station is at the prow of an army could be able to please and satisfy everyone by yielding to their wishes. Why, even Zeus, whose kingship is greater than mine, is not loved, whether he thoroughly soaks the ground or whether he dries it up; if he entered a debate with mortals, he would lose his case. How then can I, a mortal born of a mortal woman, be cleverer than Zeus at making the right decision?

Agamemnon, finding himself having to make a decision (about whether to sacrifice Polyxene?) that will cause trouble whichever way it goes.

D (525)

From the sky and from the murky cloud …

Perhaps from a prophecy of the devastating storm that fell on the Achaeans during their return voyage.

E (526)

χιτών σ' ἄπειρος, ἐνδυτήριον κακῶν ...

E (526) *Etymologicum Genuinum* α999 (*Etymologicum Magnum* 120.47) |
ἐνδυτήριον *Et.Gen.*: ἐνδυτήριος *Et.Mag.*

F (527)

παράρυμα ποδός

F (527) Hesychius π652 (Schmidt); Photius Galeanus 389.1 | παράρυμα
Musurus: παραρύμα ᵃHsch.: παρὰ ῥύμα Hsch.: παράρυμμα Photius

G (528)

(περικόπτειν τὰ ἄκρα)

G (528) Harpocration η8 Keaney ἠκρωτηριασμένοι ... ἀντὶ τοῦ
λελυμασμένοι· οἱ γὰρ λυμαινόμενοί τισιν εἰώθασι περικόπτειν αὐτῶν τὰ
ἄκρα, ὡς καὶ Σοφοκλῆς Πολυξένη (Maussac: Πολυξενῆτιν codd.)

E (526)

An endless robe, an evil festive garment, <shall entrap> you

Addressed to Agamemnon, and foretelling his murder; perhaps a continuation of the same prophecy.

The following fragments cannot be assigned to a context:

F (527)

a side-screen for the foot

From an anapaestic or lyric passage, possibly describing either the royal attire of Agamemnon or the bridal attire of Polyxene the last time she comes on stage.

G (528)

(cutting off the extremities)

Referring to the mutilation of Polyxene's brother Troilus?

POLYXENE

A (523)

For the position of this fragment in the play, see Introduction (pp. 53–54), where it is shown that it probably belongs to the prologue. The close parallel with the opening words of Polydorus' ghost in Euripides' *Hecuba* ("I have come here leaving the recesses of the dead and the gates of darkness, where Hades dwells apart from the gods") makes it likely that our fragment comes very close to the opening of the play, but we probably do not have the play's actual first words; for the ghost of a male person would not be made to use the feminine participle *lipousa* with reference to itself unless it had *previously* spoken of itself, not as "Achilles", but as "the ghost (*psūkhē*) of Achilles" (cf. Sutton 113).

1–2 black … deep below: Greek *melambatheis* "black-deep", a tragic epithet for places in or associated with the underworld (Tartarus in [Aesch.] *Prom.* 219; the dragon's cave, into which Menoeceus leaps to his death to save Thebes, in Eur. *Phoen.* 1010).

1–2 lake-shores: the shores of the Acherusian lake, which the souls of the dead had to cross to reach the realm of Hades (*El.* 138, Eur. *Alc.* 253, 443, Ar. *Frogs* 137–140, 180–270; cf. *Odyssey* 10.513–4, Pl. *Phd.* 112e-114b).

1–2 unvisited by Apollo: lit. "without Paeon" (Apollo's title as a god of healing); the same shores (or perhaps the boat that ferries souls thither) are described by a synonymous phrase at Aesch. *Seven* 859. Apollo was notorious for shunning contact with death and mourning (cf. Stesichorus *PMG* 232; Aesch. *Ag.* 1075, 1079; Eur. *Supp.* 974–5; schol. Eur. *Phoen.* 1028), and the description of him washing and dressing the corpse of Sarpedon in *Iliad* 16.666–683 seemed so inappropriate to Zenodotus that he rejected the passage as un-Homeric. The word can simultaneously be understood as meaning "without paeans (songs of joy)", cf. Eur. *IT* 183–5, Kannicht on Eur. *Hel.* 176–8.

2 barren: Greek *arsenas,* lit. "male"; Apollodorus interprets this as meaning here "causing nothing to grow", contrasting it with the epic phrase "female [i.e. nourishing] dew" (the "food and drink" of the cicada, according to Hes. *Shield* 395; cf. also Callimachus frr. 110.53, 384.27, 548, and the T-scholia to *Iliad* 22.45; in *Odyssey* 5.467 "female" seems rather to mean "moist" or "enervating").

2 **<cliffs[?]>**: the text is corrupt. The context requires a noun denoting some feature of the infernal lake-shores that can be said to "echo the sound of mourning blows and piercing wails"; and since Apollodorus' gloss on *arsenas* is a phrase in the feminine gender, it appears that the noun in the text he read was a feminine noun. The manuscripts (of Stobaeus, who is quoting Porphyry who is in turn quoting Apollodorus) offer us *khoās*; that means "libations" (especially those offered to chthonic deities or to the dead), and even if we suppose that the meaning here is "streams" (for which there is no parallel), or emend to *rhoās* "streams" (Meineke) or *guās* "fields" (Blaydes), we still would not get the desired sense, since a stream is neither a shore nor part of a shore, and neither a stream nor a field is good at echoing sounds. The two features that are found on coasts that *do* echo sounds well are caves and cliffs; and while caves (hollow and often moist) are perhaps not very well described as "male", cliffs (tall, hard and often barren) certainly might be. And cliffs were part of traditional Greek infernal geography: Circe in *Odyssey* 10.515 mentions a rock that rises where the rivers Pyriphlegethon and Cocytus flow into (Lake?) Acheron; Aristophanes (*Frogs* 470–1) makes the doorkeeper of Hades speak of "the sable-hearted rock of Styx and the blood-dripping crag of Acheron"; in Hesiod's *Theogony* (786–7, 792) the waters of Styx, on which the gods swear, flow "from a steep, lofty rock". The only feminine noun meaning "cliffs" that will fit the metre in our passage is *petrās* – which happens to be used in all four of the passages just cited. The reading *khoās* may have originated from an interlinear or marginal correction of *ēkhousās* in the following line.

3 **the sound of mourning blows and piercing wails:** lit. "sharp-beating wailings", i.e. high-pitched (a regular secondary meaning of *oxus* "sharp") wailings accompanied by head- or breast-beating such as mourners performed; cf. *Aj.* 631–4, *El.* 89–90, Aesch. *Cho.* 23, 425–8, Eur. *Andr.* 1210–1, *Supp.* 51, *El.* 148–9, *Tro.* 279–280, 1235, *Hel.* 372, 1089, *Phoen.* 1350–1, *Iliad* 18.31, 50–51, Hdt. 6.58.3. See D.C. Kurtz and J. Boardman, *Greek Burial Customs* (London, 1971) 59, 104, 144, 214, and pll. 13–16, 24, 33–35; M. Alexiou, *The Ritual Lament in Greek Tradition* (Cambridge, 1974) 6, 8, 41; R. Garland, *The Greek Way of Death* (London, 1985) 29, 32.

B (522)

Strabo (10.3.14), who cites these lines, says that Sophocles "brings on Menelaus speaking [them]" in *Polyxene* "when he portrays Menelaus as eager to depart from Troy ... and Agamemnon wishing to remain a little for the sake of propitiating Athena"; as discussed in the Introduction (pp. 57–58), this quarrel must have occupied an early episode of the play, before the attempted departure which was prevented by the epiphany of Achilles' ghost. Here Menelaus is angrily telling Agamemnon that he can do what he pleases, even (he says hyperbolically) sacrificing all the sheep on the mountains of the Troad, implying (and doubtless stating, a few lines before or after) that *he*, Menelaus, is determined to leave come what may.

1 **right here:** Greek *authi*, fairly common in epic, is found only here in tragedy, with the doubtful exception of Aesch. *Supp.* 828 (in a damaged and incoherent passage). It is doubtless used here to echo *Odyssey* 3.155–6, where in a narrative of this same dispute it is said that "half the host restrained themselves and *stayed where they were* (*authi*) with Agamemnon son of Atreus".

1 **somewhere in the land of Ida:** Menelaus professes to suppose that Agamemnon will personally lead an expedition to the mountains to collect sheep for sacrifice; cf. *Iliad* 23.110–124 where he *sends* an expedition (led by a secondary figure, Meriones) to Mount Ida to collect timber for Patroclus' funeral pyre.

2 **Olympus:** this name was borne by several mountains in Greece, Asia Minor and Cyprus in addition to the famous Mount Olympus in Thessaly, but there was no well-known Olympus in the Troad. Strabo offers, in effect, two explanations of the name: (i) four of the peaks of Mount Ida, in the region of Antandros (the southern Troad), bore the name Olympus; (ii) Sophocles has confused Ida with the "neighbouring" Mount Olympus in Mysia (actually over 100 miles to the south, above Smyrna), following an allegedly widespread practice of poets who "often beat Ida and Olympus into one mountain".

C (524)

In the Introduction (p. 61) it is shown that the speaker is almost certainly Agamemnon, and suggested that the most plausible occasion for him to say this is when he finds himself forced to take the invidious decision whether to sacrifice Polyxene – and that he perhaps in the end evades doing so by transferring the responsibility to Calchas. The substance of what he says here is adapted from Theognis 23–26 ("I am renowned among all men, but I am not yet able to please all my fellow-citizens; and no wonder, son of Polypaeus – *for even Zeus does not please everyone, either when he gives rain or when he withholds it*"; the italicized sentence became semi-proverbial, and has survived on a third-century ostrakon [*PBerol* 12319]). The argument is parallel to, but less reprehensible than, the argument sometimes heard in tragedy (*Trach.* 441–8, Eur. *Hipp.* 451–461, *Tro.* 948–950, fr. 794) and parodied in comedy (Ar. *Clouds* 1079–82, *Eccl.* 778–783) that mortals' acts of greed or lust are excusable because the gods frequently commit similar acts.

1   one whose station is at the prow: Greek *prōirātēs* "prow-man", an officer who was stationed in the bows of a ship, acting as forward lookout (Ar. *Knights* 543, Plut. *Agis* 1.4), commanding the forward section of the deck crew, and generally assisting the helmsman (*kubernētēs*) and seeing that his orders were executed; see J.S. Morrison and J.F. Coates, *The Athenian Trireme* (Cambridge, 1986) 112–3, 130, 160, 223. It is at first sight surprising that Soph. makes Agamemnon use this word, which everyone knew denoted the *second*-in-command of the ship, when *prumnētēs* "stern-man, helmsman" (cf. Aesch. *Eum.* 16, 765) was available; but if Agamemnon is thinking of himself as a *leader* of men, it is perhaps understandable that he avoids assigning himself a post at the *rear* end of the figurative vessel.

5   if he entered … he would lose his case: or, with Degani (*Eikasmos* 2 [1991] 101), "if he went to law with mortals, he would incur condemnation". Attempts at experimental verification of this assertion were considered inadvisable (as the hero of Euripides' *Bellerophon* discovered: Eur. fr. 286, 292, 293, 306–8, Ar. *Peace* 146–8) except in comic fantasy (Ar. *Peace* 105–8: "[I mean] to ask [Zeus] about the Greeks … what he's aiming to do with them. – And if he doesn't tell you? – I'll indict him for betraying Greece to the Medes!") If Neoptolemus is present, we may perhaps be reminded of his later attempt to demand satisfaction from Apollo for the killing of his father, which in Sophocles' *Hermione/Phthiotides* (*q.v.*) and Euripides' *Andromache* (52–53) and *Orestes* (1657) was the cause, or one of the causes, of his violent death at Delphi.

7   at making the right decision: Pearson's conjecture, giving the sense "how can I, *if in my right mind,* be cleverer than Zeus?", is tempting but should be rejected, because such a caveat would be pointless: even if

Agamemnon were *out* of his mind, he still would not be cleverer than Zeus – he would only *think* he was.

D (525)

This line is cited by a scholiast on Apollonius Rhodius to illustrate the adjective *lūgaios* "murky, dark". It has usually been taken as part of a prophecy of the storm that decimated the Achaean fleet on the return voyage (cf. Eur. *Tro.* 78–79 "Zeus will send rain, gigantic hailstones, and *dark* blasts from the *sky*"), though Wilamowitz (ms. ap. Radt) associated it with meteorological portents accompanying the epiphany of Achilles' ghost (cf. perhaps Accius 659–660 Warmington; also Eur. *Hcld.* 854–8 [see below]). If the context is indeed prophetic, the speaker cannot be the ghost of Achilles (see Introduction, pp. 55–57); it may be Polyxene or Cassandra, or the former reporting the utterances of the latter.

The striking phrase *lūgaion nephos* "murky cloud" appears again in Eur. *Hcld.* 855, in a description of an epiphany of Heracles and Hebe (in the form of stars) which rejuvenates Heracles' nephew Iolaus and enables him to pursue Eurystheus in his chariot from Pallene in eastern Attica to the Scironian Rocks beyond Megara, where he captures him. That cloud is a very small one, covering only the chariot itself, and the portentous epithet used to describe it seems overblown; it is more likely that Euripides was imitating a Sophoclean phrase than that he invented it himself for a not entirely appropriate context. If so, we can infer that *Polyxene* is earlier than *Heracleidae*, making ca. 430 BC the latest possible date for it.

1   **cloud:** instead of *nephous* "cloud" one of the two mss. in which the scholium survives (P) reads *skotous* "darkness", and Meineke suggested that Soph. had written *knephous* "darkness", since this could account for one of the transmitted readings as a scribal slip and the other as a gloss. In Eur. *Hcld.* 855, however, the context requires the meaning "cloud", and *skotous* in P may be merely a piece of scribal absent-mindedness (the scribe had just written that *lūgaios* meant *skoteinos* "dark").

E (526)

This time we are certainly dealing with a prophecy, addressed to Agamemnon and predicting his murder; again Polyxene or Cassandra is the likely speaker (see Introduction, pp. 56–57). Already before Aeschylus, as we know from a calyx-krater painted by the Dokimasia Painter about a decade earlier (Boston 63.1246; A.J.N.W. Prag, *The Oresteia* [Warminster, 1985] pl. A6), the story existed of how Agamemnon, on his return home, was bathed by his wife and then dressed by her in a robe that covered him completely, with no holes for head or arms, and left him a helpless victim for Aegisthus' sword; Aeschylus modified this by having Clytaemestra wield the sword herself. She describes the robe as "an *endless* net, as if for fish..., an *evil* wealth of raiment" (Aesch. *Ag.* 1382–3); Orestes, displaying it to gods and men after taking his revenge on Clytaemestra and Aegisthus, asks whether he should call it "a device for hunting a beast, or a tent to cover the feet (*podenduton*, cf. *endutērion* here) of a corpse in the bath" (*Cho.* 998–9); Apollo, addressing the Athenian court, speaks of Clytaemestra "hobbling her husband with a cunningly-made *endless* robe" (*Eum.* 634–5). Sophocles recalls this death-trap in another context when he makes Heracles speak of the death-trap of a garment that *his* wife has (innocently) caused him to don as a "woven net of the Erinyes" (*Trach.* 1051–2), a blend of phrases from Aesch. *Ag.* 1382 (above) and 1580; cf. also Eur. *Or.* 25. Prediction of Agamemnon's murder (never, of course, believed) became almost a cliché in dramas set shortly before his homeward voyage (Eur. *Hec.* 1275–84, *Tro.* 356–364, 404–5, 445–461).

The fragment, as quoted, is not a complete sentence; the verb is lacking, and presumably came in the following line.

robe: Greek *khitōn*, properly a garment worn directly over the skin. Heracles' fatal robe was also a *khitōn* (*Trach.* 580, 612, 769). The term is not used in the *Oresteia.*

festive garment: Greek *endutērion*, lit. "something for putting on"; this and cognate words are particularly used of garments specially put on for special occasions (e.g. Aesch. *Eum.* 1028, Eur. *Tro.* 257, Antiphanes fr. 38). Agamemnon's robe was ostensibly to be worn at a sacrifice to celebrate his victorious return (cf. Aesch. *Ag.* 1056–7, 1310). Heracles' robe, also to be worn at a victory-sacrifice, is called *endutēra peplon* at *Trach.* 674.

F (527)

The noun *parar(rh)ūma* is well attested as a naval term denoting curtains of linen or hair (i.e. skin with the hair left on) stretched along the sides of ships for protection against foul weather and enemy missiles; each Athenian warship was supposed to have four such screens, two of each type (*IG* ii 2 1611.244–9, 1612.73–79, etc.; cf. Xen. *Hell.* 1.6.19, also 2.1.22 where the non-technical term *parablēmata* is used); see Morrison and Coates, *The Athenian Trireme* 151. The term is also applied to the curtains of the Tabernacle (translating Hebrew *ohel* "tent") in LXX *Exodus* 35.11. The "*parar(rh)ūma* of a foot" should therefore be something that protects the sides of the foot, i.e. a closed shoe or boot as distinct from a sandal, and this is how Photius glosses the phrase ("shoes that protect the feet"). Hesychius, however, while recognizing the senses "rope [sic] in ships" and "shoe", gives first place to the following mysterious explanation of the phrase as used in *Polyxene*: "because certain woven things were hung from the chariot for beauty". Since chariots do not have feet, it is likely that *harmatos* "chariot" is corrupt, and I suggest that *ek tou harmatos* (ΑΡΜΑΤΟΣ) "from the chariot" should be emended to *ek dermatos* (ΔΕΡΜΑΤΟΣ) "<made> of skin". The commentator who is Hesychius' ultimate source may have explained that *parar(rh)ūmata* normally referred to hanging leather screens on board ship but that here the word denoted a kind of ornamental footwear worn "for beauty", and this note may then have been garbled in the process of excerption and abridgement.

If the word-order as transmitted in Hesychius and Photius is accurate, the phrase must come from an anapaestic or (less likely) lyric passage. In *Antigone* (155–161, 376–383, 526–530, 626–630, 801–5, 1257–60) each entrance of Creon, Antigone, Ismene or Haemon is greeted by a short anapaestic passage chanted by the chorus, and it is possible that our fragment comes from a similar passage. If so, and if the chorus were commenting on the entering character's luxurious footwear, it is likely that (s)he was lavishly dressed in other respects also; which suggests that the reference is either to Agamemnon in royal robes (worn with a view to officiating at his proposed sacrifice to Athena?) or, as Wilamowitz supposed (ms. ap. Radt), to Polyxene coming out in the dress of a bride (cf. Sen. *Tro.* 945–8, 1132–4) to go to her own sacrifice.

G (528)

Greek literature contains several references to the custom (sometimes called *maschalismos*) of cutting off the extremities (hands and feet, sometimes also nose and ears) of a person one has murdered, stringing them together and tying them around his neck and under his armpits (*maschalai*) with a view *inter alia* to disabling his ghost from pursuit and vengeance; see E. Rohde, *Psyche* (tr. W.B. Hillis, London, 1925) 582–6, and R.C. Jebb, *Sophocles ...: The Electra* (Cambridge, 1894) 211–2. In some accounts the corpse of Agamemnon was so treated by Clytaemestra (Aesch. *Cho.* 439, Soph. *El.* 445) and that of Apsyrtus, brother of Medea, by Jason (Ap.Rh. 4.477); Atreus' mutilation of the children of Thyestes (Aesch. *Ag.* 1594–7, Sen. *Thy.* 1004–34, [Apoll.] *Epit.* 2.13; cf. Hdt. 1.119) may once have been imagined as having had this apotropaic function as well as that of concealing from their father what it was that he was eating. See also Pausanias Att. μ8, Hesychius μ379, Suda ε928, μ275, *Et.Mag.* 118.22–36, 574.202–217, Apostolius 11.4. The amputation of extremities is also referred to as an (atrocious and barbaric) punishment (e.g. *Odyssey* 22.474–7, Aesch. *Eum.* 188, Hdt. 3.69.5, 3.118.2, 3.154–5, 9.112.1, Xen. *An.* 1.9.13). Thus when Demosthenes in his speech *On the Crown* (18.296) spoke of the pro-Macedonian politicians in the various Greek states as having "amputated the extremities of their own native cities" he was accusing them of one of the most horrendous crimes imaginable.

Sophocles' *Troilus* (q.v.), which dealt with the killing of Troilus by Achilles, contained the phrase "full of *maschalismata*" (*Troilus* fr. L [623]), so it is likely that in that play Achilles not only beheaded Troilus' corpse (see Introduction, p. 45) but "maschalized" it also. It is thus possible in principle, as was suggested by Calder (1966) 50, that Harpocration's reference to Sophocles' *Polyxene* is an error and that the mutilation was mentioned only in *Troilus* (perhaps in a speech by Polyxene); but there is no reason why it should not have been mentioned in *Polyxene* too, whether by Polyxene herself (as one of the miseries of her life, or as a reason she has for hating Achilles) or by the ghost of Achilles (perhaps in a retrospective narrative in the prologue of the play). Another possibility is that the reference is to the future mutilation of Agamemnon's corpse, as part of the prophecy of his murder to which fr. E (526) also belongs (so Bardel [2005] 97).

SYNDEIPNOI (THE DINERS) *or*

ACHAIÔN SYLLOGOS (THE GATHERING OF THE ACHAEANS)

Texts and Testimonia: Pearson i 94–103, ii 198–209; Lucas de Dios 75–76, 286–290; *TrGF* iv 163–5, 425–30; Lloyd-Jones 56–57, 280–5.

Myth: Odyssey 8.74–80 with scholia; *Cypria* Arg. §9 West; Aristotle, *Rhetoric* 1401b17–19 (cf. *CAG* xxi 2.151.16); Philodemus, *On Anger* col. 18.17–24, *On Poems* 1.213.2–9 Janko. Gantz 588–9.

Artistic evidence: none.

Main discussions: H. Weil, *REG* 3 (1890) 339–343; U. von Wilamowitz-Moellendorff in *BKT* v.2 (1907) 64–72; D.F. Sutton, *HSCP* 78 (1974) 138–140; P. von der Mühll, *Ausgewählte kleine Schriften* (Basel, 1975) 150–1; S.L. Radt, *EH* 29 (1982) 211, 214 n.51; M.G. Palutan, *SIFC*³ 14 (1996) 10–27; C. Heynen and R. Krumeich in *Satyrspiel* 396–8; P. Michelakis, *Achilles in Greek Tragedy* (Cambridge, 2002) 178–185; A.H. Sommerstein in *Shards* 355–371; P. Voelke, *ibid.* 339–340; A. López Eire, *ibid.* 399–400; M.R. Christ, *CQ* 54 (2004) 47–48.

The myth: literary and artistic evidence

The play of Sophocles[1] that is cited sometimes as *Syndeipnoi (The Diners)*,[2] sometimes as *Achaiôn Syllogos (The Gathering of the Achaeans)*,[3] and sometimes under hybrid titles like *Syndeipnon (The Dinner Party)*[4] or *Achaiôn Syndeipnon (The Achaeans' Dinner Party)*,[5] is based on what appear originally to have been two separate stories about quarrels among the leaders of the Achaean army just before, or early in, the Trojan war. One of these stories appears first, for us, in the *Odyssey* (8.74–80) and the other in the *Cypria*, the cyclic epic that narrated the

---

[1] For the question whether *Syndeipnoi* and *Achaiôn Syllogos* are one play or two, see pp. 88–90 below.

[2] Frr. B (563), N (571), O (562), and probably C (564) (where the text is corrupt) are cited in this way; the play is also referred to under this title by Cicero (*ad Quintum fratrem* 2.16.3), and Athenaeus 8.365b, mentioning that "some" argue that the correct title is the neuter *Syndeipnon*, implies thereby that *Syndeipnoi* was the title most commonly used.

[3] Frr. A (143), E (144), H (144a), P (146), Q (147) and R (148) are cited in this way; in Hesychius' citation of fr. K (145) the title is given simply as *Syllogos (The Gathering)*.

[4] Frr. F (568), M (567), S (569) and T (570) are cited in this way.

[5] Fr. G (565) is cited in this way.

Trojan War saga from its beginning up to the point where the *Iliad* commences. In the *Odyssey* Odysseus, at the court of the Phaeacian king Alcinous, hears the bard Demodocus sing

> a tale whose fame at that time reached the broad heavens, the strife of Odysseus and Achilles son of Peleus, how they once quarrelled with vehement words at a rich feast of the gods, and Agamemnon king of men rejoiced in his heart that the best of the Achaeans were quarrelling, because Phoebus Apollo had so spoken to him in an oracle at holy Pytho when he crossed the stone threshold.

The story must have been known to the original audiences of the *Odyssey*, since it is apparently not necessary to tell them what it was about the oracle given to Agamemnon that made him rejoice when a quarrel broke out between Achilles and Odysseus, respectively the best fighter and the cleverest adviser in the army.[5a] Ancient commentators[6] either knew or guessed that the oracle had said that the Achaeans would capture Troy if, or when, their best men quarrelled with each other, and that while Agamemnon took it to be referring to this quarrel between Achilles and Odysseus, it really referred to the quarrel between Achilles and Agamemnon (the "best of the Achaeans" in yet another sense, as being the most powerful among them and the leader of the expedition) which precipitated the events of the *Iliad*, culminating in the death of Hector which, as the *Iliad* implies (e.g. 22.56–76, 410–1) and comes close to explicitly stating (15.69–71), made the fall of Troy inevitable. They also agree on the subject of the quarrel: Achilles and Odysseus were disputing the relative importance of valour and ingenuity in war. They say nothing of when or where the quarrel occurred,[7] but Agamemnon's misreading of the oracle would be of little significance unless the quarrel took place very early in the war or even before it began, leading Agamemnon to suppose it would be over quickly whereas in fact it lasted ten years. No scholiast links this quarrel to the one described in the *Cypria*, let alone to Sophocles' play.

Of the quarrel narrated in the *Cypria* we know from the synopsis of that epic by Proclus (*Cypria* Arg. §9 West). After speaking of the assembly of the expedition at Aulis and the sacrifice of Iphigeneia, Proclus proceeds:

[5a] See A.F. Garvie's commentary (Cambridge, 1994) *ad loc.*

[6] Schol. *Odyssey* 8.75, 77, 80.

[7] Except that one of them (on 75) self-contradictorily places it "after the death of Hector".

> Then they sail to Tenedos; and while they are feasting, Philoctetes is
> bitten by a water-snake and is left on Lemnos because of the evil
> smell, and Achilles, having been invited late, quarrels with
> Agamemnon. Then they land at Ilium ...

There are no other references to either story earlier than Sophocles' play,
nor is the subject identifiably treated in archaic or classical art.

Among later references to the story which do not explicitly credit
Sophocles' play the most important is a brief one in Aristotle's *Rhetoric*
(1401b17–19). Aristotle is discussing fallacies, and in particular the fallacy
of treating the incidental as though it were essential, as for instance

> if someone were to say that the greatest honour one can have is to be
> invited to dinner, because Achilles was angry with the Achaeans at
> Tenedos on account of not being invited – whereas in fact he was
> angry because he was dishonoured, and it so happened that this
> dishonour related to the failure to invite him.

A commentator (*CAG* xxi 2.151.16) adds that it was Agamemnon who
failed to invite Achilles "when he invited the leading men (*aristoi*)".
Aristotle is more likely, on the whole, to be referring to the *Cypria* than to
our play, since "on account of not being invited" matches Proclus'
statement and no reference is made to what was evidently the most
celebrated feature of the play, the quarrel with Odysseus.

In Sophocles' play we have a quarrel between Achilles and Odysseus,
as in the *Odyssey* (frr. J, L, M = 566, 567), but as in the *Cypria* the quarrel
takes place when the Achaeans are "see[ing] the dwellings of Troy land"
for the first time, and when Hector is "close at hand" but has not yet,
apparently, met the Achaeans in battle – which exactly suits the stop at
Tenedos, a small island lying, at its nearest point, two or three miles off the
coast of the Troad.[8] Thus Sophocles appears to have merged the two
stories into one by inserting the *Odyssey*'s Achilles-Odysseus quarrel into
the framework of the *Cypria*'s Tenedos feast. A more detailed discussion
of the structure of the play must wait until we have considered whether
Syndeipnoi and *Achaiôn Syllogos* are or are not alternative names for the
same play.

In addition to quotations of words or passages from the play, there are
two other references to it in later authors. Philodemus (*On Anger* col.
18.17–24) speaks of people turning everything topsy-turvy "when they are

---

[8] Today it is the Turkish island of Bozcaada; it was an advanced base for British and
Commonwealth forces in the Gallipoli campaign of 1915.

dismissed (*parapemphthentes*) by the host of a banquet, like the Achilles of Sophocles"; since the host of the Tenedos banquet must certainly have been Agamemnon, this shows that, as in the *Cypria*, the dispute was initially between Achilles and Agamemnon, and the quarrel with Odysseus must have somehow arisen out of this.

More enigmatic is a reference to the play in a letter (*QF* 2.16) of 54 BC from Cicero to his brother Quintus, then serving under Caesar in Britain: "As to the *Syndeipnoi* of Sophocles, though I see that the little play has been composed [*or* performed] by you in a humorous manner, I in no way approved of it." A textual uncertainty leaves two very different interpretations possible. If with the mss. we read *actam* "performed", since it is hardly likely that Quintus had been putting on amateur theatricals in camp, it must be presumed that on some occasion he had behaved in jest (towards Caesar or one of his chief lieutenants) as Achilles in the play behaves in earnest. This view was approved by Latte[9] and apparently by Radt (*TrGF* iv 425), but is most implausible: Quintus knew very well that his brother was at this time anxious to be on good terms with Caesar;[10] he would hardly have risked giving public offence to him – and if he had, his brother Marcus would have had rather more to say to him than merely "I in no way approved". More likely we should read *factam*[11] and suppose that Quintus had translated or adapted Sophocles' play; this fits well with his intense interest in poetry and especially tragedy (a few months later he claimed to have written four tragedies in sixteen days [*QF* 3.5.7]). "I see" suggests that he had sent the script to Marcus, who now says that although he sees that the "sketch" or "skit" (Latin *fabella*) was made humorously, he was far from approving of it; this implies that he would have found it

---

[9] K. Latte, *Hermes* 60 (1925) 6 n.1 = *Kleine Schriften* (Munich, 1968) 889 n.5, following G.A. Gerhard, *Philologus* 75 (1918) 258 and arguing that Cicero's "sharp rejection" contrasts markedly with his usual courtesy regarding his brother's poetry [but might it be tongue-in-cheek?] and that in view of what precedes and follows it, the sentence about *Syndeipnoi* should have a political or social reference [but the sentence is followed by a sharp turn to an entirely new and evidently exciting subject, viz. Britain].

[10] Compare, in the same letter, Cicero's reference to "those who grieve that we are so intimate with Caesar" (§1) and his anxious inquiry (§5) as to whether Caesar had been displeased by the content or style of the poem Cicero had recently submitted to him. The same notes are repeatedly struck in earlier correspondence (2.12.1, 2.14.1–2, 2.15.2). Cicero was at this time working on an epic poem in Caesar's honour (cf. 3.7.6).

[11] This conjecture by Buecheler was adopted by D.R. Shackleton Bailey (Cambridge, 1960; Stuttgart, 1988); W.S. Watt (Oxford, 1958) had retained *actam*, as subsequently did A. Salvatore (Milan, 1989). The emendation assumes a very easy corruption (omission of F following the similar letter E in the preceding word *te*).

still more objectionable if he had thought it was made seriously, which in turn strongly suggests that the sketch was disrespectful to someone. Given that Caesar was engaged in an attempt to subdue Britain which, if successful, would rival or exceed the achievement of Agamemnon (making Caesar the first commander ever to conquer a land beyond the "ocean"), it is quite credible that Quintus' thoughts might turn to Sophocles' presentation of Agamemnon and his colleagues on the eve of their great enterprise, and that he might write (perhaps for his eyes and his brother's only) a skit on *Syndeipnoi* with Caesar and his generals substituted for Agamemnon and his. In that case Marcus' expression of disapproval may well be largely tongue-in-cheek; if Caesar got to know about the skit, and lacked the sense of humour to take it in the spirit in which it was intended, he might find it gravely offensive – but Caesar was well known to be good at taking (and making) a joke.[12] From the point of view of one interested in Sophocles' play, the passage is mainly of importance as showing that it was well known among upper-class Romans of literary tastes.

Syndeipnoi *and* Achaiôn Syllogos

As we have seen, there survive eight citations from Sophocles' *Syndeipnoi* or *Syndeipnon* (plus one from *Achaiôn Syndeipnon*) and six from *Achaiôn Syllogos* (plus one from *Syllogos*). That these two plays are one and the same was first suggested by Toup in the eighteenth century, and widely accepted until in 1907 a papyrus (*PBerol* 9908) was published[13] that seemed to refute the conjecture decisively. It contained a choral song instructing a man previously thought to be a Mysian, but now discovered to be a Greek born at Tegea – quite certainly Telephus, whose mother Auge was daughter of Aleos king of Tegea[14] – to guide the Achaean fleet to Troy, followed by the arrival of an impatient Achilles, eager to sail instantly, and a dialogue between him and the more cautious Odysseus. The expedition has been resolved on (line 14), but preparations for it are not yet complete; we are clearly not on Tenedos but somewhere in Greece, at Aulis or even Argos/Mycenae. The link with *Achaiôn Syllogos* seemed to be given by Achilles' question in line 12, "Where is the gathering (*syllogos*) of our friends?", and certain features of the language, notably

---

[12] Cf. Cic. *QF* 2.14.3, *Fam.* 7.5.3; Suet. *Jul.* 22.2, 73.
[13] By Wilamowitz in *BKT* V.ii 64–72.
[14] Eur. fr. 696.1–7; Hecataeus *FGrH* 1 F 29; Alcidamas, *Odysseus* 14; Arist. *Poet.* 1460a32; [Apoll.] 2.7.4.

pontios in the sense "sea-girt" (line 11),[15] *hoi en telei* "those in authority, the powers that be" (line 14), and *rhēsis* "speech" (line 20), were diagnosed as being distinctively Sophoclean.[16] The separate status, and the subject, of *Achaiôn Syllogos* seemed firmly established, and it was sometimes (e.g. by M. Fromhold-Treu, *Hermes* 69 [1934] 333–6) suggested that it had been part of a Sophoclean trilogy or tetralogy called the *Telepheia* and known from a fourth-century inscription (*IG* ii² 3091).

Then in 1957 E.W. Handley and J. Rea in *The Telephus of Euripides* (*BICS* Suppl. 5) 1–16 published a papyrus (now *POxy* 2460) which contained (in its frr. 17–20) parts of seventeen of the twenty-four best-preserved lines in the Berlin papyrus, but also (in its fr. 32) a few letters, on three successive lines, that coincide with a previously known fragment of Euripides' *Telephus* (Eur. fr. 716). The Berlin papyrus (now Eur. fr. 727c) thus no longer comes into consideration as a possible fragment of *Achaiôn Syllogos*, and we are free to consider afresh the evidence suggesting the identification of that play with *Syndeipnoi*.

This evidence is as follows:

(a) In fr. A (143) it is said that (part of) the fleet is at sea after dark. Since this can hardly refer to the *commencement* of a voyage (see Comm.), it must refer to the failure of some ships to *arrive* before nightfall. The port at which they are expected could in principle be either Aulis or Tenedos. The fragment also, coming as it is likely to from near the beginning of the play (since, generally speaking, arrivals are typical of the early portions of a drama and departures of the later portions), tends to suggest that the action began in the evening, which is very unusual in Greek drama but would be entirely appropriate for a play centred on a banquet.

(b) In fr. E (144) someone (presumably Agamemnon) is advised to read out the list of "those who joined in the oath" and note any absentees. This advice would be pointless unless, at the time when this was said, one (or more) of the leaders in fact had not arrived, and it is, to say the least, very tempting to link this with the quarrel involving Achilles and his

---

[15] Handley and Rea (see below) 13–14 point out that this in fact occurs in a papyrus fragment of Euripides' *Hypsipyle* (Eur. fr. 759a.73); they also draw attention to several words that occur in the Berlin fragment and frequently in Euripides but not in Sophocles, notably *eretmos* "oar" (nine times in Euripides), *strateuein* (active voice) "to campaign" (eight times), *hoplītēs* "fully armed footsoldier" (eleven times), and – *syllogos* (ten times).

[16] Wilamowitz's claim (*op.cit.* 65) that the sequence *ou ... oute* "not ... nor" (lines 16–17) is also un-Euripidean holds only if several *prima facie* instances of this sequence in Euripides (*Med.* 1354–7, *IA* 977–8, 1319–24) are arbitrarily emended away.

"dismissal" from the feast. Certainly anyone who *was* thus publicly identified as a defaulter would take grave offence when he came to know of it.[17]

(c) A further piece of evidence became available only in 1968 with the publication of some previously unknown entries from a Madrid ms. of the lexicon of Cyril, which identified fr. H (144a) as coming from *Achaiôn Syllogos*. This fragment refers to "the bald head of Nestor", an expression which *prima facie* is unsuited for serious tragedy (see Comm.) just as are several expressions in fragments cited from *Syndeipnoi* (see §5 below).

Thus both *Syndeipnoi* and *Achaiôn Syllogos* deal with the assembling at a seaport of the Achaian army and fleet en route for Troy; in both, the action probably begins in the evening and not, as usual, in the morning; an insult to one of the leaders, and a grave quarrel ensuing, are a central feature in one, while in the other they are, at the least, a possibility to be seriously envisaged; in both, there is some apparently untragic language and content but no positive evidence for a satyr chorus; and the titles of both are cited sometimes with and sometimes without the word *Achaiôn*. And now that the Berlin papyrus has proved to be irrelevant, there is no evidence whatever telling *against* an identification of the two plays.[18] Radt, Lucas and Lloyd-Jones have all regarded this identification as probable; I regard it as beyond reasonable doubt, and have accordingly edited the fragments ascribed to the two plays (plus two more that are not ascribed by our ancient sources to either) as a single unit.

The play[19]

We have seen that the scene of the play is Tenedos; more precisely, it is outside the quarters there of Agamemnon, who will be the host of the banquet. As Philodemus' reference to the play shows, Agamemnon was a character, and Achilles' dispute was initially with him, but this must have somehow developed into a quarrel between Achilles and Odysseus which

---

[17] Although I argue in the Commentary that the advice was given to Agamemnon in these terms precisely in order to *avoid* publicly identifying Achilles as a defaulter.

[18] Christ (2004) 47 n.44 argues (i) that fr. E (144) "fits the situation of an initial muster at Aulis better than a later review of the troops in Tenedos", (ii) that σύλλογος is "the normal word for muster ... and not a very likely synonym for σύνδειπνον". I would reply that once the question is raised whether one or more of the leaders may have deserted the expedition, the gathering at Tenedos effectively becomes another muster.

[19] Much of the material in this section is taken over from my chapter in *Shards* 355–371, though every issue has been considered afresh.

was the most memorable feature of the play. In thus blending the Achilles-Agamemnon quarrel of the *Cypria* with the Achilles-Odysseus quarrel of the *Odyssey*, and giving Odysseus a central role in the play, Sophocles will have been able, if he wished, to evoke recollections of the Embassy scene of the *Iliad* (9.182–657) and/or of the courteous conversation between Odysseus and the shade of Achilles in the Odyssean *Nekyia* (*Odyssey* 11.467–540).

In addition to Achilles, Odysseus and Agamemnon, it is likely that Nestor and Ajax were also characters in the play. There is a fragment cited from an unspecified play of Sophocles (printed here as fr. D [855]) in which Ajax reviles Nestor and Nestor soothingly replies "I do not condemn you; you may be injurious in speech, but you're good in action"; as the Commentary endeavours to show, this can very plausibly be assigned to the same scene as frr. B and C (563, 564) in which a character whom there are some reasons for identifying with Ajax eagerly anticipates a good meal and is criticized by an older man for gluttony. Moreover, and crucially, Nestor is known to have been mentioned in *Achaiôn Syllogos* (fr. H [144]). Thus it seems that five of the leading Achaean figures in the Trojan War were significant characters in this play, and all of them are involved, one way or another, in two quarrels, one between Nestor and Ajax, easily composed it seems, the other far more serious. The only other character we can identify is Thetis (fr. O [562]).

The Nestor-Ajax quarrel took place on stage – all the three fragments relating to it appear to be spoken by Nestor to Ajax or vice versa – and, as is shown by fr. B (563), it *preceded* the banquet that gave the play its usual title. At least one other scene must also have preceded the banquet, namely the scene containing fr. E (144), in which Agamemnon is advised to take a roll-call of the leaders and identify absentees – an idea which, together with the comment (fr. A [143]) on some ships still being at sea after dark, indicates that at least one major leader is going to be arriving late for a feast which, at such an important moment in the expedition (almost on the eve of the landing), may also be intended to serve as a council of war.

This late arrival (or the last of them, if there are more than one) will evidently be Achilles, and his lateness will be the reason or excuse for the slight he receives from Agamemnon. At the point at which fr. E (144) occurs, so much time has apparently already passed that Agamemnon can plausibly be recommended to take the drastic step of publicly identifying those not (yet) present and either declaring or plainly implying that they have broken the oath they took to defend the rights of Helen's husband. The banquet must be about to commence (having perhaps already been delayed somewhat), and it would be a nuisance dramatically if anyone other than Achilles was still awaited: all the other leaders must thus have arrived by this point. It does not, of course, follow that they have all been seen by the audience: it would be perfectly easy for the prologue-speaker (see next paragraph) to have said something like "Agamemnon has invited all the chiefs to a banquet in his quarters here, and most of them are already within, but some have yet to reach the island". Indeed it may well be that apart from Agamemnon himself, only Nestor and Ajax have been seen on stage before the moment when fr. E (144) is spoken; the tempting idea that Odysseus is the speaker of this fragment, and that he is actually scheming to provoke an outburst by Achilles, founders on the fact that Achilles had not been one of Helen's suitors, had not taken the oath they took, and so would not, under the procedure proposed, have been named as a defaulter – which suggests that the maker of the proposal is not Odysseus but that instinctive conciliator, Nestor (see Commentary on fr. E [144]).

Fr. A (143) probably does not belong in this context. It refers to several or many ships, not just one, and is therefore perhaps best spoken at an earlier stage, when Achilles is not yet the only leader still awaited. It may well, indeed, have formed part of a prologue, perhaps spoken by Nestor, which among other things will have made it clear to the audience where they are situated, geographically and chronologically, within the Trojan War saga, and also that, unusually for a Greek drama, the action is going to occupy all or part of a *night* rather than a day. He will have mentioned (see above) the banquet, the presence in the building of most of the leaders[20] (including Odysseus), the overdue arrival of others (probably Ajax and Achilles). Then ("talk of the devil")[21] enter Ajax. He perhaps explains what has delayed him; Nestor tells him of the forthcoming banquet; Ajax's exuberant reaction (fr. B [563]) earns him a rebuke from Nestor (fr. C [564]) which in turn seems to have led to some high words from Ajax, but Nestor's diplomatic skills (fr. D [855]) enable him to calm Ajax down, and Ajax presumably then goes into Agamemnon's quarters where the banquet is to be held. Nestor may go in with him, but it is also possible that he remains outside, waiting for Achilles. For an actor actually to participate in the choral *parodos* is typical of late plays of Sophocles (*El., Phil., OC*), but Euripides does it as early as *Medea*, and in *Trachiniae*, probably

---

[20] Most likely he has himself come out of the building; if he is provided with a motive, it was perhaps to see whether the latecomers were about to appear.

[21] See O.P. Taplin, *The Stagecraft of Aeschylus* (Oxford, 1977) 137–8: "in drama people often turn up just as thoughts turn to them".

Sophocles' earliest surviving play,[22] Deianeira probably remains onstage, though silent, during the *parodos*.[23]

This, at any rate, would be an appropriate moment for the chorus to appear. They must be a group who could plausibly be imagined as gathering close to Agamemnon's headquarters after dark; most likely, therefore, a party of soldiers summoned to guard the place when so many persons of such importance are to assemble within it.[24] These will make an appropriate stage-audience for the onstage part of the great quarrel that is soon to follow.

Nestor, if he has remained outside, is now joined by Agamemnon. Achilles must now be the only major leader who has not yet reached Tenedos, and Agamemnon will have asked Nestor what he should do about this, perhaps mentioning that a jealous Odysseus[25] is pressing him to name Achilles as a defaulter. Nestor, apparently assuming that it is now too late for Achilles to arrive this evening,[26] suggests a compromise (fr. E

---

[22] It must be earlier than Bacchylides 16: see E.R. Schwinge, *Die Stellung der Trachinierinnen im Werk des Sophokles* (Göttingen, 1962) 128–133; H.G.T. Maehler, *Bacchylidis carmina cum fragmentis* (Leipzig, 1968) xlviii, liv; T.F. Hoey, *Phoenix* 33 (1979) 214–5; and J.R. March, *The Creative Poet* (*BICS* Suppl. 49 [1987]) 62–64. The suggestion by M. Davies, *Sophocles: Trachiniae* (Oxford, 1991), that the Sophoclean and Bacchylidean versions both derive from the early epic *The Sack of Oechalia*, is implausible, given that the overwhelming majority of artistic representations of the death of the centaur Nessus down to 450 have him killed by sword or (as in Bacchylides fr. 64.25–31) by club, not by an arrow (see F. Díez de Velasco, *LIMC* vi.1 [1992] 838–843), leaving him no opportunity to give Deianeira his poisoned blood or anything else as a supposed love-charm.

[23] There is no indication of an exit in her words at 92–93 or of an entrance in her words at 141ff; and at least in the latter part of the *parodos* the chorus are addressing her in the second person (126, 137)

[24] One notes how closely, in *Iliad* 9.65–94, the posting of sentries is associated with a dinner for the leaders – though there the sentries are guarding the whole camp rather than just Agamemnon's quarters. The title of the play (even assuming that *Syndeipnoi* is the correct form of it) does not require us to suppose that the chorus must have consisted of persons who were actually attending the banquet (so rightly Palutan [1996] 12 n.6).

[25] Odysseus' jealousy of those who excelled him in one ability or another is a recurrent theme in tellings of the Trojan saga. Its most notorious instances are the murder of Palamedes (dramatized by all three great fifth-century tragedians) and the use of devious tactics to defeat Ajax in the contest for the arms of Achilles (Pind. *Nem.* 7.20–27, 8.23–34; also Soph. *Aj.* 1135–8 where Teucer's allegation of vote-rigging is never actually denied by Menelaus).

[26] Given Achilles' uncertain temper, it would be asking for trouble to consciously run the risk of his arriving half-way through the banquet, particularly if Odysseus was known to be eager to make mischief.

[144]): let the banquet be held without him, and let Agamemnon call the roll of those who "joined in the oath" and note any absentees (there will be none).[27] Then, if Achilles arrives next day or the day after, no slight will have been inflicted on him, and there will be no risk of this headstrong young man being lost to the army.[28]

Nestor's ingenious plans sometimes go awry – most notably when, with the best of intentions, he gives Patroclus the advice (*Iliad* 11.793–802) that will lead him straight to his death.[29] On this occasion they are frustrated by the fact that Achilles *does* arrive on the evening of the banquet. In fact, once it has been decided to hold the banquet without him, he must be the next character to arrive, since all the other participants will be fully occupied inside.

Agamemnon and Nestor will have gone inside; with no actors present, one would now expect another choral song, after which Achilles will enter. He will probably have no one to converse with except the chorus(-leader). Doubtless he will explain how he has come to be delayed. We have no sure clue to the reason. Stress of weather is possible, but would be surprising, given that we have been told in fr. A (143) that the winds were favourable; perhaps, then, Achilles had turned aside to make a rapid raid on some island community on or near his route.[30] If he gave the chorus an account of such an exploit, it might have prompted him to speak more generally of his thirst for glory and his ambition to win it in abundance at Troy; and this would provide a context, though not the only possible context, for the chorus's lyric reflections (fr. F [568]) on the power of song to preserve mortals' fame from oblivion – reflections that will sound extremely ironic

---

[27] Unless Philoctetes had already been abandoned on Lemnos. In the *Cypria* the snake-bite that led to his sequestration apparently took place at the same feast at which Achilles quarrelled with Agamemnon (cf. [Apoll.] *Epit.* 3.27); but in Soph. *Phil.* 269–270 (cf. 194, 1326–8, Dio Chrys. 59.9, Paus. 8.33.4) it happens on the (unidentifiable, and according to Pausanias subsequently submerged) island of Chryse. There is no evidence that the Philoctetes story figured either directly or indirectly in *Syndeipnoi*.

[28] The fact that he is not oath-bound, as his colleagues are, makes it all the more important to avoid offending him.

[29] Cf. also *Iliad* 23.304–350 where he gives lengthy, sage advice to his son before the chariot-race – which proves to be of no relevance or assistance whatsoever.

[30] I owe this suggestion to André Lardinois (at the Nottingham Sophocles Fragments Conference in July 2000). The Aegean island nearest to Achilles' route (other than Scyros, which is obviously out of the question – his son was being brought up there – and Lemnos which has a different role in the saga) is Imbros, which is mentioned in conjunction with Tenedos at *Iliad* 13.33, and to which Achilles is said in *Iliad* 24.753 to have sold some of Priam's sons as slaves.

if the next we hear of Achilles is an account of behaviour by him that any hero, and most other men too, would desperately wish to be forgotten! One may wonder whether the chorus tried to warn Achilles what might be in store for him, or at least urged him to keep calm and not allow himself to be provoked; if they did, it evidently had little effect.

Achilles went into the building; the chorus sang an ode of which fr. F (568) may have been part; and then came the great quarrel. This took place partly offstage, partly onstage; we know this because in fr. G (565) and probably also in fr. H (144a) one of those involved is *narrating* something that happened in the banqueting room, whereas in frr. J, L, M (566a, 566b, 567) – and also in frr. K (145) and N (571) if they are rightly assigned to this context – Odysseus and Achilles are actually addressing hostile words to each other. There are good analogies for such a sequence. One is in Euripides' *Hippolytus*, where the early stages of the quarrel between Hippolytus and Phaedra's nurse are overheard and reported by Phaedra (565–600) after which Hippolytus bursts out of the house, followed by the nurse, and they continue arguing outside (601–668); but the closest is probably in Aristophanes' *Clouds*. Strepsiades is holding a feast for his son Pheidippides, to celebrate Pheidippides' graduation from Socrates' *phrontisterion* as a fully qualified sophist, able to defeat any opponent, however bad his case. Suddenly the old man rushes out of the house, crying in pain, followed by his son. Strepsiades tells the chorus how, as a result of a quarrel over poetry, his son had fallen upon him and beaten him up (*Clouds* 1321–90); Pheidippides robustly asserts that he had had every right to do so, having so often been beaten by his father when a child (1399–1436). In Sophocles' surviving plays we do not have a sequence of this precise form,[31] but we do have some sequences in which an important event or situation is first *narrated* and then *displayed* — the humiliation of Ajax among the slaughtered animals, of which we hear from Tecmessa (*Aj.* 201–330) before we see it for ourselves (346ff), or the words of the self-blinded Oedipus which we hear first from the Messenger (*OT* 1271–4, 1287–91) and then from his own lips after he appears at 1297.

It is Odysseus who comes out first (see Commentary on fr. G [565]) and narrates what happened inside, including the throwing of a chamber-pot at his own head and perhaps the throwing of some other object at "the bald pate of Nestor" (fr. H [144a]). We have no direct evidence as to how

---

[31] Though there may have been a somewhat similar sequence in *Tereus* (see Intr. to *Tereus*, pp. 152–3).

the quarrel came to such a violent climax; we only know (from Philodemus) that initially Achilles was angry with Agamemnon, and (from fr. G [565].2) that the chamber-pot did not strike Odysseus by accident – it was aimed at him, and hit its target. It follows that Odysseus must have intervened in the dispute between Achilles and Agamemnon and said something that inflamed Achilles' anger more strongly and diverted it from Agamemnon to himself. We have a Sophoclean model for just such an intervention in the false tale told by Achilles' son Neoptolemus in *Phil.* 359–384. Neoptolemus says that he went to the Atreidae in a friendly fashion and asked them for his father's armour and other property (361–2); they replied that he could have the rest of Achilles' property but not his armour, which now belonged to Odysseus (363–6). Neoptolemus burst into tears, stood up in a rage, and asked them how they dared give *his* property to someone else without consulting him (367–370); whereupon Odysseus, who "happened to be close by", said "Yes, boy, they were entitled to give it as they did; I was there to save his armour and his body" (371–3). At which Neoptolemus gave him a thorough tongue-lashing (374–7) until Odysseus, "despite his calm temperament", was stung to reply:

> You weren't where we were; you were away where you shouldn't have been (379) –

a monstrous charge of evasion of military duty, against a youth who had not been called up and probably was not even of age to be –

> and since you do speak so audaciously, be sure that you will never sail back to Scyros with this armour (380–1).

Which was enough to provoke him to set sail for Scyros without it, and with (he says) an undying hatred of Odysseus and the Atreidae.

Our evidence about the indoor quarrel in *Syndeipnoi* can be fitted into a very similar pattern. Achilles arrived late, and unexpectedly, for the banquet. It had begun without him; he no doubt asked why, perhaps in terms or tones that hinted at insubordination (cf. *Iliad* 1.88–91). Agamemnon replied with his usual lack of tact.[32] Achilles reacted angrily, perhaps with personal insults to Agamemnon (cf. *Iliad* 1.122), perhaps by railing against everyone present; Odysseus may then, as in Neoptolemus'

---

[32] See the devastating but accurate analysis of the Agamemnon of the *Iliad* by O.P. Taplin in C.B.R. Pelling ed. *Characterization and Individuality in Greek Literature* (Oxford, 1990) 60–82. The Agamemnon of Aeschylus' *Oresteia*, or of Sophocles' *Ajax*, is not much of an improvement.

story, have joined in the argument on Agamemnon's side with particular venom,[33] whereupon Achilles, provoked beyond his powers of self-control, picked up the nearest chamber-pot, flung it at Odysseus, and perhaps began flinging other things around too, one of which hit Nestor (fr. H [144a]).

All this Odysseus will narrate to the chorus, evidently hoping to persuade them to share his indignation against Achilles and probably to demand his punishment. Our next glimpses of the play show Odysseus and Achilles in furious onstage argument with each other. Achilles, then, must have come outside as well, either shortly after Odysseus appears or after his speech has ended. Our scanty fragments suggest that the tone of the argument is as crudely personal as are the arguments that Teucer has in *Ajax* with Menelaus (1047–1162) and Agamemnon (1226–1315). Odysseus taunts Achilles with cowardice (fr. J [566a]); Achilles says (as he will say to Odysseus nine years later, *Iliad* 9.356–363) that he is going to sail home (Plut. *Mor.* 74b, cf. perhaps fr. K [145]); Odysseus again claims that Achilles is motivated not by honour but by fear (fr. L [566b]); and at some point or points before, during or after these exchanges, Achilles denounces Odysseus as a villainous trickster, possibly employing a colourful colloquialism to convey the point (fr. N [571]) and certainly calling him the true offspring of two notorious cheats, his alleged father Sisyphus and his maternal grandfather Autolycus (fr. M [567]).

How did the action proceed from this point? All we can be sure of is that in the end Thetis intervened. She says (fr. O [562]) that she has "rushed" from among the Nereids beneath the sea, which strongly suggests that a truly dangerous situation has developed which only divine intervention can avert. This situation is unlikely to be merely the quarrel at the banquet, serious as that was — if only because, had Thetis intervened at that stage, the play would have ended too soon. Rather, it will have been something graver still, probably therefore a plot aiming at murder — perhaps a plan by Achilles to kill Odysseus, more likely (since Achilles is never much of a schemer) a plan by Odysseus (possibly with the aid of Agamemnon) to murder Achilles. There are various lines that the action could then have taken: Achilles might be treacherously invited to a reconciliation meeting, and be just about to walk into the plotters' trap when Thetis intervenes to stop him; or he might get to know of the plot

---

[33] He could even have said, in these or other words, "You weren't where we were; you were away where you shouldn't have been".

and be rushing to take revenge on the plotters;[34] or he might be so
overwhelmed with disgrace, distress and despair as to be on the point of
suicide, as he is near the beginning of *Iliad* 18 when Thetis, sitting among
the Nereids, hears his cry (18.34–38) and comes to comfort him; and that
by no means exhausts the possibilities. At any rate, the action, like that of
Philoctetes, is likely to have been headed in a direction which, if it had
been allowed to continue, would have been fatal not merely to one or two
major Achaean heroes but to the entire Trojan War saga. This is bound to
be prevented, and it is.

Several times in the *Iliad* (9.410–6, 11.794–5 = 16.36–37, 17.408–9,
18.9–11, 18.95–96) we hear of Thetis giving privileged knowledge of the
future to her son;[35] on this occasion she will be revealing such information
to a wider circle. The crucial fact that she must disclose is that if Achilles
does not fight against Troy, Troy will never fall: if Odysseus (and
Agamemnon, if acting as his confederate) cause the death of Achilles or
drive him to leave the army, they will be ruining their own cause. How
much more she revealed we cannot tell, but it would have been prudent of
her to forestall any future jealousies by assuring Odysseus that Achilles'
glory in the war would not diminish his.

Perhaps the most striking feature of *Syndeipnoi*, if it went roughly as I
have sketched, is its relationship to the *Iliad*. On one level, the feast given
by Agamemnon recalls that of *Iliad* 9.89–178, and all the principal human
dramatis personae have important roles in that section of the poem.[36] On
another, the action of the play as a whole anticipates that of the *Iliad* as a
whole.[37] A seemingly small dispute involving Achilles escalates with
terrifying speed and nearly leads to disaster for the entire expedition. In the

---

[34]As he takes revenge on Hector in the *Iliad*, on Thersites and Memnon in the *Aethiopis*;
or as he would have taken revenge on Agamemnon in *Iliad* 1.188–194, had not Athene
intervened. However, this is perhaps the least likely of the listed alternatives: that Thetis
rushes to the scene with such urgency suggests that, devoted mother as she always is in the
Iliad, she is concerned to save her son rather than to restrain him. If it were Odysseus or
Agamemnon who had to be saved, one would have expected the *dea ex machina* to be
Athena or Hera, the two deities who in the *Iliad* are most inflexibly determined on the
success of the Achaean expedition and the destruction of Troy.

[35] Cf. also [Apoll.] *Epit.* 3.26, Plut. *Mor.* 297e-f: Thetis warns Achilles that if he kills
Tenes, he will himself be killed by Apollo.

[36]Odysseus and Ajax are two of the three envoys who are appointed on the advice of
Nestor to convey Agamemnon's offer of compensation to Achilles.

[37] "C'est une première colère d'Achille, espèce de parodie de celle de l'Iliade" (Weil
[1890] 341) – though for "parody" I would substitute something like "dry run".

Iliad (1.495–530) Thetis secures the support of Zeus for her partisan cause; the result is that a reconciliation is reached only after Patroclus is dead and Achilles himself doomed by his own choice to an early death. In *Syndeipnoi*, she is able to intervene when nothing irrevocable has been done, but not before we have been reminded of many things that will happen in the future which Thetis is unlikely to have mentioned. Nestor's success in placating Ajax will recall his repeated failures to compose the Iliadic quarrel between Agamemnon and Achilles.[38] Achilles' fury at being excluded from Agamemnon's feast, and his ensuing quarrel with Odysseus, prefigure, with several inversions, *Iliad* 19, where Achilles is reconciled with Agamemnon, argues with Odysseus over whether the army should eat before battle, and adamantly refuses to eat anything himself — but also, in a different way, *Iliad* 1. I have no doubt that if we had the whole of this play we would see, as we can in *Ajax*,[39] many more ways in which Sophocles exploited the *Iliad* as an intertext.[40] But we can see enough already to be sure that this is an important part of what he is doing. And putting his story and Homer's together, a thoughtful spectator might well feel that what Thetis has done is to give the feuding chieftains a second chance — but that then they went to Troy and made almost exactly the same mistake again. That time, however, they had the Trojans and Hector to cope with as well as themselves, and that time, for Achilles at least, there was no second chance.

The possible structure of the play, as it has emerged from this discussion, may be set out thus:[41]

Prologue (Nestor)	A (143)
Nestor and Ajax (quarrel, resolved)	B, C, D (563, 564, 855)

---

[38] *Iliad* 1.247–291; 9.92–173; 11.654–802.

[39] On which see especially P.E. Easterling, *BICS* 31 (1984) 1–8.

[40] And perhaps not only the *Iliad*. André Lardinois, in discussion at the Nottingham Sophocles Fragments Conference in July 2000, suggested that the play may have looked back as well as forward – to the feast held at the wedding of Achilles' parents, when likewise a guest (Eris) arrived late, threw something (the 'apple of discord'), and caused a quarrel that had dire consequences. Eris's intervention at the feast already figures in the *Cypria* (Arg. §1 West); the apple is not mentioned explicitly in archaic or classical texts, but it appears in at least two representations of the Judgement of Paris from the first half of the fifth century (*LIMC s.v.* Paridis Iudicium 37, 38). May the story of that wedding feast have been recalled in a choral ode – or even by the bride, Thetis, herself?

[41] The location within the play of those fragments not listed in the table (all of them single-word citations) cannot be determined, except that fr. S (569) must come from a lyric or anapaestic context.

Parodos (chorus of soldiers)
Nestor advises Agamemnon   E (144)
First Stasimon
Arrival of Achilles (narrative of exploits?)
Second Stasimon   F (568)?
Odysseus narrates fracas at feast   G, H (565, 144a)
Odysseus and Achilles quarrel onstage   J, K, L, M, N (566a, 145,
                                                  566b, 567, 571)

Third Stasimon
Crisis escalates until fatal violence (by or
    against Achilles) is imminent
Thetis intervenes   O (562)
Reconciliation; *Exodos*

Several other Sophoclean fragments have at various times been assigned to *Syndeipnoi* or *Achaiôn Syllogos*,[42] in no case are there compelling grounds for the ascription, and in some it can be definitely ruled out.[43]

Tragedy, satyr-drama, or something between?

It has long been a matter of dispute whether *Syndeipnoi* was a tragedy or a satyr-drama.[44] There is evidence for both positions.

---

[42] Soph. fr. 91, 735, 769, 799, 848, 913, 929; *trag. adesp.* 35. One might add fr. 887 ("May Zeus bring about a return with victory in battle, an end to grief, and an absence of fear") which could come from any Trojan War play which had a chorus of soldiers or sailors and whose action was set *before* the final capture of the city.

[43] Soph. fr. 769 is addressed to someone who is clothed as, or like, a female at the time of speaking, and hence, if the addressee *is* Achilles, the location must be Scyros, not Tenedos; fr. 799 comes from a quarrel between Odysseus and Diomedes, and such a quarrel in our play is neither attested nor likely; in *trag. adesp.* 35 the addressee has a choice between "going on the expedition" and "remaining", whereas in *Syndeipnoi* Achilles' choice is rather, as in fr. L (566b), between *remaining* with the expedition and *departing* for home.

[44] The suggestion that it was a satyr-drama was first made in the eighteenth century by L.C. Valckenaer, and has been supported in recent decades by W.N. Bates (in *Classical Studies Presented to E. Capps* [Princeton, 1936] 21), Sutton (1974), Palutan (1996), A. López Eire (in *Shards* 401–2), and J. Redondo (*ibid.* 424, 431, 432, 435). S.L. Radt, *EH* 29 (1982) 194, included *Syndeipnoi* in a list of "not improbable candidates" for identification as satyr-plays. Most of those who did not regard the play as satyric have nevertheless suspected that it might well have been "prosatyric" like Euripides' *Alcestis* (so Wilamowitz [1907] 72, Pearson ii 200–1); my own earlier treatment (in *Shards* 368–370) cited

In favour of taking Syndeipnoi *as a tragedy:*

(a)   There is no evidence whatsoever for a chorus of satyrs,[45] or for Silenus as a character, both of which are obligatory for all satyr-dramas.

(b)   The plot, involving a serious quarrel between major heroic figures and a hurried intervention by a deity to prevent irrevocable harm from being done to one or more of them, is not suitable for the farcical treatment required in satyr-drama, and more resembles the common type of tragedy in which a catastrophe is narrowly averted.[46]

(c)   The praise of fame, especially poetic fame, in fr. F (568) would be very surprising coming from a chorus of satyrs, shameless creatures whose every act demonstrates their indifference to reputation.

(d)   The foreshadowing of the tragic conflicts of the *Iliad* (see above).

In favour of taking Syndeipnoi *as a satyr-drama:*

(e)   The frank avowal of gluttony by the speaker of fr. B (563), and the warning given to him that he is in danger of getting the reputation of "a son of the belly" (fr. C [564]).[47]

(f)   The incident of the chamber-pot (fr. G [565]) and the emphasis laid on its offensive smell.

(g)   If *masthlēs* "leather strap" in fr. N (571) is used, as it may well be, in the metaphorical sense "supple rogue", such an expression is better suited to comedy or satyr-drama than to tragedy (see Commentary).[48]

Aeschylean parallels to argue that the play *could* have been tragic in the full (ancient) sense. Radt, Lloyd-Jones, and C. Heynen and R. Krumeich (in *Satyrspiel* 396–8) are non-committal.

[45] But the title of the play is not in itself evidence that the chorus was not composed of satyrs: see Sutton (1974) 138–140, and B. Seidensticker in *Satyrspiel* 18 (cf. also note 24 above).

[46] Regarded as the best type of tragedy by Arist. *Poet.* 1454a2–9, in the specific context of murder of kinsfolk averted by recognition, citing (among other plays) Euripides' *Iphigeneia in Tauris* as an example. Other surviving tragedies of narrowly averted catastrophe are Euripides' *Ion* and *Orestes* and, in a rather different way, Sophocles' *Philoctetes* (where the catastrophes that are averted are first the starvation or suicide of Philoctetes and later, at 1300–2, the shooting of Odysseus).

[47] One might compare Eur. *Cycl.* 334–7 "I sacrifice [my animals] to none but myself – not to the gods – and to the greatest of divinities, this belly: to eat and drink well day by day, *that* is Zeus for men of sense!"

[48] In addition, J. Redondo (*Shards* 424) suggests that the high frequency of crasis (the phonetic blending of two words where one ends, and the next begins, with a vowel) in the fragments of *Syndeipnoi* (four times in 19 spoken verses, compared with one instance per 8.4 spoken verses in *Ajax*) might indicate that it was satyric; but (i) the only fully preserved

I consider points (a–d) to be strong evidence that the play was not satyric; but points (e–g), while individually they can be explained away,[49] are collectively of considerable weight, and one further piece of evidence, not so far mentioned, seems to me decisive. Fragment H (144a) speaks of "the *phalanthon* head of Nestor". I here summarize the discussion of this fragment in the Commentary. The adjective *phalanthos*, in every place where its meaning is made clear by the context, means "bald in the front part of the head". Baldness is typically satyric (Silenus is frequently bald in art) and comic, and is never mentioned in any undisputedly tragic text. It follows, almost inevitably, that our play was not, in the full sense, tragic.[50] But the two lexicographers who cite the phrase insist, against all other indications, that *phalanthon* here means "grey/white-haired"; they must have derived this gloss from a commentator on *Syndeipnoi*,[51] who evidently was not prepared to admit that the word could mean "bald" in this play. If the play had been satyric, there would have been nothing objectionable about a reference to baldness. It follows, almost inevitably, that our play was not satyric. The only remaining possibility is that it was "prosatyric", i.e. that like Euripides' *Alcestis*, it was produced *in place of* a satyr-drama as the fourth play of a tragic tetralogy.

Like *Alcestis*, *Syndeipnoi* both is and is not tragic. It presents a conflict which could have had terrible consequences and which involves a fundamental value both of heroic and of fifth-century Greece, the male sense of honour; but the heroes, except perhaps Nestor,[52] are none of them admirable – Ajax with his gargantuan appetite, Achilles with his hair-trigger temper, Agamemnon with his tactlessness, Odysseus with his inferiority complex – and like a group of reckless children, they have to be

---

satyr-drama, Euripides' *Cyclops*, has a considerably *lower* incidence of crasis than *Ajax* (one instance per 15.1 spoken verses); (ii) the 200 or so reasonably well-preserved iambic trimeters in the papyrus of Sophocles' *Ichneutai* contain only ten instances of crasis; (iii) there are many passages of tragedy in which four crases occur within 19 lines: if we divide the 133–line prologue of *Ajax* into seven 19–line stretches, one of these (39–57) will contain four crases and another (96–114) will contain five.

[49] As I sought to do in *Shards* 368–370. All three have epic or tragic parallels: with (e) compare *Odyssey* 9.8–10 and 7.216–221; with (f), Aesch. *Cho.* 756–7 and Aesch. fr. 180; with (g), the descriptions of Odysseus cited in Comm. on fr. N (571).

[50] Radt (1982) 211, indeed, takes this fragment as evidence that *Achaiôn Syllogos* was a satyr-play "and so almost certainly identical with *Syndeipnoi*".

[51] Or rather *Achaiôn Syllogos*, which is the title used for the play in these citations.

[52] And even Nestor may have been shown to be dangerously overrating his own wisdom.

rescued from themselves by one of their mothers, who is luckily a goddess. And this when all they were trying to do is feast! What will it be like when they have to fight? We know the answer – the same, only worse – but even after Thetis has spoken, and revealed *some* of what is to come, they probably do not.

ΣΥΝΔΕΙΠΝΟΙ ἢ ΑΧΑΙΩΝ ΣΥΛΛΟΓΟΣ

Selected Testimonia

Aristotle, *Rhetoric* 1401b16–19: ἢ εἴ τις φαίη τὸ ἐπὶ δεῖπνον κληθῆναι τιμιώτατον· διὰ γὰρ τὸ μὴ κληθῆναι ὁ Ἀχιλλεὺς ἐμήνισε τοῖς Ἀχαιοῖς ἐν Τενέδῳ· ὁ δ᾽ ὡς ἀτιμαζόμενος ἐμήνισεν, συνέβη δὲ τοῦτο ἐπὶ τοῦ μὴ κληθῆναι.

ἐπι τοῦ F: διὰ τὸ Δ Vet: διὰ τὸ ἐπι τοῦ A.

Commentarii in Aristotelem Graeci **xxi 2.151.16:** ἐμήνισεν ὁ Ἀχιλλεὺς διὰ τὸ μὴ κληθῆναι παρὰ τοῦ Ἀγαμέμνονος τοὺς ἀρίστους καλέσαντος.

Philodemus, *On Anger* col. 18.17–24: ἐπ[ειδὰν τὰ κάτω] ἄνω μιγνύωσι [π]αραπεμφθέντες ὑπό [τ]ινος ἑστιῶντος, ὥσπερ [ὁ] Σοφοκλέους Ἀχιλλεύς, [ἢ] κατά τι τοιοῦτο παρολιγωρηθέντες, οὔπω γὰρ ἀδικηθέντας λέγω...

    all supplements by Gomperz

THE DINERS *OR* THE GATHERING OF THE ACHAEANS

Selected Testimonia

Aristotle, *Rhetoric* 1401b16–19: Or if someone were to say that the greatest honour one can have is to be invited to dinner, because Achilles was angry with the Achaeans at Tenedos on account of not being invited – whereas in fact he was angry because he was dishonoured, and it so happened that this dishonour related to the failure to invite him.

Commentarii in Aristotelem Graeci **xxi 2.151.16:** Achilles was angry because he was not invited by Agamemnon when he [Agamemnon] invited the leading men.

Philodemus, *On Anger* col. 18.17–24: Wh[en] they turn [everything topsy-]turvy when they are [d]ismissed by [t]he host of a banquet, like the Achilles of Sophocles, [or] slighted – I cannot go so far as to say "wronged" – in some such matter …

A (143)

ὡς ναοφύλακες νυκτέρου ναυκληρίας

πλήκτροις ἀπευθύνουσιν οὐρίαν τρόπιν

A (143) Pollux 10.133 (ἐν Ἀχαιῶν συλλόγῳ) | 1 ὡς om. S | ναυκληρίας cett.: ναυαγίας FS || 2 πλήκτροις cett.: πλήθροις FS

B (563)

φορεῖτε, μασσέτω τις, ἐγχείτω βαθὺν

κρατῆρ'· ὅδ' ἀνὴρ οὐ πρὶν ἂν φάγῃ καλῶς

ὅμοια καὶ βοῦς ἐργάτης ἐργάζεται

B (563) Athenaeus 15.685f-686a (ἐν Συνδείπνοις) | 1 φορεῖτε A Epit.: φυρᾶτε Bergk

C (564)

οὔτοι γένειον ὧδε χρὴ διηλιφὲς

φοροῦντι κἀντίπαιδα καὶ γένει μέγαν

γαστρὸς καλεῖσθαι παῖδα, τοῦ πατρὸς παρόν

C (564) Athenaeus 15.678f-679a (Συνδείπνοις [Ald.: συνδείπνοι A, Συνδείπνῳ Casaubon]) | 1 διηλιφὲς Casaubon: διηλειφὲς A: διηρεφὲς van Herwerden

D (855*)

ΝΕΣΤΩΡ   οὐ μέμφομαί σε· δρῶν γὰρ εὖ κακῶς λέγεις

D (855) Plutarch, *Moralia* 504b-c ("Sophocles' Nestor calming down an angry Ajax"), 810b ("Sophocles' Nestor replying when reviled by Ajax")

A (143)

For the guardians of the ships on their night-time voyage are
guiding their keels with the helm, with the wind behind them.

*Probably from the prologue, with the speaker (Nestor?) explaining that
some of the Achaean ships have yet to reach Tenedos.*

B (563)

Bring the stuff – let someone knead – let someone fill the
mixing-bowl deep! This man, just like a ploughing ox,
doesn't work till he's eaten well!

Ajax(?) impatient for the coming feast.

C (564)

It does not befit someone sporting so sleek a beard, someone
so youthful and of such high birth, to be called the son of
Belly when he could be called his father's son.

The speaker of fr. B is rebuked (by Nestor, cf. fr. D?) for his gluttony.

D (855*)

I do not condemn you; you may be injurious in speech, but
you're good in action.

Nestor's soft answer to angry insults from Ajax.

E (144)

σὺ δ᾽ ἐν θρόνοισι γραμμάτων πτυχὰς ἔχων

νέμ᾽ εἴ τις οὐ πάρεστιν ὃς ξυνώμοσεν

E (144) Σ^{BD} Pindar *Isthmian* 2.47 [68] (ἐν Ἀχαιῶν Συλλόγῳ) | 2 νέμ᾽ εἴ Bergk: ἀπόνειμον νέμει codd. (ἀπόνειμον Pind. loc. cit.) | πάρεστιν ὃς ξυνώμοσεν Bergk: πάρεστι τίς ξυνώμοσε codd.: πάρεστι τῶν ξυνωμοτῶν Hartung

F (568)

λάθα Πιερίδων στυγερὰ

κἀνήρατος· ὢ δύνασις

θνατοῖς εὐποτμοτάτα μελέων,

ἀνέχουσα βίου βραχὺν ἰσθμόν

F (568) Stobaeus 3.26.1 (ἐκ Συνδείπνου) | 1 Πιερίδων codd.: Πιερίσι(ν) Grotius || 2 κἀνήρατος Jebb: καὶ ἀνάρατος SMA: καὶ ἀνάρετος Tr.: καὶ ἀνάρεστος Voss, Arsenius | ὢ (ὤ) δύνασις Buecheler: ὠδυνάσεις vel sim. codd. || 3 θνατοῖς Grotius, εὐποτμοτάτα Schneidewin: θανάτοις εὐποτμότατε codd.

G (565)

ἀλλ᾽ ἀμφὶ θυμῷ τὴν κάκοσμον οὐρανὴν

ἔρριψεν, οὐδ᾽ ἥμαρτε· περὶ δ᾽ ἐμῷ κάρα

κατάγνυται τὸ τεῦχος, οὐ μύρου πνέον·

ἐδειματούμην δ᾽ οὐ φίλης ὀσμῆς ὕπο

G (565) Athenaeus 1.17c-d (ἐν Ἀχαιῶν Συνδείπνῳ), whence Eustathius, *Commentary on the Odyssey* 1828.27ff

E (144)

And you, in the chair, holding the inscribed tablets, record
anyone that joined in the oath who is not present.

Nestor(?) advising Agamemnon.

F (568)

To be forgotten by the goddesses of Pieria is hateful
and not to be wished for. O the power
of song, supreme giver of happiness to mortals,
sustaining the narrow isthmus of their life!

From a choral song, possibly reflecting on an avowal (by Achilles?) of ambition to attain everlasting glory.

G (565)

But in his rage he threw the evil-smelling chamber-pot, and
did not miss his aim; the vessel, whose odour was not of
perfume, broke over my head, and I was terrified by the
unfriendly smell.

Odysseus narrates Achilles' assault on him (or, less likely, vice versa).

H (144a)

φάλανθον Νέστορος κάρα

H (144a) Cyrillus, *Glossary* ed. M. Naoumides, *GRBS* 9 (1968) 269 (Ἀχαιῶν Συλλόγῳ); Hesychius φ91 (without attribution)

J (566.1–2*)

ΟΔΥΣΣΕΥΣ
    ἤδη τὰ Τροίας εἰσορῶν ἐδώλια
    δέδοικας

J (566a) Plutarch, *Moralia* 74a–b

K (145)

ἐκκεκώπηται

K (145) Hesychius ε1434 (Συλλόγῳ) | ἐκκεκώπηται I. Voss: cf. *IG* ii^2 1604.73: ἐκκεκόπηται codd.: ἐκκεκώπευται Meineke

L (566.3–4*)

Οδ.   ἐγῷδ' ὃ φεύγεις· οὐ τὸ μὴ κλύειν κακῶς,
       ἀλλ' ἐγγὺς Ἕκτωρ ἐστίν· οὐ μένειν καλόν

L (566b) Plutarch, *Moralia* 74b | 2 οὐ μένειν καλόν most mss.: οὐ μαίνειν κ. F: θυμαίνειν κ. GXΛ F^{mg} υ^{mg}: οὐ θυμαίνειν κ. K: perh. οὐ καλὸν μένειν?

H (144a)

… the bald head of Nestor.

Possibly from the same narrative, reporting further outrageous behaviour by Achilles.

J (566.1–2*)

Now you can see the dwellings of Troy land, you're

frightened.

Odysseus taunting Achilles.

K (145)

… is fully equipped with oars.

Achilles, in reply, declaring that he is in a position to sail home forthwith?

L (566.3–4*)

I know what you're running away from. It's not that you

don't like being insulted. No, Hector is close at hand – so it's

not proper to stay!

Odysseus' sarcastic retort to Achilles' threat to depart.

M (567)

ὦ πάντα πράσσων, ὡς ὁ Σίσυφος πολὺς
ἔνδηλος ἐν σοὶ πάντα χὢ μητρὸς πατήρ

M (567) Σ^{LFHG} Sophocles, *Ajax* 190 (ἐν Συνδείπνῳ) (H has line 1 only) | 1
πάντα LFH: πάνδαρε G: πᾶν σὺ Blaydes ‖ 2 πάντα χὢ Vater, Conington:
πάντα χωρὶς (abbreviated χ) G: πανταχοῦ LF | μητρὸς LG: μητρὶ F

N (571)

μάσθλης

N (571) Hesychius μ333 | μάσθλης (or μάσθλη) Pearson: μάσθλητας
Nauck: μάσθλητας τομούς Wecklein: the Hesychius entry is corrupt (the
ms. has μάσθλη· τὰς τομουτὰς ἡνίας. καὶ γὰρ ἡ μάσθλη. Σοφοκλῆς
Ἀνδρομέδᾳ [cf. fr. 129] καὶ Συνδείπνοις) and it is not clear precisely what
word or phrase he was ascribing to *Syndeipnoi*

O (562)

ΘΕΤΙΣ   λιποῦσα μετὰ σὲ πόντιον χορὸν

          Νηρηΐδων ὤρουσα

O (562) Anon. περὶ τρόπων ed. C. Fredrich, *NGG* (1896) 340; Σ^{AE}
Dionysius Thrax 1 p.460.3 Hilgard (ἐν Συνδείπνοις ἡ Θέτις πρὸς τὸν
Ἀχιλλέα) | 1 perh. <ὦ παῖ,> λιποῦσα or <τέκνον,> λιποῦσα? | λιποῦσα
Anon.: λείπουσα Σ Dion. | μετὰ σὲ Sommerstein: cf. Σ Dion. (after
quotation) ὅτι μετὰ σὲ ἀντὶ τοῦ πρὸς σὲ καὶ παρ' Ἡσιόδῳ: μὲν Anon., Σ
Dion. ‖ 1–2 πόντιον χορὸν Νηρηΐδων ὤρουσα Σ Dion.: πόντιον χορὸν
ὤρουσα Νηρηΐδων Anon.: Νηρηΐδων ὤρουσα πόντιον χορὸν Wilamowitz

M (567)

You'll stop at nothing! What a great deal of Sisyphus there plainly is in you, in every respect, and of your mother's father as well!

Addressed to Odysseus, doubtless by Achilles during the quarrel.

N (571)

thong [i.e. supple rogue]

Again probably Achilles reviling Odysseus.

O (562)

<My child,> I have left the band of the Nereid sea-goddesses and rushed to you.

Thetis hastily intervening to save, or to restrain, Achilles.

P (146)

ἐπιξενοῦσθαι

Hesychius ε5017 (Ἀχαιῶν Συλλόγῳ)

Q (147)

ἐπισειούσης

Hesychius ε5150 (Ἀχαιῶν Συλλόγῳ)

R (148)

ξυμβόλους

Hesychius ξ112 (Ἀχαιῶν Συλλόγῳ)

S (569)

Ἀζειῶται

Hesychius α112 (Συνδείπνῳ)

T (570)

βέβηλος

Σ^{LRM} Sophocles *OC* 10 = *Etymologicum Magnum* 194.5–6 (ἐν Συνδείπνῳ)

The following fragments cannot be assigned to a context:

P (146)

to live abroad *or* to call to witness

Q (147)

shaking out the reins over, *i.e.* urging on

R (*148*)

omens

S (569)

the people of Azeia

From a lyric passage.

T (570)

layman

THE DINERS *or* THE GATHERING OF THE ACHAEANS

A (143)

The interpretation of this fragment depends on its first word, *hōs*, which could mean either "as" (introducing a simile) or "for" (introducing a causal clause); the latter is more likely because (i) almost all Sophoclean similes take the form of a nominal or participial phrase rather than a complete clause, (ii) a simile would normally be expressed in the singular rather than the plural, and (iii) in a play set in the early stages of the Trojan expedition (before it landed in the Troad) reference to *actual* sea-voyages is only to be expected.

Since no one would *begin* a voyage after dark, except for special reasons of danger or secrecy (as in *Odyssey* 2.388–434, 4.842–7, and *Sack of Troy* Arg. §2 West; cf. *Iliad* 14.74–81), the passage probably refers to ships, presumably of Agamemnon's expedition, which put to sea by day in the ordinary way, have been delayed en route for some reason (perhaps by adverse winds), and now, "with the wind behind them", are hastening to reach their destination as soon as possible. Such an impending arrival suggests we are near the beginning of the play, very likely in the prologue. The explicit reference to night confirms this view, because it serves to tell, or perhaps remind, the audience that they are to imagine it is dark: it was important for the dramatist, writing for an open-air daylight performance, to emphasize this to his audience early on, and in the only surviving Greek drama whose action is nocturnal, the pseudo-Euripidean *Rhesus*, there are twelve references to night, darkness, sleep, etc., in the first 25 lines (cf. also e.g. Aesch. *Ag.* 4, 22, Ar. *Clouds* 1–2, *Wasps* 2, *Eccl.* 1–20).

The passage gives no clue to the identity of the speaker; my suggestion that it is Nestor depends on the assignment of fr. D [855] to this play (see below). I have argued elsewhere (*RhM* 143 [2000] 118–127, at 124) that Nestor was the prologue-speaker in Aeschylus' *Palamedes*, another play about a quarrel between Achaean leaders early in the Trojan campaign; one wonders if Sophocles made him later attempt to reconcile Achilles with Odysseus as he persistently tries to reconcile Achilles with Agamemnon in the *Iliad* (1.247–284, 9.92–113, 11.655–802).

Nocturnal navigation figures in three other episodes of the Trojan saga; one of these, perhaps significantly, involves Achilles and another involves Tenedos. (1) According to the cyclic epics, the Achaeans were scattered by a storm on the way back from their mistaken attack on Telephus' city of

Teuthrania, and Achilles' ship was driven to Scyros, "where he came to a painful harbour that night" (*Little Iliad* fr. 4 West with *Cypria* Arg. §7 West); this appears to be an older alternative to the better-known story of Achilles being hidden by his mother at Lycomedes' palace on Scyros disguised as a girl. (2) After leaving the Wooden Horse outside the walls of Troy, the Achaeans burned their camp and sailed off to Tenedos, returning by night when their agent in the city, Sinon, raised a fire-signal (*Little Iliad* fr. 14 and *Sack of Troy* Arg. §2 West). (3) On the return voyage, after many ships had been lost in a storm, many more were wrecked during the night on the rocks of Euboea, on to which they had been lured by the deceptive fire-signals of Nauplius ([Apoll.] *Epit.* 6.7, Hyginus *Fab.* 116; Aesch. *Ag.* 654ff ignores Nauplius and instead has the fleet shattered by a night-time storm in the open sea); Sophocles dealt with this story in his *Nauplios Pyrkaeus* (see vol. ii). There is no known tradition that mentions night-sailing on the voyage from Aulis to Troy, and it is likely that Sophocles has devised this as a means of accounting for Achilles' late arrival – though his ships will not necessarily have been the only ones still awaited. Aristophanes' *Acharnians, Lysistrata* and *Ecclesiazusae* also begin with the delayed arrival of a number of persons expected to attend a meeting; for the "[s]he should be here by now" motif near the start of a play cf. also *Trach.* 43–48, *OT* 73–75.

1 guardians of the ships: elsewhere (Ar. fr. 388, cf. Soph. *Phil.* 543) this word (*nāophylakes* or *nauphylakes*) refers, as we might expect, to persons responsible for protecting ships from damage when docked, beached or in harbour; its use here to denote helmsmen may well be based on Aesch. *Seven* 2–3 where Eteocles speaks of himself as "one who *guards* the city's fortunes, wielding the *helm* at its stern, and not letting his eyes rest in *sleep*".

B (563)

This frank avowal of a hearty appetite and an urgent need to satisfy it is one of the passages that have often been seen as indicating that *Syndeipnoi* was satyric or prosatyric; cf. Eur. *Alc.* 753–9, 787–798 where a tipsy Heracles acts and talks rather similarly, to the great exasperation of the household of the mourning Admetus. The passage is strikingly reminiscent of *Odyssey* 9.8–10 (censured by Pl. *Rep.* 390a-b) where Odysseus, who is just about to reveal his true identity and tell the story of his wanderings, says to Alcinous that there is nothing more pleasant than to be at a feast where "the tables are full of bread and meat, and the wine-steward draws wine from the mixing-bowl, brings it and pours it in the cups": of the first six words of our fragment, three (*phorein* "bring", *enkhein* "pour in [wine], fill [cup/bowl]", and *krātēr* "mixing-bowl") occur in a stretch of seven words in the *Odyssey* passage.

The sentiment is not well suited to Achilles (who famously, in *Iliad* 19.145–237, wishes to lead the Achaean army into battle without any breakfast) or even to Odysseus (a warrior of guile and ingenuity rather than of brute muscle); of the major figures in the army it best fits Ajax (cf. fr. D [855]), the slow, defensive fighter whose trademark was his enormous shield and whose standard epithet was *megas* "large", the "big-chested, broad-backed man" who, after his death, is sneeringly compared to an ox by Agamemnon in *Aj.* 1250–4 (cf. *bougāïe* "big [lit. ox-] clod", the insult flung at Ajax by Hector in *Iliad* 13.824).

1–2   fill the mixing-bowl deep: or "fill a deep (i.e. capacious) mixing-bowl".

2   this man refers to the speaker; cf. *Aj.* 822, *OT* 534, 815, *OC* 1329, Eur. *El.* 43.

C (564)

A rebuke to a young man, the son of a distinguished father, who is bringing disgrace on himself and his ancestry by a display of gluttony. It may be regarded as virtually certain that the young man is the speaker of fr. B (563), since it is unlikely that *two* characters in the same play would flaunt a heroic appetite in this manner; and the apparent play on the name of Ajax's father (see on 3) helps to confirm that he is the man (it can hardly be Achilles; see on 1–2). The speaker is evidently a considerably older man with a strong sense of what constitutes proper heroic behaviour; Nestor (cf. fr. D [855]) would be highly appropriate. Even if one refuses to assign fr. D (855) to this play, the speaker here is not likely to be Odysseus: Odysseus (whose son is still a baby) can be only a few years older than Ajax, and in Homer he is no contemnor of the importance of food (*Iliad* 19.154–237; *Odyssey* 7.215–221, 9.5–11).

1–2   sporting so sleek a beard: the well-groomed state of his beard indicates that he is rich and leisured. The fact that he *has* a beard points strongly to his being Ajax rather than the much younger Achilles, who in fifth-century art is normally beardless.

2 so youthful: Greek *antipais* normally means (i) "like a child" (Aesch. *Eum.* 38) or (ii) "little more than a child; an adolescent" (Eur. *Andr.* 326, D.S. 16.86.1 [Alexander at Chaeroneia, aged 18], Josephus *Life* 9 ["about my fourteenth year"]). Since this addressee is bearded, *antipais* must here bear a relative sense: the addressee is very young indeed *from the speaker's point of view.*

3 the son of Belly: his belly is, as it were, his mother (since *gastēr* "belly" – also "womb" – is a feminine noun). Two ideas are combined here. (1) It is a son's duty to cherish and maintain his mother; this man cherishes and maintains his belly. Perhaps the closest parallel is Men. *Dysk.* 88 where Pyrrhias calls Knemon "son of Grief", i.e. one who loves causing grief to others. Cf. also *OT* 1080–5 ("I reckon myself the son of Fortune and ... will never show myself other than that", i.e. will always trust loyally in Fortune), Ar. *Ach.* 1150 ("Antimachus the son of Showers", i.e. the splutterer), Cratinus frr. 258–9 (Zeus-Pericles the son of Stasis, i.e. the fomenter of civic dissension, and Hera-Aspasia the daughter of Lust). (2) It was considered disgraceful for a man to be publicly spoken of as his mother's son rather than his father's (cf. Eur. *El.* 933–5, fr. 1064.6–7; in Soph. *El.* 365–6 the somewhat unconventional Electra applies the same principle to her sister), because this would imply that his mother was a publicly known figure – which in turn would imply, almost by definition, that she was in breach of the norms of womanly behaviour (see D.M. Schaps, *CQ* 27 [1977] 323–330).

3 his father's son: particularly appropriate if the addressee is Ajax; his father's name, Telamon, meant "Shield-strap", so that to call Ajax his father's son was in effect to call him a born warrior.

D (855*)

This line is cited twice by Plutarch (*Mor.* 504b-c, 810b), in very similar terms, as having been spoken in Sophocles by Nestor in an attempt to calm down an angry Ajax who was reviling him. The attempt was evidently successful, since in the second passage Plutarch proceeds to point out that such "blame mixed with praise ... creating not anger but remorse and repentance, comes across as friendly and courteous". Plutarch does not specify the play, and Wilamowitz (1907) 72 n.1 argued that Ajax could be spoken of as "good in action" only after he had demonstrated his outstanding fighting qualities in the great defensive action he fights in books 15–16 of the *Iliad*. He is clearly, however, one of the leading figures in the Achaean army right from the start of that poem (e.g. 1.138, 145; 2.768; 7.179) and is nominated by Nestor himself as an appropriate envoy to go to Achilles (9.169); and even before the fighting against the Trojans began Ajax would have had a chance to show his prowess in the mistaken attack on Teuthrania. The indications (see above) that Ajax is the speaker in fr. B (563), and that in fr. C (564) he is the addressee and the speaker is a substantially older man, point strongly to the conclusion that the present fragment comes from the same context as these two and therefore (as Brunck first proposed) from *Syndeipnoi*, which will thus have contained a minor and easily resolved quarrel between Nestor and Ajax as prelude to the major quarrel between Achilles, Agamemnon and Odysseus.

With Nestor's summing-up of Ajax cf. *Aj.* 119–120 (Athena) "what man was found ... *better* than this one at *doing* what the situation required?", Pind. *Nem.* 8.24 "oblivion enfolds one [such as Ajax] who is unskilful of tongue but valiant of heart".

E (144)

These lines, quoted by a scholiast on Pindar from *Achaiôn Syllogos*, are spoken, evidently to Agamemnon, at or shortly before a meeting which all participants (or at least all contingent leaders) in the expedition against Troy were expected to attend. If *Achaiôn Syllogos* was the same play as *Syndeipnoi*, this meeting will doubtless have been combined with the feast, as in *Iliad* 9.65–178. The reference to the oath (evidently that administered by Tyndareos to the suitors of Helen: Hes. fr. 204.78–85, Stesichorus *PMG* 190, Eur. *IA* 55–66, Thuc. 1.9.1, [Apoll.] 3.10.9, Paus. 3.20.9; unknown to, or ignored by, Homer, and absent from our evidence for the cyclic epics) might seem to identify the occasion as the first muster of the expedition at Aulis; but the oath would remain binding until Helen was recovered, and it would have been easy for a reluctant ally to present himself at Aulis, separate from the fleet after it put to sea, and sail home instead of to the rendezvous at Tenedos.

I was wrong to argue in *Shards* (357, 359, 360–1) that the proposal to call the roll of the leaders and identify any absentees is aimed at shaming Achilles. If it were, it would not have been expressed in the terms used here, because by (almost) all accounts Achilles had not been one of those who "joined in the oath". The oath was taken by the suitors of Helen. We have three lists of these suitors. The oldest of these (Hes. frr. 197–204) is incomplete, but it is made clear (fr. 204.87–93) that Achilles was not among the suitors: his tutor, the centaur Cheiron, kept him on Mount

Pelion because he was too young, and by the time he got back home (whence he could have sent a message, and gifts, to Tyndareos at Sparta) Helen was already married. The two later lists ([Apoll.] 3.10.8; Hyginus *Fab.* 81) are presented as being complete, and neither includes Achilles. (He is, to be sure, said to have been one of Helen's suitors at Eur. *Hel.* 99; but as Dale *ad loc.* in effect points out, Euripides is there modifying tradition for convenience, since otherwise Helen, isolated in Egypt since the time of Paris's visit to Menelaus, would have had no idea who Achilles was.) Yet Achilles must already be regarded as a crucial member of the expedition (Agamemnon, when summoning Iphigeneia to Aulis on the pretence that she was to be married, named Achilles as the bridegroom; and in *Odyssey* 8.75–78 he is represented as regarding Achilles and Odysseus as "the best of the Achaeans") and his presence or absence could not have been treated as a matter of no importance. Either, then, the speaker must be assumed to have forgotten that Achilles was not one of those who had taken the oath, or (perhaps more likely) he is deliberately – and perhaps surreptitiously – engineering a diplomatic ploy. Probably (see Introduction, p. 93) all the main leaders have now reached Tenedos except Achilles. It is reasonable to assume that on leaving Aulis, all had been told that they must be present at Tenedos for a feast and council of war on a specified day, which has now arrived; anyone not present is *ipso facto* a defaulter. But if the proposal made here is adopted, even if Achilles does fail to appear, he will not be publicly *named* as a defaulter; the roll that is to be called over, evidently, will not be the roll of those who came to Aulis, but of those who swore Tyndareos' oath – and so Achilles will not have failed to answer to his name, because his name will not have been called. Thus the army will be able to avoid a public shaming of Achilles that would almost certainly provoke him into quitting the expedition, especially seeing that he is not bound to it by oath.

If this interpretation of our passage is correct, it is likely that, of the two regular counsellors of Agamemnon who appear to have had roles in our play, the speaker here is Nestor rather than Odysseus: the latter, that "much-enduring" hero, if he had devised a subterfuge to avoid jeopardizing the expedition by stigmatizing Achilles as a deserter or latecomer, would hardly, later the same evening, even after being himself insulted, stigmatize him even more woundingly as a coward (frr. J+L [566]). To the arch-conciliator Nestor, on the other hand, the idea is entirely appropriate: several times in the *Iliad* we find him anxiously seeking ways to save Achilles from losing face (1.275–284, where he urges Achilles once to be less intransigent but Agamemnon twice; 9.111–3, where he is the first to propose an approach to Achilles; 11.793–802, where he suggests a way in which Achilles can save the army without yielding on principle).

In the *Iliad* Agamemnon normally accepts Nestor's advice (the only exception is 1.285–291, where he has been asked, in effect, to swallow some very gross insults), and it is likely that he accepted this piece of advice as well; but if so, he may well not have been aware of Nestor's underlying objective, since we know from Philodemus (*On Anger* col. 18.17–24) that he did give offence to Achilles when Achilles eventually arrived at the feast. Probably the planned roll-call never took place, because of the violent quarrel that interrupted the feast; Nestor's proposal would have worked perfectly had Achilles missed the feast altogether – but he had not foreseen the possibility of Achilles' arriving half-way through. Just so, in *Iliad* 11.793–802, it does not occur to Nestor that Patroclus might press his attack further than he or Achilles or Nestor had intended and thereby meet his own death.

As is pointed out by Christ (2004) 47, the procedure here envisaged is very similar to that followed at the mustering of a military expedition in classical Athens: "the taxiarchs had a written list of those in the muster-roll, on which they made a mark against the names of those who failed to appear by the specified time" (Pollux 8.115).

1 in the chair: Agamemnon will be presiding over the feast and the meeting.

1 the inscribed tablets: lit. "the foldings of the writing". In tragedy, following the precedent of *Iliad* 6.169, written documents tend to be referred to as folded (presumably waxed) tablets (*deltoi* or, as here, *ptykhai*); cf. *Trach.* 47, Aesch. *Supp.* 947, fr. 281a.21–22, Eur. *Hipp.* 856, *IT* 584, 727, 760, *IA* 35, 98, 112. In Eur. fr. 369.6–7 the same terminology is applied even to literary texts, most of which would be far too lengthy for such a tablet.

2 record: this sense of Greek *nemein* is found otherwise only in the technical phrase *prostatēn nemein*, used of a metic (resident alien) at Athens registering the name of his citizen patron (Isoc. 8.53, Hyp. fr. 21, Arist. *Pol.* 1275a12) and in a reference by Polybius (6.47.8) to "unregistered athletes". The Pindar scholium which quotes our passage adds at this point *aponeimon*, the aorist imperative of a compound of the same verb; this is not a textual variant in the Sophoclean passage – it is the word in Pindar (*Isthm.* 2.47) on which the scholiast is commenting, inserted here either because a scribe's eye wandered or as an attempted "correction" of a text corrupted by wrong word-division (the mss. have the unconstruable *nemei tis* for *nem' ei tis* "record anyone who ...").

2 anyone that joined in the oath: see above.

F (568)

This lyric reflection on the hope of posthumous fame as a source of comfort and happiness in this brief life could fit various contexts, but it would be particularly appropriate in a choral song that followed a scene in which some character had expressed a strong desire to gain undying glory; and if so, that character is most likely to have been Achilles, the paradigm case of a hero whose short life is compensated by eternal renown (*Iliad* 9.412–3). A plausible moment for such a speech and such a song would be soon after Achilles' first appearance: he might express his ambitions to the chorus and then go in to the feast, leaving them to reflect on what he has said. Their thoughts will then have an ironic ring when we hear of Achilles' undignified behaviour and witness his furious argument with Odysseus and his threat to quit the expedition – all things which he would doubtless dearly love the Muses to forget, but which they will in fact remember perfectly, as is proved by the very fact that we, centuries later, are watching a play on the subject!

The metre is dactylic. The first three cola each consist of a hemiepes (– ∪∪–∪∪–) preceded by one, two or three long syllables; in the fourth, which is catalectic (indicating that a pause followed), the dactylic rhythm is more strongly emphasized by the substitution of double-short for the initial long. The overall effect is of a single long sequence of dactyls and spondees, fifteen feet in length, concluding (from the middle of line 3 to the end) with a pure dactylic hexameter – highly appropriate for a song in praise of heroic fame.

1 to be forgotten by: lit. "the forgetfulness of", taking *Pīeridōn* "of the goddesses of Pieria" as subjective genitive (cf. Pl. *Phdr.* 275a, Xen. *An.* 1.2.18, Plut. *Mor.* 650e). With Grotius' emendation *Pīerisi(n)* the meaning becomes "Oblivion is hateful ... to the goddesses of Pieria"; but this is neither true (for poetry preserves the memory, not of everything indiscriminately, but only of persons and events of special significance) nor relevant (the next sentence, closely linked to this one by rhythm and asyndeton, is about the happiness brought to mortals by the prospect of gaining fame, not the happiness brought to the Muses by the prospect of conferring it). For the loathsomeness of being dead and unremembered cf. Sappho fr. 55, Pl. *Symp.* 208c–e, Xen. *Mem.* 2.1.33 (paraphrasing Prodicus).

1 **the goddesses of Pieria:** the Muses, who had been associated with Pieria in Thessaly ever since Hesiod (*Thg.* 53, *Works* 1).

2 **power:** Greek *dynasis,* used twice elsewhere by Sophocles (*Ant.* 604, 951) as a lyric substitute for the everyday word *dynamis* (which in both passages has displaced it in part of the manuscript tradition).

3 **sustaining the narrow isthmus of their life:** life is a short, precarious interlude, like a narrow isthmus parting the two seas of eternity before birth and after death (cf. M.Aur. 4.3.7). It is not clear, and perhaps was not meant to be, whether the idea is that the *hope* of winning immortal fame can sustain the will to live, or that the *fact* of immortal fame prevents the memory of a man's life from being submerged in oblivion (cf. Radt [1982] 214 n.51).

G (565)

We have here evidently an incident in the quarrel between Achilles and Odysseus which was the most celebrated feature of *Syndeipnoi*. It is narrated by the victim, who must therefore have come out of the banqueting hall and be speaking to the chorus. We cannot tell whether his adversary is yet on stage. (That he is spoken of in the third person of course proves nothing; in Ar. *Clouds* 1353–90 – likewise an account of an assault during a banquet, narrated by the victim – the assailant, who is on stage and has already had an altercation with his victim, is spoken of exclusively in the third person until he interrupts at 1378.)

The most striking feature of the passage is that the incident is virtually identical to one narrated by Aeschylus, almost certainly in *Ostologoi (The Bone-collectors)* – and much of the wording is also identical or nearly so (one stretch of ten words is quoted verbatim). In *Ostologoi* Odysseus, apparently standing over the bodies (or perhaps rather the ash-urns) of Penelope's suitors, had delivered a speech detailing the assaults and insults they had committed against him while he had been posing as a beggar in his own palace. One fragment (Aesch. fr. 179) accuses Eurymachus, the second most prominent of the suitors, of having repeatedly thrown the dregs of his wine-cup at Odysseus' head; another (Aesch. fr. 180), cited by Athenaeus in the same context as the parallel Sophoclean passage (but without mention of a play-title or identification of the speaker), speaks of a person (unnamed) who "threw at me a missile that caused laughter, the evil-smelling chamber-pot" which, as in Sophocles, broke over the speaker's head and "breathed on me an odour quite different from that of pots of scent". Nothing quite like this occurs in the *Odyssey*, where the objects thrown at Odysseus are solid and heavy, and none of them hits his head (Antinous hits Odysseus on the shoulder with a footstool, 17.462–4; Eurymachus throws another footstool and misses, 18.394–7; and Ctesippus misses his head with an ox-hoof, 20.299–302): for attempts to hurt the unrecognized beggar, Aeschylus substitutes attempts to humiliate him. Sophocles has taken the incident over, emphasizing the connection by verbatim quotation and other echoes as he does in *El.* 1415–6 where he makes the dying Clytaemestra utter the same cries as Aeschylus' dying Agamemnon does in *Ag.* 1343–5; but this time the outrage is committed, not by an unworthy pretender against a supposed beggar, but with full knowledge by one of "the best of the Achaeans" against another. Its physical foulness makes it grosser than any of the insults that give rise to the great quarrel of the *Iliad*, and it could easily have provoked fatal violence: Odysseus, after all, did kill the offending suitors for similar behaviour, and but for divine intervention Achilles would have killed Agamemnon for less (*Iliad* 1.188–221). In Dem. 54.4 it is considered to be *hybris* when a group of drunken men sprinkle the contents of their chamber-pots over other men's *slaves*, let alone their masters.

Who is the narrator, Odysseus or Achilles? Or, equivalently, who is the aggressor, Achilles or Odysseus? Has Sophocles made Odysseus undergo the same experience at Achilles' hands as he will undergo nineteen years later at the hands of the anonymous suitor, or has he, on the principle "the doer shall suffer" (Aesch. *Ag.* 1563–4, *Cho.* 313), made him commit an act which he will later expiate like-for-like? A passage of Philodemus (*On Poems* 1.213.2–9 Janko), which speaks of "a chamber-pot being smashed over the head of Odysseus", unfortunately does not specify whether the reference is to Aeschylus or Sophocles or both; but there are other considerations that do tell in favour of Odysseus as the narrator, Achilles as the aggressor. Firstly, the narrator says that he was frightened by the smell, which is much more appropriate to Odysseus (who seems to act like a coward in *Iliad* 8.92–98, and who is never ashamed to admit to fear in the *Odyssey*, e.g. 9.236, 11.43, 11.633, 12.244) than to Achilles who is never in the *Iliad* afraid of anything bar a god (or himself: *Iliad* 24.560–586). And secondly, he says that his assailant acted in anger (in contrast to the Aeschylean suitor whose motive is said to have been derision), which of course fits Achilles perfectly and does not suit the calculating, patient Odysseus at all.

Why should Achilles attack Odysseus, though, when we are told (Philodemus, *On Anger* col. 18.17–24) that the person who had given offence to him was his host, namely Agamemnon? Just possibly Achilles threw the pot wildly in the general direction of Agamemnon (or of no one in particular) and it hit Odysseus by accident; but Odysseus specifically says (line 2 of our fragment) that Achilles did not miss his target, and if Achilles had no hostile feelings towards Odysseus as an individual the ferocity of the quarrel is hard to account for. More probably, therefore, we are meant to believe Odysseus when he says the throw was aimed, which implies that Odysseus must have intervened in the dispute between Achilles and Agamemnon and somehow, whether intentionally or not, inflamed Achilles further. He could have done this by an insufficiently tactful attempt at reconciliation (as in the Embassy scene of the *Iliad* where, as here [see on fr. K (145)], the argument culminates in a threat by Achilles to sail home) or he could have done it by telling Achilles that Agamemnon was in the right (as he tells Achilles' son, with similar consequences, in the false tale of *Phil.* 359–384; cf. Introduction, pp. 96–97).

The subject-matter of this fragment might well be thought beneath the dignity of tragedy, and it has been one of the prime pieces of evidence for those who argue that *Syndeipnoi* was a satyr-play (see e.g. Palutan [1996] 10–27, A. López Eire in *Shards* 399–400); but *Ostologoi* was probably a tragedy (see T.R. Gantz, *AJP* 101 [1980] 151–3; P. Grossardt, *Die Trugreden in der Odyssee in ihre Rezeption in der antiken Literatur* [Bern, 1998] 299–301; id., *HSCP* 101 [2003] 155–8; and my discussion in *Shards* 369–370), and elsewhere in Aeschylean tragedy we find references to urination (*Cho.* 756–7) and to the "unapproachable exhalation" of the Erinyes as they belch in their sleep (*Eum.* 53).

1 **chamber-pot:** regularly available in dining-rooms for the convenience of the diners; cf. Ar. *Frogs* 544, Eupolis fr. 385.5, Epicrates fr. 5.4, *com. adesp.* 133. In Men. fr. 252, at what is evidently a large party, there are sixteen of them on the floor. The everyday word for one is *(h)amis*: *ouranē*, the word used here and in Aesch. fr. 180, is found nowhere else except in grammarians' citations of these passages.

3 **whose odour was not of perfume:** cf. Aesch. *Ag.* 1306–12 where Cassandra, about to enter Agamemnon's palace in the knowledge that she is going to her death, recoils because to her inspired perception "the

house breathes blood-dripping murder … such a smell as comes from a tomb", and the chorus, who can detect only the familiar smells associated with sacrifice, remark "It is of no Syrian embellishment [i.e. frankincense] in the house that you speak" (1312).

4 **I was terrified:** fear might seem an inappropriate response to a disgusting smell, but cf. *Phil.* 869–876 where Neoptolemus is said to show the "nobility" of his character and birth (in contrast to the Atreidae, sarcastically called "those brave commanders") by enduring the evil smell of Philoctetes' wound and his cries of pain, and Ar. *Wasps* 1031–7 (≈ *Peace* 752–760) where the poet prides himself on his Heracles-like courage in standing up to a loathsome monster (Cleon) whose attributes include "terrible smells of leather" (*Peace* 753) and "the smell of a seal, the unwashed balls of a Lamia, and the arse of a camel" (*Wasps* 1035 = *Peace* 758), implying that a lesser man would have fled in terror.

H (144a)

It is thanks to the interest of two lexicographers in the first word of this short fragment, *phalanthon*, that the phrase has been preserved for us; and as it happens, both the assignment of the fragment to a context, and its significance for our understanding of the play as a whole, depend crucially on the meaning of this word. The two lexicographers, Cyril and Hesychius, define it as *polion* "grey, hoary", but add that "some" say it means *phalakron* "bald". Other lexicographers give only the meaning "bald" (e.g. *Et.Mag.* 786.59, Photius s.v. *phalanthoi*, Suda α2518, φ41) or "bald in front" (*Anecd. Bekk.* 71.17–20) – though Photius does seem to have been aware of the alternative explanation, since he adds that *anthos* can mean "white hair". And "(wholly or partly) bald" is certainly what we find the adjective *phalanthos* means whenever we can see it in context: D.L. 7.164 treats *phalanthos* and *phalakros* "bald" as synonyms in telling the story of how the philosopher Ariston of Chios (nicknamed *Phalanthos*) died of sunstroke, Eusebius *Praep. Ev.* 3.11.13 allegorizes the "*phalanthon* and gleaming" appearance of the head of Silenus (traditionally bald in front, both in art and in poetry) as a symbol of the celestial sphere, and *AP* 9.317 has Hermaphroditus laughing at the undignified spectacle of the "noisy god" (probably Priapus, or his statue) being hit on the *phalanthon* top of his head by a pear. Cf. also the related noun *anaphalanthiasis* "forehead-baldness" in Arist. *HA* 518a28. It is very unlikely (*pace* M. Naoumides, *GRBS* 9 [1968] 270) that the same word could have denoted both the *colour* of hair (in old age, for men and women alike) and the complete or partial *absence* of hair (in men of any age). To be sure, as Mary Bachvarova has pointed out to me, English *bald* (probably a cognate of the Greek root *phal-*) refers both to absence of hair in humans, and (nowadays only in *piebald, skewbald,* and the inn-name *Bald Faced Stag*) to white patches on the coats of animals (see OED^2 s.v. bald a.); but this is not an adequate parallel, since the two English usages, unlike the two supposed usages of *phalanthos*, do not overlap so as to carry the risk of ambiguity.

So it is almost certainly Nestor's bald head, rather than Nestor's grey head, that is being spoken of in the passage from which this fragment comes. And bald heads tend, in Greek texts, either to be laughed at or to be struck by something (for the latter cf. Eur. *Cycl.* 227, *AP* loc. cit., and the story about the death of Aeschylus in *Life of Aeschylus* 17 Radt, Val. Max. 9.12 ext. 2, Aelian *NA* 7.16). It is thus tempting to suggest that the fragment may come from a narrative (presumably the same narrative that included fr. G [565]) of hybristic behaviour by Achilles in which he attacked Nestor as well as Odysseus, no doubt when Nestor attempted to compose Achilles' quarrel with Agamemnon and/or Odysseus as he had successfully, a little time before, composed his own quarrel with Ajax. What was thrown at Nestor we cannot tell; possibly wine as in Aesch. fr. 179. It is striking that a series of scholia to *Aj.* 237–8 (where Ajax is described as seizing two "white-footed rams", cutting off the head and tongue of one, and tying up and flogging the other) claim that he took the second for Odysseus (cf. *Aj.* 101–113) *and the first for Nestor* even though Nestor is nowhere directly mentioned in the play: it is as if these two, heroes of outstanding mental qualities, tend to be thought of together as natural targets for the resentment of heroes of outstanding physical qualities who feel themselves slighted.

Now baldness is a theme for satyr-drama and comedy, not for tragedy. Except for our fragment, no tragic or possibly tragic text ever mentions baldness. Silenus, on the other hand, is regularly bald (Soph. fr. 173, Eur. *Cycl.* 227); and some degree of baldness seems to have been ubiquitous for old (and some not so old) men in comedy (this is illustrated by many of the plates in O.P. Taplin, *Comic Angels and Other Approaches to Greek Drama through Vase-Paintings* [Oxford, 1993]), while comic *dramatists* could make fun of each other's baldness (Ar. *Ach.* 850, cf. C. Carey, *LCM* 18 [1993] 54; Eupolis fr. 89) and defiantly take pride in their own (*Knights* 550, *Clouds* 540, *Peace* 767–774). And it is hard to see what special reason there could be, in a fully serious tragedy, for ascribing this physical characteristic, which clearly was regarded in such contexts as somewhat undignified, to a person who, while he sometimes has his foibles, is always, in epic and tragedy alike, a respected counsellor, and who had apparently shown himself to good advantage in his scene with Ajax. This seems to me to be stronger than any of the various pieces of evidence which at one time or another have been adduced to show that *Syndeipnoi* is satyric or prosatyric – though curiously the fragment seems to have only once been *itself* cited for this purpose since its Sophoclean origin became known in 1968 (viz. by Radt [1982] 211), largely no doubt because Cyril ascribes it to *Achaiôn Syllogos*.

But there is still another question to ask. The entries in Cyril and Hesychius, having as they do the lemma *phalanthon* in the neuter gender, evidently derive ultimately from a commentary on our play (cf. M. Naoumides, *GRBS* 9 [1968] 271). The author of this commentary is, so far as we know, solely responsible for the claim that *phalanthon* here means "hoary". Given that he must have known perfectly well that this word normally meant "bald", why did he attach an abnormal meaning to it in just this passage? If the play were satyric, *phalanthon* "bald" would have seemed, and been, unobjectionable. But if this commentator thought the play was a tragedy, he might well have arbitrarily given the word a different meaning because he felt that it was improper for anybody, especially a person of high status, to be called "bald" in a tragic drama. If this explanation of the surprising gloss is correct, it proves that *Syndeipnoi* was not satyric, i.e. did not have a chorus of satyrs. But if the gloss itself is wrong, if the adjective *phalanthos* here as everywhere else does mean "bald", that all but proves – what various other pieces of evidence, none decisive in itself, tend to suggest (see especially on frr. B [563], G [565]) – that *Syndeipnoi* was not a tragedy in the full sense. Thus this fragment provides the key to the riddle of the generic identity of *Syndeipnoi*: it was a prosatyric play like Euripides' *Alcestis*.

J (566.1–2)

Whether or not Achilles was on stage during Odysseus' narrative of the quarrel indoors (see on fr. G [565]), he is definitely present now and arguing with Odysseus in front of the audience and presumably in the presence of the chorus. Plutarch (*Mor.* 74a-b), who cites these words, gives some of the context: Odysseus, "provoking Achilles", said that he (Achilles) was not angry on account of <his treatment at> the feast, but [here follow the words of this fragment]; Achilles in response "was fiercely indignant and said he was sailing off" (cf. on fr. K [145]), to which Odysseus retorted in the words of fr. L (566.3–4). Plutarch does not name the play he is quoting, but the situation (a quarrel between Odysseus and Achilles, when the Achaeans are in sight of "the dwellings of Troy land" for the first time) identifies it with certainty.

Both Odysseus' accusation, as partly paraphrased and partly quoted by Plutarch, and Achilles' "fierce indignation" and threat of departure, would have taken at least several lines, and it is perhaps most likely that both formed part of set speeches constituting an *agon* such as is found at some point (sometimes more than once) in most of Sophocles' surviving plays; this may have been followed by an altercation in distichomythia (perhaps shifting into single-line stichomythia later, as in *Ant.* 726ff; in *OC* 800ff there is an irregular alternation between the two), of which fr. L (566.3–4) could have been part.

Odysseus' taunt of cowardice is almost as gross an insult as one could possibly offer to a warrior by words alone. Plutarch's discussion implies *prima facie* that Odysseus' offensiveness was calculated; he introduces frr. J+L (566) as an example of what should be done "when we either [i] have to knock someone off course who is about to go wrong, or [ii] wish to give a boost of encouragement to those who are [a] standing up to the attack of a powerful opposing impulse or [b] weak and unenthusiastic in an honourable endeavour". Of the three possible objectives set out here, it must be [i] that Plutarch takes Odysseus to have in mind, since Achilles' current mood is one of rage against Odysseus himself, Agamemnon, and perhaps the whole army, and Odysseus would certainly be wanting to "knock [him] off course" rather than to strengthen his resolve. But can Plutarch really have believed, as his treatment in context implies, that Odysseus was speaking as a friend, trying to shock Achilles into changing his behaviour by making him think he was giving the impression that he was a coward? If so, his first attempt was clearly a disastrous failure, and the second (fr. L [566.3–4]), saying very much the same thing in different words, can hardly have had a much greater prospect of success; nor is it in the least plausible that Odysseus would be presented as having the best of amicable intentions towards a man who had just showered him with urine. More probably, then, Plutarch was taking the passages out of context (either carelessly or deliberately) to illustrate his point that when one wants to achieve any of the above three objectives, it can be effective to "ascribe what is happening [i.e. the friend's actions or inactions] to improbable and unseemly causes". If Odysseus' words are calculated at all, they are calculated to inflame; but it is also possible, despite Odysseus' reputation for self-control (see p. 126), that they are the product of sheer rage. The risk that such an insult to such a man would provoke personal violence, which could very well be fatal either to Odysseus himself or to Achilles, was so great and so obvious that it is quite hard to believe that Odysseus can have been represented as consciously deciding to run it. Indeed, it is somewhat surprising to the modern mind that Achilles does *not* in fact instantly resort to the sword; but an audience knowing the *Iliad*, and knowing also that physical violence on stage was not normal in tragedy, would not be too surprised when his response, like his response in *Iliad* 9.308–429 to Odysseus' careful and courteous appeal, consists of angry words and a declaration that he is about to depart (doubtless for home).

Pearson, Radt, Lucas and Lloyd-Jones all print and/or translate the fragment as a question, but the run of Plutarch's sentence, in which the quotation of the fragment in *oratio recta* is made grammatically parallel to a statement by Odysseus in *oratio obliqua* that Achilles is not really angry about his treatment at the feast, indicates that Odysseus' words about Achilles' alleged fear are also to be read as a statement – or at least that Plutarch (without benefit of punctuation marks, but with the full context before him) so read them.

1 **the dwellings of Troy land:** not the city of Troy itself (which is visible from the higher parts of Tenedos, but not from sea level); rather, towns or villages on the Aegean coast of the Troad facing the island. In Homer *Troiē* can denote either the city (e.g. *Iliad* 1.129, *Odyssey* 1.2) or the Troad as a whole (e.g. *Iliad* 2.237, 9.329); for the latter usage in tragedy cf. *Aj.* 1021, *Phil.* 1297, 1332, 1376, Eur. *Andr.* 11, 58, 968, *Hec.* 140, *Tro.* 816, *Or.* 522.

K (145)

This one-word fragment is preserved by the lexicographer Hesychius. Both the word itself and Hesychius' definition of it are corrupt in the only manuscript (of the fifteenth century), but two easy emendations (both postulating confusions of vowels which in medieval Greek sounded alike) yield the form *ekkekōpētai* (lit. "is thoroughly oared", if the noun from which it is derived, *kōpē*, bears its most common classical meaning) and the definition *exērtūtai* "is fully equipped"; uncompounded forms of the same verb, *kekōpētai* (singular) and *kekōpēntai* (plural), are found in another entry in Hesychius (κ2124) – where the subject is a ship – and in a fourth-century Athenian naval inventory (*IG* ii² 1604.73). The metrical form of the word (– ∪ – – –)is consistent with its coming from an iambic trimeter.

We know (see on previous fragment) that in answer to Odysseus' taunt Achilles was "fiercely indignant" and threatened to sail away, and (so far as our information goes) this provides the likeliest context for someone to say that a single ship was "fully equipped with oars". There is, however, yet another Hesychius entry (κ2123) in which the cognate verb *kekōpeutai* has an army (*stratos*) as its subject, and conceivably therefore the reference might be to Achilles' whole contingent of ships (fifty, according to *Iliad* 2.685) or even to the entire fleet's state of readiness for crossing to the mainland of the Troad.

L (566.3–4)

Odysseus affects to perceive further evidence of cowardice in Achilles' threat to quit the expedition, and with heavy sarcasm says that (sc. in Achilles' view) the proximity of Hector makes it "improper" (dishonourable) to remain with the army – intending to be understood as meaning the opposite, viz. that Achilles is dishonourably running away from Hector. In a passage of Aelius Aristides (*Or.* 16.32) which seems to be based on this one (though set much later in the war), the speaker (not Odysseus, *pace* Pearson, since he has more than one child, cf. 16.13) tells Achilles with similar sarcasm that "it's honourable now to put in to Scyros" and asks him what he will say to his son when he gets there.

This fragment is understood quite differently by Lloyd-Jones, who places a question-mark at the end of each line and translates: "I know what you wish to flee from! Is it not from ill-repute? But Hector is near! Does not honour demand that you remain?" This gives us an Odysseus who, presumably for the sake of the army, is willing to swallow Achilles' insults and gives him advice whose acceptance will benefit both Achilles himself and the Achaean cause. However, the emphatic *egōida*, "*I* know", implying that Odysseus has perceived something that most other people could not have perceived, would then be out of place, since Achilles must by now have explained the cause of his indignation and that cause must have to do with a slight to his honour, for which he must retaliate or else suffer in reputation. Rather, what Odysseus claims to have perceived is that Achilles' alleged concern for his honour is a sham (for *egōida* carrying this kind of implication cf. Ar. *Ach.* 118, *Knights* 469, *Thesm.* 502, *Frogs* 836) and that he is really frightened for his skin.

1 **I know:** the contracted form *egōida* (for *egō oida*) is otherwise found in tragedy only at *OC* 452.

1 **being insulted:** Greek *kluein kakōs*, lit. "hearing ill", i.e. "being ill spoken of"; this could refer either (as I have taken it) to the insulting treatment of Achilles by Agamemnon in connection with the feast and the subsequent taunts of Odysseus, or to the loss of face and reputation that would result if Achilles accepted such humiliations and remained with the army.

2 **Hector is close at hand:** we are expected to assume that the Achaeans are already familiar with the reputation of "manslaughtering Hector" (*Iliad* 1.242 and often). No story survives of any martial exploits of his before the Achaean landing near Troy when he killed Protesilaus (*Cypria* Arg. §10 West). Perhaps Sophocles invented some local conflicts for him to win fame in; these could have been mentioned earlier in the play by almost any of the characters and/or the chorus.

M (567)

The scholiast on *Ajax* 190 who quotes these lines makes it clear (as we could have deduced in any case) that they were addressed to Odysseus; in effect they call him, three times over, a clever trickster and cheat. In view of what is known about our play, Achilles is much the most likely speaker.

1 **You'll stop at nothing!:** lit. "O you who (will) do anything"; cf. *OC* 761 "O you who (will) dare anything" (Oedipus to Creon). Phrases of this kind may be regarded as elegant alternatives to the colloquial term *pan(t)ourgos* "villain, trickster", though the latter is also found in tragedy (it is applied to Odysseus at *Aj.* 445 and *Phil.* 408).

1 **Sisyphus,** king of Corinth, "the craftiest of men" (*Iliad* 6.153) who temporarily outwitted death (Alc. fr. 38.5–10; Theognis 702–712, Pherecydes of Athens *FGrH* 3 F 119) but eventually suffered dire punishment in the underworld (*Odyssey* 11.593–600), is several times spoken of by Odysseus' enemies in tragedy as Odysseus' real father (*Aj.* 190, *Phil.* 417, 1311, Aesch. fr. 175, Eur. *IA* 524, 1362). The story was that he had slept with Anticleia when visiting her father Autolycus (see below) to reclaim his stolen cattle (schol. *Aj.* 190 [i]; schol. Lycophron 344) or had raped her when she was travelling to Ithaca to be wedded to Laertes (schol. *Aj.* 190 [ii]; Plut. *Mor.* 301d), so that she was already pregnant with Odysseus when Laertes married her; this embarrassing situation is the theme of an Apulian vase-painting of about 420 BC (*LIMC* Antikleia 1).

2　**your mother's father:** Autolycus, son of Hermes (Pherecydes of Athens *FGrH* 3 F 120) and father of Odysseus' mother Anticleia, according to *Odyssey* 19.395–6 (cf. *Iliad* 10.266–7) "excelled all men in stealing and swearing" (i.e. in formulating oaths in terms that were misleading but not actually false); he was able to evade detection of his thefts by his power to make anything he touched invisible (Hes. fr. 67) or transform it into any shape he pleased (Pherecydes loc.cit., Hyginus *Fab.* 201). He was outwitted only by Sisyphus (see above); he got away with his depredations from Sisyphus' herds for a long time, but was detected when Sisyphus began to mark his animals' hooves with his monogram (schol. *Aj.* 190; schol. Lycophron 344).

N (571)

This fragment is derived from a desperately corrupt entry in Hesychius. It is about a word which appears elsewhere as *mas(th)lēs* (masculine) and means either "leather strap" (Sappho fr. 39.2, of a sandal; Alc. fr. 143.12 [?] and Soph. fr. 129, of a whip) or, metaphorically, "supple rogue" (Ar. *Knights* 269, *Clouds* 449). The Hesychius entry defines either this word, or an otherwise unattested variant form *masthlē* (feminine), or a phrase which may be *masthlētas tomous* (lit. "cutting straps") as "reins", mentions specifically that the form *masthlē* exists, and adds the reference "Sophocles in *Andromeda* and *Syndeipnoi*". Since the word is rare, the *Andromeda* reference is likely to be to fr. 129 where the masculine form appears in a different phrase (*daphoinon masthlēta digonon* "bloody double whip"; cf. Aesch. *Ag.* 642–3). Does that imply that *masthlētas tomous* (if that is indeed the lemma of our Hesychius entry) appeared in *Syndeipnoi*? Or are the two Sophoclean plays only being cited as parallels for the use of the noun itself? And which noun, the masculine one or the feminine? It is impossible to answer these questions with any confidence. All we can say is that one of these two nouns was used, either in the literal or in the figurative sense, in *Syndeipnoi*.

If the word was used literally, we cannot tell who used it and in what context. If it was used figuratively, it is very likely to have been applied to Odysseus, as similar opprobrious, half-slangy epithets are by other speakers hostile to him: he is called "the damnable fox" (*Aj.* 103, cf. Ar. *Clouds* 448), "filthy fine-ground meal" (i.e. someone who slips through your fingers: *Aj.* 381, 389, cf. Ar. *Clouds* 260), "subtle-minded soft-talking populist <word->chopper" (Eur. *Hec.* 131–2), "clever piece of metalwork" (Soph. fr. 913, [Eur.] *Rhes.* 498–9). And if so, the most probable speaker is once again Achilles, either during the quarrel or when reflecting on it afterwards (none of the above insults whose context is known is uttered when Odysseus is known by the speaker to be present – although Silenus in Eur. *Cycl.* 104 does greet Odysseus' announcement of his name with "I know the man – the sharp-sounding castanet [cf. Ar. *Clouds* 260, 448] – the son of Sisyphus!").

O (562)

The two grammarians who quote this fragment state that it is spoken by Thetis to Achilles, and it is probably the first, or nearly the first, thing she speaks on entering; this is shown both by *lipousa* "leaving", which is semi-formulaic in entrance-speeches by deities or ghosts (*Polyxene* fr. A [523] 2, Eur. *Andr.* 1232 [Thetis again, "leaving the house of Nereus"], *Hec.* 2, *Tro.* 1, *Ba.* 13) and by *ōrousa* "I have rushed", implying an urgent intervention (cf. *OC* 890, Eur. *Ion* 1556). Thetis comes thus to the side of her son when he is in distress (*Iliad* 1.357–363, 18.35–77; Aeschylus, *Nereids*), but her haste here suggests that Achilles is not merely in distress but in danger – either from a vengeful Odysseus, or because he himself, in pursuance of the quarrel, has done or is about to do something that risks bringing down the wrath of the army on him. We can reasonably call Thetis a *dea ex machina* in functional terms, without committing ourselves as to whether she actually appeared on the *mēkhanē* (flying-machine) – though she apparently did so in Euripides' *Andromache* (cf. 1226–30), and the suddenness of an airborne arrival could be useful if (as in Eur. *Hel.* 1642ff, *Or.* 1625ff) instant intervention was necessary to prevent serious harm being done.

The fragment consists either of parts of two iambic trimeters, or of part of one line and the whole of a second. Its text, in particular the word-order and the placement of the line-division, are uncertain – paradoxically, because the two grammarians actually quote it as an example of abnormal word-order (*anastrophē*).* They quote it, however, in two different forms,

---

* I give here the relevant passages in the two grammatical texts, unemended. The texts are an anonymous treatise περὶ τρόπων (*On Figures of Speech*), published by Carl Fredrich in *NGG* 1896 (at p.340), and a scholium to Dionysius Thrax (vol. i p.460.3 Hilgard). They begin alike: γίνεται δὲ ἀναστροφὴ καὶ διὰ πλειόνων μερῶν τοῦ λόγου, ὡς παρὰ Σοφοκλεῖ ἐν Συνδείπνοις ἡ Θέτις πρὸς τὸν Ἀχιλλέα φησί ("Displacement also occurs through a distance of several words, as in Sophocles' *Syndeipnoi* Thetis says to Achilles ..."). The

both of which are unmetrical; one of them, professing to show what the normal word-order (*to hexēs*) would have been, offers a sequence which itself does violence to grammatical bonds, viz.

pontion khoron lipousa Nērēïdōn ōrousa

(lit. "maritime chorus leaving of-Nereids I-have-rushed", with the object phrase divided in two by the verb); and the other adds a note on the use of *meta se* (lit."after you") in the sense of *pros se* ("to you"), although *meta se* does not appear in the fragment as quoted by either writer.

My restoration of the fragment is premised on the assumption that *meta se* originally appeared in its text – as it must have done, unless the note on this phrase has been accidentally interpolated from some totally different context – and the fact that if the second word in the fragment as transmitted, the particle *men*, is taken to be a corruption of *meta se*, the whole fragment falls into correct iambic rhythm without there being any need to emend the transmitted word-order as we have to if *men* is retained. The disappearance of *meta se* from the quotation appears also to have confused copyists attempting to make sense of what was being said about the word displacement (*anastrophē*) in the passage. The common source of our two grammarians probably wrote that the normal order would have been

lipousa pontion khoron Nērēïdōn ōrousa meta se

(lit. "leaving maritime chorus of-Nereids I-have-rushed after you"), where every syntactic constituent of the sentence is a continuous string of one or more words; whereas in the actual text *meta se* appeared four words early, in the middle of the participial phrase *lipousa ... Nērēïdōn* with which it had no syntactic connection. This makes an excellent illustration of what the grammarians say they are illustrating, "displacement ... through <a distance of> several words" (they have previously given examples in

---

anonymous treatise then quotes our fragment (in the form λιποῦσα μὲν πόντιον χορὸν ὤρουσα Νηρηΐδων) and continues τὸ γὰρ ἑξῆς οὕτως ἐστί ("for the straightforward order is as follows")· πόντιον χορὸν λιποῦσα Νηρηΐδων ὤρουσα. The Dionysius Thrax scholium quotes the fragment in the form λείπουσα μὲν πόντιον χορὸν Νηρηΐδων ὤρουσα, and continues ὅτι μετὰ σὲ ἀντὶ τοῦ πρὸς σὲ καὶ παρ' Ἡσιόδῳ ("note that *meta se* 'after you' is used for *pros se* 'to you' also by Hesiod" – referring probably to *Works* 199). If, as here argued, what Sophocles wrote was λιποῦσα μετὰ σὲ πόντιον χορὸν Νηρηΐδων ὤρουσα, the common source of the two grammatical texts probably gave the "straightforward order" as λιποῦσα πόντιον χορὸν Νηρηΐδων ὤρουσα μετὰ σέ.

which the distance of displacement is only one word). When *meta se* in the quotation became *men*, the copyists found themselves faced with a text in which the "displaced" word-order of the quotation was identical with the "normal" word-order with which it was being contrasted – and proceeded to "correct" the latter, not realizing that the error that had caused the problem was not an error of word-order at all.

If this restoration is correct, and if these words are spoken by Thetis immediately on her entrance, then two syllables (× –) are missing at the beginning of the first line. Since they were apparently never included in the grammarians' quotation, they were probably not an integral part of the syntactic structure of the sentence, and they are very likely to be a vocative: of the ten speeches by divinities intervening near the end of Sophoclean and Euripidean plays which survive intact, nine contain a vocative or equivalent in their first sentence. The only vocatives that Thetis might use to Achilles which fit the available space are *ō pai* and *teknon*, both meaning "my child" – or, less likely, the synonym *tekos*, which mothers use in addressing their children in tragic lyrics (Eur. *El.* 1215, *Phoen.* 317) but not in spoken tragic iambics. In the *Iliad* Thetis invariably addresses Achilles as *teknon, tekos* or *teknon emon* (1.362, 414; 18.73, 95, 128; 19.8, 29; 24.128).

1 **band:** lit. "chorus". Tragedy often envisages the fifty Nereids (like other bands of nymphs) as a chorus of dancers, normally in or under the sea; cf. Eur. *Andr.* 1267, *El.* 432–444, *Tro.* 2, *IT* 274, 427–9, *Ion* 1081– 6, *IA* 1054–7. They function as a chorus in lamenting for Achilles in *Odyssey* 24.58–64 and also (while he still lives) in *Iliad* 18.35–64; and they formed the chorus of, and gave their name to, the second play of Aeschylus' tragic trilogy based on the *Iliad.*

P (146)

For this verb, *epixenousthai*, Hesychius gives two senses, *marturesthai* "to call to witness" and *poreuesthai* "to travel"; the latter sense is more accurately glossed by Pollux (3.58) as "to go to another city as a foreigner" and is attested in Isoc. *Letter* 6.2, Arist. *Pol.* 1327a13, and in many later texts. Hesychius cites the verb both from our play (as *Achaiōn Syllogos*) and from Aeschylus' *Cretan Women* (Aesch. fr. 120); this might mean, as Pearson supposes, that the verb bore one of its senses in one of these plays and the other sense in the other play, but it is also possible that both citations refer to the second sense. It is in fact highly dubious whether the sense "to call to witness" exists at all; it bears no relation to *xenos* "foreigner, stranger, guest, host", from which the verb is derived, and is probably no more than a conjectural interpretation of Aesch. *Ag.* 1320 where (see Fraenkel ad loc.) it is most likely that the verb actually means something like "I demand (this) as my right as a guest". In its regular sense "travel abroad, live abroad" the verb might have been used e.g. in reference to Achilles' sojourn on Scyros.

Q (147)

The verb *episeiein*, usually "brandish (something) at (someone)", could also mean "shake out (the reins) over (a team of horses)" and hence "urge on", taking an accusative of the person (etc.) incited and normally a dative of the target: cf. Eur. *Or.* 255–6 (parodied in Alexis fr. 3), 613–4. Hesychius' citation is *episeiousēs*, the genitive singular of the feminine present participle; possibly the subject was a goddess (e.g. Aphrodite encouraging Paris to abduct Helen). As it stands, the form *episeiousēs* cannot be accommodated in an iambic trimeter; its initial vowel must have been absorbed by ("aphaeresis") or blended with ("crasis") the vowel of a preceding monosyllable, e.g. *ē* "or" (*ē 'piseiousēs*) or *kai* "and" (*kāpiseiousēs*).

R (148)

The noun *symbolos* (or, in its older Attic spelling, *xymbolos*) originally meant a chance meeting. Since some such encounters (especially those with certain animals or certain kinds of person, and especially an encounter which took place immediately on leaving one's house in the morning) were good or bad omens (cf. [Aesch.] *Prom.* 487, Ar. *Birds* 721, *Frogs* 196, *Eccl.* 792, Xen. *Mem.* 1.1.3, *Apol.* 13, Thphr. *Char.* 16.3, Luc. *Pseudologistes* 17), *symbolos* came to have the more general meaning of "omen", including for example omens derived from words and from sneezes (see below). The extension of the meaning of *symbolos* was doubtless aided by confusion with the cognate neuter noun *symbolon*, which had independently come to bear the meaning of "omen" (e.g. Pind. *Olymp.* 12.7) through a specialization of its established sense of "token" (an omen being a token of what the future would bring).

Hesychius' entry for the word runs: "*Xymbolous*: they spoke of omens derived from sneezes <by this name>, and these were treated as sacred to Demeter; some <say it denotes> prophetic inferences derived from utterances, which Philochorus [*FGrH* 328 F 192] says Demeter first discovered. Sophocles in *Achaiôn Syllogos*." For "omens derived from sneezes" cf. *Odyssey* 17.541, Ar. *Birds* 720, Xen. *An.* 3.2.9; for "prophetic inferences derived from utterances" cf. *Odyssey* 20.105–121 (Odysseus hears a maidservant pray for the destruction of the suitors), Ar. *Lys.* 391–7 (laments for Adonis heard during a debate on the Sicilian expedition). The omen(s) mentioned in our play must have been of one of these two classes, but we cannot tell which (though no other surviving tragic, or even satyric, text or fragment makes any mention of sneezing).

S (569)

Azeia was a town in the Troad. It was mentioned by the historian Hellanicus (*FGrH* 4 F 58) in his account of Lydia, probably in connection with a campaign by one of the two Lydian kings who controlled the Troad, Gyges in the seventh century (cf. Strabo 13.1.22) and Croesus in the sixth (cf. Hdt. 1.6, 1.28). In what part of the Troad it lay we do not know, though it is not very likely to have been on the west coast facing Tenedos (see below). Its people were called *Azeioi, Azeiês* or (as here) *Azeiōtai.* Like many towns in the north (Black Sea coast), north-west (Hellespontine coast) and interior of the Troad, Azeia was a member of the Athenian alliance at least by the 450s, paying a modest annual tribute of 400 drachmae, of which Athena's quota of one-sixtieth (6 dr. 4 ob.) is several times recorded in the so-called Athenian Tribute Lists (*IG* i^3 261 IV 28, 270 II 26, 277 IV 18, 279 I 106, 281 III 27). The towns on the western (Aegean) coast of the Troad, such as Larisa, Colone and Hamaxitus, do not appear to have been assessed for tribute until the great reassessment of 425/4 (*IG* i^3 71 III 125–137, cf. 77 IV 15–23). It is thus not very likely that Azeia was singled out for special mention in this play because it was close to, or visible from, Tenedos; more probably it was mentioned in a choral song (*Azeiōtai* cannot fit into a spoken iambic trimeter) as part of a survey of the peoples of the Troad comparable to the survey of lands lost to Persia in Aesch. *Pers.* 865–902, or to the lyric Catalogue of Ships in Eur. *IA* 231–302.

T (570)

The adjective *bebēlos* (usually "profane, non-sacred") is cited from our play in the sense *idiōtēs*, i.e. person who is not of whatever special category the situation requires. In practice, not surprisingly, *bebēlos* in this sense appears most frequently in religious contexts referring to the exclusion of those not qualified (by initiation or otherwise) to take part in a cult: cf. Eur. fr. 648, Pl. *Symp.* 218b (a humorous parody of sacral language), *Orphica* frr. 7, 23.20 D–K, Callim. *h.Dem.* 3. We cannot tell in what connection the word was used in *Syndeipnoi.*

TEREUS

Texts and Testimonia: Pearson ii 221–238; Buchwald (see below) 33–42; Lucas de Dios 303–310; *TrGF* 435–445; Lloyd-Jones 290–301. *POxy* 3013; Tzetzes on Hes. *Works* 566; schol. Ar. *Birds* 212.

Myth: Odyssey 19.518–23; Hesiod, *Works* 568 and fr. 312; Sappho fr. 135; Pherecydes *FGrH* 3 F 124; Aeschylus, *Suppliants* 58–67 and *Agamemnon* 1140–51; Livius Andronicus frr. 24–29 Warmington; Accius frr. 639–655 Warmington; Conon *FGrH* 26 F 1.31; Ovid, *Metamorphoses* 6.424–674; [Apollodorus], *Bibliotheca* 3.14.8; Hyginus, *Fabulae* 45; Achilles Tatius 5.3 and 5.5; Antoninus Liberalis, *Metamorphoses* 11; Pausanias 1.5.4, 1.41.8–9, 10.4.8–10; Nonnus 4.320. I. Cazzaniga, *La saga di Itis nella tradizione letteraria e mitografica graeco-romana. Vol. 1, Da Omero a Nonno Panopolitano* (Varese, 1950); N.J. Zaganiaris, *Platon* 25 (1973) 208–32; G. Mihailov, *Annuaire de l'Université de Sofia, Faculté des Lettres* 50.2 (1955) 77–199; Gantz 239–41; E. Touloupa, *LIMC* vii.1 (1994) 527; J.R. March in N.K. Rutter and B.A. Sparkes ed. *Word and Image in Ancient Greece*, (Edinburgh, 2000) 123–134.

Artistic evidence: E. Touloupa, LIMC vii.1 (1994) 527–9; March op.cit.

Main discussions: F.G. Welcker, *Die griechischen Tragödien mit Rücksicht auf den epischen Cyclus i* (Bonn, 1839) 374–88; W. Buchwald, *Studien zur Chronologie der attischen Tragödie 455 bis 431* (Diss. Königsberg, 1939); W.M. Calder, *Thracia* 2 (1974) 87–91; Sutton 127–132; Kiso 51–86, 139–147; N.C. Hourmouziades in J.H. Betts et al. ed. *Studies in Honour of T.B.L. Webster i* (Bristol, 1986) 134–142; G. Dobrov, *AJP* 114 (1993) 197–214; A.P. Burnett, *Revenge in Attic and Later Tragedy* (Berkeley, 1998) 177–91; J.R. March in N.K. Rutter and B.A. Sparkes ed. *Word and Image in Ancient Greece* (Edinburgh, 2000) 119–139; D.G. Fitzpatrick, CQ 51 (2001) 90–101; K. Zacharia in F. Budelmann and P. Michelakis ed. *Homer, Tragedy and Beyond: Essays in Honour of P.E. Easterling* (London, 2001) 91–112; J.R. *March in Shards* 139–161; F. McHardy in McHardy et al. ed. *Lost Dramas of Classical Athens* (Exeter, 2005) 141–5; P. Monella, *Procne e Filomela: dal mito al simbolo letterario* (Bologna, 2005).

The subject matter of this play is not in doubt; but although the testimonial evidence for the tragedy is relatively good,[1] and although *Tereus* has probably attracted more attention than almost any other lost tragedy of Sophocles, it is still difficult to reconstruct the dramatic action with any precision. The outline of the story is as follows: Tereus, king of Thrace, received Procne in marriage from the Athenian king, Pandion. They had a son, Itys. Procne missed her sister Philomela and asked Tereus to bring her from Athens. During the journey to Thrace, Tereus raped Philomela and cut out her tongue to prevent her from speaking the truth. But Philomela made the truth known to her sister through a piece of weaving. When Procne learnt the truth, she exacted a terrible revenge. Itys was killed, cooked, and fed to an unsuspecting Tereus. Tereus' attempt to take revenge on the women was frustrated when the gods intervened and turned the two sisters and Tereus into birds.[2] Procne was transformed into a nightingale; Philomela was turned into a swallow;[3] Tereus became a hoopoe in Sophocles, though he may have become a hawk in earlier versions. The tragedy could not have encompassed all of this narrative and it is generally agreed that the dramatic action covered the final parts of this outline.

The myth: literary and artistic evidence[3a]

The evidence for the myth shows that two versions of the myth, both aetiologies explaining the nightingale's song, existed from an early period.

---

[1] Particularly since the publication in 1974 of a papyrus (*POxy* 3013) containing what is most likely the Hypothesis to Sophocles' tragedy. Although the papyrus is damaged – the right-hand side of the second of the two columns is completely lost – it is, nevertheless, possible to retrieve an overall reading in which important features are not in doubt because the Hypothesis is similar to several other summaries of the story. These are Tzetzes (on Hes. *Works* 566) and two Aristophanic scholia (on *Birds* 212). D.F. Sutton, *GRBS* 29 (1988) 90 n.13, thinks that the version in Tzetzes is indebted to the Aristophanic scholia which in turn had followed the Hypothesis. In this edition the Hypothesis has been printed before the fragments of the text.

[2] P.M.C. Forbes Irving (*Metamorphosis in Greek Myths* [Oxford, 1990]) 96–107 has argued that the pattern of bird transformation in this myth gives metaphorical expression to the perversion of order in house and family.

[3] In Roman versions, there was a tendency to have Procne turn into the swallow and Philomela into the nightingale.

[3a] We regret that the valuable study by Monella (2005) reached us too late for us to do more than draw attention to it here.

In one, Aëdon (Nightingale)[4] killed her son by mistake when attempting to murder a son of her brother-in-law because she was jealous of his wife who had more children than her.[5] In the other, which was the version followed by Sophocles, Aëdon is assisted in the, presumably, deliberate killing of her son by Chelidon (Swallow). Unfortunately, the evidence for this version can only be pieced together from some literary references and iconographic material,[6] and it is thus impossible to establish some aspects with certainty. The name of the child suggests that the two versions developed from a similar source. It is Itylus in some versions, but Itys has become the established name by the time of *Tereus*.[7]

The earliest pieces of evidence for the version followed by Sophocles are a painting, dated to the last third of the seventh century BC, on a metope in the temple of Apollo at Thermon, and a citation from an unidentified poem of the Hesiodic corpus. The metope depicts two women, one of whom is identified as Chelidon (= Swallow),[8] holding the body of a child (*LIMC* 1, March fig. 7.1). The Hesiodic citation goes as follows (Hes. fr. 312):

> Hesiod says that the nightingale is the only bird that has no care for sleep and is awake the entire night; the swallow is not awake for the complete night but loses half its sleep.[9]

---

[4] There is no evidence for the names Procne or Philomela in the early myth, though I sometimes use these names (and also that of Tereus) below, purely for convenience, in referring to early versions of the story. Were the two actually sisters in early myth? There is no evidence either way.

[5] It is referred to by Homer (*Od.* 19.518–523) and a scholiast on the passage gives a more detailed version of the same story and attributes it to Pherecydes (*FGrH* 3 F 124).

[6] The iconographic evidence in *LIMC* is discussed by Touloupa (1994) with some reproductions. It is also discussed by March (2000) with a fuller set of reproductions. We have included the references for both discussions, citing the *LIMC* numbers and the figure numbers for March.

[7] The fact that the name Itys appears on two red-figure cups which depict the different versions of the myth (Munich 2638 [= *LIMC* 2 and March fig. 7.1] and Cahn HC [= *LIMC* 3 and March fig. 7.5]) tends to support the argument that the two versions developed from the same source.

[8] Some, e.g. Gantz 240, say that the A of Aëdon is visible.

[9] The final sentence of this fragment as presented in MW has been excluded because it is in *oratio recta* (whereas the statements quoted above are in *oratio obliqua*) and should therefore be regarded as a statement by the citing author (Aelian *VH* 12.20) rather than by "Hesiod". The omitted line says, 'They pay this penalty because of the audacious act they undertook in Thrace relating to that impious banquet'. As Aelian was writing at the beginning of the third century AD, he may well have been influenced by later versions of

This evidence shows that the future nightingale and swallow were partners in the murder of Itys from an early period. The sleeping patterns of the birds in Hesiod indicate that the main responsibility for killing the child lies with the nightingale (= Procne). This aspect of this version of the myth is further corroborated in several vase paintings which date to the beginning of the fifth century BC. Some fragments of an Attic red-figure kylix depict the murder of Itys whose name appears on the vase (Cahn HC 599 = *LIMC* 3, March fig. 7.5). The fragments show that two women were involved in the killing, though neither of their names appears among the surviving fragments. Only one women has survived substantially, and she appears to be about to strike the fatal blow: this must be Procne. Some have thought that a red-figure cup (Louvre G 147 = *LIMC* 4, March fig. 7.4) shows Philomela taking the initiative in killing Itys, while Procne actually attempts to protect her son.[10] The woman on the left is armed with a sword, while the woman on the right has a child gripped by both arms. If the cup depicted this myth, as it surely does, then the woman with the sword must be Procne. Although Philomela assists in the killing of Itys, the main horror is that of a mother killing her son and in no known version is the killer anyone else.[11]

While the evidence for the early myth suggests that Sophocles inherited a coherent and established form of the story, there are, nevertheless, some serious gaps in what can be recovered from the earlier material. For example, there is no specific evidence for Tereus' treatment of Chelidon (=

---

the myth which had been influenced, in turn, by Sophocles' tragedy. However, while there are good grounds (see below) for the view that the Thracian location of the story was a fifth-century innovation, there is no positive reason for denying the filicide or the cannibalism to "Hesiod".

[10] B.A. Sparkes in C.G. Boulter ed. *Greek Art, Archaic into Classical: A Symposium held at the University of Cincinnati 2–3 April, 1982,* (Leiden, 1985) 31; Hourmouziades (1986) 141 n.28; Gantz 240; March (2000) 129–131.

[11] March (2000) has discussed the iconography related to this myth and expressed scepticism about the attribution of some vases to the myth. This sceptical treatment of the iconography is a vital part of March's unconvincing argument (further developed in *Shards* 143–151) that there is no clear evidence that Procne deliberately murdered Itys in versions of the myth before Sophocles. Her suggestion that the Makron kylix (Louvre G 147 = *LIMC* 4, March fig. 7.4) might depict the daughters of Minyas is unconvincing. Even less convincing is her interpretation of the surviving fragments of a kylix by Onesimos (Cahn HC = *LIMC* 3 and March fig. 7.5). We believe both pieces can be interpreted as showing the mother taking the lead in killing her son and indicate that this was a feature of the early myth.

Philomela), either for the rape or for the tongue removal.[12] It is highly probable that the cannibalism was a part of the early myth. The earliest evidence is a vase dated to the 460s (Villa Giulia 3579 = *LIMC* 6, March fig. 7.6);[13] there may be a reference to the cannibalism in Aesch. *Ag.* 1144–5.[14]

The various lacunae in our knowledge of the early myth make it difficult to gauge the extent of Sophoclean innovation in the tragedy. However, it may be possible to discern two features of the Sophoclean tragedy which subsequently became canonical features of the myth.[15] First, there is no evidence in earlier versions of the myth for the metamorphosis of Tereus into a hoopoe. A reference in Aeschylus' *Suppliants* suggests that Tereus may have been turned into a hawk: the chorus sing about "Aëdon, the hawk-chased wife of Tereus" (*Supp.* 62). And in a later version of the myth, Hyginus (*Fab.* 45) has Tereus turned into a hawk. The second aspect is his locating of the dramatic action in Thrace. Thucydides (2.29.3) writes:

> Tereus lived in Daulis, which is now called Phocis, but was then inhabited by Thracians. And the women did the deed concerning Itys in this land (indeed many poets when referring to the nightingale call it the Daulian bird).

Except for Sophocles' play, this passage is the earliest explicit connection of the myth with Thrace, and Thucydides' protestations are significant. His assertion that Tereus lived in Phocis, together with the claim that the

---

[12] There may be some implicit evidence for the tongue removal. The twittering of the swallow was a traditional metaphor for people, particularly non-Greeks, who spoke inarticulately or unintelligibly: see Dunbar on Ar. *Birds* 1680–1 and Dover on Ar. *Frogs* 93. Is it possible that this myth with its tale of tongue-removal originated in part as an aetiology for the twittering of the swallow?

[13] March (2000) 133 suggests that the vase might depict the Thyestes myth, but does not argue for this view which is extremely unlikely. Why would two women serve Thyestes' sons to him on behalf of Atreus? And who are they?

[14] As the passage follows Cassandra's allusion to the murder and cannibalism in the house of Atreus (Aesch. *Ag.* 1090–2), this interpretation is a strong possibility. It would be strengthened by Page's emendations of the text at 1145–6; see J.D. Denniston and D.L. Page, *Aeschylus: Agamemnon* (Oxford, 1957) 173–5.

[15] It is generally accepted that the Sophoclean tragedy gave the myth its canonical version. See Dobrov (1993) 198–200 for references.

nightingale is known as the Daulian bird,[16] suggests that the Thracian setting was a Sophoclean innovation.[17] The association of the story with Athens, on the other hand, appears to be of much earlier origin: both Hesiod (*Works* 568) and Sappho (fr. 135) describe Chelidon as the daughter of Pandion.[18]

The preceding discussion has looked at aspects of the myth before, and including, Sophocles' tragedy. Before looking at the literary and artistic material after Sophocles, there are some contemporaneous versions to examine briefly. The only other fifth century tragedian who is known to have created a tragedy from the myth was Philocles (though both Aeschylus and Euripides refer to it). His *Pandionis* tetralogy, like Sophocles' play (see §4 below), must have been produced before 414 when Aristophanes' *Birds* (281–2) alludes to it; moreover, the *Birds* passage appears to suggest that Philocles' tetralogy was produced later than Sophocles' tragedy and was heavily influenced by it.[19] At any rate, so little survives of this tetralogy that it is impossible to say anything about it. The myth and its handling by the tragic poets provided some paratragic potential for Aristophanes, and also for other comic dramatists: one Old Comic poet – Cantharus (frr. 5–9) – and two Middle Comic poets – Anaxandrides (frr. 46–48) and Philetaerus (frr. 15–16) – wrote plays entitled *Tereus*, presumably burlesques of the myth and perhaps of the tragedies based upon it, but the surviving fragments of these comedies throw little light on their treatment of the story.

---

[16] There is no surviving instance of this 'Daulian bird' in Greek poetry, but there are several in Latin poetry (Catullus 65.14 and Ovid *Her.* 15.154). It is unlikely that the phrase would have found its way into Latin poetry, if it were not an established one in Greek.

[17] S. Hornblower (*A Commentary on Thucydides. Volume 1, Books 1–3* [Oxford, 1991]) 287 thinks that Thucydides may even be correcting Sophocles.

[18] March (2000) 127–8 (also *Shards* 146) urges great caution about assuming that the Pandions of Hesiod and Sappho are to be identified as the Athenian king. Admittedly, establishing a precise genealogy of Pandion is very difficult, but the two occurrences of Pandion in two different authors seem irresistible, and we know of no other mythical Pandion who could have been the father of the future swallow. We do not think that, as in the case of the names Itylus and Itys, Pandion is a simple doublet for the Pandareos of *Odyssey* 19.518. If anything, it is more likely that 'Pandareos' there is an error (by the poet) for 'Pandion', due to confusion with the quite different story about the daughters of Pandareos which is told in Odyssey 20.66–78. Pausanias (1.41.8) says that Pandion was king of Athens and Megara. Zacharia (2001) 101–4 examines this connection in respect of the tragedy's possible exploitation of supposed mythical links for political purposes.

[19] See Sommerstein, and Dunbar, on Birds 281–2.

Given the gaps in the earlier versions of the myth, there has been a tendency to rely on later versions – especially literary versions and references in mythographers – to reveal the likely plot of Sophocles' lost play. It is important, for this reason, to make a clear distinction between the early versions of the myth and later versions when examining *Tereus*, and to exercise caution in the use of the latter, in view of the risk of importing backwards into the lost tragedy ideas and motifs which do not belong there.

Two Roman tragedians, Livius Andronicus (late third century BC) and Accius (170–c.86 BC), wrote *Tereus* plays which, like all other Roman tragedies before Seneca, survive only in fragments,[20] six of Livius' play and seventeen of Accius'. In some discussions of Sophocles' play, there has been a tendency to assume that Accius was simply a Latin translation of the Sophoclean play, and the Accian fragments are taken as actual Sophoclean fragments![21] Notwithstanding the Roman tendency to borrow, it is sheer folly to assume identification where there is no clear evidence to support this assumption.[22] At any rate, neither the fragments of Accius nor those of Livius permit a reconstruction of their plots. It is, therefore, impossible to see how either may have been influenced by Sophocles and to establish retrospectively aspects of the Sophoclean tragedy.

The most detailed surviving literary treatment of the myth in Latin literature is in Ovid's *Metamorphoses* (6.424–674). This narrative has had a profound and, arguably, a detrimental effect on reconstructing Sophocles' tragedy.[23] As there is discussion of Ovid's handling of the myth in other parts of this Introduction and in the Commentary on several of the fragments, it will not be discussed in detail at this point. However, it is worth stating clearly that the narrative style of the *Metamorphoses* allowed Ovid to develop aspects of the myth which could not have been handled in a dramatic version.[24] So, for example, there is some

---

[20] Accius frr. 639–655 Warmington and Livius Andronicus frr. 24–29 Warmington.

[21] See, for example, Kiso 63–74 and Sutton 127–132.

[22] See the remarks by Dan Curley in *Shards* 180–2. Although arguing that Ovid was following Sophocles, Curley shows clearly that Ovid was familiar with, and influenced by, the Accian tragedy.

[23] One of us has contended elsewhere (Fitzpatrick [2001] 90–101), and we still believe, that any reconstruction of the tragedy should be guided by *POxy* 3013. Curley, however, has argued recently (*Shards* 183) that "the *Metamorphoses* upholds the plots of extant tragedies, especially those which forever changed their respective myths, [and therefore] it is reasonable to expect the same treatment of innovative lost tragedies like the *Tereus*".

[24] Cf. Curley *Shards* 168.

development of, and concentration on, the ordeal of Philomela. This is, undoubtedly, a very significant contrast with Sophocles' play, especially the fact that Ovid actually allows Philomela to speak and denounce Tereus (6.533–548).

As indicated earlier, artistic evidence is an important element in establishing the versions of the myth which inspired the Sophoclean tragedy. There is not, however, much in the way of artistic evidence to assist the reconstruction of *Tereus* itself. Two vases are thought to be representations of the play, one possibly and the other certainly, though neither assists reconstruction of the dramatic action in any serious way.

The first vase is a Lucanian bell crater (Louvre CA 2193) dated to the second half of the fourth century BC. In his catalogue of Lucanian red-figured vases, Trendall attributed the scene to Euripides' *Medea*,[25] but many who have considered the *Tereus* believe that it relates to the *anagnorisis* (recognition scene) in this play.[26] The vase depicts four people, but none of them are specifically identified. Moving from left to right, the figures are male, female, female and male. If the scene does represent *Tereus*, then the male and female figures on the left must be Tereus and Procne respectively. The other two figures are more problematical and their identification depends on how one reconstructs the plot. The woman presenting a gift to Procne might be Philomela herself or, along the lines of Ovid (6.578–580), some servant. The second male figure is more difficult. It seems from his worried expression and gesture that he knows the true meaning of the situation. The vase poses many problems. Even if it does represent *Tereus*, it cannot be assumed to be presenting a specific scene from the play.

The second depiction is on a Campanian fragment from a vase by the Caivano Painter (Dresden PV 2891 = *LIMC* 9) which is dated to the second half of the fourth century BC.[27] The architectural feature of an open door and the elaborate costume of the central male figure, who is rushing out of the door, indicate the "dramatic" nature of the scene. There are two women, one on either side of the male figure, of which one survives substantially. So, if the scene is from Sophocles' *Tereus*, it appears to show Tereus rushing from the palace in pursuit of the two sisters when he

---

[25] A.D. Trendall, *The Red-figured Vases of Lucania, Campania and Sicily* (Oxford, 1967) 100. For a reproduction of the vase, see *LIMC* vi.2 under Kreousa 2.1.

[26] For references, see Dobrov (1993) 209 n.47.

[27] For a reproduction, see M. Bieber, *The History of the Greek and Roman Theater*[2] (London, 1961) 29 fig. 105.

has realised what he has eaten. The vase is often considered in the context of the following reference in Aristophanes' *Lysistrata* (563):

> There was another, a Thracian, brandishing a light shield and a javelin, just like Tereus, and he frightened the fig vendor.

If this reference is inspired by the Sophoclean tragedy, it suggests that an aggressive and armed Tereus appeared on stage to pursue the women and exact revenge upon them. The vase fragment does not obviously depict an armed Tereus, but he appears to have originally had something in his right hand.[28] Such a scene presumably belongs near the end of the tragedy. The scene bears some comparison with the mid fifth-century column-krater discussed earlier (Villa Giulia 3579 = *LIMC* 6 and March 7.6).

The play

No fragment survives with its known dramatic context.[29] For a number of fragments there has been general consensus on where they belong, but it is far from certain that such consensus is merited except, perhaps, in respect of those fragments which are thought to belong at the end of the play. As the Commentary will discuss each fragment in detail, this section examines several matters related to the reconstruction of the play – characters, plot and theme – in light of the arguments which are articulated in the Commentary.

Dramatic location and characters

It was shown earlier that the play was innovatively set in Thrace (cf. fr. A [582]). The *skene* must have represented the royal palace of Thrace. Identifying all of the *dramatis personae* is impossible, though it has been attempted several times.[30] The fragments confirm only one character for certain and this is Procne (fr. C [585]). It can be assumed that Tereus and

---

[28] Dobrov (1993) 209 n.47 suggests that Tereus holds an axe and, citing M. Bieber (*MDAI[A]* 101 [1925] 11–18), a part of a bone in his right hand.

[29] As presented by Radt, there are seventeen fragments. Four are, or appear to be, from choral songs and do not assist reconstruction. There are three non-choral fragments of five lines or more, six that consist of one or two lines, and four that comprise only one or two words each.

[30] e.g. Calder (1974) 88, Kiso 60–2, Dobrov (1993) 199.

Philomela were characters, though the latter was mute.[31] The child, Itys, might also have made a silent appearance.[32] A fragment addressed to a man who can hardly have been Tereus suggests that there was another male character (fr. G [588]). It has been supposed that Procne had some sort of female confidant, but this is conjecture.[33] Such a role could have been taken by the chorus which almost certainly consisted of Thracian women (see fr. B [584]). The play concluded with a *deus ex machina* and there have been several suggestions about the likely identity of this deity (see frr. M [581] and N [589]).

A central interpretative problem

Before considering the likely course of the dramatic action, it is necessary to address what is arguably the central interpretative issue bearing on the reconstruction of the plot. Until recently, there had been a fairly consistent line from the earliest considerations of the play in which the reconstruction of the plot was heavily influenced by the narrative in Ovid's *Metamorphoses* (6.424–674). Now, however, there is growing scepticism about the wisdom of this reliance.[34] Nevertheless, once the dependence on Ovid crept into analyses of the play, it has been hard to break free from its influence entirely. In Ovid, Tereus, having fallen in love with Philomela on the journey from Athens, incarcerates her in a hut in the countryside when he arrives in Thrace. It is there that he rapes her and cuts out her tongue, and then, having returned home, tells Procne that her sister died on the journey to Thrace. After a year has passed, Philomela contrives to have the truth revealed to Procne by weaving a *peplos* and having a servant convey the article to Procne. Dressed as a Bacchic maenad, Procne effects

---

[31] In light of Sophocles' early retirement from acting because of a weak voice (*Life of Sophocles* §4), it is sometimes thought, e.g. by Calder (1974) 88, that Sophocles may have played this role. This is no more than fanciful speculation.

[32] Both Sophocles and Euripides made great dramatic use of silent children, where appropriate. Some Sophoclean examples are Eurysaces in *Ajax* 545–82 and Oedipus' daughters in *OT* 1471–1523.

[33] e.g. Calder (1974) 87, Sutton 129, Kiso 61, Dobrov (1993) 199. It is based on an analogy with *Trachiniae* which, in turn, assumes that the prologues of the two plays were similar. Fitzpatrick (2001) 92–93 suggested that Procne ought to be in a mood of happy anticipation because of Philomela's imminent arrival. But we no longer subscribe to the implications of this view. Sophoclean tragedies begin with a dramatic situation in which something is amiss and needs to be addressed. As in *Trachiniae*, the *Tereus* could have opened with some ominous reference to the absence of Tereus and his anticipated return.

[34] Cf. Burnett (1998) 180.

the release of Philomela and this leads towards the revenge and metamorphoses. Incorporating all aspects of the Ovidian narrative poses a serious problem for establishing a dramatic performance which retains the semblance of continuity of action within a single day that is common in tragedy.[35] In many respects, the problem with using the narrative in Ovid can be reduced to one feature which one of us has called elsewhere 'the internment of Philomela' (Fitzpatrick [2001] 96). A handful of other problems are all related to this feature. Some are very significant, e.g. the *anagnorisis*, and others, arguably, are minor, e.g. the Dionysiac element. While many aspects of the plot will always remain unclear, it has been increasingly recognised that solving the issue of internment has a significant impact on how the plot is reconstructed and how the surviving fragments are interpreted and arranged. There has also been a growing consensus that the internment was not part of the Sophoclean tragedy.[36] The removal of the internment creates a canvas on which it is possible to see typical (Sophoclean) tragic situations around which to build a credible Sophoclean tragedy. The general move against including the internment has been accompanied by a growing, though often implicit, acceptance that *Tereus* was a *nostos* play and that Tereus returned to Thrace with a mute Philomela.[37]

The plot of Tereus

The following outline of the play will not break the action into specific episodes.[38] Working from the Hypothesis, and mindful of some typical scene types in a (Sophoclean) tragedy, this outline suggests a possible arrangement of scenes or, more accurately, action sequences. Based on the outline below, the fragments in the following text/translation section have been placed in an order which reflects this outline.

The play begins at a point before Tereus' return from Athens. The opening scenes would have set up the return, possibly employing a palace servant

---

[35] On this semblance of continuity of action, see the remarks by O.P. Taplin, *The Stagecraft of Aeschylus* (Oxford, 1977) 290–4 and 377–9.

[36] Dobrov (1993) 201 offers what is, perhaps, the most persuasive dramatic situation for the internment by making Tereus' return an event before the beginning of the dramatic action. However, this view is dependent on Ovid and also on a misunderstanding, we believe, of the place of fr. E (583) in the play.

[37] On the *nostos* pattern in tragedy – wife home alone, husband due to return – see the remarks by Taplin *op.cit.* 125–6 and 302–3.

[38] This has been attempted several times without much success; e.g., Kiso 63–74, Hourmouziades (1986) 138–9.

or a Herald of Tereus (fr. A [582]). The audience would have been
introduced to Procne through her exchange with this figure and the chorus
of Thracian women (fr. B [584]). When Tereus returns, he lies to Procne
about Philomela (fr. C [585]). The nature of this lie is the subject of
contrary opinions. Did Tereus lie about Philomela's dumbness, claiming
that it was an affliction that had struck her spontaneously as if by divine
visitation? Or did he, as March has suggested, tell Procne that Philomela
had died, but actually introduce her into the palace as a servant?[39] The
former alternative has some attractions, in view of the possible thematic
status of communication in the play; but the latter appears to be supported
by the first words of fr. E (583), "Now … I am nothing *on my own*", which
show that at some stage of the action Procne believed that she was entirely
isolated. At any rate, the lie is subsequently undone in an *anagnorisis*
which, as Aristotle's *Poetics* confirms, was effected in a dramatically
contrived manner through a piece of weaving (fr. F [595]), so that Procne
learns that her sister is alive, dishonoured, and mutilated. It is very likely
that Procne and Philomela were on stage during the recognition scene.
Earlier reconstructions, under the influence of Ovid's narrative, have
tended to assume that this potentially powerful scene occurred off-stage. It
is also possible that a male character confirmed the truth (fr. G [588]) of
the 'shuttle's voice' (fr. F [595]). The sequence of events after the
anagnorisis which leads to the revenge is very uncertain. It undoubtedly,
however, included the hatching of Procne's revenge plan. This was
presumably articulated on stage and may have involved an appearance of
Itys. Next will have come, offstage, the murder and the banquet (doubtless
with a break in the stage action filled by a choral song). What followed
then? As noted earlier, there is some evidence that Tereus' pursuit of the
sisters was a feature of the play (see pp.148–9 above); and fr. K (587)
suggests that the play included a bitter *agon* between Procne and Tereus.
Since such a quarrel between them *before* the banquet would have put
Tereus on his guard against his wife, it is more likely to have taken place
afterwards. Perhaps the sisters rushed out of the palace in flight from an
enraged Tereus, who must have somehow become, or been made, aware
that he had eaten the flesh of his son; Tereus, coming out after them,
denounced them and explained what had happened at the feast;[40] Procne

---

[39] March (2000) 135–6 n.44, and *Shards* 158, on the basis of Ant. Lib. *Met.* 11.

[40] There may have been a rather similar sequence, involving Achilles and Odysseus, in
Syndeipnoi (see pp.[65–66]); in extant drama the nearest parallel is in Aristophanes' *Clouds*
(1321ff).

defended herself and in turn denounced Tereus' crimes, Tereus' fury was unabated, and the women fled along an *eisodos* with Tereus following shortly after. A choral ode may have separated this sequence from the dénouement. Perhaps a messenger returned to relate details of the chase (fr. L [586]). It is virtually certain that the action culminated in a *deus ex machina* scene in which some deity related details of the metamorphosis (fr. M [581]) effected by another god, probably Zeus, and commented on the action (fr. N [589]).

The revenge of Procne

As the myth is an aetiology which explains the mournful song of the nightingale, the emphasis of the tragedy itself must have been on the revenge of Procne.[41] If the tragedy were a *nostos* play, then Procne would, most probably, have been on stage from a point close to the beginning and for a considerable length of the dramatic action thereafter.[42] As with several characters in the extant Sophoclean tragedies, Procne may have experienced several emotional highs and lows: initial anxious anticipation of her sister's arrival; the shock of her sister's reported death (or of her dumbness); the 'recognition' of the truth; and the devastation which is then overturned by an extreme and gruesome revenge. How would the original Athenian audience, which, at least predominantly, would have been made up of men, have reacted to the extreme revenge of this Athenian princess? As the recognition of Tereus' mistreatment of Philomela leads to the revenge, it may seem that the rape and mutilation of her sister provokes Procne's revenge. It is true that rape, or the avenging of rape, might not necessarily in itself have guaranteed the sympathy of the male audience. The legal status of rape in Athens is not altogether clear, but, as women had little standing in Athenian law except in relation to men, it is possible that Procne's revenge could have been viewed negatively.[43] It was not

---

[41] Hourmouziades (1986) 138 proposed the inclusion of the Dryas episode which is mentioned in Hyginus *Fab.* 45. Hyginus says that Tereus, having been warned by divination that a relative would kill his son, murdered his brother, Dryas. Dobrov (1993) 202 n.34, however, observes that if this were a feature of Sophocles' tragedy, it would have been cited in more post-Sophoclean sources.

[42] Several Sophoclean tragedies have one figure with a lengthy stage presence: e.g. Electra in *El.*, Creon in *Ant.*, Oedipus in *OT*. In fact, Electra and Procne share a common goal – to avenge paternal honour.

[43] A.H. Sommerstein (in D.L. Cairns and V. Liapis ed. *Dionysalexandros: Studies on Greek Tragedy Presented to Alexander F. Garvie* [Swansea, forthcoming]) has shown, contrary to a currently popular view about rape, that a classical Athenian male would have

unusual for rape to be punished, but, as rape was essentially an act of dishonour against a man, such redress would have been sought by the woman's husband, father or *kyrios*. However, what we have here is a rape that is aggravated by a cruel mutilation of a kind that Greeks abhorred. There is also another aspect to the matter. Although Tereus has physically assaulted Philomela, he has also insulted Procne and their marriage.[44] In Athenian marriages, a woman was essentially 'lent' to the husband by her father and, consequently, a father retained some influence and interest in the life of a married daughter.[45] This also illuminates an aspect of a wife's relationship to her husband and his *oikos*: a woman never fully severed her connection to the paternal home. The plot of many tragedies is built around the tensions between husbands and wives. As a woman retained strong loyalty to her natal family, this loyalty could manifest itself in displaying support for her natal family should their interests clash with those of her husband or his family. The woman could abandon her husband's interests in favour of her father's, or even go so far as to kill her husband or his relations.[46] As the children from her marriage were considered part of her

---

been concerned with issues relating to a (free) woman's consent to sex in these circumstances. If this is correct, since the sources clearly indicate that Tereus raped Philomela against her will, the original audience might well have viewed her plight, and Procne's anger, sympathetically, even apart from the considerations presently to be mentioned. On the other hand, a fragment from the *Tereus* of the Old Comedy poet, Cantharus (fr. 7), looks as though it was addressed to Philomela by someone who is suggesting, in an all too familiar way to a rape victim, that she had "asked for it".

[44] The Hypothesis (lines 24–26) indicates that Procne was motivated by jealousy. Although the papyrus is lacunose at this point, it does describe Procne as "driven mad by jealousy" when she learnt the truth. While this jealousy may reflect the sexual jealousy of Aëdon in the Theban version of the myth, it also suggests that Procne appears to have been as much angered by Tereus' betrayal of herself as by his treatment of her sister. (Or was she at first irrationally angry *with Philomela*, only later to realize – maybe with the assistance of the chorus – against whom her anger ought properly to be directed? But for a gap of seven lines or so in the Hypothesis papyrus, we might have known.) Although the situation is not identical, see the comments on the 'disastrous' *ménage à trois* in Eur. *Andr.* by M. Lloyd ([ed.] *Euripides: Andromache* [Warminster, 1994]) 6–9. Athenian men were free to pursue sexual relations outside the home, but there were limitations on what was socially acceptable. In tragedy (e.g. Aesch. *Ag.* and Soph. *Trach.*), introducing a mistress into the wife's home is a fatal error; and this is in effect what Tereus has done, though the "mistress" is an unwilling victim and the wife becomes her ally.

[45] A woman's dowry was a tangible sign of her ongoing connection with the paternal home. See L. Foxhall, *CQ* 39 (1989) 32–39.

[46] In this context, it is important to note Antigone's argument in Soph. *Ant.* 905–12 that brothers are more important than husbands or sons. The passage is considered by some to

husband's family line, a mother might even kill her own child in support of her natal family.[47] Ultimately, Tereus' actions towards the women are a betrayal of their father's trust in him. Burnett has given the correct lead in understanding the revenge theme when she says that Procne kills Itys "to restore the honour of her paternal house, in retaliation against a husband who had broken faith with her father".[48] Although Procne's infanticide is often compared to Medea's in the Euripidean tragedy, there is a very significant difference in the contexts of both acts: Medea abandoned her natal family to follow Jason (cf. Eur. *Med.* 165–7 and 483–5), whereas Procne obeyed her father's wishes in marrying Tereus. While their act of revenge is similar, its reception by the original audience would have been radically different. The Athenian men would have considered Procne's act of revenge as justifiable.[49]

The revenge theme in *Tereus* should not be understood solely as a clash between husband and wife, conjugal and natal families. As noted earlier, the Thracian setting was an innovation. Sophocles' relocation of the dramatic action to Thrace was undoubtedly due to the fact that the Thracians were firmly established in Athenian consciousness as a stereotypical barbaric race.[50] It seems, therefore, that Sophocles was deliberately placing the tragedy in the context of an Athenian and Thracian

---

be an interpolation, but was known to Aristotle (*Rhet.* 1417a32–33) as Sophoclean; for a discussion of its authenticity and references, see Griffith on *Ant.* 904–915.

[47] McHardy (2005) stresses the element of personal revenge and suggests that the original audience would have viewed Procne unfavourably because she was acting under the influence "of excessive passion associated with madness" (144).

[48] Burnett (1998) 179. This idea is present in Ovid *Met.* (cf. 6.496–501, 534–5) too.

[49] Burnett (1998) 190 and Zacharia (2001) 106–8 have noted that Sophocles could not have condemned the revenge. It is worth pointing out that Procne's action, though deliberate, was not taken without sadness. Her transformation into the nightingale which mourns her dead son indicates this. Euripides, in contrast, does not allow Medea to express any grief for her children after their death (*Med.* 1317–1404).

[50] See E.M. Hall, *Inventing the Barbarian: Greek Self-definition through Tragedy* (Oxford, 1989), 104–5 and 126. There are examples of several other treacherous Thracians on the Attic stage, e.g. Polymestor in Eur. *Hec.* and Eumolpos in Eur. *Erechtheus*. R. Degl'Innocenti Pierini (in S. Faller and G. Manuwald ed. *Accius und seine Zeit* [Würzburg, 2002] 127–139) has shown that the barbaric character of Tereus which is present in Accius, and indeed Latin literature, is probably a motif that had its origins in the Sophoclean tragedy. D. Tsiafakis (in B. Cohen [ed.] *Not the Classical Ideal: Athens and the Construction of the Other in Greek Art* [Leiden, 2000] 364–389) has highlighted the apparent paradox of fifth century Athenian fascination with, and repulsion by, the Thracian race.

(= barbarian) conflict too.[51] This, in turn, suggests that Sophocles was incorporating this stereotype about barbaric Thracians to enhance both the character and the tragedy of Procne. While Sophocles played up the horror of a mother sacrificing her child to uphold the honour of her paternal family, he was also reinforcing Athenian chauvinist attitudes.

A potential difficulty with this notion of a 'positive' Procne is that there is no evidence for it earlier than Sophocles' tragedy.[52] However, it can be established indirectly that Procne was viewed favourably in the Athenian imagination. An important example is the funeral speech attributed to Demosthenes (60). In this speech, the speaker praises each of the ten tribes in turn by recalling an event associated with its history. When it comes to the Pandionidae, the speaker declares (60.28),

> The Pandionidae had inherited the tradition of Procne and Philomela, the daughters of Pandion, who took vengeance on Tereus for his crime against them. They [the Pandionidae] hold that life is not worth living for them, if they do not show themselves as having the same spirit as those women, when an outrage is committed against Greece.

Notwithstanding the rhetorical nature of the speech, it is impossible to imagine that this point would have had any effect on its audience unless the idea was firmly established in the Athenian consciousness that Procne and her act ought to be viewed in favourable terms. It is, of course, impossible to say how much influence Sophocles may have had in establishing this tradition about Procne. An example more contemporaneous with Sophocles is a piece of sculpture on the Acropolis by Alcamenes, a pupil of Pheidias, which depicted Procne and Itys.[53] Pausanias described it as follows (1.24.3):

---

[51] Kiso 81 denies that this is an important element of the tragedy and reads it in a more liberal light: either simple Sophoclean interest in the non-Greek world or a text about the latent barbarity in both sides of the opposition. When Kiso 56 observes that Sophocles was "second to none in his love for his country and yet was free from racial prejudice", this betrays a desire to view Sophocles in terms which we would now describe as 'politically correct'.

[52] In this context, it is worth noting that some passages in Cicero mention a posthumous performance of Accius' *Tereus* in which the audience's reaction to the revenge implied support for the conspirators who had assassinated Caesar: Cic. *Att.* 16.2, 16.3 and *Phil.* 1.36.

[53] It is sometimes thought that the statue was erected on the occasion of Sophocles' victory in the tragic festival with his *Tereus*: see, most recently, March *Shards* 154. Assuming such a connection, J. Carter (*AJA* 85 [1981] 189) suggests an emendation of the text of Pausanias to make him say that the sculpture was "dedicated [by Sophocles and

Alcamenes dedicated Procne and Itys, when she has taken her decision against the boy.

Item 1358 in the Acropolis Museum is what remains of the depiction of Procne and Itys (*LIMC* 11). Although the precise nature of the pose is not evident from what remains,[54] it shows Itys within his mother's grasp. As Pausanias makes clear, the sculptor chose to depict the moment when Procne has decided to kill her son and is about to strike the fatal blow. It illustrates an Athenian mother sacrificing her child to uphold Athenian honour, and this, in turn, indicates that Procne was a significant figure in the Athenian imagination of the late fifth century BC.[55] Was Sophocles following an established myth? Or was he the myth-maker?

Date

The performance date of *Tereus* is uncertain, though the parody in Aristophanes' *Birds* establishes a *terminus ante quem* of 414 BC.[56]

---

made] by Alkamenes". This is no more than speculation and is unlikely to be true. At any rate, the sculpture, as J.M. Hurwit (*The Athenian Acropolis: History, Mythology, and Archaeology from the Neolithic Era to the Present* [Cambridge, 1999]) 231 has observed, "does not much look like a victory monument".

[54] It is generally thought that Procne is about to strike Itys fatally with her left hand, but P.N. Boulter ('Review of *Antike Plastik Lieferung XVII*', *AJA* 84 [1980] 385–7, at 386) observes that "muscles of Prokne's right forearm indicate that she held the knife in that hand, instead of the left as it is often restored. This explains the movement of the child, who looks back at the murder weapon and attempts to hide in the folds of the peplos".

[55] Touloupa (1994) lists two other possible representations of Procne on the Parthenon. The first is metope 20 from the south side of the temple (*LIMC* 12). The metope belongs in a sequence of nine metopes which, unlike the rest of the metopes on this side, do not depict the battle between the Centaurs and Lapiths. Although the relationship between these nine metopes and the rest of the sequence remains unexplained, A. Mantis ('Parthenon Central South Metopes: New Evidence', in D. Buitron-Oliver ed. *The Interpretation of Architectural Sculpture in Greece and Rome* [Washington, 1997] 67–81, at 76) has now shown that metopes 19 and 20 are to be taken together and illustrate the making of a new piece of cloth. This sequence should not be considered as depicting the *anagnorisis* between the sisters. The second possible depiction is from the West Pediment (*LIMC* 13). The central scene depicted the struggle between Athena and Poseidon for the land of Attica. On either side of this scene, there are the fragmentary remains of several female figures which are thought to be figures from Attic myth. The poor state of preservation makes identification impossible. And in her recent consideration of the West Pediment, O. Palagia (*The Pediments of the Parthenon* [Leiden, 1993]) does not refer to the presence of Procne at all.

[56] It is, perhaps, possible to bring the *terminus ante quem* back to the late 420s. Cantharus, the Old Comic poet who wrote a *Tereus*, won first prize at the City Dionysia of

Attempts for anything more precise, or even an approximation, are speculative. A variety of methods have been tried, e.g. historical data[57] and metrical evidence,[58] but without success. One of the most significant issues in respect of dating is the relationship between *Tereus* and Euripides' *Medea*. The Euripidean tragedy is securely dated to 431 BC and debate focuses on the question which tragedy influenced the other in respect of the filicide.[59] In this context, the case for the priority of Sophocles rests on the fact that the filicide was an established part of the myth while it appears to have been an innovation in Euripides. Certainly the fact that *Tereus* was parodied by Aristophanes in 414 cannot be taken to exclude the possibility of its having been produced in the early 430s; one need only think of the period between Euripides' *Telephus* (438) and its parody in Aristophanes' *Thesmophoriazusae* (411).[60] In fact, Sophocles' production of 438 BC, the titles of which are unknown, defeated a production by

---

422 (Cantharus testt. 2 and 3 K-A). Since there are more fragments attributed to his *Tereus* (five) than to all his other plays combined, the *Tereus* may well have been his 422 comedy and might, in turn, provide a *terminus ante quem* of 422 for Sophocles' play. Interestingly, two of Cantharus' four other known plays were called *Nightingales* and *Medea*. The appearance of an apparent quotation from *Tereus* (fr. R [595b]) in a papyrus fragment of Eupolis' comedy *Taxiarchs* is not as helpful as one might have hoped, since there is no agreement on the date of *Taxiarchs*, some favouring 428 or 427, others 415 (see I.C. Storey, *Eupolis, Poet of Old Comedy* [Oxford, 2003] 246–8).

[57] Such discussions tend to place it between 431 and 425. For references, see *TrGF* 436 and Kiso 146 n.86.

[58] See comm. on fr. D (591). Discussions of the subject tend to place the play in the 430s or earlier: see *TrGF* 436 and Kiso 145–6 n.85 for references. As there are similarities between the lyric metres of *Tereus* and *Trachiniae*, the issue is complicated by the uncertainty over the date of the latter play which might be anything between 457 and 430 BC (P.E. Easterling, *Sophocles: Trachiniae* [Cambridge, 1982] 19–23).

[59] We can almost certainly rule out the possibility that the two plays were produced simultaneously, even though we know that Sophocles did compete in the Dionysia of 431: the combination, in both plays, of a Greek/barbarian couple, the deliberate killing of a son or sons by their mother, and a speech by that mother deploring the lot of women with special reference to marriage (fr. E [583] ~ *Med.* 214–266) cannot be coincidental. One of the two plays must have been composed by an author, and for an audience, that knew the other; the only question is which. The somewhat comparable uncertainty over the relative dating of Sophocles' and Euripides' *Electra* plays still remains unresolved, despite our having both plays complete; contrast M.J. Cropp, *Euripides: Electra* (Warminster, 1988) xlviii-l with J.R. March, *Sophocles: Electra* (Warminster, 2001) 20–22.

[60] It is worth bearing in mind that Philocles' version was produced at a point between Sophocles' and *Birds*, and it could have functioned as the reminder for the Athenian audience of Sophocles' play.

Euripides which included *Telephus* and *Alcestis*. Was *Tereus* part of this production? The case for the priority of *Medea* has been stated recently at length by March,[61] who bases her argument on the fact that the Euripidean chorus, in the ode immediately after the murder of Medea's children, sing that Ino is the one and only precedent for what Medea has done (Eur. *Med.* 1282–3). One would *prima facie* take this as implying that the story of Itys being deliberately murdered by his mother did not yet exist in 431; but, as we have seen (pp. 143–5), it is very hard to square such an inference with the iconographic evidence. We should therefore conclude, not that *Tereus* is necessarily later than *Medea*, but that *if* it is earlier, then Euripides has made his chorus ignore the Procne/Itys precedent – and expected his audience, or many of them, to notice this. Could this be because of a crucial difference between Ino's case on the one hand, and both Procne's and Medea's on the other? Ino was "maddened by the gods" (*Med.* 1284), and her killing of her son was apparently motiveless;[62] Procne, like Medea, had the powerful, and socially recognized, motive of revenge for a grave wrong. The chorus think of Medea as a second Ino, i.e. mad; Jason (*Med.* 1339–40) says that "no Greek woman would ever have dared to do this"; the audience know that a Greek – indeed an Athenian – woman *did* dare to do it, and for the same kind of reason. This line of thought does not prove that *Tereus* was indeed earlier than *Medea*; but it does show that such a chronology is not ruled out by *Med.* 1282–3.

---

[61] March (2000); March *Shards* 139–161.
[62] Euripides (cf. Mastronarde *ad loc.*) is apparently following a version of the story somewhat similar to that now found in [Apoll.] 3.4.3, in which Ino and her husband Athamas were both driven mad by Hera because they had cared for the child Dionysus, and each killed one of their children. Cf. R.M. Newton, *AJP* 106 (1985) 496–502.

ΤΗΡΕΥΣ

Hypothesis

Τηρεύς [· ἡ ὑ]πόθεσις.[2] [Π]ανδίων ὁ τῶν Ἀθηναίων δυν<άστ>ης,[3] [ἔ]χων
θυγατέρας Πρόκ<ν>ην καὶ Φιλο[4][μ]ήλαν, τὴν πρεσβυτέραν[5] Πρόκ<ν>ην
Τηρεῖ γάμῳ ἔζευξεν [τ]ῷ[6] [τῶ]ν Θρᾳκῶν βασιλεῖ, ὃς ἔσχεν ἐξ[7] [αὐ]τῆς
υἱὸν προσαγορεύσας[8] Ἴτυν. χρόνου δὲ διελθόντος καὶ[9] βουλομένης τῆς
Πρόκνης θεά[10]σασθαι τὴν ἀδελφήν, ἠξίωσε τὸν[11] Τηρέα πορεύσασθαι εἰς
Ἀθήνας[12] ἄξειν. ὁ δὲ παραγενόμενος εἰς[13] Ἀθήνας καὶ ἐπ[ιτρε]φθεὶς ὑπὸ[14]
τοῦ Πανδίονος [τὴν πα]ρθένον καὶ[15] μεσοπορήσας [ἠράσθ]η τῆς παι[16]δός·
ὁ δὲ τὰ πισ[τὰ οὐ φ]υλάξας[17] διεπαρθένευ[σεν, εὐλ]αβούμε[18]νος δὲ μὴ τῇ
ἀ[δελφῇ μηνύσῃ][19] ἐγλωσσοτόμη[σε τὴν παῖδα.][20] παραγενάμενος [δὲ εἰς
τὴν][21] Θρᾴκην καὶ τῆς Φ[ιλομήλας οὐ][22] δυναμένης [ἐκλαλεῖν τὴν][23]
συμφοράν, δι' ὕφο[υς ἐμήνυσε.][24] ἐπιγνοῦσα δὲ ἡ Πρ[όκνη τὴν ἀλή][25]
θειαν ζηλοτυπ[ίᾳ ....][26] οἰστρηθεῖσα καὶ [ca. 7][27] νη †υ . ερεινοις†
λα[βοῦσα τὸν][28] Ἴτυν ἐσφαγίασε [καὶ καθεψήσα][29]σα παρέθηκε [τῷ
Τηρεῖ, ὁ δὲ τὴν][30] βορὰν ἀγνοῶν [ἔφαγεν. αἱ δὲ φυγα][31]δευθεῖσαι
ἐγέ[νοντο ἡ μὲν][32] ἀηδών, ἡ δὲ χε[λιδών, ἔποψ][33] δὲ ὁ Τηρεύς.

Hypothesis *POxy* 3013 ed. P.J. Parsons (1974); supplements and
corrections are by Parsons unless otherwise noted | 5 πρεσβυτέραν Rea:
πρεσβυτερωτέραν pap. ‖ 25 τῇ ἐσχάτῃ suppl. Parsons ‖ 26–27
[μεμανημέ]νη ὑπ' Ἐρινύος Rea

TEREUS

Hypothesis

Tereus: [the Hy]pothesis. [P]andion, the ruler of Athens, who [h]ad two daughters, Procne and Philo[m]ela, gave the elder, Procne, to be united in marriage to Tereus, [t]he king of [th]e Thracians, who had a son by [h]er whom he named Itys. After some time had passed, when Procne wanted to see her sister, she asked Tereus to travel to Athens to bring her. He came to Athens, was en[trus]ted with [the ma]iden by Pandion, and midway on his journey he [became enamour]ed of the girl; [not k]eeping his pled[ge], he deflowe[red] her, and as a [pr]ecaution against her [revealing it] to her s[ister] he cu[t] out [the girl's] tongue. When he arrived [in] Thrace, Ph[ilomela was not] able [to speak about her] plight, [but she revealed it] through wea[ving]. Pr[ocne,] learning [the tr]uth, was stung by [the utmost(?)] jealous[y] and [madden]ed by a Fury (?) she to[ok] Itys, slaughtered him, [boil]ed him and served him [to Tereus, and he,] not knowing what [the] food was, [ate it. The women] were forced to [flee] and [one of them] be[came] a nightingale, the other a sw[allow], and Tereus [a hoopoe.]

A (582)

῞Ηλιε, φιλίπποις Θρηξὶ πρέσβιστον σέλας

A (582) Σ A *Iliad* 15.705 | Θρηξὶ Bekker : θριξὶ A | σέλας A: σέβας Bothe

B (584)

πολλά σε ζηλῶ βίου,
μάλιστα δ' εἰ γῆς μὴ πεπείρασαι ξένης.

B (584) Stobaeus 3.39.12 | μάλιστα Brunck : κάλλιστα codd.

C (585)

ἀλγεινά, Πρόκνη, δῆλον· ἀλλ' ὅμως χρεὼν
τὰ θεῖα θνητοὺς ὄντας εὐπετῶς φέρειν.

C (585) Stobaeus 4.44.58

D (591)

ἓν φῦλον ἀνθρώπων, μί' ἔδειξε πατρὸς
καὶ ματρὸς ἡμᾶς ἀμέρα τοὺς πάντας· οὐδεὶς
ἔξοχος ἄλλος ἔβλαστεν ἄλλου.
βόσκει δὲ τοὺς μὲν μοῖρα δυσαμερίας,
τοὺς δ' ὄλβος ἡμῶν, τοὺς δὲ δουλεί-   5
ας ζυγὸν ἔσχεν ἀνάγκας.

D (591) Stobaeus 4.29.12; Favorinus fr. 96.11 Barigazzi (ἓν – ἀμέρα) | 1
ἓν φῦλ[ο]ν Favorinus (confirming a conjecture by Bergk) : ἓν φύλων vel
sim. Stobaeus ‖ 2 ἡμᾶς Dindorf : ἡμέας codd. ‖ 6 ἀνάγκας Grotius :
ἀνάγκης codd.

A (582)

O Sun, light most revered by the horse-loving Thracians.

Spoken by a Thracian (a servant or herald of Tereus?).

B (584)

I envy your life a lot, but especially if you have not
experienced a foreign land.

Spoken by Procne to the chorus of Thracian women.

C (585)

Procne, these things clearly are painful; but nonetheless it is
necessary for those who are mortal to bear the things sent by
the gods readily.

*Probably spoken by Tereus to Procne, hypocritically consoling her for her
sister's supposed death.*

D (591)

There is one race of human beings, a single day produced us all from a
father and mother; no one was born superior to another. But some of us are
nurtured by a fate of misfortune, others by prosperity, while others again
are held in slavery's yoke of compulsion.

From a choral ode.

E (583)

νῦν δ' οὐδέν εἰμι χωρίς. ἀλλὰ πολλάκις
ἔβλεψα ταύτῃ τὴν γυναικείαν φύσιν,
ὡς οὐδέν ἐσμεν. αἳ νέαι μὲν ἐν πατρὸς
ἥδιστον, οἶμαι, ζῶμεν ἀνθρώπων βίον·
τερπνῶς γὰρ ἀεὶ παῖδας ἀνοία τρέφει.   5
ὅταν δ' ἐς ἥβην ἐξικώμεθ' ἔμφρονες,
ὠθούμεθ' ἔξω καὶ διεμπολώμεθα
θεῶν πατρῴων τῶν τε φυσάντων ἄπο,
αἱ μὲν ξένους πρὸς ἄνδρας, αἱ δὲ βαρβάρους,
αἱ δ' εἰς ἀγηθῆ δώμαθ', αἱ δ' ἐπίρροθα.   10
καὶ ταῦτ', ἐπειδὰν εὐφρόνη ζεύξῃ μία,
χρεὼν ἐπαινεῖν καὶ δοκεῖν καλῶς ἔχειν.

E (583) Stobaeus 4.22.45 | 2 ταύτην A ‖ 3 αἳ Brunck : αἱ codd. | μὲν ἐν Valckenaer: μὲν γὰρ SMA, μὲν γὰρ ἐν B ‖ 5 παῖδας F.W. Schmidt : πάντας codd. ‖ 6 δ' A², om. SMA | ἔμφρονες Dobree: εὔφρονες codd. ‖ 7 διεμπολώμεθα Valckenaer : διεμπολούμεθα codd. ‖ 10 ἀγηθῆ (after Scaliger) van Herwerden : ἀληθῆ SMA, ἀήθη B

F (595)

κερκίδος φωνή

F (595) Aristotle, *Poetics* 1454b36–37

E (583)

Now, however, I am nothing on my own. But often I have regarded the whole female sex in this way – that we are nothing. As young girls in our fathers' homes, I think, we live the most pleasant life of all mortals; for ignorance always gives children a happy upbringing. But when we come to adolescence and awareness, we are pushed out and sold, away from our parents and our family gods, some of us to foreign men, some to barbarians, some into homes empty of joy, some into homes full of abuse. And this, when a single night has yoked us, we have to approve and regard as good.

Spoken by Procne to the chorus of Thracian women, probably after she has been told that Philomela is dead.

F (595)

(the) shuttle's voice

Referring to the tongueless Philomela's use of weaving to reveal Tereus' crimes against her.

G (588)

θάρσει· λέγων τἀληθὲς οὐ σφαλῇ ποτε.

G (588) Stobaeus 3.13.21 | σφαλῇ L : σφάλλῃ vel sim. MSA

H (593)

ζώοι τις ἀνθρώπων τὸ κατ' ἆμαρ ὅπως
ἥδιστα πορσύνων· τὸ δ' ἐς αὔριον αἰεὶ
τυφλὸς ἕρπει.

H (593) Stobaeus 4.34.40 | 1 ζώοι codd.: ζῴη Wagner | ἆμαρ Gleditsch : ἦμαρ codd. ‖ 3 τυφλὸς Friedländer: τυφλὸν codd.

J (592.4–6)

ΧΟΡΟΣ   τὰν γὰρ ἀνθρώπου ζόαν
        ποικιλομήτιδες ἆται
        πημάτων πάσαις μεταλλάσσουσιν ὥραις.

J (592.4–6) Stobaeus 4.34.39 | 1 γὰρ Bergk : δ' codd. | ζόαν Dindorf : ζωὰν codd. ‖ 3 ὥραις SM : ὥρας A

K (587)

φιλάργυρον μὲν πᾶν τὸ βάρβαρον γένος.

K (587) Stobaeus 3.10.25

G (588)

Have no fear! If you speak the truth, you will never come to harm.

Probably Procne, encouraging some man (the speaker of fr. A?) to corroborate her understanding of the "shuttle's voice".

H (593)

Let any human being live so as to provide for himself, day by day, the maximum possible pleasure; he is always walking blind into tomorrow.

From a choral song.

J (592.4–6)

For the life of man is transformed by the cunning wiles of ruinous error that bring calamities at all seasons.

From a choral song – probably the same one.

K (587)

The entire barbarian race is money-loving.

Spoken by Procne, perhaps to Tereus.

L (586)

σπεύδουσαν αὐτήν, ἐν δὲ ποικίλῳ φάρει

L (586) Herodian *On Words with Two Quantities* 2.16.3

M (581)

τοῦτον δ' ἐπόπτην ἔποπα τῶν αὐτου κακῶν
πεποικίλωκε κἀποδηλώσας ἔχει
θρασὺν πετραῖον ὄρνιν ἐν παντευχίᾳ·
ὃς ἦρι μὲν φανέντι διαπαλεῖ πτερὸν
κίρκου λεπάργου· δύο γὰρ οὖν μορφὰς φανεῖ   5
παιδός τε χαὐτοῦ νηδύος μιᾶς ἄπο·
νέας δ' ὀπώρας ἡνίκ' ἂν ξανθῇ στάχυς,
στικτή νιν αὖθις ἀμφινωμήσει πτέρυξ·
ἀεὶ δὲ μίσει τῶνδ' ἀπαλλαγεὶς τόπων
δρυμοὺς ἐρήμους καὶ πάγους ἀποικιεῖ.   10

M (581) Aristotle, *Historia Animalium* 633a18–27 (ascribing the lines to Aeschylus; Welcker first assigned them to this play) | 4 φανέντι Nauck : φαίνοντ(α)ι codd. | διαπαλεῖ Gilbert : διαπάλλει Ald.: διαβάλλει codd. ‖ 6 χαὐτοῦ (sic) Sylburg: καὐτοῦ codd. ‖ 7 ἡνίκ᾽ ἂν ξανθῇ (-ῇ) β: ἵνα καταξανθῇ αγ ‖ 8 στικτή (στικτῆ) α: τίκτει vel sim. βγ | νιν β: νιμ α: (τίκτειν) ἵν᾽ P: νῖν KᶜMᶜ: νῦν EᵃLᶜn | ἀμφινωμ- EᵃP: ἀμφινῶν- vel sim. KᶜMᶜ: ἀμφινομ- αβ n: κἀμφινομ- Lᶜ | -μήσει β: -μήση α EᵃMᶜP: -μίση KᶜLᶜn ‖ 9 τῶνδ᾽ α: τὸν δὲ or τόνδε βγ | ἀπαλλαγεὶς Heath: ἄπ' ἄλλον vel sim. (ἀσπάλλον P, ἀπαλῶν Aᵃ) εἰς codd. ‖ 10 ἀποικιεῖ Dindorf : ἀποικίσει codd.

L (586)

... as she herself was hurrying, and in a dappled coat ...

Spoken by a messenger, perhaps describing the pursuit of the sisters by Tereus.

M (581)

While him, the hoopoe which is a viewer of its own sufferings, he has adorned with varied colours and has revealed as a bold rock-dwelling bird wearing full panoply. When spring appears he will spread the wing of a white-feathered hawk; for he will show two forms from a single womb, his child's and his own. And when the harvest is new and the grain is threshed, again a dappled wing will cover him. But he will always hate these regions and separate himself from them, making his home far away in the lonely woods and mountains.

Spoken by the deus ex machina (Apollo?), describing the transformation of Tereus effected by another god (Zeus?)

N (589)

ἄνους ἐκεῖνος· αἱ δ' ἀνουστέρως ἔτι
ἐκεῖνον ἡμύναντο <πρὸς τὸ> καρτερόν.
ὅστις γὰρ ἐν κακοῖσι θυμωθεὶς βροτῶν
μεῖζον προσάπτει τῆς νόσου τὸ φάρμακον,
ἰατρός ἐστιν οὐκ ἐπιστήμων κακῶν.　　　　　5

N (589) Stobaeus 3.20.32 | 1 ἀνουστέρως ἔτι Pflugk : ἀνούστερ' ἔτι codd. ||
2 πρὸς τὸ καρτερόν Bamberger : καρτερόν codd.

O (590)

ΧΟΡΟΣ　θνητὴν δὲ φύσιν χρὴ θνητὰ φρονεῖν,
　　　　　τοῦτο κατειδότας, ὡς οὐκ ἔστιν
　　　　　πλὴν Διὸς οὐδεὶς τῶν μελλόντων
　　　　　ταμίας ὅ τι χρὴ τετελέσθαι.

O (590) Stobaeus 3.22.22 | 1 θνητὴν δὲ φύσιν χρὴ θνητὰ φρονεῖν Grotius:
θνητὰ φρονεῖν χρὴ θνητὴν φύσιν codd.

N (589)

He was foolish; but they were more foolish still to fight against him with violence. For whoever of mortals is enraged when in distress, and applies a cure which is worse than the illness, is like a doctor who does not understand the disease.

Spoken either by the deus ex machina, or possibly by a messenger reflecting on events he has narrated.

O (590)

Human nature must think human thoughts, knowing this,

that Zeus and no one else is the dispenser of what is

to be accomplished in the future.

Probably the final lines of the play, delivered by the chorus.

P (594)

αἴγλη

P (594) Hesychius α1730

Q (595a)

λίβανος

Q (595a) Herennius Philo, *On Words of Different Meanings* κ108 Nickau;
Phrynichus, *Ecloge* 157

R (595b)

] εις νιν εἰς φθορ[

R (595b) *POxy* 2740 fr. 1.8 = Eupolis fr. 268.8; line 6 reads τουτου
Σοφοκλέο[υς] (τοῦτ' οὐ Σοφοκλέο[υς ἐστίν;] Austin), lines 10–11 (a
scholium) Σοφοκλέους ἐσ[τὶν ἐκ] Τηρέως δοκῶ vel sim. | προ]θεὶς Lobel:
ἀ]φεὶς Austin | φθόρ[ον] Austin: φθορ[άν] Lobel

The following fragments cannot be assigned to a context:

P (594)

gleaming ornament

Q (595a)

frankincense

R (595b)

exposing (*or* abandoning) her (*or* him) to ruin

TEREUS

Hypothesis

This text declares itself to be the hypothesis of a work entitled *Tereus*, and there can be no reasonable doubt that the work in question is Sophocles' tragedy. Every work we know of entitled *Tereus* is a tragedy or a comedy; the story narrated here, climaxed by the death of the innocent Itys at his mother's hands, is certainly a tragic, not a comic one; the only other known tragedy of this name is that by Philocles, whose work never became the object of large-scale ancient scholarly effort; nothing in the Hypothesis is inconsistent with our other information about Sophocles' play (though see below on 27–29), and the detail that Philomela revealed her plight "through weaving" (line 21; cf. fr. F [595]) is known to have been one of the play's most memorable features.

Like some other tragic hypotheses (e.g. those to Euripides' *Hippolytus*, *Hecuba* and *Stheneboea*), this one seems to have devoted as much space to the "back-story" of the play as to the events actually included in it; the events narrated in lines 1–19 (the marriage, Procne's request for a visit by her sister, and Tereus' journey to Athens and back) can have been mentioned in the tragedy only retrospectively. On the plot of the play itself, the Hypothesis does not give us as much new information as we might have hoped, though this is partly due to the corruption in line 33.

16 [not k]eeping his pled[ge]: this pledge is more likely to have been given to Pandion (who was Philomela's *kyrios* and had a very strong interest in her safety and in the preservation of her virginity) than to Procne; Pandion requests, and is given, just such a pledge (by joining of hands; cf. *Phil.* 813) in Ovid *Met.* 6.496–510.

23–24was stung by [the utmost(?)] jealous[y]: Parsons' supplement here can only be tentative, but the structure of the sentence all but requires the missing word(s) to have included either an adjective describing Procne's jealousy, or an adverb modifying *oistrētheisa* "stung, driven mad". This is perhaps the most important new information about the plot of *Tereus* with which the Hypothesis supplies us. It is not clear whether Procne's jealousy involved, even initially, any hostile feelings towards Philomela (cf. Introduction, p. 154 n.44); that it need not have done is evident from *Trachiniae*, where Deianeira, though she is deeply hurt by Heracles' apparent rejection of her (cf. *Trach.* 531–551) – and is said to be suffering from jealousy (*zēlotypiā*, the same word used here) by a scholiast on *Trach.* 434 – never wishes her rival Iole any ill.

27 [madden]ed by a Fury(?): restoration of the text is again very uncertain, but it is not unlikely that the nonsensical *ereinois* conceals some form or compound of *Erīnys* "Fury" – which would have been identically pronounced by most Greek speakers in Egypt at the time (about AD 200) when our papyrus was written. If this is correct, there was probably some reference to Furies in the text of the play, whether by Procne herself or another; depending on the identity and attitude of the speaker, this might be meant to suggest that Procne's crime was a natural act of revenge in the circumstances (cf. *Aj.* 836–844, *El.* 112, 276, 1080), or that she is out of her mind (cf. *Ant.* 603) – or both.

27–29 she to[ok] Itys, slaughtered him … : it is tempting to take this as indicating that in Sophocles' play Procne acted alone without Philomela's aid, but fr. N (589) shows that both sisters were involved in the crime: the summarizer has concentrated on the leading (and only speaking) figure. It is, however, reasonable to assume that it was Procne's hand that actually slew Itys and also that it was she, as Tereus' wife, who brought him the dish with his son's flesh on it. For the attribution of responsibility for the murder in other literary and artistic versions of the myth, see Introduction, pp. 142–149, 156–7.

32 [a hoopoe]: known from fr. M (581) and from Aristophanes' *Birds.*

A (582)

This fragment could well be the first line of the play. Five of the extant Sophoclean tragedies begin with a vocative, although in each case the opening speaker is addressing another character. Such an opening line for *Tereus* would combine two standard opening devices in Sophocles' tragedies: the invocation or vocative and the identification of the location of the dramatic action (for which cf. *OT* 1, *Phil.* 2). The juxtaposition of a Thracian deity together with a familiar epithet about Thrace makes it an appropriate line to use in an introductory context indicating the general location of the action; at any later stage, the audience would not have needed to be given this information. The Thracian setting was a Sophoclean innovation (Introduction, pp. 145–6).

Buchwald (1939) 36 was the first to suggest that this line began the play (cf. Sutton 128). He attributed it to a speech by Procne in which she complains about the misery of her married life, but this view is, in many respects, dependent on a long interpretative tradition which imagines the play beginning with a *rhesis* by an unhappy Procne. See further on fr. E (583) below. Is an unhappy Procne likely to call upon the god of her conjugal home? In fact, fr. E (583) suggests that she would more likely call upon the gods of her *paternal* home. At any rate, the invocation to Helios can easily be attributed to a Thracian (cf. Hourmouziades [1986] 136). It is common in tragedy for a person returning home to apostrophize the land on arrival (cf. *Hermione* fr. A [202] and Comm.). In such a context, it could belong to a Thracian herald (or other subordinate) arriving ahead of Tereus. It is unlikely that the speaker is Tereus himself: it is not usual for a tragedy in which a hero returns unwittingly to disaster, such as *Trachiniae* or Aeschylus' *Agamemnon*, to begin with the hero's entrance. In both of these tragedies, a herald arrives ahead of the returning hero to announce his arrival. The line could be given to such a herald, or to a palace servant awaiting Tereus' return.

In many discussions of *Tereus*, the fragment has been attributed to Tereus and placed in a later part of the play: it is usually placed at the moment when Tereus discovers that he has dined on his son's body (Welcker [1839] 383, followed by Kiso 71, Hourmouziades [1986] 139 and Dobrov [1993] 208–9), and thought to be a call on Helios to witness the outrage he has suffered at the hands of the two women. Helios, however, is here being addressed not as the "all-seeing" god (as in [Aesch.] *Prom.* 91 and *Iliad* 3.277) but merely as the principal god of the Thracians.

Buchwald (1939) 36 thought that the first line of Philocles' tetralogy, "I address you [sc. the Sun], master of all things" (Philocles fr. 1), was modelled on the opening invocation in Sophocles' tragedy. On the relationship between the versions of Sophocles and Philocles, see note on fr. M (581) below. Another play that begins with an invocation to Helios is Euripides' *Phoenissae* (1–3); the resemblance to our passage becomes even stronger if lines 1–2 are spurious as is now generally thought (see M.W. Haslam, *GRBS* 16 [1976] 149–74, at 152). There, however, the mention of Helios is purely decorative; the Sun is told that he lighted a day of misfortune for Thebes when Cadmus first came there (4–6) and is not mentioned again.

O Sun: for the association of the Thracians with sun-worship, see Pearson 227 and M.L. West, *CQ* 21 (1971) 303 n.7. The cult worship of Helios in Thrace appears to be well established in the minds of the fifth-century Athenians through the myth of the Thracian king, Orpheus. Although the early evidence for this myth is thin, several references in tragedy show that it was known by the time of Sophocles' play; e.g. Aesch. *Ag.* 1629–32, and Eur. *Alc.* 357–62. An important reference is [Eratosthenes], *Catasterisms* 24, which states that its source is a tragedy of Aeschylus, almost certainly *Bassarae*. The passage describes how Orpheus, discontinuing his worship of Dionysus after his trip to the underworld, considered Helios the greatest of gods and equated him with Apollo. Dionysus punished Orpheus by sending the Bassarae, the Thracian equivalent of maenads, to tear him apart on Mount Pangaeus where he had gone to witness the rising sun. A fragment from *Bassarae* hints at this latter episode (Aesch. fr. 23a). The plot of *Bassarae* is uncertain and the corrupt nature of the fragment adds to the obscurity. It may belong in a messenger speech relating events on Pangaeus, or in a choral ode (see Radt ad loc.)

horse-loving Thracians: this epithet is a familiar one in Greek literature. It is present as early as Homer (*Il.* 10.436–7) and Hesiod (*Op.* 505), and it persists in tragedy, e.g. Eur. *Hec.* 9, 428, and *Rhesus* passim. One might also include Heracles' eighth labour when Eurystheus sent him to Thrace to tackle Diomedes' team of man-eating horses. When the Thracian king Sitalces invaded Macedonia in 429, he is said to have had 50,000 cavalry, forming about one-third of his army (Thuc. 2.98.4).

B (584)

The fragment is generally attributed to Procne, and this is undoubtedly correct: she is the only speaking character in the play (so far as we know) who is living outside her native land. It is most likely that Procne is addressing her observation to a female interlocutor or interlocutors; even if we can imagine her saying to a man or men that she envies their life (i.e. that she wishes she were a man), it would be nonsense for her, or anyone, to say that the main advantage men have over women is that they are unlikely ever to have been abroad, when in fact, as every spectator knew, men were far more likely than women to leave their native land temporarily or permanently (for reasons of military service, business, exile, etc.) Several discussions of the play have assumed that Procne had a female confidant such as the Nurse in Soph. *Trach.*, but there is no evidence for this (see Introduction, p. 150 and note 33); if these lines were addressed to some such character, she would have to have been Thracian. It is most likely, however, that the addressee is the chorus or its leader. Many discussions of *Tereus* have assumed that the chorus consisted of Thracian men, but the arguments to support this view are weak. For example, Calder (1974) 88 (followed by Kiso 61 and Dobrov [1993] 199–200) put forward three arguments. One is that the choral lyrics of frs. 590–3 are only appropriate for a male chorus, but, as T.B.L. Webster (*An Introduction to Sophocles* [Oxford, 1936] 4) noted, there is a close correspondence between the metre and thought of these fragments and the lyrics sung by the chorus of young maidens in *Trach.* (cf. Pearson 234 on fr. D [591]). Another is that Sophocles may have wished to emphasise Procne's isolation by making her share the acting space with a chorus of Thracian men; this is mere speculation and not an argument. The third argument, which relies on the assumption that Accius' *Tereus* is a more or less direct translation of Sophocles, suggests that the Roman tragedy had a male chorus because Procne is addressed in one fragment as 'woman' (*mulier*, frr. 643–4 Warmington); but (i) the underlying assumption is anything but certain, and (ii) we cannot in any case be sure that the chorus actually spoke this line. One of the important elements when considering the identity of the chorus is to imagine their reaction to the proposed infanticide, which must have been planned in their presence; it is extremely hard to imagine a chorus of Thracian men tolerating, and being prepared to keep secret, a plot to murder the only son of their king, whereas a female chorus would at least, as in Euripides' *Medea*, have had the motive of gender solidarity. It is not possible to be any more precise about the identity of the chorus, but it is presumably a group of Thracian maidens or Thracian women. See Fitzpatrick (2001) 94–95 for discussion and references.

Helen Bacon (*Barbarians in Greek Tragedy* [New Haven, 1961] 81) thought that the chorus consisted of Athenian women – in which case, of course, this sentence could not be addressed to them. It is quite possible in itself that Sophocles had Procne come to Thrace after her marriage with some attendants who formed the play's chorus; but she could hardly then complain of being completely isolated as she does in fr. E (583).

The fragment is often placed in the same speech as, or the same context as, fr. E (583) (Welcker [1839] 377, followed by Calder [1974] 89 and Dobrov [1993] 203), but this need not be the case. It may also belong quite independently in the early stages of the play when the chorus has come on stage and when it is usual for a main character and the chorus to establish a relationship: cf. *Trach.* 141–3.

1 I envy your life a lot: this is often thought to be addressed, in apostrophe, to the absent Philomela (Welcker [1839] 377, followed by Calder [1974] 89, Kiso 64, Dobrov [1993] 203). This placing is usually derived from an assumption that this fragment belongs with fr. E (583) in the prologue of the play; see comm. on that fragment. There is, in fact, no reason why we should assume an apostrophe to an absent addressee, when there is no difficulty (except the unwarranted assumption that the chorus must be male) in the supposition that Procne is addressing someone on stage in the ordinary way.

2 **you have not experienced a foreign land:** cf. fr. E (583) 6–10 where emphasis is laid on the separation of brides from their "parents and ... family gods, some [going] to foreign men, some to barbarians".

C (585)

There are a number of views on the identity of the speaker who addresses these words of advice to Procne and also on its position in the play. Some suggested identifications of the speaker are the chorus-leader (J.A. Hartung, *Sophokles' Fragmente* [Leipzig, 1851] 166), a female confidant or servant (Welcker [1839] 381), and Tereus (Buchwald [1939] 40, Kiso 65, Dobrov [1993] 204, Fitzpatrick [2001] 101). The interpretation of the fragment depends, to a large extent, on whether one believes Tereus returned from Athens (i) openly bringing a dumb Philomela with him, or (ii) pretending Philomela was dead and either (a) bringing her into the palace in the guise of a servant or (b) imprisoning her elsewhere (see Introduction, pp. 151–2); in case (i) the "painful" event is Philomela's dumbness, in case (ii) her death – and either way, if the speaker is Tereus, his words are almost unbearably hypocritical (cf. Polymestor in Eur. *Hec.* 954–961). Another proposed placing of the fragment is at a time when Procne has learnt the truth about the ordeal of Philomela; for example, Welcker [1839] 381 and Pearson 225 have suggested that the words are spoken to Procne when she had discovered Tereus' crimes. But a consolation of this kind is grotesquely inappropriate when addressing a woman who has just learned that her husband has raped and mutilated her sister.

1 **these things clearly are painful:** the precise cause of the pain, which is, of course, mental, is unclear for the reasons outlined above.

2 **things sent by the gods:** the adjective *theios* appears elsewhere in tragedy to attribute some event or affliction to an indefinite or undetermined *daimon* or deity. In *Ajax*, the chorus use it twice to describe Ajax's madness (185, 611); the Guard in *Antigone* (421) describes the storm which covered Polyneices' body with dust as a

'divine visitation'; Neoptolemus in *Philoctetes* uses it to describe Philoctetes' diseased foot (192, 1326); and the chorus in *OC* use it in reference to Oedipus' death (1585). Some instances in fragmentary plays are *Epigonoi* fr. 201f.1 and (with different adjectives of the same meaning) *Tyro* fr. 650 (see vol. ii) and *Phaedra* fr. B (680).

D (591)

The fragment is part of a choral ode. Following Welcker [1839] 379, Jebb had seen in the fragment "a principle which belonged to the spirit of the Dionysiac cult – the freedom and equality of men" (Pearson 233). This was influenced by the belief that there was a significant Dionysian element in the tragedy, but this need not have been the case (see further on fr. L [586]). The sentiment of the ode simply reflects generalisations about human life which are expressed throughout ancient Greek poetry; the idea of the oneness of the human race is perhaps particularly appropriate if a sympathetic 'barbarian' chorus is addressing a Greek woman in distress. In fact, the sentiments of the surviving choral lyrics from *Tereus* all reveal a similar concern about the fortunes of human life.

Jebb thought that the fragment belonged to the first *stasimon* (Pearson 233), but it is not really possible to place it with any certainty. The contrast between good and bad fortune suggests, perhaps, that it belongs at a point further into the dramatic action when some of the problems and issues have arisen. However, an equally good argument could be made for an earlier placement.

The metre is dactylo-epitrite, based on the units $-\cup\cup-\cup\cup-$ (*D*) and $-\cup-$ (*e*), usually with so-called link-syllables separating each unit from the next; thus the first line has the structure $-e-D$. Dactylo-epitrites are fairly common in Sophocles' earlier plays (e.g. *Trach.* 94–111, *Ajax* 172–192, *OT* 1086–1109) but are almost completely absent from those produced after 420.

1   one race of human beings: the idea of a single race of human beings echoes Pind. *Nem.* 6.1–2, where it is added that gods too share the same ancestry.

1–2   a single day produced us all from a father and mother: i.e. all humans are descended from the same progenitors – presumably Deucalion and Pyrrha, the central figures of the Greek version of the Flood story (on which see M.L. West, *The East Face of Helicon* [Oxford, 1997] 489–493).

E (583)

This is, perhaps, one of the best known fragments of Sophocles. Given its criticism of the social position of women in respect of marriage, it is cited, not unsurprisingly, in many books and articles about women in ancient Greek society. Although it has come down to us without any indication of the speaker, it is unanimously accepted as spoken by Procne. The speech is often compared to that by Medea on the same theme, inspired by Jason's betrayal of her (Eur. *Med.* 214–66): both speak of marriage, though from different points of view, as equivalent to slavery (line 7 ~ *Med.* 232–4), and both emphasize the wife's complete dependence on the character of her husband (lines 9–10 ~ *Med.* 228–9, 235–247). There are, however, some significant differences between the two speeches; (i) Procne has yet to learn about her husband's treachery, and (ii) Procne is an Athenian princess (married to a 'barbarian') while Medea is a 'barbarian' (married – if marriage it was – to a Greek prince).

This fragment has long been placed close to the beginning of the play. For example, Dobrov (1993) 201 observes that "an account of the expedition to Athens and its tragic conclusion fits quite naturally in the context of Prokne's famous lament (fr. 583 Radt), which most likely belongs to an expository prologue". There are, however, very strong arguments against this view. Not once in his surviving tragedies does Sophocles employ an 'expository prologue' like the ones favoured by Euripides. Even *Trach.* which is closest to the Euripidean type of prologue is radically different. This fragment is a lengthy generalisation which is not comparable to the opening speeches in either *Trach.* or Euripidean prologues. Moreover, a speech like this would hardly be appropriate at a time when Procne would be looking forward to a reunion with her sister in the very near future, as a result of an act of kindness by her husband. The fragment is better placed in the midst of the dramatic action and probably belongs at a point at which Procne believes Philomela to be lost to her for ever (whether by death or by inability to speak; see Introduction, p. 152) so that she is now completely isolated in a foreign land (cf. fr. B [584]), apparently with a not very congenial husband (cf. lines 9–10).

1 **Now, however:** As the fragment begins with the contrast, it follows that an earlier section of Procne's speech has been lost. It is most likely that in this lost section Procne dwelt upon the happy prospects of which she has been so unexpectedly deprived.

1 **I am nothing:** this expresses a particularly tragic sense of desperation, cf. *Phil.* 951, 1030, 1216, *El.* 677. Procne's description of herself in these terms must therefore be taken to reflect an extreme situation and is not, as has sometimes been suggested, a simple expression of loneliness.

3 **as being nothing:** lit. "how we are nothing". Procne's use of the first person plural, here and throughout the passage, suggests that she is speaking in the presence of at least one other female. It is very likely that she is addressing a female chorus (on the identity of the chorus, see on fr. B [584]).

3–4 **As young girls … we live the most pleasant life:** cf. *Trach.* 144–50. For a boy, too, it could be said that childhood was the only really happy time of life (*Aj.* 552–9).

5 **ignorance always gives children a happy upbringing:** cf. *Aj.* 553–5.

7 **sold:** i.e. treated as slaves; cf. Aesch. *Cho.* 132–5, 915. In *Medea* (232–4) the wife is the purchaser rather than the purchased; but what she buys (with her dowry) is "a master for [her] body".

10 **empty of joy:** Greek *agēthē*, a brilliant emendation of the nonsensical *alēthē* "true" read by most mss. and of B's *aēthē* "unfamiliar" (which cannot be right, since a major point of the passage is that the bride virtually *always* finds her new home unfamiliar); in medieval Greek *agēthē* and *aēthē* would have been pronounced almost identically.

10 **full of abuse:** Greek *epirrothos* (a purely poetic word) normally means "giving help" (probably in origin "answering a shout for help", from *rhothos* "noise, clamour"), but in *Ant.* 413 it seems to be used to mean "noisy, abusive", and Hesychius (ε5131) says that the neuter plural form of a cognate adjective, *epirrothēta*, was used somewhere (the author and text are not stated) to mean *epipsoga* "full of blaming, censorious". The sense "full of shouted rebukes" (for alleged breaches of duty by the wife) would suit our passage well.

11 **a single night** (the wedding night) seems to have been a catch-phrase; cf. Eur. *Tro.* 665–6 (tr. Kovacs) "They say that a single night dispels the hatred a woman feels for her bedmate" (the speaker, Andromache, strongly disagrees).

F (595)

This fragment is preserved in a passage from Aristotle's *Poetics* (1454b36–37). In the late eighteenth century, Tyrwhitt first suggested that the two substantive words in Aristotle's phrase were taken directly from the text of Sophocles' tragedy, and this has been accepted ever since. The passage confirms that Procne learnt the truth about her husband's treachery through a piece of weaving, as stated in the Hypothesis and its parallel versions (see Introduction p. 142 n.1). It is worth citing the fragment's context because this may provide a clue to the overall arrangement of the *anagnorisis*.

> The second kind are those contrived by the poet, and inartistic for that reason. As when Orestes in *Iphigenia [in Tauris]* causes recognition that he is Orestes. She [Iphigenia] reveals herself through the letter, but he himself says what the poet, not the plot, wants. So it is close to the fault which I mentioned [in 1454b20–30], for he might have carried some [tokens] as well. And in Sophocles' *Tereus* it is the "shuttle's voice".

Reconstructions influenced by Ovid *Met.* follow that narrative in presuming that Philomela dispatched the weaving to Procne via an intermediary. This presumption, however, removes the possibility of a dramatic scene in which the two sisters are on stage together. Aristotle's juxtaposition of the letter in Eur. *IT* and the *peplos* in *Tereus* may suggest that he was using two comparable scenes in which the recognition between siblings took place when they were on stage together. At any rate, the *peplos* or embroidered artefact has been long overlooked as a potentially potent stage prop which ought to be considered in the context of other notable props in Sophoclean tragedy such as Hector's sword in *Ajax*, the urn in *Electra*, and the bow in *Philoctetes*. It is worth stating explicitly something which has, perhaps, been taken for granted in respect of this fragment and, therefore, overlooked; the *anagnorisis*, i.e. the use of a piece of weaving to reveal the truth, is clearly a Sophoclean dramatic innovation. If it had been an element in earlier versions of the myth, it would not have attracted attention and comment from Aristotle.

The suggestion by Nauck that the rather similar fragment 890 ("the songs of the shuttle, which awakens sleepers") also belongs to this play, for which there was never much justification (the singing shuttle was a poetic cliché: see Dover on Ar. *Frogs* 1316), can now be definitively ruled out. The fragment's context has appeared in a new papyrus (forthcoming in

POxy lxxi; made available to us in advance of publication through the kindness of Dr Dirk Obbink), which shows that the passage was concerned with the making of arms and armour (the shuttle was being used to weave linen for corslets). The editor of the papyrus, C. Mülke, by a convincing emendation of schol. Ar. *Wealth* 541, where fr. 890 is quoted, has shown that the fragment is actually from Sophocles' *Epigonoi*; it will be discussed fully in vol. ii of this edition.

voice (Greek *phōnē*) clearly refers here, not to the noise of the moving shuttle (cf. above), but to the way in which the mute Philomela 'spoke' to Procne by means of woven work. There has been debate on the nature of Philomela's embroidered work and whether she wove images or words: the scholium to Ar. *Birds* 212, which in general reads like a paraphrase of the Hypothesis, says specifically that Philomela in her weaving revealed the truth "by means of letters" (*dia grammatōn*) – as she does in Ovid (*Met.* 6.577, 582) – but this detail might conceivably be due to contamination with some later (Hellenistic?) version of the story. It could be argued that images run the risk of interception (Fitzpatrick [2001] 97–8), but few if any theatre spectators would be likely to think of this. Given the sophistication of ancient tapestries, the weaving of images is very possible. Only J. Cahill (*Her Kind: Stories of Women from Greek Mythology* [Peterborough, Ont., 1995]) 29–30 n.8, has developed this view at length. On the other hand, there is no difficulty in supposing that Procne and Philomela could have been assumed to be literate: women in Greek tragedy can be literate whenever it is dramatically appropriate or necessary, as Phaedra is in Euripides' surviving *Hippolytus* (apparently also in his lost *Hippolytus* – see Introduction to *Phaedra,* pp. 257–8) and Iphigeneia in his *IT*. The use of a text would complement two overlapping themes in *Tereus*, those of communication and the Greek-barbarian antithesis. The illiterate Tereus believes that the removal of Philomela's tongue is sufficient to prevent her revealing the truth, but the literate mute Philomela 'speaks' her words through the domestic act of weaving.

G (588)

The identities of the speaker and addressee of this line are impossible to determine with certainty; there is, nevertheless, almost universal consensus on who the speaker is and where the fragment belongs in the play's action. The speaker is generally thought to be Procne in the context of the *anagnorisis* or recognition scene. In this scenario, the line is spoken to someone (male, as the masculine participle *legōn* shows) who is in a position to confirm the truth of the "shuttle's voice" – in other words, a man who had been with Tereus and Philomela on their journey. Hourmouziades (1986) 137 has suggested that the tone indicates that the line is addressed to a social inferior who is to report something unpleasant, or to retract a lie previously told by himself or another superior person (the latter scenario corresponds to the position of Lichas in *Trach.* 436–489: Deianeira, like Procne, has been able to expose the falsehood with the help of information from another source). If we are right to suppose that fr. A (582) was spoken by a herald or other subordinate of Tereus announcing his impending return, the addressee here is most probably the same man. Possibly he is the mysterious fourth person on the bell-crater Louvre CA 2193 (see Introduction, p. 148).

Have no fear: evidently the addressee fears punishment by Tereus if he reveals the latter's crime. Deianeira (*Trach.* 457–8) thinks Lichas may be afraid to tell the truth for a different reason (fear of hurting Deianeira's own feelings).

if you speak translates the Greek masculine participle *legōn* "speaking". Kiso (67 and n. 60) suggests that the masculine participle is here used generically and does not necessarily show that the addressee is male; but here, in contrast with passages such as Eur. *Med.* 1018 which she cites, the speaker is not making a universal statement but is reassuring a particular individual in a particular situation – the participle is closely linked with the two second-person verbs.

you will never come to harm: the strength of the truth was proverbial, cf. *Ant.* 1195.

H (593)

In the editions of Nauck and Pearson this fragment was combined (as Bergk had first suggested) with another from a different source (fr. 879a in *TrGF*: "One should never fix one's gaze on great human prosperity; for a man who is as old as a tall poplar tree, and who loses his livelihood ..."), on the ground that their themes were similar and their (dactylo-epitrite) metrical schemes almost identical. However, it is far from rare for separate dactylo-epitrite songs to resemble each other closely, the two passages cannot be combined into one without substantial textual surgery, and they are making different points: fr. 879a is giving advice on how happiness should be *judged* (the familiar "call no man happy until he is dead", cf. *OT* 1524–30, *Trach.* 1–3), whereas our fragment gives advice on how happiness can be *attained* so far as this is possible in human life.

The fragment is evidently from a choral song. A recommendation to live for the pleasure of the moment might in principle be either (i) a short-sighted utterance like that of Iocaste in *OT* 977–9, made just *before* a disaster which the audience can foresee but the speaker cannot, or (ii) a *reaction* to a disaster that seems to make nonsense of all imaginable ethical principles, like that of the chorus in Eur. *Hipp.* 1115–9 to the banishment of Hippolytus (cf. also Eur. *HF* 503–512, on which Bond collects numerous parallels). It is hard to find a plausible context in *Tereus* for an utterance of type (i) by the chorus; (ii) is more likely, and the chorus may well be reacting to the terrible fate of the innocent Philomela.

2–3   he is always walking blind into tomorrow: cf. Eur. *Alc.* 783–6 (Heracles, advocating hedonism) "There is no mortal who knows whether he will be alive when tomorrow comes: the outcome of his fortune is invisible, and one cannot learn it nor hunt it down by any skill".

J (592.4–6)

What Radt, following Nauck and Pearson, presents as the single six-line fragment 592, actually consists of two distinct book fragments. The first three lines ("But what pleasure is there in many good things, if ill-counselled thinking is going to ruin wealth and happiness?") are preserved in Plutarch's treatise *How a Young Man should Study Poetry* (*Mor.* 21b); he ascribes them to Sophocles but does not name the play. The other three lines are preserved in Stobaeus (4.34.39) and have a specific attribution to Sophocles' *Tereus*. Bergk had originally conjectured that the two belong together because their metre is identical (suggesting that they may be in strophic responsion) and their theme similar. As in the case of fr. H (593), and for similar reasons, this argument is dubious: note that whereas the quotation in Plutarch ascribes reversals of fortune to the "ill-counselled thinking" of humans, the quotation in Stobaeus ascribes them to the "cunning wiles" of, one must assume, a malevolent deity. Accordingly, the lines cited in Radt as fr. 592.1–3 are not considered here to be part of *Tereus*.

The metre is dactylo-epitrite, as in frr. D (591) and H (593); but the relationship of this fragment with fr. H (593) may be closer than that. In the present fragment the chorus state, by way of explaining or justifying some earlier utterance, that human life is full of calamities caused by "ruinous error"; and fr. H (593), recommending a hedonistic approach to life that takes no thought for the morrow, is just the sort of utterance that might be justified in this way (compare the passages from Euripides' *Hippolytus* and *HF* cited in the discussion of the previous fragment). It is therefore quite possible that these two fragments come from the same ode.

2 the cunning wiles of ruinous error (Greek *ātē*, either "ruin", or the mental blindness that can lead to ruin, or the divine power imagined as causing these phenomena): cf. Aesch. *Ag.* 386 "Ruin who plans beforehand".

K (587)

This condemnation of barbarians can only have been spoken by a Greek – that is, by Procne. As Pearson 231 noted, it was "no doubt spoken with particular reference to the Thracians"; indeed the presence in the line of the particle *men* "on the one hand", indicating that a contrasting sentence will follow, makes one wonder if that sentence was not something like "but the Thracians are most avaricious of all". Greed and violence were firmly established in the Athenian stereotype about Thracians. In Eur. *Hec.* (710, 774), for example, the Thracian king Polymestor kills Polydorus in order to steal the gold which he had taken with him. Other passages reflecting these stereotypes include Archilochus fr. 93a and Thuc. 2.97.4 ("the law, which holds good for Thracians in general, that one should receive rather than give").

The context may have been an *agon* between Tereus and Procne, in which Procne perhaps denounced her husband for his treatment of Philomela; such an *agon* is likely to have followed rather than preceded the cannibalistic feast (see Introduction, pp. 152–3). Sophocles puts an almost identical line (with *mantikon* "of prophets" in place of *barbaron*, and a different word-order) in the mouth of Creon, accusing Teiresias (falsely), at *Ant.* 1055.

L (586)

This line is preserved in Herodian who cited it for a metrical peculiarity (the use of *pharos* "cloak" with a short *a*; he also cites Soph. fr. 360). While the words are understandable *per se*, it is difficult to make overall sense out of them. It is part of a description relating to a woman by a third person and, for this reason, may well have been part of a messenger-type speech. It has been variously interpreted.

Most significantly but, we believe, erroneously, this fragment is supposed to provide evidence for a significant Dionysian element in the Sophoclean tragedy. Many analyses of *Tereus* presume that the dramatic action was closely linked to a biennial festival (*trietēris*) of Dionysus. This is supposed to provide the context for two aspects of the action. One is Procne's covert operation to release Philomela from incarceration in the countryside; the other is Procne's scheme which leads to Tereus' cannibalism. This festival is thought to have featured in Sophocles' tragedy because of its presence in Ovid (*Met.* 6.587 ff.) and, though less explicitly, Accius' tragedy (Accius 647 Warmington). The basic problem is that there is no evidence for the Dionysian element in any early source (unless this fragment itself offers such evidence), and its presence in Sophocles depends upon these later Roman sources. In these sources the Dionysiac element is inextricably combined with the internment of Philomela, and if we introduce the internment into Sophocles' play we are forced to exclude from it some typical tragic dramatic situations such as an on-stage *anagnorisis* between the sisters. On the other hand, a festival could offer Procne the opportunity to seduce Tereus into the *skene* for the cannibalistic feast (thus Calder [1974] 90; cf. Curley *Shards* 188).

Under the influence of Ovid, the fragment is thought to refer to Procne wearing the attire of a maenad on the way to release Philomela from her incarceration (cf. Welcker [1839] 381 and Dobrov [1993] 206). There are other quite different possibilities. Pearson 230–1 (cf. Hourmouziades [1986] 136–7) thought that the fragment was a reference to the piece of embroidery through which Philomela revealed the truth. Alternatively, it may belong to a report of the women's activities in the house leading up to the killing and cooking of Itys. Then again, it might belong, as we are inclined to think, in the build-up to the appearance of the *deus ex machina*. It is difficult to imagine how the play worked towards its dénouement. It seems likely that the sisters fled the royal palace and that Tereus pursued them. This is mentioned briefly in the Hypothesis (lines 30–31) and more extensively in its parallel versions in Tzetzes and the Aristophanic scholia, but there is nothing in the fragments that clearly relates to it. If there were such a sequence, then it is necessary to guess what happened between the flight from the palace and the entrance of the deity. The bridging of this gap with a messenger speech which relates details of the chase is very attractive. One detail in the line, as indicated below, strongly suggests that the metamorphosis of the characters into birds is not far away.

she was hurrying herself: the subject may be either Procne or Philomela, more likely the latter (see below).

in a dappled coat: As noted above, the garment is sometimes thought to be a Bacchic fawnskin. Curley (*Shards* 177 n.25) draws attention to fr. M (581) 2 where the *deus ex machina* describes the "varied colours" of Tereus' wings after his transformation, and wonders whether our passage refers to "Procne or Philomela ... after the metamorphoses". It cannot refer to Procne, since the nightingale's body is monochrome; but in Ar. *Birds* 1412 the swallow is called *poikilā* "of varied colours", a word which "aptly describes all the five hirundine species found in Greece" (Dunbar ad loc.) Possibly, therefore, as Curley supposes, the line describes the swallow that was once Philomela; but *pharos* (properly "piece of cloth") is never used to denote the skin, fur or plumage of a living bird or beast, and it is more likely that Sophocles represented Philomela as wearing, shortly *before* her transformation, a garment that prefigures her future appearance as a bird.

M (581)

This fragment is preserved in Aristotle (*HA* 633a 18–27) who attributed it to an unnamed play of Aeschylus. As there is no other evidence that Aeschylus (or Euripides either) ever wrote a play about this myth, Pearson and Radt follow the view of Welcker that the fragment belongs to Sophocles' tragedy: it would not be the only Sophoclean fragment misattributed to Aeschylus (fr. 15, from *Aias Lokros*, is cited by Zenobius 6.14 from the non-existent *Aias Lokros* of Aeschylus). Nauck and Mette, however, attributed the fragment to an unknown play of Aeschylus (Aesch. fr. 304 Nauck, 609 Mette). There have been some recent objections to its identification as Sophoclean or even Aeschylean (Burnett [1998] 183 n.22 and March *Shards* 161 n.55), though these dissenting voices go no further than expressing a view that the lines are not worthy of Sophocles. There are several possible approaches to the issue. One is to accept that the fragment is Aeschylean. As the fragment is clearly part of a fairly extensive speech, we would have to presume, without any supporting evidence, that Aeschylus wrote a play about the Tereus myth, and that he turned Tereus into a hoopoe when we know that in *Suppliants* (62) he made him a hawk. Moreover, the conjunction *hēnika* "when" (line 7) never occurs in Aeschylus (whereas it is found 25 times more in Sophocles and 38 times in Euripides, excluding *Rhesus*). Secondly, we may ascribe the fragment to Sophocles, in which case it surely comes from *Tereus*. A third possibility is that the fragment belongs to another poet altogether. It can hardly be from a fourth-century poet, since Aristotle would not have attributed to Aeschylus the composition of one of his own contemporaries; the most likely candidate, therefore, is Philocles (cf. Introduction, p. 146). He is the only other fifth-century tragic poet who is known to have dealt with this myth. It may be significant that Philocles was the nephew of Aeschylus, because the family connection could conceivably explain Aristotle's error. But given that our fragment is perfectly consistent with the plot of Sophocles' play as outlined in the papyrus Hypothesis (see Comm. on Hypothesis), and given that ancient authors quote Sophocles hundreds of times more often than they quote Philocles, to attribute the fragment to Sophocles remains the most reasonable conclusion.

A study of the vocabulary of the fragment confirms that Sophocles is its most likely author: of twenty significant lexical items in the passage (excluding overwhelmingly common words such as *neos* "new, young" and *kaka* "evils, sufferings", heavily context-dependent words like *epops* "hoopoe" and *kirkos* "hawk", and words that occur nowhere else in tragedy), a clear majority (eleven) are, by their proportional frequency (after allowing for the relative sizes of the three corpora), more characteristic of Sophocles than of either of the other two major tragedians (seven are most frequent in Euripides, one in Aeschylus, and in one case Aeschylus and Sophocles stand equal). For the purpose of these counts, "Aeschylus" is taken to exclude *Prometheus Bound*, "Euripides" is taken to exclude *Rhesus*, and "Sophocles" is taken to exclude this fragment.

This passage, describing an action of Zeus (cf. on line 2 below) from knowledge (rather than conjecture) and predicting the future behaviour of the transformed Tereus, must have been spoken by a god, presumably a *deus ex machina* (this expression is not intended to imply that we can be sure the *mechane* was used to bring the god on stage). The deity has been identified as Hermes (Welcker [1839] 383–4, Kiso 62–63, Dobrov [1993] 212), as Athena (Burnett [1998] 183 n.34, March *Shards* 161), and as Ares (Calder [1974] 88) – though Ares is surely ruled out by the god's condemnation of violence in fr. N (589) 1–2. More likely is Apollo, who was equated with the Thracians' supreme god Helios (fr. A [582]) in Aeschylus' *Bassarae* ([Eratosthenes] *Catast.* 24), Euripides' *Phaethon* (fr. 781.11–13 = 224–6 Diggle), and possibly also in Euripides' *Hecuba*

(1067–8) where the Thracian Polymestor calls on Helios (rather than Apollo) to heal him; the identification is supported by the concentration of medical language in fr. N (589) 4–5. See Fitzpatrick (2001) 98–100.

Dobrov (1993) 202, 210–1, suggested that the *ekkyklema* was used during the speech of the *deus ex machina* and that tokens representing each character appeared on the *ekkyklema* to symbolise the metamorphoses. Nothing that is known or reasonably conjectured about the use of the *ekkyklema* in tragedy, however, offers any parallel for this, and it is not clear how it could be intelligibly arranged, particularly since Dobrov (p.209) accepts the consensus view that the sisters fled from the palace pursued by Tereus, so that the metamorphosis must be imagined as taking place somewhere at a distance from the performing area. Nothing that is said in Aristophanes' *Birds* (e.g. 100–1), or even in its scholia, requires us to posit an onstage appearance of the transformed Tereus, or anything representing him, in Sophocles' play (see Dunbar ad loc.); nor does the demonstrative pronoun *touton* in line 1 of our fragment, which need mean no more than "the person just referred to".

1 While him: i.e. Tereus. This contrastive opening to the account of Tereus' transformation suggests that it was preceded by a description of the metamorphoses of Procne and Philomela (effected by the same god who transforms Tereus, since no new subject is indicated).

1 the hoopoe which is a viewer: the Greek has a pun (*epoptēn epopa*), and Burnett complains that it creates an almost comic mood; but puns in Greek poetry did not necessarily have that effect (consider the famous pun on the name of Helen in Aesch. *Ag.* 681ff).

1 its own sufferings: the use of *kaka* "evils, troubles, afflictions" here may be echoed in fr. N (589.3, 5).

2 he has adorned: the use of the third person and perfect tense indicates that the *deus ex machina* is speaking about another deity who has effected the metamorphoses already. As Zeus is responsible for the metamorphosis in many versions of the myth, including one (schol. Ar. *Birds* 212) which appears to be largely a paraphrase of the Hypothesis to our play, Zeus is most likely the subject of this sentence

2 has revealed does not require us to suppose that the transformed Tereus, or anything representing him, was visible on stage (cf. above); Greek verbs meaning literally "reveal (as)" sometimes in practice mean no more than "make, render" (cf. LSJ *apodeiknūmi* II 2).

3 full panoply: Tereus had probably appeared in the play accoutred as a warrior (cf. Ar. *Lys.* 563 "brandishing a light shield and a javelin, just like Tereus"). As regards the hoopoe, the reference is primarily to the bird's prominent crest (cf. Ar. *Birds* 94).

4–8 A reference to a belief, attested by Arist. *HA* 633a17 (who quotes this passage in support), that the hoopoe and the (sparrow-)hawk are the same bird in different seasonal guises; see Dunbar on Ar. *Birds* 15. As she points out, Sophocles (if Sophocles it is) appears to have got the seasons the wrong way round: the hoopoe is found in Greece only in spring and summer, the sparrowhawk mainly in winter. Before Sophocles, Tereus seems regularly to have become a hawk (see Introduction, p. 145); the enmity of hawk and nightingale was proverbial as early as Hesiod (*Works* 202–212). But he is not always changed into a bird. For example, in the Megarian version mentioned by Pausanias (1.41.9), Tereus killed himself because he could not catch the women, who had fled to Athens (and were changed into birds there).

6 from a single womb, his child's and his own: there must surely be an allusion to Tereus' act of cannibalism, whereby he took his son into his own belly. Since the hawk pursues, attacks and eats smaller birds, while the hoopoe is "so timid that [it has] been observed fleeing in terror when a swallow as much as flew above" (Dunbar loc.cit.), it is evident that the hawk is being thought of as having the personality of Tereus, the hoopoe that of Itys.

9 these regions: presumably cities and cultivated lands, in contrast with the "lonely woods and mountains".

N (589)

As with all the fragments of *Tereus* preserved by Stobaeus, there is no accompanying evidence for the dramatic context. The authoritative tone suggests that these may be the words of a *deus ex machina*, but there have been several other suggestions. Welcker [1839] 383 thought that they were spoken by the chorus, but Jebb (*ap.* Pearson 231) noted that a comment by the chorus would be confined to two verses and suggested that they were the closing words of a messenger speech. Burnett (1998) 182 has attributed the lines to a servant who is reporting on an indoor scene.

Even if the speaker is indeed a god, his views are not necessarily meant to be accepted automatically. After all, we surely are expected to admire Odysseus when he rejects Athena's invitation to gloat over the humiliation of Ajax and instead expresses pity for his fallen enemy (*Aj.* 121–6); see M.W. Blundell, *Helping Friends and Harming Enemies* (Cambridge, 1989) 60–64.

1   they: the Greek pronoun is feminine, and must denote Procne and Philomela.

4–5   cure ... illness ... doctor: the heavy medical references may support the identification of the speaker as Apollo (see on fr. M [581]).

O (590)

These anapaestic lines are generally accepted as the closing lines of the play; their sentiment and language are reflected to a greater or lesser extent in the endings of *Trachiniae, Ajax* and *Antigone* and also in some Euripidean choral tailpieces (e.g. *Med.* 1415), though the authenticity of many of the latter is disputed (see, on opposing sides, W. S Barrett, *Euripides: Hippolytos* [Oxford, 1964] 417–8 and D.H. Roberts, *CQ* 37 [1987] 51–64).

1   human nature ... human thoughts: this idea is proverbial and appears with slight variations throughout Greek poetry. Cf. *Aj.* 758–777, *Trach.* 473, Soph. fr. 346, Aesch. *Pers.* 821, Pind. *Isthm.* 5.16.
4   Zeus and no one else: this may have a specific reference to the metamorphosis, which was probably effected by Zeus (see on fr. M [581] 2); in *Trach.* 1278 the concluding reference to Zeus carries even greater weight.

P (594)

Hesychius (α1730) states that Sophocles used the word *aiglē* (usually "gleam, splendour") in this play to mean *khlidōn* "ornament (esp. necklace, bracelet, or anklet)"; that such a sense of the word existed in the fifth century is confirmed by Hesychius' further citation of Epicharmus (fr. 17) who used *aiglē* to mean "fetters" (presumably a humorous usage like the policeman's "bracelets" for handcuffs). No doubt the word was applied primarily to *golden* ornaments. Thrace, as abundant archaeological evidence has shown, was extremely rich in gold (see R.F. Hoddinott, *The Thracians* [London, 1981] and I. Venedikov, *Thracian Treasures from*

Bulgaria [London, 1976]); in the pseudo-Euripidean *Rhesus*, the Thracian Rhesus wears golden armour and his chariot has a golden yoke (*Rhes.* 301–6, 382). The ornaments referred to here may be worn by the women of the chorus, or they may be gifts made by Tereus to Procne, or they may even be worn by Tereus himself (in which case they would stamp him as a typically luxurious and effeminate barbarian; cf. E.M. Hall, *Inventing the Barbarian* [Oxford, 1989] 127–8).

Q (595a)

Several ancient grammarians state that *libanos*, properly the frankincense tree, can be used to denote the aromatic resin itself (more usually *libanōtos*), as indeed it is in Sappho fr. 44.30 and Eur. *Ba.* 144; and one, Herennius Philo (*On Words of Different Meanings* κ108 Nickau) says that Sophocles used the word thus in *Tereus*. We cannot determine the context, but the burning of incense regularly accompanied sacrifices, and sometimes in tragedy a character will burn incense on an altar on stage when making a prayer (e.g. *OT* 911–923). Conceivably the reference is to a sacrifice in honour of the return of Tereus (cf. Aesch. *Ag.* 1312); such a sacrifice would be the normal prelude to a great banquet.

R (595b)

This fragment comes from a papyrus commentary on a comedy, almost certainly Eupolis' *Taxiarchs*; the papyrus (*POxy* 2740) appears in *PCG* as Eupolis fr. 268. It appears that a new lemma begins with, or just before, the letters *toutousophokleo* (fr. 1, line 7 of the papyrus), which is plausibly read and supplemented by Austin as *tout' ou Sophokle[ous estin?]* "is that not by Sophocles?" This, if correct, would of course refer to some words spoken previously, which have not survived. But in the next line (8) we read *eisnineisphthor*, and this sequence contains the pronoun *nin* "him, her" which is common in tragedy and alien to the ordinary language of comedy; and two lines later (10–11) the commentator (at, or very near, the end of the note) is saying "It is by Sophocles, from *Tereus*, I think". (The intervening line 9 contains material which may come from the comic text, or be by the commentator, or partly one and partly the other; there is no positive reason to ascribe any of it to a tragic source.)

It is not clear why the commentator only *thought* that the words he was discussing came from *Tereus*; the most likely explanation is that Eupolis, as often happens, had slightly misquoted the tragedy (through a lapse of memory, or for comic effect), and therefore the words in the commentator's text of *Taxiarchs* did not quite match the words in his text of *Tereus*. We cannot tell, however, whether any of the words in line 8 were misquoted; there is nothing untragic about them or about their metrical pattern.

It thus appears that a speaker in Eupolis' play quoted (perhaps with minor changes) from Sophocles, and probably from *Tereus*, a line (or so) that included the sequence of syllables *–eis nin eis phthor-* "(?) him/her to ruin" (the last word was almost certainly either *phthoron* or its near-synonym *phthorān*). The first word, of which only the ending survives, might in principle be a second-person present-tense verb, but it has usually, and probably rightly, been taken to be the masculine nominative participle of some compound of *tithenai* "place" or *hīenai* "let go"; the participles that fit best with "to ruin" are *protheis* "exposing" and *apheis* "abandoning". The surviving syllables would fit in any of several positions in a comic iambic trimeter.

What man can have been said in *Tereus* to have exposed or abandoned someone to ruin? The expression does not well suit the actions of Tereus, whether towards Procne or Philomela or Itys; but it describes perfectly what Pandion did when he gave Philomela into the care of Tereus and thereby became the innocent cause of her rape and mutilation. Someone in the play, then, after Philomela's 'ruin' had become known, must have referred to this action of Pandion's: possibly Procne, possibly the man who had accompanied Tereus on his journey and who confirms Philomela's accusations against him (see on fr. G [588]), possibly the *deus ex machina* (cf. Eur. *Hipp.* 1283–1341 where Artemis manages to blame Phaedra, her nurse, *and* Theseus, as well as Aphrodite – but not Hippolytus himself! – for Hippolytus' impending death).

TROILUS

Texts and Testimonia: Pearson ii 253–262; Lucas de Dios 317–321; *TrGF* 453–8; Lloyd-Jones 306–7.

Myth: Iliad 24.257 with scholia; *Cypria* Arg. §11 West; Ibycus *SLG* 151, 224 = *GL* 282 (a)41–45, 282B (v); Phrynichus trag. fr. 13; Strattis frr. 42–43; Callimachus fr. 491; Lycophron 307–313 with scholia; Plautus, *Bacchides* 953–4; Virgil, *Aeneid* 1.474–8; [Apollodorus], *Bibliotheca* 3.12.5, *Epitome* 3.32; [Clement of Rome], *Homilies* 5.15.2; Dictys Cretensis 4.9 = *FGrH* 49 F 7a; Dares Phrygius 33; Dio Chrysostom *Or.* 11.77–78, 11.91, 21.17; Libanius *Decl.* 5.1.12; schol. Lycophron 168; Servius on *Aeneid* 1.474; Quintus of Smyrna 4.155, 418–435; *Mythographi Vaticani* 1.210 Mai = 1.207 Kulcsár. A. Lesky, *RE* viiA.1 (1939) 602–615; W. Kullmann, *Die Quellen der Ilias* (Wiesbaden, 1960) 291–3; A. Kossatz-Deissmann, *LIMC* i.1 (1981) 72–74 and viii.1 (1997) 91–92; Gantz 597–603; E. Cavallini, *Eikasmos* 5 (1994) 39–42; E.A.B. Jenner, *Prudentia* 30.2 (1998) 1–15.

Artistic evidence: E. Kunze, *Archaische Schildbänder* (Berlin, 1950) 141–2; C. Zindel, *Drei vorhomerische Sagenversionen in der griechischen Kunst* (Diss. Basel 1974) 63–80; A. Kossatz-Deissmann, *LIMC* i.1 (1981) 72–95 and viii.1 (1997) 91–94; G. Camporeale, *LIMC* i.1 (1981) 202–5, 210–1; B. d'Agostino in *Poikilia: Études offertes à Jean-Pierre Vernant* (Paris, 1987) 145–154; A. Cambitoglou in J.H. Betts et al. ed. *Studies in Honour of T.B.L. Webster* ii (Bristol, 1988) 1–21; M. Robertson in J.P. Descoeudres ed. *Eumousia: Ceramic and Iconographic Studies in Honour of Alexander Cambitoglou* (Sydney, 1990) 63–70; T.H. Carpenter, *Art and Myth in Ancient Greece* (London, 1990) 17–21.

Main discussions: Lesky (above) 605–9; Sutton 148–150.

The myth and the play

Perhaps the most vicious of all the actions traditionally attributed to Achilles is the killing of Troilus, a son of Priam hardly out of boyhood, at least as the episode was regularly imagined by artists of the archaic and early classical period, from which numerous surviving images[1] present a

---

[1]See Kossatz-Deissmann (1981) and Gantz 597–602.

series of moments in a fairly consistent, and horrific, story. First we see Troilus and his sister Polyxene together at a spring or fountain; presumably therefore Polyxene has come out of the city to fetch water, with Troilus as her escort. Troilus has a horse, often two,[2] but is normally unarmed. The pair are ambushed by Achilles. Polyxene runs away, bringing to Troy the news that her brother is in danger, whereupon the Trojans send out the armed force which subsequently confronts Achilles. Troilus also flees, on horseback, but "swift-footed" Achilles, unmounted, pursues and overtakes him, and kills him in a sanctuary, which literary sources[3] identify as that of Apollo Thymbraios; Achilles beheads the corpse, and is sometimes shown brandishing or even throwing its head at the Trojans who attack him.

It is not surprising that this combination of murder, sacrilege and mutilation was too rich for the poet of the *Iliad*: his Achilles can certainly be brutal, but there are limits to his brutality, and it emerges only under the influence of a grievance, or a grief, that is of properly heroic proportions. The *Iliad* mentions Troilus only once, and then (24.257) in such a way as to imply, without actually stating, that the young prince (who is called a "chariot-fighter") was slain by Achilles in battle like so many of his brothers. Nevertheless, one detail in the subsequent scene between Achilles and Priam suggests that the poet was aware, and expected his audience to be aware, of the darker version of the story that he was suppressing. When Priam enters Achilles' hut, he grasps the hero's knees and kisses "the terrible manslaying (*androphonous*) hands that had killed many of his sons" (24.478–9). Then Priam speaks, bidding Achilles remember his father, comparing Peleus' lot with his own, and speaking of the fifty sons he had had "when the sons of the Achaeans came", most of them now dead, the latest Hector; and he ends by saying (24.505–6) that he has brought himself to do "what no other man on earth has done, to raise to his lips the hand of a child-slaying man (*andros paidophonoio*)".

---

[2] The second horse finds no explanation in the artistic record taken alone, since there is no one to ride it and no sign of a chariot. Several written sources, however, say that Troilus had gone out of the city to "exercise his horses" (the T-scholia on *Iliad* 24.257, who ascribe this version to Sophocles; Dio Chrys. 11.78; *Mythogr. Vat.* 1.210 Mai = 1.207 Kulcsár; Eustathius on *Iliad* 24.257) – though none of them mentions Polyxene. Probably the artistic tradition is ultimately based on a poetic account – most likely that of the *Cypria* – in which Troilus and Polyxene went out of the city together so that Troilus could exercise his horses *and* simultaneously provide some protection for his sister while she fetched water.

[3] Sophocles ap. schol. T *to* Iliad 24.247; schol. Ibycus *SLG* S224 = *GL* 282B (v); [Apoll.] *Epit.* 3.32; schol. Lycophron *Alex.* 307; Eustathius on *Iliad* 24.257.

He means, of course, the hand of the man who had killed his, Priam's, children;[4] but for anyone who knows the traditional version of the killing of Troilus, Achilles *is* a child-slayer as well as a man-slayer.

That there was something sinister in the Troilus story from an early date is confirmed by Proclus' summary of the cyclic epic in which it was told, the *Cypria*, in which he says Achilles "murders" (*phoneuei*) Troilus.[5] And considering its early popularity in art, the story makes remarkably little showing in literary or mythographic texts.

The written sources can be broadly divided into two groups: those which follow the story, implied by the *Iliad*, of a killing in battle, and those in which the killing takes place when Troilus has gone out of the city alone, or almost alone, on some non-military business. Beyond the basic fact that Troilus was slain by Achilles, the two types of account have little in common except that Troilus is often described as a person of exceptional beauty[6] and that he usually meets his end when riding or driving horses.[7]

The Homeric version is followed by two epic poets for whom Homer served as a model, Virgil (*Aeneid* 1.474–8) and Quintus of Smyrna (4.155, 4.418–435); neither provides a context for the event within the story of the war, any more than Homer had. A remarkable variant is provided in the pretended "war diaries" of Dares the Phrygian (33) and Dictys the Cretan (4.9 = *FGrH* 49 F 7a), at least one and probably both of which are now known, thanks to *PTebt* 268 and *POxy* 2539, to have originated no later than AD 200.[8] In both of these the death of Troilus is placed much later in the war, after the death of Hector and not long before that of Achilles.[9]

---

[4]Just as when the disguised Athene reminds Telemachus (*Odyssey* 1.298–301) of how Orestes had killed the "father-slayer" (*patrophoneus*) Aegisthus, she means the man who had killed his, Orestes', father.

[5]*Cypria* Arg. §11 West.

[6]Ibycus *SLG* 151 = *GL* 282a41–45; Phrynichus trag. fr. 13; Dictys 4.9 = *FGrH* 49 F 7a; Strato *AP* 12.191; Dio Chrys. 21.17; Q.S. 4.155, 430.

[7]In the "murder" versions this is several times stated or implied, and never contradicted. In the "battle" versions it is found at Virg. *Aen.* 1.476–7 (chariot) and Dares 33 (riding).

[8]See S. Merkle, *Die Ephemeris belli Troiani des Diktys von Kreta* (Frankfurt, 1989) 243–6, who reviews earlier discussions and favours a date (for the original Greek text) relatively late in the interval between AD 66 (the purported date of the "discovery" of Dictys' narrative) and c.AD 200 (the date of *POxy* 2539; *PTebt* 268 is a little later).

[9]This version – more precisely, that of Dictys – was also known to a scholiast on Lyc. *Alex.* 307, who after expounding the version obscurely prophesied in the text on which he was commenting (that Achilles was in love with Troilus and killed him for refusing his advances) says that "these people talk that sort of nonsense about Troilus, but *I* know …"

Dares makes Troilus the most prominent warrior on the Trojan side after Hector; he takes over command after Hector's death, routs the Greeks more than once, wounds Achilles, but is killed after being thrown from his wounded horse, his body being rescued for the Trojans by Memnon. In Dictys, on the other hand, Troilus is taken prisoner *after* the death of Memnon, and together with his brother Lycaon is put to death by Achilles who is angry with their father for his failure to fulfil their agreement;[10] in retaliation for this a plot is set in motion that leads to the death of Achilles in, significantly, the precinct of Apollo Thymbraios.

Dictys is evidently blending elements from the "battle" and "murder" versions of the story. Our first literary evidence for the latter – and the only written source for it that gives any direct indication of Polyxene's involvement – comes from a papyrus fragment that gives us six or seven words of a poem by the sixth-century lyricist Ibycus (*SLG* 224 = *GL* 282B [v]) and a few tattered lines from its scholia.[11] The scholia make it clear that the passage related to Troilus, and the surviving words of text speak of him as a boy "like the gods" and as being killed "outside the citadel of Troy",[12] the scholia also refer to a sister (*adelphē*), and an isolated word surviving from a slightly later part of the text appears to be *kasis* "sibling" and to be glossed as *adel[phos]* "brother" or *adel[phē]* "sister". In Ibycus' poem, then, Troilus was killed somewhere outside the city, and a sister of his (surely, in view of the artistic evidence, Polyxene[13]) was somehow involved in the episode; furthermore, the scholia speak of someone, evidently Achilles, "watching out" (*epitērēsās*) evidently for Troilus' approach, and of a "murder" (*phonos*) committed in the sanctuary of

---

and proceeds to retail an abbreviated version of Dictys' story. This commentator seems to have known, and given credence to, Dares also; in a note on *Alex.* 168 he criticizes Lycophron for what he makes Cassandra say about Deiphobus, on the ground that "after Hector it was his brother Troilus, not Deiphobus, who ranked second as a warrior".

[10]The writer seems to be thinking of an agreement to arrange a marriage between Achilles and Polyxene; the next event in his narrative is, in fact, the initiation of negotiations for this purpose (4.10). He has not, however, previously reported any such undertaking on Priam's part. Priam had indeed begged Achilles to take Polyxene under his protection forthwith (3.27), but Achilles' reply had been that this was not the time or the place to decide the matter, and the issue had been left there; nothing is said about any stipulation as to who should make the next move or when.

[11]On this fragment see Cavallini (1994) and Jenner (1998).

[12]"Boy" and "killed" are not in the surviving text, but the scholiast's explanation makes it virtually certain that they stood in the lost parts of the sentence.

[13]Jenner (1998) 3 rightly rejects the speculation of Cavallini (1994) 42 that it might be Cassandra.

Apollo Thymbraios. These details could in principle have been derived by the scholiast from later texts[14] rather than from that of Ibycus; but they fit so exactly with the evidence of artistic representations from Ibycus' own time, which are most unlikely to have been known to the scholiast, that it is hard to resist the inference that Ibycus was narrating – perhaps at length, perhaps allusively – a version of the story essentially identical to that which underlies these representations.

Of subsequent authors, Lycophron, ps.-Apollodorus, Dio Chrysostom, the first *Vatican Mythographer*, and Eustathius[15] all speak of Troilus as having been killed by Achilles outside a battle context; a Homeric scholiast[16] tells us that Sophocles also adopted this version of the story – but to Sophocles we shall return later. Most of these writers[17] make some mention of the precinct of Apollo Thymbraios, thereby at least implying[18] that the killing was sacrilegious; the *Vatican Mythographer*, however, presents a version which elides the sacrilege by having Achilles, on the model of *Aeneid* 1.474–8,[19] tie Troilus to his horses which drag him back to the city *exanimis*.[20] Servius on *Aeneid* 1.474 reports a version which extenuates Achilles' guilt still further by apparently making the killing accidental: Achilles, being in love with Troilus (more on this in a moment), lured him close by releasing some doves, of which Troilus was fond, and then seized the boy who "perished in his embrace".[21]

---

[14]Or indeed from an earlier text such as the *Cypria*.

[15]Lycophron *Alex.* 307–313 with scholia; [Apoll.] *Epit.* 3.32; Dio Chrys. 11.77–78; *Mythogr. Vat.* 1.210 Mai = 1.207 Kulcsár; Eustathius on *Iliad* 24.257.

[16]Schol. T to *Iliad* 24.257.

[17]The exceptions are Dio (who is making only an incidental reference to the episode) and the *Vatican Mythographer*.

[18]Lycophron (*Alex.* 313) makes it explicit, at least for those who can decipher his riddling phraseology. Lycophron (*ibid.*) is also the only author known to have mentioned that Troilus was decapitated, and our earliest source for the story (which must, however, already have been known to his readers) that Troilus was actually the son of Apollo rather than Priam (cf. [Apoll.] 3.12.5).

[19]Where, however, the situation is different: Troilus has encountered Achilles in battle, taken to flight discarding his weapons, been hit in the back by Achilles' spear, fallen from his chariot, and is being dragged along with his hands still on the reins.

[20]It is not clear from what the writer says whether he imagined Troilus as already dead (as Hector is in *Iliad* 22.395–404) or only as mortally wounded (as he is in the *Aeneid* passage, and as Hector is in the version of Soph. *Aj.* 1029–31); a moment earlier he had written of Troilus being "wounded" by Achilles. Very likely the writer was not clear about this in his own mind.

[21]The ancient sexual predator, unlike the modern one, was not thought of as likely to go on to murder his victim, nor is there anything in Servius' language that points to the idea of

But in most of the accounts in this second group, Achilles' act is plainly being viewed as an impious atrocity. What can have motivated Achilles to commit it? Still leaving aside Sophocles for now, our written sources offer two kinds of answer. One version starts from the tradition of Troilus' exceptional beauty, which as we have seen goes back at least to Ibycus, and supposes Achilles to have been in love with him. This idea may have been used by the tragedian Phrynichus in the early fifth century,[22] traces of it seem to appear in archaic art,[23] and it must have been familiar to the first readers of Lycophron (*Alex.* 309–312) who makes Cassandra grieve over the coming fate of the "whelp" Troilus, who will strike a "savage serpent" with an arrow of love though "himself unwounded by his victim". Lycophron's scholiast explains that Achilles,

> being in love with Troilus ... was pursuing him and about to catch him, when he fled into the temple of Apollo Thymbraios. Achilles tried to force him to come out, but when he refused, he went in and killed him at the altar; in revenge for which, they say, Apollo [who in this version is Troilus' father] forthwith planned the slaying of Achilles.

Still a terrible crime, to be sure, but not entirely out of character for a hero who was notoriously often the slave of his passions. Servius, as we have seen, knew of a different version in which the murder itself disappears from the story.

An entirely different idea appears in two Latin sources – an idea, moreover, that has strong tragic potential, since it can be seen as putting Achilles in a position in which it becomes his *duty* to kill the unarmed, innocent young lad. In Plautus' comedy *Bacchides* (953–4)[24] the slave

---

an intentional killing; he seems rather to be supposing that Achilles without any evil design crushed or suffocated Troilus by the sheer strength of his arms. This version of the story is now known to go back to archaic times; a sixth-century Etruscan amphora in Rome (*LIMC* Achle 13) shows two doves flying towards Troilus and his horse, with Achilles about to release a third. See d'Agostino (1987).

[22] Phryn. trag. fr. 13 (lyric) "the light of love shines on his crimson cheeks".

[23] In addition to the Etruscan amphora mentioned above (n.21), there are a series of early sixth-century shield-bands from Olympia (*LIMC* Achilleus 274) depicting the killing of Troilus in the sanctuary, which show a cock standing on the altar, and this has been interpreted as a love-gift (see Kunze [1950] and, with discussion of possible further evidence, Zindel [1974]).

[24] *Bacchides* was an adaptation of Menander's *Dis Exapaton*; but the Trojan War comparison fills a lengthy (and internally inconsistent) *canticum* by Chrysalus (925–977) during which no other character is present and which does not advance the action, and which must have been created, or at least elaborated out of all recognition, by Plautus

Chrysalus, in the course of an elaborate comparison between the Trojan War and the situation in the play, says he has heard that there were three occurrences which had to happen if Troy was ever to be captured. The first was the taking of the Palladium; the third was the breaking of the upper lintel of the Phrygian (or Scaean) gate[25] – and the second was the death of Troilus. This might seem to place Troilus' death very late in the war – the taking of the Palladium is the last event mentioned in Proclus' summary of the *Little Iliad*[26] before the building of the Wooden Horse – and even, uniquely, to make it impossible for Achilles (by then dead) to have been his slayer; but the events are not necessarily being mentioned in their actual sequence in the story. The first *Vatican Mythographer*,[27] at any rate, brings the idea of Troilus as Troy's talisman into direct connection with the story of his being ambushed and murdered by Achilles early in the war; after giving a brief account of the murder, he adds that "he [presumably Achilles] had been told that if [Troilus] reached the age of twenty, Troy could not be overthrown". That this idea does not appear in any surviving Greek source is probably accidental:[28] the reference to it in Plautus is so brief that he is hardly likely to be its inventor.

All these varying versions of the story, except that of Ibycus, have two things in common. They make no mention of Polyxene, who figures so prominently in the artistic record; and while some of them give Achilles more or less adequate motives for wishing to *kill* Troilus, none of them comes near enabling us to understand why he should have hated Troilus so

---

himself. See E. Fraenkel, *Elementi plautini in Plauto* (Florence, 1960) 57–67, 403; K. Gaiser, *Philologus* 114 (1970) 72–78; E. Lefèvre, *Hermes* 106 (1978) 525–8; J.A. Barsby, *Plautus: Bacchides* (Warminster, 1986) 169–173, 176; M. Skafte Jensen, *C&M* 48 (1997) 315–323. Pearson ii 254 is thus on very unsafe ground when he states as a fact that "[the] legend that Troy could not be taken, if Troilus reached the age of twenty … was referred to by Menander in his Δὶς ἐξαπατῶν".

[25]When the Trojans took the Wooden Horse into their city, they broke down part of the wall to enable it to be taken through (*Little Iliad* Arg. §5 West; Virg. *Aen.* 2.234); Servius (on *Aeneid* 2.234, 241) says that it was the wall around and above the Scaean gate that was demolished, and adds that "we know" that Troy could not be taken so long as Laomedon's tomb, which was placed over this gate, remained undisturbed.

[26]*Little Iliad* Arg. §4 West.

[27]*Mythogr. Vat.* 1.210 Mai = 1.207 Kulcsár.

[28]The presence of Athena as a supporter of Achilles in several archaic representations of episodes of the Troilus story (*LIMC* Achilleus 218, 286, 288, 298, 317, 322, 323, 359a) may indicate that already at that time there was a tradition according to which Troilus' death was a *sine qua non* of Greek victory in the war: in the *Iliad* and the epic tradition generally, Athena's concern is to secure such a victory, rather than to promote the interests or glory of Achilles or any other individual hero (except Odysseus).

much as to mutilate his corpse by decapitation or, as we know occurred in Sophocles (fr. L [623]), by *maschalismos*. In the *Iliad* Achilles' greatest hate is for Hector, and he vows not to bury Patroclus until he has brought him Hector's armour and head (18.334–5); this would certainly be taken by Homer's audience as meaning that the enraged Achilles will decapitate Hector's corpse as Ajax son of Oileus had decapitated the corpse of Imbrius (13.202–3) and as Hector had intended to decapitate that of Patroclus (17.126) – but in fact, though Achilles inflicts many indignities on Hector's body over many days, from this one he refrains. For Troilus' corpse to be thus treated more atrociously even than Hector's, one would have expected, at the very least, that he should have committed some great injury or insult against Achilles; yet all that we hear of (and then in one source only, Lycophron) is that he persistently rejected Achilles' amorous advances (and so far as we know, not even in favour of another suitor). It must be regarded as possible, to say no more, that there may be some connection between these two apparent weaknesses in the versions of the story that we find in written sources of the Hellenistic period and later.

But it is now time to revert to Sophocles and ask what evidence we have for *his* version of the story of Troilus' death.

In the first place, we know that Sophocles' version belonged to the "murder", not the "battle" group of accounts:

> Sophocles in *Troilus* says he [Troilus] was ambushed by Achilles while exercising his horses near the Thymbraion and killed.[29]

The mention of the Thymbraion makes it highly likely that Sophocles followed the artistic tradition (and probably Ibycus) in placing the killing in the sanctuary and thereby making it an act of sacrilege; and fr. F (621), "we were making for the flowing springs of drinking water", indicates that he may well also have followed the artists in setting the initial ambush at a spring or fountain-house, a detail not repeated in any surviving later written source.[30] Moreover, there is evidence that Polyxene had a role in the plot. She is not mentioned in any surviving fragment attributed to the play or in any ancient statement about it; but the comic dramatist Strattis wrote a *Troilus* in which someone says, in tragic language, "Never come

---

[29]Schol. T to *Iliad* 24.257.
[30]This is in no way inconsistent with the *Iliad* scholiast's statement that the ambush took place "near the Thymbraion", which is probably just a (perfectly reasonable) inference from the fact that Troilus, fleeing after the ambush, was caught and killed *at* the Thymbraion.

together with her, child of Zeus!" (fr. D = *trag. adesp.* 561 = Strattis fr. 42.1), and this makes it likely that in Sophocles' play the sexual and/or matrimonial fate of Polyxene was an important issue. Late sources speak of Achilles having been in love with Polyxene,[31] and recent discoveries have made it virtually certain that they are reflecting an early tradition;[32] but since Achilles was not a "child of Zeus", the addressee in any Sophoclean model for the Strattis fragment must have been someone else, and the only plausible candidate is Sarpedon (see commentary on fr. D) – though this of course does not exclude the possibility that Achilles too may have been presented in the play as desiring Polyxene.

Three other features of the play emerge clearly from the limited evidence. In the first place, fragments A (620), E (619) and F (621) between them indicate with high probability that a prominent character in the play was a eunuch slave of Troilus, who accompanied his master on his final journey and returned with news of his death. The fact that it is he, rather than Polyxene, who brings back the news suggests that in Sophocles' play Polyxene did *not* accompany Troilus on that journey; rather, Troilus, wishing to exercise his horses, goes out of the city with the eunuch (who can both serve as his escort, and look after one of the two horses while Troilus is giving the other a work-out) and they can go to the spring, not for water to take home (that was women's work) but to give themselves and the horses a drink.

That Troilus' slave is a eunuch is one manifestation of the second feature I wish to highlight, the strong "orientalizing" – indeed Persianizing – tendency evident in many of the fragments of this play.[33] The very word *asoloikos* "unbarbaric" (fr. B [629]) in itself suggests that the contrast between barbarians and Greeks was an important theme. Trojan soldiers are referred to by the Persian term *orosangai* (fr. G [634]), their main weapon may have been the bow rather than the spear (fr. H [626]), their men wear garments that to a Greek looked feminine (fr. P [622]) and they utter "barbarian lamentations" like *iai* and *iē* (frr. N [631], O [632]); it will have been all the easier for the dramatist to emphasize their alienness if, as is not unlikely,[34] he created a character *within* the play who saw them as

---

[31]Dictys 3.2–3, 4.10–11; Hyginus *Fab.* 110; schol. Eur. *Tro.* 16; schol. Lycophron 323; Dio Chrys. 6.18; Servius on Virg. *Aen.* 3.321.

[32]See G. Schwarz, *MDAI(A)* 116 (2001) 35–50; the evidence is more fully discussed in the Introduction to *Polyxene*, pp. 45–47.

[33]For fuller discussion see Commentary on the fragments cited below. Cf. Sutton 149.

[34]See Commentary to fr. B [629].

alien, by making the eunuch slave a Greek. And yet there can be little doubt that *ethically,* at least in most respects, Achilles, whether or not he appeared on stage (he probably did not), was by far the most barbarous character concerned in the action of the play.[35]

This is most strikingly shown by the third salient feature, his systematic mutilation (*maschalismos*) of the corpse of Troilus (fr. L [623]). Our sources (discussed in the Commentary on *Polyxene* fr. G [528]) associate this procedure sometimes with the murder of kindred, sometimes with plotted or treacherous murders.[36] Other than Troilus, the only individual who is stated in any pre-Hellenistic text to have been subjected to this treatment is Agamemnon, at the hands of Clytaemestra (Aesch. *Cho.* 439, Soph. *El.* 445), and it surely implies in Achilles either a very great hatred of Troilus or a very great fear of his vengeful spirit – or both. We do not know whether in Sophocles, as in the artistic tradition and as in Lycophron, Achilles also cut off Troilus' head; all one can say is that Sophocles' apparent addition of *maschalismos* to the story suggests that he was concerned to increase the atrociousness of Achilles' actions, so it may be thought unlikely that he would simultaneously diminish it by omitting the decapitation.

In principle *maschalismos* could be viewed as a rational precaution against revenge – though that is not how Aeschylus invites us to view it in the case of Clytaemestra, whose son is told by the chorus of *Choephori* (439–442) that his mother's objective had been "to make [Agamemnon's] death something worse than your life could endure",[37] in other words that her treatment of the corpse was an act of degradation. Decapitation can be nothing but an act of hatred or rage. It was certainly out of hatred and rage that Achilles vowed to bring to Patroclus the head of Hector; Euphorbus hoped to take the head of Menelaus home to his parents to assuage their

---

[35]On "barbaric Greeks" in tragedy who are shown as ethically no better, or worse, than non-Greeks cf. E.M. Hall, *Inventing the Barbarian* (Oxford, 1989) 201–223.

[36]Murder of kindred: schol. Soph. *El.* 445; schol. Ap.Rh. 4.477; *Et.Mag.* 574.202–7; Suda μ274; Apostolius 11.4. Murder planned in advance: Paus. Att. μ8; Hesychius μ379; Suda μ928, μ275. Murder effected by trickery: *Et.Mag.* 118.23–25. The statement of Sutton 149 that "those slain in battle" were sometimes thus treated lacks all support.

[37]Since Clytaemestra cannot be supposed to have wished to make Orestes implacably determined to avenge his father's death, the meaning must be that she wished to make him feel so disgraced and humiliated that he would be driven to suicide; this is in harmony with her reported (though concealed) rejoicing at the false news of her son's death (*Cho.* 737–740) and with her call for a "man-slaying axe" (*ib.* 889) on learning that he is alive, is in her house, and has killed Aegisthus.

grief over his brother Hyperenor whom Menelaus had killed (*Iliad* 17.34–40); and the only person actually to decapitate a corpse in the *Iliad*, Ajax son of Oileus, did so because he was "angry over [the death of] Amphimachus" (*Iliad* 13.203).[38] We must therefore seek a reason for Achilles to feel hatred and rage against Troilus. The motives for the killing that are to be found in the rest of the literary tradition do not furnish him with such a reason. If Troilus is treacherously killed because his death is necessary if Troy is to be captured, that might well give Achilles cause to fear the wrath of his ghost, but it does not require there to be the least personal hostility between the two. And if he is killed for rejecting Achilles' amorous advances, that would indeed be a killing in anger, but one would expect that anger to be quickly followed by remorse as Achilles contemplated the corpse of one who had been, as Patroclus was to be, both his beloved and his victim.[39]

As indicated above, we might do well to link this problem with that of the role of Polyxene in the play. So far we have established with reasonable confidence, on the one hand that Polyxene did not accompany Troilus on his fatal excursion, on the other hand that she was sought in marriage by Sarpedon and someone tried to warn him off her – perhaps, if Strattis fr. 42.2 K–A ("but hand her over to the Lesbians and forget about her") is a comic makeover of Sophocles, by casting aspersions on her chastity; see Commentary on fr. D, where it is also argued that the likeliest person to have given this warning is Troilus himself.

Why should Troilus have done this? It is almost impossible to imagine a more appropriate bridegroom for Polyxene than Sarpedon, a son of Zeus, a man (to judge by the *Iliad*) of the highest valour and virtue, and the most distinguished figure among the Trojans' foreign allies. What could have

---

[38]Though a worthier hero than the lesser Ajax might find this an inadequate motive: Amphimachus was neither his relative nor his close colleague (he came from a quite different region of Greece, cf. *Iliad* 2.615–624); he had been killed by Hector, not by Imbrius whose corpse Ajax beheaded; Imbrius had actually died *before* Amphimachus; and it had not even been Ajax who killed Imbrius – that honour belonged to Teucer, who had been trying to strip the corpse when Hector threw a spear at him which he managed to avoid and which hit Amphimachus instead (*Iliad* 13.170–187).

[39]One thinks also, in this connection, of Achilles' grief over the dead Penthesileia, which probably goes right back to the *Aethiopis* (what else could have made Thersites imagine [*Aethiopis* Arg. §1 West] that Achilles had been in love with her – unless we adopt the grotesque fantasy of later writers who had Achilles actually perform an act of necrophilia?); cf. Paus. 5.11.6 (a fifth-century painting), schol. Lycophron *Alex.* 999, schol. D to *Iliad* 2.219, Eustathius on *Iliad* 2.220.

induced Troilus to attempt to prevent such a splendid marriage for his sister, and to do so, it may be, by slandering her in a manner that would seriously hamper her prospects of finding any other husband? It is almost as if he did not want her to marry at all. Might one speculate that that was indeed what Sophocles imagined, and that in keeping with the "orientalizing" atmosphere of the play, discussed above, and with a stereotype about the sexual preferences of barbarians of which we have other attestations,[40] he presented Troilus as being *himself* in love with Polyxene?[41]

Such a Troilus would also, and more creditably, be a zealous protector of his sister against any danger of violation by members of the invading army – including Achilles. Someone in the play appears to be interested in Achilles' family background, about which someone else provides information which is literally accurate though highly tendentious (fr. C [618]); a Greek slave (see above) would be an obvious person to provide such information, and the addressee might be either Troilus or Polyxene. That the information has been sought indicates that either the brother or the sister has particular cause to be curious about Achilles. I suggest that in Sophocles' play Troilus came to know of Achilles' passion for Polyxene; that, in keeping with the tone of fr. C (618), he warned Achilles off her in a contemptuous and insulting manner; and that it was this treatment, perceived by Achilles as gross *hybris*, that provoked Achilles, in an extremity of rage, to murder and then mutilate the Trojan prince. It will be noted that on a later occasion when Achilles is told in an insulting manner that he shall not have a woman whom he desires, he nearly kills Agamemnon in open assembly (*Iliad* 1.188–221) and subsequently asks for the Greek army to suffer defeat and heavy casualties (*ibid.* 407–412) merely because they had not protested.

If Troilus in this play is indeed secretly in love with his sister, it will be necessary for this to be somehow made known to the audience: the idea had probably not appeared in any previous version of the story, and even if

---

[40]Eur. *Andr.* 173–5; Hdt. 3.31, 3.68, 3.88; Xanthus *FGrH* 765 F 31; *Dissoi Logoi* fr. 2.33 D-K; Heracleides of Cyme *FGrH* 689 F 7.

[41]The theme of a brother's incestuous passion for his sister had already (if *Troilus* is correctly dated after 420 – see pp. 215–6) been central to Euripides' *Aeolus*, which most probably belongs to the middle 420s (see Cropp & Fick 71–72). If Sophocles used the idea in *Troilus*, he palliated its offensiveness (for which cf. Ar. *Clouds* 1371–2, *Frogs* 1081) by placing it in a setting strongly marked as barbarian and by leaving the passion unconsummated.

it had, the audience would need to know whether Sophocles was using it or not. Such a revelation could most conveniently be made in the absence of the chorus,[42] i.e. in the prologue. If Troilus had taken his eunuch slave into his confidence the revelation might come in a monologue by the latter or in a dialogue between the two; but if the slave was indeed Greek, he would hardly continue to admire Troilus as he evidently does (cf. fr. E [619]) after learning of his incestuous passion, and it is more likely therefore to be Troilus himself, alone on stage, who reveals this passion to the audience.[43] This cannot, however, have been the only soliloquy in the prologue, since we know from fr. A (620) that the eunuch gave a narrative of his personal history, evidently for the information of the audience rather than of Troilus (who would already know it). Hence the structure of the prologue is likely to have been: soliloquy by the slave, then dialogue between him and Troilus, then soliloquy by Troilus.[44]

The scene of the action will have been Troy, to which the slave (taking the role performed by Polyxene in the artistic tradition) would have brought his report of the ambush and killing of Troilus (frr. E [619], F [621]), from which the rescue/revenge expedition would have been sent out (frr. G [634], H [626], J [630], and to which Troilus' body would have been brought back for lamentation and burial (frr. L [623], N [631], O [632]).[45] More specifically, it will have been outside the palace of Priam,

---

[42]Otherwise it would be necessary to swear the chorus to secrecy as e.g. in Eur. *Hipp.* 713–714, *IT* 1075–7.

[43]The closest known parallel in tragedy is perhaps Euripides' *Melanippe the Wise*, in whose prologue Melanippe told of how she had become pregnant by Poseidon and given birth to twin sons; when in due course the boys are discovered in the ox-byres, they are thought to be the miraculous offspring of the cattle (Eur. fr. 481 and *Melanippe Sophe* test. i Kannicht). In New Comedy cf. Men. *Sam.* 31–57 where Moschion in soliloquy confesses that he is the father of the baby now being looked after by Chrysis, the mistress of his adoptive father Demeas, and that its mother is the girl he has promised to marry – facts, admittedly, which are already known to all members of the two families concerned except the fathers, who have been abroad together on business and have independently decided to arrange a marriage between their children.

[44]For a similarly structured prologue cf. Euripides' *Alcestis* (Apollo-Death). Ar. *Peace* 1–179 has a more elaborate version of the same pattern: in 1–81 two slaves (later one) are alone on stage; in 82–149 there is dialogue between the remaining slave (joined later by Trygaeus' daughters) and Trygaeus; in 150–179 Trygaeus, flying on his Pegasus-beetle, is alone.

[45]Pearson ii 254 placed the scene "somewhere in the neighbourhood of the temple of the Thymbraean Apollo", apparently because he thought that without the actual presence of Achilles the play would have been "rob[bed] ... of its chief dramatic motive" (*ib.* 255); but he offered no suggestion at all as to what the play's action could have consisted of, given

in which Troilus and Polyxene would be living. This makes it likely, but not certain,[46] that Priam and/or Hecuba appeared in the play, possibly taking part in the concluding lamentations.

The following is a very tentative account of how the play may have gone. To avoid the constant use of hedging expressions like "may have been" and "perhaps", I have instead marked its tentative status by printing it in italics.

Prologue: *the play begins with a soliloquy by Troilus' eunuch slave-tutor (*paidagōgos*), by origin a Greek, in which he narrates in summary his life history – how he became a slave, how Hecuba castrated him (fr. A [620]), and how she put him in charge of her two youngest children, Troilus and Polyxene.*[47] *He praises the character and behaviour of Troilus – handsome, intelligent, and already an expert horseman – who seems spiritually more like a Greek than a barbarian (fr. B [629]). Troilus' beautiful sister Polyxene is being sought in marriage by Sarpedon (a union to which her father Priam seems disposed to consent); messages about her have also come to Troilus from Achilles in the enemy camp, who has apparently seen her (perhaps on the city walls, perhaps when going outside them to sacrifice or fetch water) and fallen in love with her. The tutor is then joined by Troilus, who asks him for information about Achilles; in reply the slave, devoted as he has become to the welfare of Troilus and his family, gives a highly slanted and hostile account of his parentage (fr. C [618]) and no doubt of his character. Troilus sends him off with instructions to reply to Achilles' messages with a firm and contemptuous rejection, and then, left alone, confesses in soliloquy that he himself is hopelessly in love with his sister and desperately anxious to prevent her marriage. He then goes back into the palace.*

---

that neither the ambushing, nor the seizure, nor the killing of Troilus could have been represented on stage.

[46] Euripides' *Hippolytus* is set outside the house in Trozen of Pittheus, the maternal grandfather of Theseus, where Hippolytus has lived since childhood and where Theseus and Phaedra have been staying during Theseus' temporary exile from Athens (*Hipp.* 11, 24, 34–37, 794); but Pittheus is given no role in the action, on or off stage.

[47] On the even younger Polydorus of Euripides' *Hecuba* see the Introduction to *Polyxene* (p. 48 n.37).

Parodos: *entrance of the chorus, who are slightly more likely to have been male than female Trojans (cf. fr. P [622]), and if so, probably old men of high status[48].*

First Episode: *Sarpedon arrives to secure the final consent of Priam for his betrothal to Polyxene. Troilus intercepts him and warns him against the marriage (fr. D), alleging or at least hinting that there is some doubt about Polyxene's chastity.[49] Sarpedon departs, grateful to have avoided a marriage that might have shamed him. Troilus is presently joined again by his tutor who reports that the message of rejection has been conveyed to Achilles, and both go inside.*

First Stasimon *(content undeterminable).*

Second Episode: *Troilus comes out of the palace with Polyxene. With an ulterior motive obvious to the audience but unimaginable by Polyxene or the chorus, he asks her to join him when he goes out of the city to exercise his horses. She refuses, fearing that she may be waylaid by Achilles or some other Greek and that Troilus will not be strong enough to protect her, and nothing he can say will make her change her mind.[50] She goes back inside, and Troilus calls out his tutor; they go off together to the stables, whence they will depart on their ride.*

Second Stasimon *(content undeterminable).*

Third Episode: *The tutor returns alone, in acute distress, and announces that his young master is dead (fr. E [619]). Either to the chorus, or to a member of the family (most probably Hector[51]) who comes outside to*

---

[48]By making them old men, Sophocles would make it easy and unproblematic for them to stay where they are when a force of younger Trojans is sent out to do battle with Achilles.

[49]He may even for this purpose have exploited the fact that messages regarding Polyxene had come to Troy from Achilles: he might well have been able, without telling any actual falsehoods, to present the information in such a way as to make it seem that an intrigue existed between Achilles and his sister.

[50]There is, it will be seen, no direct evidence at all for this scene. I have posited it for the following reasons: (i) the pattern of surviving Sophoclean tragedies suggests that the play requires at least one further episode besides the prologue and the scenes involving Sarpedon, the report of the ambush, and the return of the body; (ii) the scene brings Polyxene on stage before as well as after her brother's death; (iii) it initially sets up a misleading expectation that Sophocles will follow the well-known version of the story in which it is Polyxene who is with Troilus when he is ambushed, thus enhancing the surprise effect when he proceeds to depart from it.

[51]The tutor's interlocutor is perhaps more likely to be male than female, since he may well later in the scene be giving orders for the despatching of an armed force; and Hector has the advantage over Priam that he will in any case need to be seen departing as the

speak to him, he then gives a detailed narrative of what has happened.[52] *After the horses had been exercised, both they and the two men were thirsty, and they made their way to a spring (fr. F [621]) not far from the sanctuary of Apollo Thymbraios. Achilles was hiding there in ambush, and leaped out at them; they narrowly escaped being seized, and fled in different directions, the tutor making for Troy,*[53] *Troilus, on horseback, galloping towards the Thymbraion. Looking back as he fled, the tutor had seen Achilles on foot pursuing the mounted Troilus, and rapidly gaining ground on him; he is convinced that Troilus must have been caught and killed. His interlocutor, however, points out that this is by no means certain, and orders the immediate mustering of the best available troops (fr. G [634]), including both hoplites and archers (frr. H [626] and J [630]), who will march out under Hector*[54] *to confront Achilles and, if possible, to rescue the young prince.*

Third Stasimon: *The chorus express anxiety about the battle that is going on even as they sing, fearing that Achilles may wreak havoc among the Trojans facing him (fr. K [625]).*

Fourth Episode: *Hector returns with the corpse of Troilus; the head had been severed, but has been recovered and placed on the bier with the body, and a grisly necklace of cut-off body parts (*maschalismata, fr. L [623]*) has been removed. He tells how the rescue expedition found Achilles inside the Thymbraion, with the headless corpse spreadeagled over the altar, and how Achilles brandished and threw Troilus' head at his enemies, thus shocking and panicking them sufficiently to give him*

---

leader of this force (see below), so that by using him as the interlocutor too a character, an exit, and an entrance can be saved.

[52] Another surviving line of Strattis' *Troilus* (Strattis fr. 43) may be based on a passage of this speech; it refers to a wild fig-tree (cf. *Iliad* 6.433, 11.167, 22.145) near some other landmark. In the *Iliad* the tree seems to be fairly near the city walls; perhaps it was the point at which Troilus mounted his horse and began his practice gallop.

[53] In the artistic tradition, Polyxene flees on foot; but Sophocles, having substituted the tutor for her, may have made him flee on horseback instead, to avoid begging the question why Achilles should pursue Troilus on foot when he could have taken Troilus' second horse.

[54] Hector, who had distinguished himself on the very first day of the war by killing Protesilaus (*Cypria* Arg. §10 West), was the best warrior in Troy, and had all the greater incentive to valour because he would be trying to save his brother; he is mentioned – we do not know in precisely what connection – by the scholia on Ibycus *SLG* 224 = *GL* 282B (v) in a note on the death of Troilus.

time to escape unscathed, leaving them to recover the body and bring it home.

Fourth Stasimon: *The chorus lament over Troilus; either they, or individual lamenters later, give voice to "barbarian" cries of woe (frr. N [631] and O [632]).*

Exodos: *Hecuba and Polyxene come out to join the lyric laments; one or both of them comment on Troilus' beauty and especially his hair, still dark and sleek with the oil he had applied to it a few hours ago (fr. M [624]). Possibly Cassandra also appears, with or after them,[55] speaking of the anger of her patron Apollo at the desecration of his sanctuary,[56] and prophesying that Achilles will die at his hands, but also that Troy will fall[57] and that Polyxene will become in death the bride of Achilles – a fate she would have avoided had not Troilus prevented her marriage to Sarpedon. Finally Troilus' body is taken off for burial.*

The *dramatis personae*, in addition to the chorus, would be the tutor, Troilus, Sarpedon, Polyxene, Hector, Hecuba and Cassandra.

---

[55]For this prophecy by Cassandra there is again no direct evidence, and it is the feature of this reconstruction about which I am most doubtful. One might well think that Achilles' sacrilege could hardly have been left hanging (according to schol. Lycophr. *Alex.* 307 some authors saw it as the cause of Achilles' death) and that it also needed to be made clear how Troilus' incestuous passion was destined to be fatal not only to him but to Polyxene. However, as N.J. Lowe has pointed out to me, Sophocles frequently leaves his audience to recall from their own prior knowledge how the future is destined to turn out, as he does in *Trachiniae* with the deification of Heracles, in *OT* with the future of Oedipus' children, in *Philoctetes* with the sacrilegious acts of Neoptolemus (cf. *Phil.* 1440–1), and in *Oedipus at Colonus* with the fate of Antigone. This technique could have been applied in *Troilus* in the confidence that the audience would indeed recall what the future held, since that future had already been dramatized in Sophocles' own *Polyxene* and in Euripides' *Hecuba.* If there *was* a prophecy at the end of *Troilus*, it must almost certainly have been Cassandra rather than Apollo that made it, since it would be essential that the predictions should not be believed and therefore should not affect the behaviour of the Trojans or the subsequent course of the war.

[56]We cannot tell whether Sophocles here used (or even invented) the story (Lycophr. *Alex.* 313; [Apoll.] 3.12.5) that Troilus was actually a son of Apollo.

[57]If Sophocles knew and used the idea that Troy could not fall while Troilus lived, this is the likeliest place for him to bring it in. It could not have been known to the Trojans earlier, else they would have protected Troilus like glass and certainly not allowed him to wander ill-protected outside the walls or indeed to ride horses.

Two surviving fragments whose play of origin is unknown or doubtful have at one time or another been tentatively assigned to *Troilus*. The one-word fragment 652 ("boar-mad", i.e. "lustful", said of a female) is ascribed by the quoting author, Hesychius (κ873), to the non-existent play *Tyrilaus*; it might just possibly have been applied by Troilus to the allegedly unchaste Polyxene, but it would probably be too dangerous for him to risk such plain speaking in the presence of the chorus, and anyway the alternative ascription to one of the *Tyro* plays (see vol. ii) is at least as plausible in itself and makes the textual corruption easier to account for. It has been suggested[58] that fr. 789 also might come from *Troilus*, but its sole point of contact with the play is the word *eunouchoisin*, and the lexicographer who quotes the line[59] makes it clear that Sophocles was not here using the word to mean "eunuchs" but in its literal, etymological sense of "bed-watching", i.e. "wakeful at night".

In addition, it has occasionally been suggested that the Sophoclean play *The Phrygians*, from which we have only two fragments cited (frr. 724, 725), is merely *Troilus* under another name; but the fragments themselves seem to rule this out. In fr. 724 a knowledgeable older person tells a younger one that the "noble and brave" are killed in war while "those who are bold with their tongues" keep safe (cf. *Phil.* 410–450); this can have nothing to do with the death of Troilus, who was neither warrior nor politician, and would be more appropriate *either* near the end of the war (as in *Philoctetes*) as a sad reflection on its effects, *or* before its commencement (or shortly after) as a warning against getting involved in war in the first place (or as advice to end it quickly).[60] Fr. 725 appears to be a denunciation of a wedding actually in progress, and this can hardly be any other than that of Paris and Helen.[61] If *The Phrygians* was indeed an

---

[58]More accurately, assumed: E. Maass, *RhM* 74 (1925) 437, in a discussion of the meanings and history of the word *eunoukhos*, spoke of Soph. fr. 721 [Nauck = 789 Pearson, Radt] as coming from *Troilus* as if this were already an accepted and acknowledged fact.

[59]*Et.Gud.* 560.17–19 de Stefani = *Anecd.Bekk.* 1376b = *Et.Mag.* 1131a. No sense can be got out of the line as a whole in its transmitted form, and serious corruption is all but certain.

[60]F. Blass, *RhM* 62 (1907) 272, suggested the lines were spoken by Priam to Paris; but whatever Paris himself thought of his own virtues, Priam would hardly consider him "noble and brave", and Hector is a more likely addressee.

[61]So R. Reitzenstein, *Der Anfang des Lexikons des Photios* (Leipzig/Berlin, 1907) xiii, very plausibly suggesting Cassandra as the speaker. The suggestion of Blass *loc.cit.* that the wedding was that of Achilles and Polyxene is untenable; the fragment refers to wedding celebrations actually in progress, and those late sources which speak of Achilles being

alternative title for another Sophoclean play, *Helen's Wedding [Helenēs Gamos]* is a much more likely candidate.

One work of art and one fragment of papyrus have been thought to throw light on *Troilus*, and one damaged inscription has been thought to reveal its date. An Italian *stamnos* of about 330 BC (LIMC Achilleus 274) shows Troilus leading his horse towards a spring; on the other side of the spring stands an Asiatic figure; behind Troilus waits Achilles, and Athena points him in Troilus' direction. It was suggested by Albin Lesky[62] that the Asiatic figure, taking the place once occupied by Polyxene, is the eunuch *paidagōgos* and that the painting is based on our play (though on a scene narrated, not enacted, in it). If so, the presence of Athena may possibly suggest that Sophocles knew and used a tradition according to which the death of Troilus was an essential condition for the ultimate capture of Troy.[63] I have suggested above (p. 212) that this idea might have figured in a prophecy by Cassandra at the end of Sophocles' play. It is very unlikely, however, that Sophocles presented *Achilles* as aware of this talismanic property of Troilus, and as killing him under divine guidance: if he knew he was fulfilling the will of Athena, he would hardly have felt the need to "maschalize" Troilus' corpse in order to restrain his vengeful spirit. Rather, if the painter was indeed inspired by Sophocles' *Troilus*, then by including Athena in his composition he may have wished to indicate that she *objectively* favoured the killing of Troilus and maybe that, unknown to Achilles, she had been working behind the scenes to bring it about[64] – and that this was clearly indicated at some point in Sophocles' play, though not necessarily in the scene in which the ambush and pursuit were narrated.

A papyrus fragment which appears to come from a headnote (Hypothesis) to Aeschylus' *Women of Aetna* (*POxy* 2257 fr. 1) consists, in its surviving portion, mainly of an account of the numerous changes of scene which that play seems to have contained (apparently there were five

---

lured to his death by an offer of negotiations for a marriage with Polyxene (see Introduction to *Polyxene*, pp. 45–46 n.25) give no hint that the plotters pushed their deception as far as that. Certainly Hyginus *Fab.* 110, which Blass cites in support of his suggestion, does not; it merely says that Achilles was killed by Paris and Deiphobus "when he was seeking her hand and had come for a discussion (*ad colloquium*)".

[62]Lesky (1939) 606–7; the vase had already been linked with *Troilus* by L. Séchan, *Études sur la tragédie grecque dans ses rapports avec la céramique* (Paris, 1926) 216–8.

[63]Cf. note 28 above. However, it is entirely possible that the artist was merely following an existing *iconographic* tradition associating Athena with this episode.

[64]As she works in *Ajax* to save the other Greek leaders from Ajax and to punish him for insulting her; or as Apollo works in *Oedipus the King* to ensure the fulfilment of his oracles, or in *Electra* to ensure that Agamemnon is avenged.

acts, with no two successive acts set at the same place). This account is introduced by the particle *gar* "for", showing that the previous sentence (at least) had also been concerned with changes of scene. It may mention Aeschylus' *Eumenides* (line 7 is plausibly restorable as "(the scene) is transferred to Athens from Delphi") and certainly, at the start of line 8, mentions Sophocles' satyr-play *The Lovers of Achilles*.[65] In between there originally stood some nineteen letters,[66] of which only six can now be read; these include the four consecutive letters τρωϊ, which might be the first four letters of *Troilus*[66a] – though they might also be the first four letters of some form of the adjective *Trōikos* "Trojan", or even (if the diaeresis over the fourth letter has been wrongly read) the last four letters of the dative case of some word ending in *–tros* or *–tron*. It has not proved possible to reconstruct anything grammatically coherent, and involving a reference to *Troilus*, between the sentence about *Eumenides* and the sentence about *The Women of Aetna*, and it is perhaps more likely that the whole of this sentence was concerned with *The Lovers of Achilles*.[67]

The small surviving portion of that section of the so-called *Didascaliae* inscription (*IG* ii[2] 2319–23) concerned with tragic productions at the Lenaea includes the entry for the year 419/8 (the archonship of Archias) in which a dramatist whose name is not preserved won first prize with *Tyro* and another play[68] of whose title only the first two letters survive: of recent editors, Snell[69] is certain that these letters were Τι-, but Mette[70] indicates doubt about the reading of the second, and H. Hoffmann[71] suggested that

---

[65]Nothing in the rest of what we know of this play either proves or disproves that it contained a change or changes of scene. One surviving Sophoclean play, *Ajax*, certainly does.

[66]But it is very difficult to base any argument on the space available for this or that word, since the writer often abbreviates words (including play-titles) drastically.

[66a]At the last minute I note that L. Poli-Palladini, *RhM* 144 (2001) 288–9, has re-examined the papyrus and finds that the surviving traces of the fifth and sixth letters of the word definitely rule out the possibility that Troilus (the person or the play) was mentioned here.

[67]Cf. B. Snell, *Gnomon* 25 (1953) 440. The writer of the Hypothesis may abbreviate his *words* (see previous note), but his *sentences*, so far as they can be read, seem always to be complete and grammatical.

[68]Competitors for the tragic prize at the Lenaea produced at this time two plays each, not four as at the City Dionysia.

[69]DID A 2b 78 (in *TrGF* i).

[70]H.J. Mette, *Urkunden dramatischer Aufführungen in Griechenland* (Berlin, 1977) III D1.14.

[71]*Chronologie der attischen Tragödie* (Diss. Hamburg 1951) 53 (*non vidi*).

this second letter was a *rho* rather than an *iota*, that the winning dramatist was Sophocles (who wrote two plays about Tyro – no such play is known to have been written by any other fifth-century dramatist), and that his second play was *Troilus*.[72] If this is right, we know the date of the play, we know that it won first prize, and we are left with not too great an interval between Sophocles' play and Strattis' parody on it.[73]

---

[72]Sophocles wrote no play whose title began with *Ti-*; he did write one other play whose title began with *Tr-* (*Triptolemus*), but this was produced in or about 468 (Plin. *NH* 18.65).

[73]Strattis seems to have preferred to choose fairly recent tragedies for parodic treatment. His *Anthroporestes* refers (fr. 1) to Euripides' *Orestes* of 408, his *Lemnomeda* perhaps to Euripides' *Andromeda* of 412, his *Philoctetes* probably to Sophocles' play of 409, his *Phoenician Maidens* certainly to Euripides' play of 410; on the other hand his *Medea* reflects a Euripidean play of 431.

ΤΡΩΙΛΟΣ

Selected Testimonia

Scholia to *Iliad* 24.257: (Τ) ἐντεῦθεν Σοφοκλῆς ἐν Τρωΐλῳ φησὶν αὐτὸν λοχηθῆναι ὑπὸ Ἀχιλλέως ἵππους γυμνάζοντα παρὰ τὸ Θυμβραῖον καὶ ἀποθανεῖν. ὑπονοήσειε δ' ἄν τις ... εἶναι ... τὸν Τρωΐλον οὐ παῖδα, διότι ἐν τοῖς ἀρίστοις καταλέγεται. (Α) Τρωΐλον ἱππιοχάρμην: ὅτι ἐκ τοῦ εἰρῆσθαι ἱππιοχάρμην τὸν Τρωΐλον οἱ νεώτεροι ἐφ' ἵππου διωκόμενον αὐτὸν ἐποίησαν. καὶ οἱ μὲν παῖδα αὐτὸν ὑποτίθενται, Ὅμηρος δὲ διὰ τοῦ ἐπιθέτου τέλειον ἄνδρα ἐμφαίνει· οὐ γὰρ ἄλλος ἱππόμαχος λέγεται.

A (620)

σκάλμῃ γὰρ ὄρχεις βασιλὶς ἐκτέμνουσ' ἐμούς

A (620) Pollux 10.165 | βασιλὶς Casaubon: βασιλεῖς codd.

B (629)

ἀσόλοικον

B (629) Hesychius α7734

TROILUS

Selected Testimonia

Scholia to *Iliad* 24.257: (T) On the basis of this passage Sophocles in *Troilus* says that he [Troilus] was ambushed by Achilles when exercising his horses near the Thymbraion, and killed. One may infer [from the Homeric text] that ... Troilus was more than a boy, since he is listed among the leading warriors. (A) "Troilus the chariot-fighter": note that on the basis of his being called a "chariot-fighter" later authors had him pursued [by Achilles] when riding a horse. And they [*or* some] suppose him to be a boy, but Homer by means of this epithet presents him as a grown man, since no one who is not is called a horse-fighter.

A (620)

For the queen, cutting off my testicles with a knife ...

The speaker is Troilus' eunuch paidagogos, *probably narrating his personal history in the prologue.*

B (629)

unbarbaric

This may be the paidagogos *again, praising the character and behaviour of his young master; if so, he is presumably of Greek origin.*

220

Sophocles

C (618)

ἔγημεν ὡς ἔγημεν ἀφθόγγους γάμους
τῇ παντομόρφῳ Θέτιδι συμπλακείς ποτε

C (618) Σ Pindar, *Nemean* 3.60 | 2 παντομόρφῳ Casaubon: παντα- BP: ποντο- D

D (trag. adesp. 561 = Strattis Fr. 42.1 K-A)

ἦ μήποτ᾽, ὦ παῖ Ζηνός, ἐς ταὐτὸν μόλῃς

D (trag. adesp. 561) Σ Aristophanes, *Wasps* 1346 | ἦ (ἦ) Γ: ἦ V | ἐς ταὐτὸν μόλῃς Dobree: ἐς ταὐτὸ μόλης V: ἐστ᾽ αὐτομόλης Γ

E (619)

τὸν ἀνδρόπαιδα δεσπότην ἀπώλεσα

E (619) Σ Pindar, *Pythian* 2.121 Σοφοκλῆς ἐπὶ τοῦ Τρωΐλου (BCFP: τῷ Τρωΐλῳ EGQ): cf. Hesychius α4768 ἀνδρόπαις· ... Σοφοκλῆς Τρωΐλῳ | ἀπώλεσα BCEFP: ἀπώλεσε(ν) GQ

F (621)

πρὸς ναρὰ καὶ κρηναῖα χωροῦμεν ποτά

F (621) Orion, *Etymologicum* 110.1–3 Sturz; *Lex.Haem.* p.627.14–15 Sturz; *Etymologicum Genuinum* s.v. νάρων = *Etymologicum Magnum* 597.46 | πρὸς cett.: ναρὸς Orion | καὶ *Et.Mag.*ᴹ: om. *Lex.Haem.*: δὲ cett. | perh. κρηναῖ᾽ ἐχωροῦμεν

C (618)

He married as he married, a marriage in which there was no
talking, when he eventually got a wrestling hold on Thetis as
she changed into every shape.

The person spoken of is Peleus; perhaps the paidagogos *is telling his
master about Achilles' family background.*

D (trag. adesp. 561 = Strattis Fr. 42.1 K-A)

Never come together with her, child of Zeus!

Troilus warning Sarpedon against seeking to marry Polyxene?

E (619)

I have lost my adolescent master

A servant of Troilus, probably the paidagogos, *returning with the first
news of his master's death.*

F (621)

We were making for the flowing springs of drinking water

From the paidagogos' *narrative of the fatal expedition.*

G (634)

ὀροσάγγαι

G (634) Claudius Casilon p.243 *LGM*; *Lexicon Rhetoricum Cantabrigiense* p.83 *LGM*

H (626)

τόξ᾽ ἀπεσκῆ

H (626) Hesychius α6043 (glossed as γυμνὰ θήκης τόξα): cf. Photius α2361 and Bekker, *Anecdota* i 422.33 | τόξ᾽(α) Salmasius: τόξον cod.

J (630)

ἔρκη (= ὅπλα)

J (630) Hesychius ε5932

K (625)

ἀμάσεται

K (625) Hesychius α3495

L (623)

πλήρη μασχαλισμάτων

L (623) Suda ε928, Photius ε681

G (634)

bodyguard

From a description of the Trojan force sent out to rescue Troilus' body and avenge his death?

H (626)

bows without their leather cases

From the same passage?

J (630)

defences (*in sense of* armour)

From the same passage?

K (625)

he will mow down (*in sense of* slaughter)

From a lyric passage predicting carnage (to be wrought by Achilles upon the rescue expedition?)

L (623)

full of cut-off body parts

Referring to the maschalismos *of Troilus' corpse by Achilles (see comm. on* Polyxene *fr. G [528]); probably said at the time when the body is brought back to Troy.*

M (624)

ἐλαιοῦται θρὶξ

M (624) Hesychius ε1847

N (631)

ἰαί

N (631) Hesychius ι59

O (632)

ἰήιος

O (632) Hesychius ι363

P (622)

καταρβύλοις χλαίναις

P (622) Hesychius κ1375 | καταρβύλοις χλαίναις ed. Haguenauensis (1521): κ. σχλαίναις Ald.: καταρβύλοι σχλαίνας cod.

Q (624a)

ψεφαυγοῦς νυκτός

Q (624a) Cyrillus, *Glossary* ed. M. Naoumides, *GRBS* 9 (1968) 279–280 (ψεφαίας νυκτός· σκοτεινῆς ... γράφεται δὲ καὶ ψεφαυγοῦς [-οὺς cod., corr. Naoumides]), ὡς λυκοφῶς [Λυκόφρων tent. Naoumides])

R (627)

ἄπειστος

R (627) Hesychius α6214 (glossing the word as ἀπαράπ<ε>ιστος, ἀπειθής) | ἄπειστος Küster: ἄπιστος cod.

M (624)

(his) hair is oiled

From a lyric passage (if the text is sound); probably referring to the dead Troilus.

N (631)

iai!

A "barbarian lamentation", doubtless from a lament for Troilus.

O (632)

of wailing

Another word typical of lyric laments.

The following fragments cannot be assigned to a context:

P (622)

in thick robes that cover their shoes

From a description of a luxuriously dressed group of men (the chorus?)

Q (624a)

in the dark-rayed night

R (627)

uncompliant

S (628/628a)

ἄσας

S (628/628a) Hesychius α7625–6 ἀσαρόν (ἀσαρδαν cod., corr. M.Schmidt)· λυπηρόν, ἀηδές. ἄσας· βλάψας. Σοφοκλῆς Τρωΐλῳ | Latte suggested that Σοφοκλῆς Τρωΐλῳ might refer to ἀσαρόν rather than ἄσας

T (633)

μέλλει

T (633) Σ Pl. *Rep.* 566d, cf. Hesychius μ743

U (635)

σακοδερμηστής

U (635) Bachmann, *Anecdota* i 361.9, Photius Galeanus 497.3; cf. Hesychius σ76 | σακο- *Anecd. Bachm.*, Photius: σακκο- Hesychius | -ηστής Hesychius: -ήτης *Anecd. Bachm.*: -ίτης Photius

S (628/628a)

deluding

T (633)

(a)waits

U (635)

eater of shield leather

Probably from a passage of "recitative" anapaests.

TROILUS

A (620)

The speaker is a eunuch, therefore a slave, and since we know from fr. E (619) that a slave of Troilus was a character in the play, it is highly likely that this is the same person. He appears to have accompanied Troilus on his last journey (cf. fr. F [621]), and Greek spectators are therefore likely to have thought of him as Troilus' *paidagōgos*, the trusted and esteemed slave whose main duty was to escort a boy when he was out of the home alone: cf. Eur. *El.* 287, *Ion* 725, *Ba.* 193, Hdt. 8.75.1, Lys. 32.28, Pl. *Lys.* 208c, 223a, *Prot.* 325c, *Symp.* 183c, *Rep.* 600e, [Dem.] 47.56, Arist. *EN* 1119b14, Thphr. *Char.* 9.5, Men. *Aspis* 14. The slave in Sophocles' *Electra* who rescued Orestes at the time of his father's murder, and who brings him back to Mycenae to take his revenge, was identified as his *paidagōgos* by ancient editors; so, with clearer justification, is the slave who escorts the children of Jason and Medea in Euripides' *Medea* (cf. *Med.* 46–48, 53). The only eunuch in surviving tragedy is the Phrygian in Eur. *Or.* 1369–1530 (cf. especially 1528 "for you were neither born a woman, nor are you in <the category of> men"), but we know that a eunuch at the Persian court was the prologue-speaker in (one of) Phrynichus' play(s) about the Persian War (Hypothesis to Aesch. *Pers.*), and there may have been other eunuchs in lost plays, particularly those set in non-Greek, especially Asian, societies. Castration was seen as an appallingly un-Greek practice (cf. Aesch. *Eum.* 187–8, Hdt. 8.104–6) and was stereotypically associated with "barbarians", especially Persians (see E.M. Hall, *Inventing the Barbarian* [Oxford, 1989] 94, 157–8), who were said to regard eunuchs as the most trustworthy of servants (Hdt. 8.105.2). For the possibility that the present speaker is of Greek birth, see on fr. B (629). In this fragment he is evidently explaining how he came to be Troilus' personal servant; since he and his background would already be well known to members of the family, he is likely here to be speaking in soliloquy, and it is reasonable to suppose that our fragment comes from the prologue of the play.

Mary Bachvarova has pointed out to me that the mutilation of the *paidagōgos* foreshadows the later mutilation of the dead Troilus (cf. fr. M [623]).

the queen: *pace* Pearson and earlier scholars, there is no need to evade the plain implication of the text that Hecuba personally wielded the instrument of castration (e.g. by taking "cutting off" to mean "ordering someone to cut off"): if Sophocles had thought it improper to have a woman do this, he could easily have replaced *basilis* "the queen" by *Priamos* and thereby avoided any possible misunderstanding. It is, after all, Hecuba and other Trojan women, in Euripides' play bearing her name, who put out the eyes of Polymestor and kill his sons. Possibly this detail is evidence that in this play Hecuba was a more forceful figure than Priam and/or that she later appeared on stage (and Priam did not?); on the Greek perception of the powerful, dominant, sometimes violent barbarian woman, see Hall *op.cit.* 95, 203–210. One would normally have expected that a eunuch would be bought ready castrated from a slave-dealer (cf. Hdt. 8.105); that this man was castrated *after* purchase implies either that it was done as a punishment (cf. Xen. *Cyr.* 5.2.28, where the setting is the Assyrian [i.e. Babylonian] court), or, perhaps more interestingly, that he had been selected from among the palace slaves by Hecuba for a position of trust which only a eunuch could hold. Has he been given charge of Polyxene as well as Troilus?

testicles are explicitly mentioned only here in tragedy, so far as we know (fr. 1130.11 is satyric).

a knife: the rare word *skalmē* is said by Pollux 10.165, on the basis of our fragment, to be "apparently a barbarian word for 'sword'", but Hesychius σ818 glosses it "Thracian knife", and this is to some extent confirmed by M.Aur. 11.15 who metaphorically describes "the affectation of simplicity" as a *skalmē*, i.e. a deadly weapon treacherously concealed. Certainly a short rather than a long weapon is more appropriate here, and (as Mary Bachvarova has suggested to me) it might well be curved, like the sickle/scimitar (*drepanon* or *harpē*) which Cronus used to castrate his father Uranus (Hes. *Thg.* 161–182), Perseus to behead the Gorgon, and Lityerses to behead all and sundry (Sositheus trag. fr. 2.12–21); the *harpē* was sometimes said to have been a Thracian invention (Clem. Alex. *Strom.* 1.16.75). G.I. Kazarow [Katsarov], *Beiträge zur Kulturgeschichte der Thraker* (Sarajevo, 1916) 71, identifies the *skalmē* with the short curved "sickle-sword" (the example he illustrates [fig. 18] is 395mm in length) found in some Thracian tombs of the classical period (see R.F. Hoddinott, *The Thracians* [London, 1981] 112).

B (629)

The word *soloikos* appears first in sixth-century poetry (Anacreon *PMG* 423 = *SLG* S313a; Hipponax fr. 27), where it seems to mean exactly the same as *barbaros*, i.e. "non-Greek" with particular but not exclusive reference to language; in fifth-century prose (Protagoras fr. 28 D-K, Hdt. 4.117.2) its derivative verb *soloikizein* means "to speak one's language badly" (as a foreigner might), e.g., in the case of Greek, by making errors of grammatical gender (Protagoras *loc.cit.*) Later writers (e.g. Xen. *Cyr.* 8.3.21, Zeno fr. 81 von Arnim) extend the word's application to other kinds of social or technical incompetence or clumsiness. The supposed derivation of "solecism" from the inhabitants of the remote Greek colony of Soli in Cilicia is not heard of before Strabo (14.2.28), and the word is more likely to be a borrowing from an Anatolian language.

Thus the negative adjective *asoloikon*, which Hesychius quotes from *Troilus*, is likely to refer either (i) to someone who is a native speaker of the language of the community in which he currently resides (or speaks it as fluently and accurately as a native) or (ii) to someone who is, or resembles, a Greek rather than a barbarian in speech or behaviour; in the latter case, moreover, the speaker describing this person would himself have to be Greek. These possibilities can be whittled down with the help of Hesychius' glosses ("gentle, kindly, not barbarous"), which show clearly that the speaker was thinking primarily of someone's behaviour and character rather than his speech, and therefore favour (ii) above rather than (i).

The speaker, then, is likely to be a Greek. In a play set in Troy, at a time when no Greek ambassadors, infiltrators or spies were in the city, the only possible Greek character (other than Helen, for whose presence in the play there is no evidence) would be a slave; and the only slave character we know of is the *paidagōgos*. He, then, is probably a Greek, who had become a slave at Troy through capture (by pirates? during an unsuccessful Greek raid early in the war?) or otherwise. The person whose gentle, kindly, "unbarbarian" disposition he is most likely to be praising is his young master, whose high personal qualities will make his early and brutal death all the more poignant. As a barbarian who is said to behave like a Greek, he will contrast notably with his slayer, Achilles, a Greek who in more than one way will be presented as behaving like a barbarian.

The praise of Troilus' character could possibly come during the narration of his death (cf. on frr. E-F [619, 621]); but it is perhaps better placed in the prologue, where the chance to serve so relatively agreeable a master could be presented by the *paidagōgos* as giving him a measure of consolation for the loss of his freedom, his manhood, and the company of his compatriots.

One of the three glosses in Hesychius (*prosēnes* "kindly") is given in a form which shows that the gender of the adjective in Sophocles' text was neuter, not masculine; in other words, the adjective described not the person directly but some attribute of his such as his mentality (*lēma*) or his heart (*kear*).

C (618)

A decidedly jaundiced view of the courtship and marriage of Peleus and Thetis; it is made to sound almost like a rape (and of a goddess, too!), and if the addressee knows no more than he is told here he would never be able to guess that there had been a formal wedding attended by almost all the gods, nor that Peleus was wooing Thetis by their permission. It is stressed, moreover, that Peleus was never able to speak to his wife (on the source of this idea see below); it is true that ancient Greek husbands often did converse little with their wives (cf. Xen. *Oec.* 3.12), but what kind of marriage would it be thought to be if the husband could not even tell his wife her duties for the day? The speaker, evidently, is hostile to Peleus – or rather (since Peleus himself would be a figure of little interest in Troy) to Achilles, about whose family background he is giving information to another person. On the other hand, nothing he says is actually false; it is merely selected and phrased so as to present Peleus in the worst light.

The person most likely to be seeking information about Achilles is the youthful Troilus (or possibly Polyxene); Trojans of military age would know about him already. The person most likely to be *giving* the information is the *paidagōgos*, who as a Greek (see on previous fragment) would be in a better position to know about the past of Achilles and his family than any Trojan. As to the question why Troilus or Polyxene might have desired to know (more) about Achilles, see Introduction, pp. 207–8. This tale of the violent conquest (as the speaker portrays it) of Thetis by Peleus – who never, then or later, says a word to her – may well arouse apprehension in Polyxene and her brother about the possible intentions of

Peleus' son towards her; the audience know, though, that both will fare far worse at his hands than they fear.

1 **he married as he married:** tautological expressions of this kind tend to be used as evasive devices when explicitness would be ill-omened, embarrassing or inconvenient. Cf. *Trach.* 1234 "responsible for your being as you are" [dying in agony], *OT* 1376 "having been born as they were born" [incestuously], Eur. *El.* 1122 "I fear [Aegisthus] as I fear him" [not at all, he being dead, unknown to the addressee], *Or.* 79 "I sailed as I sailed to Troy" [in an adulterous elopement], *IA* 721 "after making the sacrifice I have to make to the gods" [of our daughter]. See H.W. Johnstone, *Glotta* 58 (1980) 49–62. Here the speaker may be using the turn of phrase to imply that there was something, unspecified, wrong with the marriage in addition to the particular points that he is actually going to mention. In fact he will probably be leaving nothing unsaid that could possibly have been said in disparagement of the marriage; its greatest flaw – Thetis' eventual abandonment of her husband and return to her old home in the sea – will almost certainly have been mentioned in the lost lines that followed.

1 **a marriage in which there was no talking:** this mysterious phrase was convincingly explained by Bernhard Schmidt, *Das Volksleben der Neugriechen und das hellenische Alterthum* i (Leipzig, 1871) 116 n.1 (cf. Schmidt, *NJbb* 27 [1911] 648–650; J.G. Frazer, *Apollodorus: The Library* ii [London, 1921] 383–5) on the basis of a modern Cretan tale which is manifestly close kin to that of Peleus and Thetis (including the motifs of the shape-changing sea-maiden and the child in the fire): the wife never speaks until her child's life is in danger, when she cries out, seizes him, and vanishes. Evidently in at least one widely known version of the Peleus-Thetis story, Peleus (conversely) was told that Thetis would stay with him only so long as *he* never spoke to *her*; the cry he gave when he saw she had placed Achilles in the fire (she was trying to make him immortal), which caused her immediate disappearance (Ap.Rh. 4.873–9, [Apoll.] 3.13.6, schol. Ar. *Clouds* 1068), will then have been the first sound he had ever uttered in her presence. To an addressee with no prior knowledge, the speaker's words here might also be understood in a quite different way (see below).

2 when: or "after"; the Greek aorist participle is capable of being taken in either sense, but it suits the speaker's disparaging purpose best if he is trying to insinuate that Peleus' successful wrestling of Thetis into submission *was* the act by which she became his wife – i.e. that there was no wedding but merely a seizure (cf. schol. Lycophron 178 – though the scholiast's claim that Euripides describes the couple's union thus may be mere over-interpretation of Eur. *Andr.* 1278). It fits with this that the phrase *aphthongous gamous*, which I have rendered "a marriage in which there was no talking", could also be understood as "a marriage achieved without words", implying that Peleus did not use words to woo Thetis but overpowered her by force.

2 got a wrestling hold on Thetis: Greek *sumplekesthai*, lit. "get tangled up with" is often used in contexts of wrestling or other kinds of conflict, e.g. Hdt. 3.78.4, 8.84.1, Eur. *Ba.* 800, Ar. *Ach.* 704 (referring to the son of a famous wrestling trainer), Men. *Epitr.* 236. That Peleus, in order to win Thetis, had to keep hold on her like a wrestler as she tried to escape him by repeated transformations, is clearly a very old story; it is depicted scores of times in archaic and early classical art, beginning in the seventh century, and Pindar (*Nem.* 3.35–36) evidently expected his audiences to be familiar with it. But *sumplekesthai* is also often used in erotic contexts (as are *palaiein* "wrestle" and other verbs of similar meaning): cf. Pl. *Symp.* 191a, 192a, Arist. *HA* 541b3, 542a16, Lucian *The Ass* 8–11, and see F. García Romero, *Nikephoros* 8 (1995) 57–73. Hence it is being insinuated that Peleus' exploit was less a heroic feat of strength, endurance and determination than an act of rape: a far cry from the tradition according to which the gods awarded Thetis to him because he was the most virtuous man of his generation (Pind. *Nem.* 5.26–37, *Isthm.* 8.27–53, Ar. *Clouds* 1067, Ap.Rh. 4.805; cf. *Iliad* 24.61) and in particular because he had rejected the adulterous advances of the wife of Acastus (see on this J.R. March, *The Creative Poet = BICS* Supp. 49 [1987] 3–23).

2 as she changed into every shape: in *The Lovers of Achilles* (fr. 150) Peleus mentions "lion, serpent, fire, water" (cf. Pind. *Nem.* 4.62–65, [Apoll.] 3.11.5), and in art Thetis is also depicted turning into a fish, a sea-monster, a panther, an eagle, or into several creatures at once. Other shape-changing water deities who are wrestled down by heroes include Achelous (*Trach.* 9–26: bull, serpent, ox-headed man), Proteus

(*Odyssey* 4.456–8: lion, serpent, leopard/panther, boar, water, tree) and Thetis' father Nereus (Pherecydes fr. 16a Fowler, [Apoll.] 2.5.11: fire and water).

D (trag. adesp. 561 = Strattis fr. 42.1 K-A)

This is the first line of a two-line fragment quoted by a scholiast on Aristophanes' *Wasps* from the comedy *Troilus* by Strattis. This play cannot be precisely dated, but Strattis' career falls within the period 415–380, and he based several of his comedies on plays of Sophocles or Euripides: his titles include *Anthrop-orestes, Chrysippus, Lemnomeda* (presumably some blend of the story of Andromeda with that of the Lemnian women), *Medea, Philoctetes,* and *The Phoenician Maidens.* It is therefore highly likely that his *Troilus* was based on Sophocles' play of that name, particularly since no other tragedy about Troilus is attested.

The first line of the Strattis fragment is strongly tragic in diction (with *Zēnos* instead of *Dios* as the genitive case-form of *Zeus, es* "to" for Attic *eis,* and the poetic verb *molein* "come, go") and there is every reason to believe that it is quoted from Sophocles' play. The accuracy of the quotation cannot, of course, be guaranteed. Aristophanes in *Thesmophoriazusae* (855–912) quotes about twenty-three lines of Euripides' *Helen,* and while twenty of these lines are in faultless tragic diction and metre, only eleven are quoted without alteration; however, most of the discrepancies are minor, and our uncertainty about the text of this line of *Troilus* need not be significantly greater than for any other fragment indirectly transmitted. Strattis' second line is another matter, being comic both in metre and in content: "but hand her over to the Lesbians and forget about her". Lesbos was proverbially the home of oral sex (Ar. *Wasps* 1346, *Frogs* 1308, *Eccl.* 920, Pherecrates fr. 159, Theopompus fr. 36; see H.D. Jocelyn, *PCPS* 26 [1980] 31–34), so the speaker is implying that the woman referred to is (no better than) a prostitute. This may be pure comic invention, or it may be a distorted reflection of some feature of the tragic model; we cannot tell.

It appears, at any rate, that in Sophocles' play someone warned a "child of Zeus" against making an approach, presumably with sexual or matrimonial intent, to a certain woman: that the addressee is being warned off a *woman* excludes the possibility of a reference to the story ([Clement of Rome], *Homilies* 5.15.2) according to which Apollo was in love with

Troilus. If the sexual or matrimonial fate of a woman is being discussed in a play that focuses on Troilus, the presumption must be that this woman is the one who in art is inseparably connected with the story of Troilus, namely Polyxene. There is no story of her having attracted the interest of a divine lover, and Achilles, who is often said to have been in love with her (see Introduction, p. 204; also Introduction to *Polyxene*, pp. 45–47), was not a son of Zeus. Rather, the addressee must be a human son of Zeus *among the Trojans or their allies* who has either been offered, or is thinking of seeking, Polyxene's hand in marriage, and is here being warned or advised to leave her severely alone. There is thus only one possible candidate: Sarpedon, the leader of the Lycians, son of Zeus and Laodameia (according to *Iliad* 6.198–9) or of Zeus and Europa (according to Aesch. fr. 99). In the *Iliad* he is much the most prominent of the non-Trojan allies, an example and an expositor (e.g. 12.310–328) of the highest heroic standards, and his slaying is the greatest achievement of Patroclus during the latter's *aristeia* in book 16; if available, he might well be thought to be an ideal bridegroom for a daughter of Priam. It is true that according to *Iliad* 5.480 he has a wife and young son at home, but this is the kind of detail that could easily be set aside for the sake of a tragic plot.

The speaker of our fragment is evidently anxious to prevent such a marriage. Who could have an interest in doing so? Achilles maybe, but we can hardly bring him into Troy to issue the warning; unlike Odysseus, Menelaus or Diomedes, Achilles never enters the city of Troy until moments before his death at the Scaean Gate. The figure of Cassandra, vainly warning her kinsfolk and others against actions that prove to be disastrous, is a familiar one in tragedy and elsewhere, but would be inappropriate here, for it is Sarpedon's *obedience* to this warning that proves disastrous for Polyxene: in the tale of the sacrifice of Polyxene, as in most other Greek myths of human sacrifice (especially as told in tragedy), virginity is a significant factor (see W. Burkert, *Homo Necans* tr. P. Bing [Berkeley, 1983] 64–68; N. Loraux, *Tragic Ways of Killing a Woman* tr. A. Forster [Cambridge MA, 1987] 32–48), and whereas Priam's virgin daughter made both an appropriate sacrificial victim for Achilles and an appropriate posthumous bride for him, Sarpedon's widow would have been another matter. The most plausible objector to the marriage, then, is perhaps Troilus himself. On his possible motives, see Introduction, pp. 207–8. The second line of the Strattis fragment *may* indicate that he dissuaded Sarpedon from accepting the marriage by casting suspicions on Polyxene's chastity.

together: Greek *es tauton* "to the same <place>": for this phrase in sexual or erotic contexts cf. Eur. fr. 898.11, Men. *Perik.* 550.

E (619)

The Pindar scholiast who quotes this line states that it is said "in relation to Troilus", i.e. that Troilus is the "adolescent master" referred to. (He does not explicitly say that the line comes from the play *Troilus*, but Hesychius does tell us that the word *andropais* "adolescent" was used in the play.) The speaker, then, is a slave of Troilus, doubtless the *paidagōgos* who we already know was a character in the play. His plain statement of a crucial fact is typical of messengers (and their equivalents) announcing the "headline" of their story (often news of a death) before embarking on their detailed narrative: cf. *Trach.* 739–740, *Ant.* 1173, *OT* 1235, *El.* 673, *OC* 1579–80, Eur. *Med.* 1125–6, *Hipp.* 1162–3, *Andr.* 1173–4, *IT* 1289–92, *Bacch.* 1030. The *paidagōgos* thus appears to have himself been the messenger who first reported the death of Troilus.

adolescent: Greek *andropais* is given two glosses by Hesychius: (i) "a boy who is already becoming a man", (ii) "a boy with the intelligence of a man"; there follows the reference "Sophocles in *Troilus*", but it is not clear whether this is meant to apply to both the senses given or to (ii) alone. The Pindar scholiast makes the definite claim that when Sophocles used *andropais* of Troilus it meant "a boy in years, but a man in intelligence". Perhaps it did; but it is significant that when one of the Seven against Thebes, Parthenopaeus, is described in Aesch. *Seven* 533 as "an *andropais* man", the scholia again offer the double gloss ("either one who has just come to man's estate, or one who is courageous even when only a boy in age") even though the text (in 547 as well as 533) explicitly calls Parthenopaeus a man. One lexicographer, too (*Anecd. Bekk.* i 407.16–17), uses *andropais* to gloss another word (*antipais*) as a near-synonym of "close to adulthood" and "above the age of a boy". All this suggests that interpretation (ii) is an invention of ancient commentators and that Sophocles used the word in the same sense as Aeschylus did, to denote a person who was more than a boy but less than fully adult. It may nevertheless be true that Troilus, that "unbarbaric" Trojan (cf. fr. B [629]), was in fact portrayed by Sophocles as a youth of high mental endowments, and that this was what persuaded some ancient scholar(s) to suggest that he was called *andropais* because of his intellect.

F (621)

In archaic art, the ambushing of Troilus by Achilles normally takes place when he and Polyxene go to get water at a spring or fountain-house, and it is reasonable to suppose that the journey being narrated here leads up to an ambush by Achilles at such a spot – though probably Polyxene is not present (see Introduction, p. 204). For the theme "We went / were going to..." in the early part of a messenger-narrative, cf. *Ant.* 1196–7, Eur. *Hipp.* 1195–7, *IT* 1327, *Helen* 1530, *Ba.* 1043–7.

we were making for: Greek *khōroumen* could in principle be ("historic") present, but this would be more appropriate to the vivid narration of events than to an exposition of the situation that existed before anything significant had yet happened. The tense is thus more likely to be imperfect, with the augment (the prefix *e-* indicating past time) omitted as it sometimes is in extended narratives in tragedy (see L.S. Fotheringham in L. Hardwick et al. ed. *Theatre: Ancient and Modern* [Milton Keynes, 2000] 225–231; T.H. Talboy in *Shards* 234–6, on *Phaedra* fr. J [687a]). However, there are no clear cases of such omission of the augment where the preceding word, in the same line, ends with a short vowel (Eur. *IA* 404 may well be corrupt), and here, where omission of the augment would leave the tense of the verb ambiguous, it is at least as likely that Sophocles retained it, and that later a text in which both words were written in full without elision (*krēnaia ekhōroumen*) was wrongly "corrected" by a copyist. This leaves an iambic line with a word-break at its midpoint ("medial diaeresis") instead of the more usual caesura in the middle of the third or fourth foot, but medial diaeresis is quite legitimate in tragic iambics when, as here, it is softened by an elision (this occurs 76 times in Sophocles; see M.L. West, *Greek Metre* [Oxford, 1982] 82–83).

flowing: Greek *nāros* (thought to be derived from the verb *naein* "flow") occurs only here and in Aesch. fr. 347.

G (634)

Greeks knew of an Iranian word which they wrote in Greek as *orosangēs*; modern scholars dispute what this Iranian word actually was, but the most widely favoured view is that it was **varusanha-* "far-famed" (see W. Eilers, *Iranische Beamtennamen in der keilschriftlichen Überlieferung* [Leipzig, 1940] 23–24 n.4; R. Schmitt, *Zeitschrift der Deutschen Morgenländischen Gesellschaft* 117 [1967] 131). Historians (Hdt. 8.85.3; Nymphis *FGrH* 432 F 6) stated that *orosangēs* was an honorific title meaning "benefactor of the King" or "guest of the King". Phylacus of Samos was granted this title and a large allotment of land for sinking a Greek ship at the battle of Salamis (Hdt. loc.cit.). Two lexicographers, however – Claudius Casilon and the *Lexicon Rhetoricum Cantabrigiense* – report that Sophocles in *The Wedding of Helen* (fr. 183) and in *Troilus* used this word to mean "bodyguards", an instance of a tendency to "persianize" the Trojans that is also evident in several other details of this play (see on frr. A [620], O [631], Q [622]) and elsewhere in tragedy (see E.M. Hall, *Inventing the Barbarian* [Oxford, 1989] 117–133). If he conceived the *orosangai* to be a body of élite troops specially trusted by the King (cf. Aesch. *Pers.* 441–3), their Trojan equivalents would be an appropriate group to send on a special mission to confront the most dangerous man in the enemy army and rescue the body of a royal prince, and they may have been mentioned in the course of giving orders for this mission (cf. generally Eur. *Ba.* 780–5).

H (626)

The rare noun *peskos* originally denoted the skin of an animal, especially a sheep (schol. Nic. *Ther.* 549; Orion p.129.8 Sturz), whence by extension any other skin-like covering such as the bark of a tree (Nic. *Ther.* 549). The noun itself is not found in any pre-Hellenistic text; what we have here is the derivative adjective *apeskē* (neuter plural of *apeskēs*) "without a *peskos*", applied to bows. The "skin" that a bow would normally have is presumably a leather case in which it was kept when not in use. Such a case (actually of wood covered with leather – or, in luxury specimens, with gold or silver), incorporating a quiver, was used by the archers of Scythia (see E.H. Minns, *Scythians and Greeks* [Cambridge, 1913] 66–68; P. Connolly, *Greece and Rome at War 2* [London/Mechanicsburg PA, 1998] 50) and would be familiar to Athenians from the equipment of the Scythian archers who performed certain policing functions in Athens; modern scholars call it a "gorytos" (after *Odyssey* 21.54), but classical Athenians seem to have called it a *subēnē* (Ar. *Thesm.* 1197, *IG* i³ 350.82). A bow without its case is a bow ready for immediate action; so this phrase too may be part of orders given for the formation of the rescue force after the news is brought of Troilus' death (cf. on previous fragment). The bow, with its long range, would be the most likely weapon to succeed against a warrior as deadly as Achilles was with the spear (it was notoriously the arrow of Paris that killed him in the end). The contrast between spear and bow was one of the stereotypical fifth-century Greek:barbarian antitheses (cf. Aesch. *Pers.* 85–86, 239–240; see Hall, *Inventing the Barbarian* 85–86, 138–9), but it is not clear whether it was exploited for this purpose in *Troilus* (cf. on next fragment).

J (630)

The noun *herkos*, originally "fence", is used in Homer in reference to defensive arms or armour, normally with a specification of what they ward off, as in *Iliad* 15.646 (a shield), 4.137 (the *mitrē*, an item of body armour) or 5.316 (a spear-proof divine garment). Sophocles apparently used the plural on its own, without further specification, to refer to a soldier's defensive equipment generally; this seems to be his own adaptation of the Homeric usage – elsewhere the plural of *herkos* virtually always refers to literal or metaphorical snares, nets or traps. In *Troilus* the word is likely to have been used in relation to the rescue expedition, either in a narrative of its fortunes or (cf. on previous two fragments) in the instructions for mustering it. In either case it makes it likely that the expedition included not only archers but fully armed troops, the equivalent of Greek hoplites: so the expedition which Pentheus orders to muster, but never despatches, against the bacchants of Mount Cithaeron, includes hoplites ("shield-bearers"), cavalry, peltasts and archers (Eur. *Bacch.* 780–5).

K (625)

The verb *amān* "reap, mow, cut" is used in Hellenistic epic (Ap.Rh. 3.1187, 1382) to refer to mass slaughter in battle; its synonym *th(e)rizein* appears in the same sense already in the fifth century (Aesch. *Supp.* 637, *Ag.* 536). Both usages may well derive ultimately from the simile in *Iliad* 11.67–71 (cf. also 19.221–4) where the men in two lines of battle, slaughtering each other, are compared to the men in two lines of reapers cutting corn on opposite sides of a large field.

Here the verb is in the future (and in the middle voice – but very many verbs obligatorily or optionally use the future middle in an active sense); and the form *amāsetai* (not *amēsetai*) shows that it is being quoted from a lyric passage. The most likely moment in this play at which a chorus (or indeed a solo singer) might anticipate a large-scale slaughter by one person would be after the departure of the rescue expedition against the fearsome Achilles and before its outcome is known: there must anyway have been a choral song during this interval, and it appears to have contained some fearful anticipation of what the fate of the expedition might be. In a somewhat similar situation in *OC* 1044–95 the chorus confidently predict victory (1054–8, 1079–80); on the other hand in Aesch. *Cho.* 855–868 the chorus present the two possible outcomes – liberation of family and city, or final ruin for the house of Agamemnon – seemingly as equiprobable.

L (623)

On the practice of *maschalismos* see on *Polyxene* fr. G (528); *maschalismata* were the severed extremities. The transmitted text of the Suda states, absurdly, that Sophocles "speaks of the *maschalismos* as full of *maschalismata*"; either something has been lost from the text, or *maschalismos* has replaced some other word. At any rate, the object that was actually described in Sophocles' text as being "full of *maschalismata*" was doubtless the grisly necklace that had been tied around Troilus' body and under his armpits (the body had also been decapitated, if Sophocles followed the dominant artistic tradition here). On the implications for the plot of the play, and for Achilles' motives in killing Troilus, of this sequel to the killing, see Introduction, pp. 205–8.

The terrified *paidagōgos*, speeding back to Troy as fast as his feet (or Troilus' second horse) could carry him away from Achilles with the news of his master's death, could not have known about any mutilation of the body, and it must therefore have become known to the Trojans, and the audience, at a later stage, doubtless when the rescue expedition recovered the corpse; it may thus be the leader of the expedition, presumably Hector, who speaks about it. The body may well have been brought back to Troy, and to the stage, still in the state in which it was found, just as the body of Pentheus is brought back from Mount Cithaeron, dismembered and headless, by Cadmus in Eur. *Ba.* 1216ff.

M (624)

Hair was oiled to make it look darker and sleeker (Pl. *Prot.* 334b, Arist. *GA* 785a29–30, Aelian *NA* 1.48; [Alex. Aph.] *Probl.* 4.76; Heron *Strat.* p.255.16 Wescher). Aristarchus surprisingly took *elaioutai* "oiled" here to mean "dirtied"; this makes it almost certain that the hair being described is that of the dead Troilus, since Aristarchus evidently imagined the corpse being dragged in the dust like that of Hector (*Iliad* 22.401–5) or its head falling on the ground like that of Imbrius (*Iliad* 13.205). However, *elaioutai* could not have referred to treatment like that, and another commentator rightly noted "better <taken to mean> 'made to shine'": Troilus' hair, like that of Astyanax (Eur. *Tro.* 1175–6, 1182–3) and like the downy cheeks of Pentheus (Eur. *Ba.* 1185–7, cf. *Christus Patiens* 1469), remains beautiful even in death.

Unless Hesychius has reversed the order of the words, this phrase must come from a lyric (or anapaestic) passage, not a spoken one, most likely from a scene following the return of Troilus' body to Troy for lamentation and burial. It shows that even if Troilus had been decapitated, the head was recovered. It will have been put back with the body, as decently as possible. In Euripides' *Bacchae* this was done on stage, but that was inevitable given that when Cadmus collected Pentheus' limbs on Mount Cithaeron, the head had already been taken away by Agaue; in Troilus' case there would be no reason not to place the head on a bier together with the body as soon as it was found.

The utterer of these words may either be the chorus or an individual mourner. If there is to be a prominent individual mourner, the most likely is Hecuba, the archetypal Trojan lamenter who grieves over Hector in *Iliad* 24.747–760, over Polydorus in Eur. *Hec.* 681–720, over Astyanax in Eur. *Tro.* 1156–1250. Like many other aspects of this play set early in the war, such a lament would have a grim extra layer of ironic poignancy if, as is plausible, Troilus is the *first* son Hecuba has lost in a conflict that will ultimately rob her of almost every one of them.

N (631)

Hesychius describes the interjection *iai* as a "barbarian lamentation", and there is no reason to doubt his statement that it was so used in *Troilus*, into whose generally "oriental" atmosphere it would fit well. Surprisingly, it is found elsewhere in drama only as a shout of joy by the (Athenian) choruses of two comedies, *Lysistrata* (1292–3) and *Ecclesiazusae* (1180); but Aeschylus' Persian chorus cry *iōa* (Aesch. *Pers.* 1070–1) and the Aristophanic Dionysus recalls their clapping their hands and wailing *iauoi* (Ar. *Frogs* 1028–9). The exclamation no doubt figured in a lyric lament over Troilus; we cannot tell whether it was uttered by the chorus or by an individual such as Hecuba (see on previous fragment). The probability that the chorus was male (see on fr. U [635]) would not, in a play like this, preclude them from giving voice to extravagant expressions of grief as the male chorus of *Persians* do (see Hall, *Inventing the Barbarian* 83–84).

O (632)

The cry *iē*, and the adjective *iēios* derived from it, are used in two entirely different kinds of context. On the one hand they are associated with Apollo, sometimes in a way that suggests a perception of an etymological link with *iāsthai* "to heal": cf. *OT* 154, Aesch. *Ag.* 146, Ar. *Lys.* 1281. On the other hand, *iē* can be a cry of grief (Aesch. *Pers.* 1004, *Ag.* 1485, fr. 132) which can be linked (Aesch. *Supp.* 114) with the noun *iēlemos* (or *iālemos*) "lament" (often one uttered by barbarians, cf. Aesch. *Cho.* 424, Eur. *Tro.* 604, 1304, *Phoen.* 1033–4, *Or.* 1390), and *iēios* several times appears in contexts that show it is being treated as a derivative of this cry (*OT* 173, Eur. *El.* 1211, *Phoen.* 1036–7). According to Hesychius, *iēios* was used in *Troilus* to "signify a lament", doubtless in the same scene as fr. N (631).

P (622)

A *khlaina* was a thick, warm outer garment, normally of wool, suitable for winter wear; see L.M. Stone, *Costume in Aristophanic Comedy* (New

York, 1981) 160–2. In comedy it is invariably a man's garment (cf. esp. Ar. *Eccl.* 507), and with the doubtful exception of Sappho fr. 92.9 nothing in any archaic or classical text suggests that a woman would ever wear one: the only connection that women have with a *khlaina* is when it is used as a blanket to cover a pair of lovers or spouses (*h.Hom.Aph.* 158, Archil. fr. 196a.45, *Trach.* 540, Eur. fr. 603.4). On the other hand, an outer garment that "covers the shoes", i.e. reaches to the feet, is something typically feminine (cf. esp. Eur. *Bacch.* 833); hence our phrase appears to come from a description of a group of men wearing clothes that would strike the average Greek as womanish – an aspect of the effeminate luxury (*habrotēs, khlidē, truphē*) often associated with barbarians, especially Asians, in tragedy (see Hall, *Inventing the Barbarian* 81–84, 126–9, 209–210). This group may or may not have been the chorus; the context cannot be determined.

Q (624a)

The two rare adjectives which Cyril's glossary gives as alternative readings for a passage somewhere in *Troilus* – *psephaios* "dark" and *psephaugēs*, lit. "dark-rayed" – were both already known from Hesychius (ψ134–7), who cites *psephaios* in three different inflectional forms, implying that it was used at least twice more in texts known to ancient scholars. It is more likely that a unique word of *prima facie* self-contradictory meaning would be corrupted into a slightly commoner and semantically simpler word than that the reverse should happen, and *psephaugous* is therefore probably what Sophocles wrote. The same oxymoron appears in another tragic compound, *melamphaēs* "black-lighted" (Eur. *Hel.* 518, Carcinus jr. fr. 5.3; cf. Ar. *Frogs* 1331 *kelainophaēs*, in a parody of Euripidean lyric).

   Can we say what it was that happened "in the dark-rayed night"? It is possible that Troilus and his *paidagōgos* might have left the city to exercise their horses very early in the morning, but they would hardly have done so in complete darkness, nor could Troilus have had a discussion with Sarpedon about his sister's marriage (cf. fr. D [*trag. adesp.* 561]) *before* so early a departure. We can only say that the context of the phrase is unknown; it could easily be part of a simile or image (cf. e.g. *Trach.* 129–136).

R (627)

The word which Hesychius quotes from *Troilus* and glosses as "intractable, disobedient" is written in his only manuscript as *apistos* – a word which is of course very common in the quite different senses "untrustworthy, incredible" and "incredulous", though it does appear four times in the mss. of tragedy (Aesch. *Seven* 842, 875, 1030; Eur. *IT* 1476) in the sense it is said to bear here. If in these passages the authors had in fact written *apeist-*, the odds are high that it would each time have been corrupted into the much more common lexeme *apist-*, which from early Hellenistic times, if not earlier, was pronounced identically: even in the cognate adjectives *duspeistos* "hard to persuade" and *eupeistos* "easy to persuade, ready to obey", whose near-twins *duspistos* "hard to believe" and *eupistos* "easy to believe" were themselves relatively rare words and so less likely to exercise a corrupting influence, the *-ei-* spelling has survived only in *Aj.* 151 (where one family of mss. has *-pist-*) and Arist. *EN* 1151b6–10. Since the *-peist-* forms were clearly available to Sophocles, and since he is known to have used them on at least one occasion, I think it reasonable to assume that he used them regularly to distinguish the sense "(in)tractable, (dis)obedient". If in *Troilus* the adjective refers to a person, that person might be Polyxene, if Troilus slanderously disparaged her to Sarpedon to discourage him from marrying her (see on fr. D [*trag. adesp.* 561]); but the reference might just as easily be e.g. to a panicking horse.

S (628/628a)

On the face of it, Hesychius straightforwardly reports that Sophocles in *Troilus* used the masculine aorist participle of the Homeric verb *a(a)sai* "delude, infatuate" (the verb from which is, or was taken to be, derived the noun *ātē*, cf. *Iliad* 8.237, 19.91, 19.136), a verb not otherwise found outside epic except that it is cited from an unknown play of Aeschylus (Aesch. fr. 417). Kurt Latte, however (*Hesychii Alexandrini Lexicon* i [Copenhagen, 1953] 507), argued that the word was too familiar to need glossing, and the gloss "damaging" too banal to have been used, by a commentator on Sophocles, and suggested that the reference to *Troilus* was misplaced and really belonged to Hesychius' previous entry, on the adjective *asāron* ("painful", either in the sense of causing or of feeling pain); accordingly *asāron* is printed by Radt as fr. 628a (with a query indicating that its ascription to Sophocles is doubtful). Latte's premise is dubious (forms of *a(a)sai* are glossed in precisely the same way by Homeric scholiasts on *Iliad* 8.237, 9.116, 9.533, 14.271, 16.685 and 19.96) and his transposition implausible: the adjective *asāros* occurs twice in our scanty remains of Sappho (frr. 91, 103.11) and nowhere else in archaic or classical literature outside medical texts (where it appears in the Ionic form *asēros*), so it is overwhelmingly probable that the ultimate source of Hesychius' citation of it is not Sophocles but Sappho or perhaps Alcaeus. I therefore continue to regard *āsās* "deluding, infatuating" as the word here being cited from *Troilus*.

When Homer uses the verb *a(a)sai*, the deluder is by no means necessarily a god: Agamemnon generally blames Zeus or Ate for his blunders (*Iliad* 8.237, 19.91–137 *passim*), but the "agent" may also be wine, sleep, negligent comrades, or even the victim himself (*Iliad* 10.68; *Odyssey* 11.61, 21.296), and most frequently it is left unspecified. A participle, however, such as Sophocles is reported as using, requires a subject, so in this case both the deluder and the victim must have been identified. Since the usual consequence of *ātē* is disaster, the victim is likely to have been Troilus (unless the reference was to an entirely different story mentioned e.g. in a choral song) who, it might well be said with hindsight, must have been out of his mind to go for a ride out of town, unarmed and with only a eunuch for company, when Achilles might be on the prowl. The supposed deluder, being male, cannot be Ate or either of the two most strongly anti-Trojan deities (Athena and Hera); it may have been a vague, non-individualized divine power (*theos* or *daimōn*), or Zeus may have been named, as he often is, as a sort of default god who, being supreme, is taken to be responsible for events which there is no positive reason to ascribe to any other god in particular.

T (633)

A scholiast on Plato's *Republic*, noting that at 566d *mellei* (usually either "is about to" or "delays") is used in the sense of "is likely to", adds that Sophocles in *Troilus* uses the same verb to mean *menei* ("remains" or "(a)waits"). As Pearson comments, this sense is not at all easy to distinguish from "delays" (in some contexts, indeed, it might also be hard to distinguish from "is about to"), but there is no reason to doubt that Sophocles did use *mellei* in *Troilus* in some context in which it bore, or could have been read as bearing, this meaning. There is no way of telling what that context may have been.

U (635)

The classical Greek hoplite shield was made of wood and bronze, except for the handgrip (*antilabē*) which was probably of leather; see e.g. A.M. Snodgrass, *Arms and Armour of the Greeks* (London, 1967) 53. However, educated classical Greeks would have been familiar with many formulaic and other expressions in Homer testifying that shields had once been made largely of leather: for instance in the duel of *Iliad* 7 between Hector and Ajax, Ajax bears a shield "like a tower" which has seven thicknesses of oxhide and one of bronze (7.219–223) while Hector boasts "I know how to ply the dried oxhide to right and left" (7.238–9). Sophocles himself had made Ajax refer to his "unbreakable shield of seven oxhides" (*Ajax* 576), and here he exploits this old epic tradition in order to be able to imagine the shields of warriors being eaten away by insect grubs. For grubs (or perhaps weevils) is what these "(shield)-leather-eaters" ((*sako*)*dermēstai*, singular (*sako*)*dermēstēs*: the shorter form was used by Sophocles in *Niobe* [fr. 449]) almost certainly are. Aristarchus (cited by Harpocration δ23) had claimed that the word denoted a kind of snake, possibly not recognizing that it incorporated the root of *esthiein* "eat" and supposing that it meant "with a skin like a shield", i.e. bronze-coloured, but Didymus (*ibid.*) etymologized it correctly.

The reference to arms and armour suffering damage and deterioration is a *topos* in the context of wishes for permanent peace; cf. Eur. fr. 369, Ar. *Ach.* 279, Bacch. fr. 4.69–72, Theocr. 16.96–97. Such wishes could reasonably be expressed by anyone (especially perhaps on the Trojan side) at any time during the Trojan War: in *Troilus* the persons most fitted to utter such a sentiment are Troilus' bereaved kin (Hecuba, Polyxene, Hector) or the chorus, particularly if it consisted of men of military age (the actual owners of the military equipment which they hope will go to rot).

The word *sakodermēstēs* ($\cup \cup - - -$) cannot be fitted into an iambic trimeter, and its vocalism (ending in -*ēs* not -*ās*) shows that it does not come from a lyric passage; it must therefore come from a passage of chanted ("recitative" or "marching") anapaestic verse. In Sophocles' surviving plays about two-thirds of chanted anapaests are uttered by individual characters and one-third by the chorus, but there are wide variations.

It is very unusual to find in tragedy a compound word made up of three lexical roots – indeed I know of no other; such compounds are a speciality of comedy (e.g. *psamma-kosio-gargara* Ar. *Ach.* 3, *kompo-phakelo-rrhēmona* Ar. *Frogs* 839, *sarkasmo-pituo-kamptai ibid.* 966). Probably the explanation is that the last element, *-estēs*, was no longer felt as a lexical root, retaining as it does not one recognizable phoneme of the verbal root *ed-* "eat" (cf. *edomai* "I shall eat", *edōdē* "food") from which it derives. The earlier Hellenistic grammarians apparently failed to recognize that the similarly formed *ōmēstēs* "eater of raw flesh" was a compound (cf. schol. *Iliad* 11.454, 22.67) – though most later grammarians and lexicographers did analyse the word correctly – and we have seen one of the greatest of the Alexandrian scholars, Aristarchus, taking the last element of *sakodermēstēs* to be merely a derivational suffix.

PHAEDRA

Texts and Testimonia: Pearson ii 294–305; W.S. Barrett, *Euripides: Hippolytos* (Oxford, 1964) 10–45, esp. 22–26; *TrGF* iv 475–481; Lucas de Dios 341–9; Lloyd-Jones 322–331.

Myth: Odyssey 11.321–325, with scholia; *Theseis* fr. 1 West; *Carmen Naupactium* fr. 10 West; Cinesias *PMG* 774; Telestes *PMG* 807; Euripides, *Hippolytos Kalyptomenos* (frr. 428–447, and Hypothesis in *POxy* 4640 = test. ii a+b Kannicht) and *Hippolytos Stephanephoros*; Asclepiades *FGrH* 12 F 28; Zopyrus, *Theseis*, in Stobaeus 4.20.75 (cf. [Plutarch] *Moralia* 314a–b); Callimachus fr. 190; [Eratosthenes], *Catasterisms.* 6.15–22; Diodorus Siculus 4.62; Virgil, *Aeneid* 6.445; 7.761–782; Ovid, *Heroides* 4, *Metamorphoses* 15.497–546, *Fasti* 3.265–6, 5.309–310, 6.737–758; Seneca, *Phaedra*; [Apollodorus] *Bibliotheca* 3.10.3, *Epitome* 1.16–19; Hyginus, *Fabulae* 47, 49, 243, 250–1, *On Astronomy* 2.14.576–587; Pausanias 1.22.1–3; 2.32.1, 3–4; Servius on *Aeneid* 6.445; schol. Plato, *Laws* 931b; Tzetzes on Lycophron 449, 610 and 1329; *Mythographi Vaticani* 1.46, 1.116, 1.201, 1.227, 2.151. H. Herter, *RhM* 114 (1971) 14–77; Gantz 285–8; P. Linant de Bellefonds, *LIMC* v.1 (1990) 445–6, vii.1 (1994) 356.

Artistic evidence: P. Linant de Bellefonds, *LIMC* v.1 (1990) 445–464, vii.1 (1994) 356–9; M.D. Stansbury-O'Donnell, *AJA* 94 (1990) 213–235; J.H. Oakley, *Numismatica e Antichità Classiche* 20 (1991) 63–83.[1]

Main discussions: P. Schröder, *Jahrbücher für classische Philologie* 26 (1880) 408; W. Fauth, *Hippolytos und Phaidra: Bemerkungen zum religiösen Hintergrund eines tragischen Konflikts* (Mainz, 1959); H. J. Tschiedel, *Phaedra und Hippolytus: Variationen eines tragischen Konfliktes* (Diss. Inaug. Erlangen-Nuremberg, 1969); H. Herter, *RE* Suppl. 13 (1973) 1183–97; A. Kiso, *BICS* 20 (1973) 22–36; Sutton 102–4; G.K.H. Ley, *Eranos* 84 (1986) 165–166, 85 (1987) 66–7; O. Zwierlein, *Senecas Phaedra und ihre Vorbilder* (Stuttgart, 1987), esp. 54–68; F.

---

[1] For an extended discussion of the artistic evidence for the Hippolytus/Phaedra story, see Chapter III and the Appendix of T.H. Talboy, *Phaidra and Hippolytos in Greek and Roman Literature with Special Emphasis on Sophocles'* Phaedra (Diss. Nottingham 2004), where it was concluded (in agreement with Barrett [1964] 17) that art had virtually nothing to contribute to the reconstruction or understanding of *HippK* or *Phaedra*. This evidence will therefore not be further discussed here.

Jouan and H. van Looy, *Euripide* viii.2 (Paris, 2000) 221–249 (on *HippK*); F. Jouan in J.A. López Férez ed. *Mitos en la literatura griega arcaica y clásica* (Madrid, 2002) 223–4; O. Zwierlein, "Senecas 'Phaedra' und ihre Vorbilder nach dem Fund der neuen 'Hippolytos'-Papyri", in Zwierlein, *Lucubrationes Philologae* (Berlin, 2004) i 57–136;[2] E. Gelli, *Prometheus* 30 (2004) 193–208; M. Magnani, and A. Casanova, in S. Orlando et al. ed. *Fedra: Versione e riscritture di un mito classico* (forthcoming).[3]

The myth and the play

(a) Non-dramatic literary treatments

The story of Phaedra, daughter of the Cretan king Minos, sister of Ariadne and wife of Theseus, and of her love for Hippolytus, son of Theseus and an Amazon,[4] is not explicitly told by any surviving author earlier than Sophocles and Euripides, though Philodemus[5] says that the "Naupactian" epic (sixth century?) treated Asclepius' raising from the dead of Hippolytus, as later did the lyric poets Cinesias and Telestes (both of whom were active around the end of the fifth century).

The first reference to Phaedra herself is of dubious pedigree: in *Odyssey* 11.321–325, Odysseus mentions Phaedra, Procris and Ariadne among the women he saw during his visit to the underworld. These lines, however, are often suspected of being an Athenian interpolation of the sixth century, since all three heroines have Athenian connections and Theseus (322) is otherwise hardly to be found in poetry or art before the sixth century.[6]

The other sources we have for the Phaedra story seem to rely heavily on Euripides, mostly on his *Hippolytos Stephanephoros* but occasionally on *Hippolytos Kalyptomenos* (hereafter *HippS* and *HippK* respectively).[7] The tale is one of a type common both in Greek mythology and in other

---

[2] This work almost entirely supersedes Zwierlein's 1987 monograph.

[3] We are most grateful to Angelo Casanova for allowing us to see his contribution to this volume in advance of publication.

[4] Sometimes named as Hippolyte or Antiope.

[5] *On Piety* N1609 v. 5, citing the *Carmen Naupactium* (fr. 10 West). Cinesias (*PMG* 774), and Telestes (*PMG* 807).

[6] For Athenian interpolation in Homer at this period, see e.g. S.R. West in A. Heubeck et al. *A Commentary on Homer's Odyssey* i (Oxford, 1988) 36 ("a few obviously Athenocentric passages") and M.W. Haslam in I. Morris and B.B. Powell ed. *A New Companion to Homer* (Leiden, 1997) 83–84.

[7] On these dramas see (b) below.

cultures[8] wherein a married woman makes advances to a (usually young) man, is repulsed, and then in revenge and/or self-defence accuses him to her husband of attempted or actual rape; among the Greek myths of this type the Phaedra story is the only one in which the accused young man is killed. The fundamentals of the story, which are the same in all or almost all accounts, are that Phaedra falls in love with Hippolytus; that at a time when they are both in the same house (either Theseus' palace at Athens, or the home of his maternal grandfather Pittheus at Trozen[9]) and Theseus is absent, an approach is made to him, by Phaedra or on her behalf, with a view to an adulterous affair, and is rejected; that Phaedra then accuses Hippolytus to Theseus of rape or attempted rape; that Theseus, who has been granted by Poseidon the right to have three prayers automatically fulfilled, prays to Poseidon that his son be destroyed; that Hippolytus, when driving his chariot by the seashore, is attacked by a monstrous bull sent by Poseidon, with the result that his horses panic and bolt, dragging him to his death (or at least leaving him mortally injured); that Phaedra commits suicide (either when her machinations are exposed after Hippolytus' death, or else, as in *HippS*, at a much earlier stage, with her accusation left behind her in writing); and that Hippolytus receives cultic honour as a hero in Trozen.

The V-scholia on *Odyssey* 11.321 cite the *Tragodumena* of Asclepiades of Tragilus (*FGrH* 12 F 28), and tell a story that contains some elements that we know from *HippS* (such as the use of *one of* the three wishes granted to Theseus by Poseidon) but whose overall tendency is different and much more discreditable to Phaedra; in particular, in Asclepiades' telling, Theseus sends Hippolytus to Trozen in order to protect him from possible plotting by his stepmother. It follows then that Asclepiades draws on a source, independent of *HippS*, in which a fierce rivalry develops between Phaedra and Hippolytus, perhaps because Hippolytus wished to preserve his place as heir before Theseus' legitimate children by Phaedra (or because Phaedra feared that he did).

Zopyrus repeats much of *HippS* and therefore very likely based his summary on that play. Eratosthenes, as reported by Hyginus (*On*

---

[8] Exemplifications of this story-pattern in Athenian tragedy are discussed under the rubric "Potiphar's wife" by A.H. Sommerstein in D.L. Cairns and V. Liapis ed. *Dionysalexandros: Essays ... Presented to Professor Alexander F. Garvie* (Swansea, forthcoming).

[9] We use the spelling "Trozen" when citing Greek sources, and "Troezen" when citing Latin sources.

Astronomy 2.578–583) in connection with the constellation Ophiuchus, mentioned the raising of Hippolytus from the dead by Asclepius, which had also featured in the *Aetia* of his teacher Callimachus (fr. 190). Diodorus Siculus also seems to repeat much of *HippS*, but he has some significant variations, mostly in the latter part of the story. After propositioning Hippolytus at Trozen and being rejected, Phaedra goes to Athens and accuses him to Theseus there; Theseus summons Hippolytus to defend himself, whereupon Phaedra, fearing exposure, commits suicide; Hippolytus, who is out chariot-driving when he receives the summons, is so distraught by the accusation that his horses bolt and drag him to his death without the appearance of a monstrous bull (as in all other versions of the story) or any other supernatural intervention; subsequently he receives "godlike" honours[10] at Trozen. The absence of the bull, and of Theseus' curse on his son, suggest that this account is not based on tragedy but on some Hellenistic rationalizer of myth.

Virgil mentions Phaedra in the underworld scene of the *Aeneid* (6.445) without giving any details; she stands first in a catalogue of women ruined by love which culminates in the appearance of Dido. In book 7 (765–780), Virgil gives an account of Hippolytus, which briefly mentions his death, caused by Theseus "through a stepmother's wiles", but focuses mainly on his resurrection, the punishment of Asclepius (Aesculapius) for effecting it, and his second life as Virbius.

Propertius (2.1.51–52) makes a brief, and unique,[11] allusion to an unsuccessful attempt by Phaedra to poison Hippolytus.

Ovid treats the Phaedra-Hippolytus story in his *Heroides*, *Fasti* and *Metamorphoses*. In *Heroides* 4, Phaedra writes to Hippolytus (they are both in Troezen) and tells him of her love for him. She encourages him to forsake his chastity and to give in to her overtures. Her reference to chastity seems to suggest *HippS* in which Hippolytus' chastity is a major

---

[10] This apparently means no more than that he had a hero-cult, since the same expression is used immediately afterwards in reference to Theseus.

[11] Unless, as was suggested by Zwierlein (1987) 55–68, it is to be linked to a story in Apuleius (*Met.* 10.2–12) about an unnamed stepmother, in love with and rejected by her stepson, who in a bungled attempt to poison him causes (or so it seems) the death of her own son, and then accuses the stepson of murder as well as attempted rape. (Apuleius' story has a happy ending, for everyone except the stepmother and her slave assistant, when at the stepson's trial the doctor who sold the poison reveals that it was actually only a long-term sleeping-draught, and the boy duly awakes safe and sound.) Zwierlein suggested that Sophocles' *Phaedra* is the ultimate source for the poisoning motif, an idea not repeated in his more recent discussion of this group of dramas.

theme. Phaedra distances herself from any responsibility for her action by blaming Amor. She tells Hippolytus that he should fear nothing from Theseus since his dear friend Pirithous is detaining him in Thessaly; apparently (as she puts it) he prefers Pirithous to both of them. This, she says, is reason enough why they should seek comfort in each other. Not only are they both deprived of Theseus, both have suffered in other ways: she has lost her brother (the Minotaur!) and her sister, Ariadne; Hippolytus has lost his mother (killed by Theseus) and he has been overlooked in favor of Theseus' legitimate children (these are, of course, Phaedra's own children, but she neatly sidesteps this by saying that Theseus, not she, took the decision to rear them). Phaedra also suggests that Hippolytus could eventually become ruler of Crete, presenting herself (falsely) as Minos' heiress.

The account given in the *Fasti* (6.737–758) reads much like Virgil's, except for the more detailed treatment of Hippolytus' death; it is noteworthy that Hippolytus is not driving away from Troezen (as in *HippS*) but *towards* Troezen – implying that the scene of the main action was Athens, which it is not in *HippS* nor, as we now know, in *HippK*.

In the final book of Ovid's *Metamorphoses* (15.497–546), while Egeria is lamenting the loss of Numa, Hippolytus appears and reproves her for claiming that his case is worse than her own. He tells his story in rather greater detail than in the *Fasti*, again setting it in Athens; he is uncertain about Phaedra's motive in accusing him ("was it mainly fear of denunciation, or anger at being rejected?") He describes in great detail his death in the wrecked chariot, his restoration to life as Virbius, and his elevation by Diana to the status of a minor god.

Ps.-Apollodorus (*Epit.* 1.17) follows the epic *Theseis* (fr. 1 West) in having Hippolytus' mother killed while trying to disrupt the wedding celebrations of Theseus and Phaedra. In his account of the consequences of Phaedra's passion (*Epit.* 1.18–19), it is not clear whether she propositions Hippolytus directly or indirectly; Hippolytus refuses her because he hates all women (as in *HippS*) and she then fabricates evidence of rape (broken doors, torn clothes) and accuses him to Theseus. Theseus prays to Poseidon for Hippolytus to be destroyed (there is no mention of this being one of "three wishes"), with the usual result; the truth about Phaedra's passion then emerged (we are not told how) and she hanged herself.

Pausanias (1.22.1–3), reporting a Trozenian version of the story, says that Theseus sent Hippolytus to Trozen as ruler, so that he might neither supplant nor be subject to the children of Phaedra; otherwise he follows *HippS* fairly closely (though with many omissions), specifically saying, however, that it was at Trozen (and not at Athens, as in *HippS*) that Phaedra saw Hippolytus for the first time. In a later chapter (2.32.1, 3–4) where he describes the Trozenian cult of Hippolytus and again claims to be reporting the Trozenian account, Pausanias adds that according to them Hippolytus did not die but was taken up to heaven as the constellation of the Charioteer (Auriga).

Hyginus, apart from brief mentions of Phaedra in a list of women suicides and of Hippolytus in a list of heroes who were killed while driving their chariots, offers a narrative (*Fab.* 47) which is indistinguishable from that of *HippS* except for some slight compression.

The Virgilian commentator, Servius, says that Phaedra accused Hippolytus directly to Theseus; Theseus prayed to Aegeus (not Poseidon; but this may be a slip) and asked him to send a seal (not a bull) to scare Hippolytus' horses. Phaedra killed herself *amoris impatientia* – which, at this point in the narrative, must mean "because she could not bear her distress at the loss of her beloved".

The Platonic scholiast on *Laws* 931b gives a rather vague account, whose only striking feature is that Phaedra's accusation is not said to be one of rape or even of attempted rape but merely of "being enamoured of her" (sc. rather than vice versa). This need not, however, reflect a distinct tradition, since the scholiast may be euphemizing, as he does when he states that Hippolytus "did not comply with Phaedra's wishes" without making it explicit what those wishes were. Other late sources (the Vatican Mythographers and Tzetzes) merely repeat material already found in earlier accounts.

Before passing to the dramatic treatments of the story by Euripides and Seneca, we may compare what is said by the various non-dramatic sources about a few key aspects of it.

Missing from all but Zopyrus and Ovid is any specific mention of *Theseus' absence* which, as we will see, is a regular feature of the dramatic treatments; on the other hand, none of the accounts gives any positive indication that he was *not* absent at the time of the actual approach and rejection. We also hear nothing in the non-dramatic sources about a *direct confrontation between Theseus and Hippolytus*, such as occurs in *HippS*, or of a *reconciliation* before Hippolytus' death.

It is usually left unclear whether Phaedra *approached Hippolytus* directly (as she does in Seneca, and as she is usually presumed to have done in *HippK*) or indirectly; most references to the approach tend to suggest the former, but Zopyrus explicitly has her send her Nurse. No source, unless directly reporting *HippS*, suggests that the Nurse acted, as she does in *HippS*, on her own initiative.

Hippolytus' presence on the shore when he is killed is accounted for in different ways. In Asclepiades and Zopyrus, he simply happens to be driving his chariot there (for exercise and for pleasure, respectively); in Diodorus he has gone driving because he is disturbed by Phaedra's accusation; in ps.-Apollodorus he flees because he hates all women and is appalled by Phaedra's advances. In Ovid's *Metamorphoses*, probably in the *Fasti* too, and also in Hyginus, he is on his way into exile.

In all the sources where *Phaedra's suicide* is mentioned, except in Diodorus and Zopyrus, she kills herself *after* Hippolytus' death. Her reason for committing suicide varies widely: in Asclepiades it is because she has been exposed; in Diodorus she fears she may be; while in Zopyrus, Servius and the Vatican Mythographers, the suicide is a lover's response to the pain of rejection.

Lastly, we can see that the *raising from the dead* of Hippolytus by Asclepius is an old element. But we should note that in the cases in which he does raise Hippolytus from the dead, Asclepius is a mortal hero; as a god he cannot raise the dead, only heal the living.[12]

(b) Euripides' Hippolytus *plays*

We know of three important ancient dramatic treatments of the Phaedra-Hippolytus story, other than that by Sophocles. Two of these survive complete, and we have a fair amount of information (substantially augmented in recent years) about the third.

We may begin with Euripides' extant play, *Hippolytos Stephanephoros* or *Stephanias* (*HippS*). A brief summary of it will suffice. As the play opens, Theseus is away from home for an unspecified reason;[13] "home" is at present Trozen, Theseus having gone into exile there for a year, taking Phaedra with him, to purge the pollution caused by his killing of the Pallantids. Aphrodite tells the audience that Phaedra is in love with Hippolytus but is keeping her passion secret; we will learn later that she is, in fact, deliberately starving herself to death because she found she could neither endure nor conquer her passion – to yield to it was not an option

---

[12] See below, p. 286 n.136.

[13] We later discover that he has been visiting a sanctuary (he refers to himself as a *theōros*, one who goes on a religious mission, at 792 and 807), most likely to consult an oracle; on his return he is wearing a garland (806–7), apparently in token of having received a favourable response – but we never learn anything more about his mission.

that she even considered. Phaedra's Nurse tries to discover the cause of her mistress's illness, and eventually induces her to reveal her love for Hippolytus. The Nurse takes it upon herself to remedy the situation, convincing Phaedra that she will use magical means to do so while leaving it very vague what she is actually intending to achieve. In fact, after first securing an oath of silence from Hippolytus, she reveals to him Phaedra's desire for him. Phaedra hears Hippolytus' furious rejection of the Nurse's proposal and is overwhelmed by the exposure of her desire, bound as it is to disgrace her and leave her children burdened by a bad reputation. Phaedra returns to her plan and, with vague words of menace against Hippolytus, goes inside and hangs herself. Theseus arrives home to the sound of loud lamentation. He is told of Phaedra's suicide. As he grieves over her death, he finds a tablet tied to her wrist. In it Phaedra has accused Hippolytus of rape. Phaedra's death serves, for Theseus, as decisive proof of the truth of the accusation. Theseus calls down the wrath of Poseidon upon Hippolytus by using one of three wishes Poseidon had given him; but being apparently unsure whether this prayer will be effective, he adds a further decree of exile. Hippolytus returns and an *agōn* ensues. Because of his oath of silence Hippolytus is unable to defend himself effectively, and Theseus confirms his sentence of exile. Hippolytus leaves, distraught at his father's refusal to believe him. Shortly thereafter a messenger reports that Hippolytus has been terribly injured in the wreck of his chariot when a bull from the sea frightened his horses. Hippolytus, barely alive, is brought back to Theseus. When he arrives, Artemis has already told Theseus the truth about his wife's false accusation; she promises Hippolytus a permanent cult in Trozen, and Hippolytus dies reconciled with his father, having formally released him from all guilt for his death.

Euripides' *Hippolytos Kalyptomenos* or *Katakalyptomenos* (*HippK*) is another (probably earlier) version of the same story.[14] The play has not survived, but we have the advantage of two overlapping papyrus copies of a Hypothesis and more than twenty quoted or paraphased fragments of the text.

---

[14] See below, pp. 266–272, for the question of the dating of the two *Hippolytus* plays. References by letter to fragments of *HippK* below are to Barrett (1964) 18–22, even where we do not agree with Barrett's sequencing; the fragments are also printed and discussed by M.R. Halleran, *Euripides: Hippolytus* (Warminster, 1996) 25–37, as well as in the complete editions of Euripidean fragments by Jouan & van Looy (2000) and Kannicht.

The first copy of the Hypothesis (*PMich* inv. 6222a) was published in 1988 by G.W. Schwendner, and re-edited in 1994 by Wolfgang Luppe.[15] The second copy was discussed briefly by M. van Rossum(-Steenbeek) in 1998[16] and published by her in 2003 in an edition (*POxy* 4640)[17] which presents both copies, first separately and then (where they overlap) in combination. The new fragment not only supplements the Michigan text, but also enables us to establish definitively the sequence of its fragments, which had previously been in dispute.[18]

Interpretation of the *HippK* fragments must now start from the Hypothesis. In the following sections we do this in order to create a framework in which Sophocles' play may then be examined.

The beginning of *PMich* fr. A may be saying that Phaedra has fallen in love with Hippolytus (1a]νεπεσ.[ ),[19] and that she then takes some action (1b]υσα, almost certainly a feminine participle). We also learn that Theseus is away in Thessaly (1d), presumably with Peirithous (cf. Ovid *Her.* 4.109–112). *HippK* fr. A (443) fits this scenario: Phaedra, perhaps in a typically Euripidean prologue, tells of her situation, providing background to the action that will soon develop.[20] She is one of "the unhappy" because she is affected by her passion for Hippolytus, and

---

[15] G.W. Schwendner, *Literary and Non-Literary Papyri from the University of Michigan Collection* (Diss. U. of Michigan 1988); W. Luppe, *ZPE* 102 (1994) 23–39 (see also his articles in *Eos* 84 [1996] 231–6 and *ZPE* 143 [2003] 23–26).

[16] M. van Rossum-Steenbeek, *Greek Readers' Digests? Studies on a Selection of Greek Subliterary Papyri* (Leiden, 1998) 16, 22.

[17] Hereafter, references to van Rossum, unless otherwise indicated, will be to the pages of *POxy* lxviii.

[18] The Hypothesis has now also been published by Richard Kannicht in *TrGF* v.1 (2004) 460–3. Kannicht prints the Oxyrhynchus and Michigan fragments separately as testimonia ii a and ii b to *HippK*. Below we use the *POxy* line-numbering (all references are to column ii of the papyrus), except for the first line of the Oxyrhynchus text and the five lines of *PMich* fr. A printed above it on *POxy* lxviii p.20; these six lines we designate as 1a-1f.

[19] Cf. Antiphanes fr. 232.3 εἰς ἔρωτά τ' ἐμπεσών 'falling in love', Eur. *IT* 1172 εἰς ἔρον γὰρ του μαθεῖν πεπτώκαμεν 'I have fallen into a desire for knowledge', Eur. fr. 138.

[20] Jouan & van Looy (2000) 233, followed by Zwierlein (2004) 69, have Aphrodite speaking the prologue, and place this speech of Phaedra's after the entrance of the chorus. There is no positive evidence for a divine prologue-speaker, and it may be judged unlikely that Euripides would thus repeat himself. It is, however, possible that Phaedra's speech followed a prologue delivered by a subsidiary human character such as the Nurse; fr. E (447b), which describes Phaedra as invoking the moon, "[can] hardly [reflect] an actual invocation on the stage [by her]" (Barrett [1964] 19), since fr. A (443) shows that it was daylight when Phaedra made her first entrance, and may therefore paraphrase something that was said in such a prologue.

because she is neglected by her husband. In the *Heroides* (4.109–128) Phaedra tries to persuade Hippolytus to join her because Theseus has wronged them both. This appeal to a shared grudge seems to be anticipated by *HippK* fr. B (447a),[21] which might be addressed to Hippolytus or might come from a soliloquy.

The new Oxyrhynchus fragments show that someone has met a violent death (1f κατέσφαξ[αν or κατέσφαξ[ε(ν) "they/he/she slew"), possibly in connection with a wedding or in a marital bedroom (1f [θα]λάμοις) and that something has been written by a woman (2 χαράξασα "making marks" [fem.]). Van Rossum (21, 22) suggests that perhaps a household servant has been killed and that Phaedra is writing to Theseus (Phaedra is still alive much later in the action, cf. 16). One quite attractive possibility, raised by Hutchinson[22] and approved by Zwierlein (2004) 64, is that the reference may be to "an attempt by Phaedra to enforce her will, from which Hippolytus escapes with violence". On this view the murdered slave would be an accomplice of Phaedra's, and would have been killed by Hippolytus; Phaedra could then have turned the incident against Hippolytus by claiming that *he* had been the one trying to enforce his will and that the slave had died defending his mistress's honour. There is also, however, another possible interpretation of this part of the Hypothesis. If Theseus is in Thessaly with Peirithous, he may well have been attending his friend's marriage to Hippodameia when (according to many accounts) the party was disrupted by the behavior of the Centaurs, who assaulted the women guests and, as Ovid makes explicit (and as we would anyway expect), tried to rape the bride herself.[23] A great battle ensued with the Lapiths ultimately defeating the Centaurs. Indeed Pausanias (1.17.2) describes a painting in which Theseus (and apparently Theseus alone) has already killed a Centaur.[24] This accounts well for the first two elements noted at the beginning of this paragraph, without unnecessarily postulating a murder unknown in any other version of the story; on the other hand it does not provide an organic link between the episode of violence and Phaedra's letter.

---

[21] With the apparent reference there to Theseus' sexual infidelities cf. *Her.* 4.127–8 *i nunc, sic meriti lectum reverere parentis,* | *quem fugit et factis abdicat ipse suis.*

[22] *ZPE* 149 (2004) 20.

[23] D.S. 4.70.3; Ovid *Met.* 12.219–226; [Apoll.] *Epit.* 1.21; Plut. *Thes.* 30.3.

[24] So in Ovid (*Met.* 12.226–240) he is the first to do so; his victim, Eurytus, is the one who had seized Hippodame (as Ovid calls her).

For it seems fairly safe to accept that Phaedra in *HippK* did write a letter to Theseus. Lines 3–4 of the Hypothesis refer to Hippolytus and to an act of violence, and by the time we reach lines 6–7 we find that an accusation has already been made against Hippolytus (κατὰ τοῦ παιδ[ός] "against the son") which Theseus has believed (πιστεύσας).[25] It seems very likely, therefore, that Theseus was already aware of the accusation before he returned from Thessaly, and was prepared to question his son upon his arrival. This makes it plausible to suppose, as Hutchinson has argued,[26] that the sending of the letter with the accusation, and therefore also the initial approach by Phaedra to Hippolytus and its rejection, were not part of the dramatic action but were part of the "back-story" narrated in the prologue, just as was the propositioning of Bellerophon by Phaedra's counterpart in infamy, Stheneboea, in the play named after her (Eur. fr. 661.8–14).[27]

In that case, Phaedra at the outset of *HippK* will be anxiously awaiting Theseus' return: if he believes her accusation he can be expected to punish Hippolytus, if he disbelieves it he will certainly punish *her*. But she also apparently still has some hope of a successful consummation of her passion: fr. C (430) shows that she still feels herself in the grip of Eros rather than of hatred. It is not entirely clear how this might come about – unless perhaps Phaedra had written her letter *anonymously* (referring to herself in the third person), thus giving herself the opportunity, ahead of Theseus' return, to make a further approach to Hippolytus with the options of confirming the accusation if he again refused or rebutting it if he consented. She may well have explained her intentions, at least in broad terms, in her first speech. If this, or something like it, was indeed her scheme, one can well understand why the author of the Hypothesis to *HippS* speaks of *HippK* as notable for "objectionable impropriety" which has been "corrected" in *HippS*.

---

[25] The next word, of which only the first letter (α) survives, could well be αὐτῇ "her" (Hutchinson).

[26] G.O. Hutchinson, *ZPE* 149 (2004) 15–28, esp. 21 (citing in comparison the Hypotheses of *HippK* and especially of *Stheneboea*). The analysis that follows, however, differs in important ways from Hutchinson's.

[27] Zwierlein (2004) 71–78, on the other hand, places the murder of the slave, and apparently the sending of the letter, *within* the action of the play – though his sketch of its structure (77–78) seems to leave little or no space for this complex and innovative sequence of events.

Phaedra must now make another approach to Hippolytus, and it is likely that, in contrast with the Phaedra of *HippS*, she made it directly.[28] Two fragments appear to come from the approach of Phaedra to Hippolytus. One of these is fr. D (434); this is seen by Hutchinson[29] as coming from a soliloquy by Phaedra or a "sympathizer", and by Zwierlein (61, 77) as coming from a dialogue between Phaedra and her nurse about action to be taken against Hippolytus; but the reference to the use of physical force (χερῶν ὑπερβολαῖς "by greater strength of hand") to achieve a goal suggests that it is a male – and therefore Hippolytus – who is being urged to make the effort. For him, the goal to be thus achieved could hardly be anything other than political power. If so, Phaedra is here descending to even greater depths of villainy by betraying not only her husband but also her children, whose inheritance she is abdicating to their bastard half-brother.[30] An allusion to this scenario must become part of the later false supplication scene, as we shall see, and it may be reflected in *HippS* 1010–1, when Hippolytus suggests that Theseus may think he was motivated to take both Phaedra and Theseus' throne.

Phaedra most assuredly swore Hippolytus to silence before embarking on her approach.[31] Without an oath, there is no guarantee that Hippolytus will not reveal Phaedra's attempts to Theseus. It is true that in one ancient account (that of Diodorus) Hippolytus has no chance to denounce Phaedra in any case, since he hears of her accusation when out driving and in his distraught state loses control of his horses with fatal results; but Phaedra could not count in advance on events developing in this way, and in any case, as will be seen below, Hippolytus and Theseus do seem to have met

---

[28] Though she may have made her plans known to her trusted Nurse – if indeed such a character existed in this play. Zwierlein (2004) offers no evidence or argument in support of his assertion (64 n.14, cf. 72) that an onstage approach by Phaedra to Hippolytus would be "hardly representable" in the Athenian theatre.

[29] *ZPE* 149 (2004) 22.

[30] No fragment of *HippK* refers directly to Phaedra's children, but they are so crucial to Attic myth (they fight in the Trojan War, where they rescue their grandmother Aethra; and one of them, Acamas, is the eponymous hero of one of Athens' ten civic tribes) that it is unthinkable that Euripides, even by silent implication, should abolish them. It is striking that in *HippS* he considers it unnecessary to mention these children in the prologue; the audience can be assumed to know all about them, and no explanation is needed when they eventually are referred to at 305–6.

[31] Even if, as here argued, she is not making the approach for the first time, she would still need to renew the oath: she is about to communicate an entirely new and even more audacious proposal, and must protect herself against any plea by Hippolytus that his original oath did not apply to this.

on stage in *HippK* as they do in *HippS*. The oath appears to be evidenced by fr. G (435) where the addressee is asked to specify "what [he is] to suffer" if he breaks his promise.[32]

Hippolytus again rejects Phaedra's advances and recoils at the shamefulness of her actions (fr. H [436]).[33] Phaedra in reply may utter fr. F (428) – "Those mortals who shun Aphrodite unduly are as unhealthy as those who pursue her unduly" – which on her lips, in the situation we have envisaged, would probably be perceived by the audience, but not by Hippolytus, as a veiled threat. Alternatively, fr. F may be addressed by Phaedra, with studied understatement, to her Nurse or to the chorus (which consists of women, as fr. J [429] shows, and can be expected to sympathize with her).

Phaedra's second failure will have changed her love into the vengeful hatred of "a woman scorned". She apparently expressed her feelings, and revealed at least something of her intentions, in the presence of the chorus, whose reaction is shown in fr. J (429), and possibly also of her Nurse; fr. P (433) may belong here, and perhaps, as suggested above, fr. F (428) too.

Now at last Theseus returns to Trozen (Hypothesis, line 6). Phaedra comes out to greet him, and we suddenly learn the depths to which she will descend in order to obtain her revenge on Hippolytus. Having already, as we have seen, written to Theseus to tell him of the alleged rape attempt, she now goes a step further by claiming that Hippolytus, in Theseus' absence, was plotting to overthrow him.[34] For the second time she is

---

[32] Zwierlein (2004) 71–77 argues, for reasons connected with the word λυθείς "released" and the treatment of supplication in tragedy (cf. Barrett [1964] 19), that this fragment does not come from the exacting of an oath (so too, on partly different grounds, Hutchinson, *ZPE* 149 [2004] 22). But who, if not a god, is to punish the addressee for betraying the speaker? The threat of punishment by the speaker herself will not be much of a sanction, since if she has been betrayed she will have lost all power to enforce such a threat.

[33] The placing of this fragment by Jouan & van Looy (2000) 233 in the mouth of Phaedra, as part of a declaration of love to Hippolytus, is perplexing. Phaedra, in making her approach to Hippolytus, is unquestionably to be regarded as shameless, and as fr. C (430) shows, she is well aware of this; she is also inviting him to commit at least one and probably two great wrongs against the person whom, of all the world, he ought to respect the most. In such a situation, a wish that Shame should drive Shamelessness out of human hearts would be the most blatant and obvious hypocrisy imaginable, and would at once ruin any prospect of successful persuasion.

[34] It is striking that in the Hypothesis to *HippS* (line 18) Phaedra is said to have accused Hippolytus, in her suicide note, of rape *and hostile plotting* (ἐπιβουλήν). Theseus in *HippS*

accusing him of himself committing, or planning, an act that he had indignantly rejected when she had suggested it to him.

Theseus calls for Hippolytus,[35] having believed Phaedra's original accusation and having been further incensed by the additional charge.[36] In *HippS* he both curses and exiles Hippolytus without waiting to hear his defence; this leads to some serious complications relating to the curse[37] in which Euripides is most unlikely to have involved himself twice over in different plays. It is therefore best to assume (*contra* Zwierlein [2004] 65, 77) that in *HippK* the order of events was the reverse. When Hippolytus arrives, Theseus immediately denounces him in what is in effect a prosecution speech. Fr. L (437) may well come from this speech, describing Hippolytus' alleged crimes as *hybris* (a term which fits both rape[38] and rebellion against legitimate authority[39]) and suggesting that he was tempted to commit them by his privileged and prosperous status;[40] fr. M (438) seems to make the same point again, perhaps later in the *agōn*.[41]

---

never makes any mention of such an allegation, and the statement in the Hypothesis may well be due to confusion with *HippK*.

[35]The suggestion of R.M. Newton, *GRBS* 21 (1980) 7–10, that the *agōn* was between Theseus and Phaedra (not Hippolytus), on the ground that "it is difficult to imagine that, if Hippolytus had been allowed to plead his innocence, Theseus would have neglected to summon Phaedra for cross-examination", is virtually ruled out by the papyrus evidence, which has Theseus arriving at Trozen, believing the allegations against his son, and apparently praying to Poseidon for his destruction, all within less than two lines. See further n.42 below.

[36]If *POxy* 4639 (= Eur. fr. 953f Kannicht) comes from this play (as was tentatively suggested by its first editor, A. Kerkhecker, a view endorsed somewhat less tentatively by Zwierlein [2004] 78–83), Theseus at this stage apparently expressed his anger at some length. That in this fragment Theseus – if it is Theseus – is speaking in Hippolytus' absence is strongly indicated by fr. 1 ii 6–10, where he first refers to the young man in the third person (ἱππευέτω "let him ride/drive his horse(s)"), then sends someone off ἐς ἀγ[ρούς?] "to the countryside(?)" presumably to fetch him, and then speaks of what will happen "when he is here" (χὤταν παρῇ[ι]). Nothing in the fragment, however, indicates that Theseus *curses* his son in this scene; indeed, a curse at this stage seems inconsistent with a summons to Hippolytus to appear before his father. In *HippS*, where we do have an early curse by Theseus, Hippolytus is not summoned but comes of his own accord. Fragment Q (432) tends to confirm that in *HippK* the curse was uttered in Hippolytus' presence (see p.262 below).

[37]On these see Barrett (1964) 41–42, 334–5.

[38]See N.R.E. Fisher, *Hybris* (Warminster, 1992) 105–7.

[39]*Ibid.* 129–130.

[40]Cf. Solon fr. 6; Aesch. *Ag.* 750–6.

[41] Barrett (1964) 20 assigns this fragment to Hippolytus as a rebuttal of Theseus' argument; but Hippolytus could hardly defend himself by arguing that *hybris* is "the child

Because of his oath, Hippolytus cannot mount an effective defence; as in *HippS*, all he can do is deny the charge, use general "arguments from probability" to suggest that he is not likely to have committed such crimes, and plead for time (fr. O [441]; cf. *HippS* 1051) to give an opportunity for evidence to emerge that will clear him.[42] This seems to Theseus mere crafty evasion (fr. N [439]) and convinces him even more firmly that his son is guilty.

If Theseus did not pray to Poseidon before the *agōn* for Hippolytus' destruction, he must do so after it; the letters]ωνι· in line 7 of the Hypothesis may be the conclusion of a statement about a prayer to Poseidon (τῷ Ποσειδῶνι),[43] and in fr. Q (432) Hippolytus may be taunting his father after the curse, saying he should not merely pray to the gods but also "do something" himself,[44] and we can safely assume that an outraged Theseus takes up this challenge and sentences his son to exile. Since this would be motivated by Hippolytus' taunt, it does not require us to suppose that Theseus is in any doubt about the efficacy of his curse, as he seems to be in *HippS* (894–8, cf. 1169–70); we can therefore assume that in *HippK* the motif of Theseus' "three wishes", which is quite inorganic in *HippS* (888, 1315) – it would have been far easier for Euripides, had it been possible, to give him only one – was put to its logical use. Poseidon had given Theseus the right to have any three prayers automatically granted; Theseus had already used this right on two occasions[45] and now uses it for

---

[42]In *HippS* he solemnly swears his innocence (1025–31) and also suggests that prophets be consulted (1055). In *HippK*, with Phaedra alive, we might expect him to suggest that Phaedra be summoned for cross-examination; but perhaps she had made him swear to her in terms (e.g. to cause her no harm) that rendered this impossible.

of wealth, not of thrift" when his favourite pastime is chariot-driving, which requires great wealth and is the very antithesis of thrift (as is amusingly exemplified by the dispute between Strepsiades and his wife over the naming of their son in Ar. *Clouds* 60–67, ending with an agreement to give him the self-contradictory compromise name Φειδιππίδης "Thrifthorse").

[43] So Luppe (*ZPE* 102 [1994] 33).

[44]There is what seems to be a reminiscence of this in *HippS* 1084–90. Theseus orders his servants to seize Hippolytus and "drag" him off; Hippolytus retorts "If any of them touches me, he'll regret it; thrust me out of this land *yourself*, if you have the heart." But Theseus does have "the heart" to do so, if necessary, and Hippolytus at last accepts that his condemnation (to exile – the curse has, for the time being, been forgotten about) is irrevocable.

[45] To escape from Hades and from the labyrinth, according to schol. *HippS* 46, 887, 1348; but this may be mere guesswork, since (i) it puts these two adventures in the wrong order, (ii) it ignores the roles of Heracles and of Ariadne in Theseus' two escapes, and (iii)

the third time[46] – so that if he afterwards discovers that his prayer was mistaken, he no longer has any sure means of revoking it. As we shall see, the time will come when he very much wants to do so, and cannot. After the *agōn* with Theseus, Hippolytus goes straight to the stables (fr. R [442]) and sets off in his chariot. Theseus, left alone, begins to have second thoughts about what he has done, and his doubts are strengthened by the remarks of a servant[47] who warns him, with a wry paradox, that he should not believe a woman "even when she tells the truth" (fr. K [440]) – particularly, perhaps, when she makes an accusation of rape against a young male resident in her house.[48] But Theseus does not immediately reverse his decision; instead he decides that he must test Phaedra.

The Hypothesis (line 13) seems to speak of someone being dressed in Hippolytus' clothes; it appears, therefore, that an attempt is being made to deceive someone by having another person pose as Hippolytus. The Oxyrhynchus fragments, by establishing the sequence of the Michigan fragments as ACB, have caused it to be generally accepted that this scheme was devised and carried out after the cursing and exiling of Hippolytus; and since Phaedra has no need now to contrive any further plots, and Hippolytus himself is no longer present, the deviser must be Theseus.[49] In addition, to make the deception work, we must assume that Phaedra does not know of Hippolytus' banishment; she must, therefore, have gone inside after making her denunciation, and stayed inside.[50]

The likeliest person to pose as Hippolytus is the slave belonging to Hippolytus whom we know from the Hypothesis (line 9) to have had a

---

one admittedly late source (Seneca, *Ph.* 951–3) says Theseus did not use any of his three prayers while in Hades.

[46] So Cicero (*Off.* 1.32) and Seneca (*Ph.* 949).

[47] Very likely the "slave of Hippolytus" who is mentioned in line 9 of the Hypothesis, and who may play an important role in a subsequent scene.

[48] Did the servant also tell Theseus that it was, in fact, Phaedra who had made adulterous and/or traitorous proposals to Hippolytus and not vice versa? The apparent request to Phaedra by the false Hippolytus for "some true proof of her love" (Hypothesis, lines 15–16 as supplemented by Luppe, *ZPE* 102 [1994] 30–31) suggests that the servant and Theseus had definite grounds for believing that she was in love with Hippolytus.

[49] So W. Luppe, *ZPE* 143 (2003) 23–26 (a conclusion he had reached, reversing his earlier views, as soon as the evidence of the Oxyrhynchus fragments was first reported; see Jouan & van Looy [2000] 238 n.27), and G.O. Hutchinson, *ZPE* 149 (2004) 19, 20, 23.

[50] And out of earshot; this could be made clear to the audience by (e.g.) having Phaedra say, on her exit, that she was going to the women's quarters (which would normally be situated well away from the outer door), thus incidentally emphasizing to Theseus, as she would wish to do, that she has behaved and is behaving as a proper wife.

significant role in the play (a slave appears to be mentioned again at line 17 [θερ]άπων). Theseus dresses him in Hippolytus' clothes so that Phaedra will think it is Hippolytus. As a suppliant the false Hippolytus covers his head (line 14),[51] ensuring that Phaedra will have no way of knowing that he is not the real Hippolytus. It is true that he must speak to her, and one might have expected her to recognize that his voice is not that of Hippolytus, but he is muffled and this will disguise his voice considerably.[52] In any case, any possible implausibility will be strongly mitigated by the fact that the conversation will not occur on stage. For since the scene between Phaedra and the false Hippolytus apparently takes place at the hearth (lines 14–15 [ἐπὶ τῆς ἑ]σ῾τ῾{θ}ίας καθ[ί]σαι "to sit at the hearth" – so Luppe[53]), it cannot have been enacted in front of the audience (*pace* Zwierlein [2004] 77, 88) and must instead have been reported – either by the slave, by Theseus (if, as is likely, he was watching the episode from a place of concealment[54]), or just possibly by a third party. Theseus is perhaps the most likely candidate, since he will be needed on stage anyway soon afterwards.

The false Hippolytus approached Phaedra with his face covered, sat at the hearth, and asked her for some true proof of her love for him;[55] Phaedra will then have said something (we cannot tell what) that made her guilt manifest to the listening Theseus, and the false Hippolytus, ostensibly reassured, will have left her. Without knowing it, she has destroyed herself, the deceiver successfully deceived.

Theseus will be distraught with rage at Phaedra, horror and shame at his own actions, and concern for his son, whom he now knows he has cursed

---

[51] Presumably, in view of the play's subtitle, the real Hippolytus had done the same thing (though not for the same reason) earlier in the action. We should not suppose, with Jouan & van Looy (2000) 238, van Rossum 11, 22, and Zwierlein (2004) 59, 66, that the subtitle actually referred to the disguise of the false Hippolytus; the subtitle speaks of Hippolytus covering his face, not of an impostor doing so. There is no reason why there should not have been multiple face-veilings in *HippK*: in *HippS* there are at least two (243–250, 1458), probably three (cf. 946–7), and perhaps even more.

[52] In Ar. *Birds* 1498–1503 this effect of muffling is made to work, as it were, in the opposite direction, as the muffled Prometheus mishears everything that Peisetaerus says to him.

[53] *ZPE* 102 (1994) 31 (where he does not reproduce the deleted letter).

[54] Unless Theseus was present to witness Phaedra betraying her guilt, he would still, just as before, have no evidence against her except the word of the servant.

[55] The pretence must have been that he was unaware of Phaedra's denunciation and had had second thoughts about his rejection of her.

and exiled unjustly. Perhaps he sends horsemen to summon Hippolytus urgently back; almost certainly he prays to Poseidon to ignore his previous request for Hippolytus' destruction. But it is too late.

A messenger arrives and narrates the terrible story of Hippolytus' last drive; we have only one fragment of his speech, fr. R (442), describing Hippolytus rushing to the stables immediately after we last saw him on stage. Theseus thus learns that Hippolytus is dead, and his anguish is intensified further; Phaedra, learning[56] that the youth she loved is dead and that her plot has been revealed, commits suicide. Hippolytus' body is brought back on stage[57] as Theseus laments the loss of his son. Fr. S (444) probably belongs to this context, but it is not clear who speaks it; its somewhat vapid sententiousness would be suitable for a comment by the chorus-leader, but the speaker could also be Theseus. In either of their mouths, the description of the disaster as "innate and god-sent" might be seen as an evasion of responsibility: Theseus is partly responsible for Hippolytus' death because he acted too quickly and drastically on Phaedra's unproven allegations, the chorus because they knew the truth and did not reveal it (though they may have been sworn to secrecy, as in *HippS*[58]).

Someone will now enter from the *skene* to report Phaedra's death; and presently there appears a *deus ex machina*[59] (we know this from fr. U [446]), since only a god could have ordained Hippolytus' hero-cult). Who is the god? Hardly Artemis, since Euripides is unlikely to have used the same divinity in *HippK* and *HippS*; a more likely candidate is Poseidon, the father of Theseus, the grandfather – and the killer – of Hippolytus.[60] He

---

[56] We cannot tell precisely how. One possible scenario would be for Phaidra to come out of the house drawn by the sound of loud laments and for Theseus then to denounce her as the "killer" of his son, whereupon she would go inside to end her life (like the Sophoclean Deianeira, Eurydice and Iocaste). Zwierlein (2004) 77 places Phaedra's suicide earlier, before the arrival of the messenger, supposing that she has by then become aware that the person she thought was Hippolytus is in fact an impostor and that she has betrayed herself.

[57] There is no evidence that he was brought back alive, as in *HippS*, and it is better to assume that Euripides varied his treatment.

[58] May, not must: in *Medea* the chorus keep Medea's plans secret from everyone even though they have never sworn to do so (they are merely asked to, and do, *promise*: *Med.* 259–268).

[59] We use the conventional term without wishing necessarily to imply that the flying-machine (*mechane*) was employed on this occasion.

[60] It is striking that Artemis in *HippS* has been assigned some qualities and functions more usually associated with Poseidon – in particular, a connection with the sea and with

cannot now reverse his action, even if Theseus were able to wish for it; but what he can do is assure Hippolytus' place among heroes.

After Poseidon has prescribed Hippolytus' cult, and presumably consoled Theseus and condemned Phaedra, the chorus apparently ended the play with an anapaestic chant (fr. U [446]), praising Hippolytus' virtues, especially his chastity (*sōphrosynē*, often treated as the antonym of *hybris*) and piety[61] – virtues that may well have stood out more clearly in *HippK* than in *HippS*, where his *sōphrosynē* is shadowed by an arrogant self-righteousness and contempt for his supposed inferiors, and his piety is a selective piety that excludes Aphrodite.

Two fragments have not been discussed above: fr. T (445), which would fit in a great many contexts (the speaker says that "the gods do not judge these things aright", by way of explanation of some fact that he/she will then proceed to mention, evidently a fact that he/she finds, or professes to find, disagreeable) and fr. 447, the single word *diopos* "captain, ruler", which probably comes from a lyric or anapaestic passage[62] and whose reference cannot be determined.[63]

What is the date of *HippK*? The hypothesis to *HippS* tells us that the play to which it is attached was produced in 428, that it won first prize (defeating Iophon, son of Sophocles, and Ion of Chios) and that it was the later of Euripides' two *Hippolytus* plays. Until recently it was taken for granted that this was reliable fact.[64] There can certainly be little doubt that the surviving play is indeed the one called in antiquity *Hippolytos Stephanephoros*; this subtitle plainly refers to the first scene in which

---

horses (*HippS* 228–231) – as if to make a connection between her and Hippolytus more credible; Hippolytus, contrariwise, has been made a devotee of hunting as well as of chariot-driving, with the same objective. (It should not be forgotten that for ancient Greeks there was no direct cultural link between "horse and hound"; they hunted on foot. In *HippS* Hippolytus appears to be in the habit of hunting before breakfast [52, 109–110] and going for a drive afterwards [110–2]) .

[61] Phaedra was wrong, then, to say (fr. D [434]) that the fortunes of mortals are not determined by their piety – wrong, at least, if posthumous reputation is taken into account.

[62] Its only two other tragic occurrences, at Aesch. *Pers.* 44 and [Eur.] *Rhes.* 741, are both in anapaests.

[63] One naturally thinks of Theseus, but the word might for all we know have occurred in a choral song referring to some entirely different myth. In *Persians* and *Rhesus* (see previous note) it denotes subordinate commanders in non-Greek armies.

[64] As it still is by Jouan & van Looy (2000), and by Kannicht in *TrGF* v.1 466 ("fabula docta est ante a. 428").

Hippolytus appears,[65] where he offers a garland to Artemis (73–87). But Gibert[66] was quite right to point out, as indeed Barrett (1964) 29 had already done, that the festival records (and probably also Aristotle's *Didascaliae*, which was based on them) will simply have recorded two productions by Euripides including plays called *Hippolytus*, one of them in 428 (winning first prize) and another at an earlier date, and that the identification of *HippS* as the play of 428 will therefore be the conjecture of a Hellenistic scholar. Indeed, the Hypothesis itself virtually tells us as much, saying that "it is apparent that [this *Hippolytus*] was written second, because in this play the objectionable impropriety [of the other *Hippolytus*] has been corrected". This conjecture may or may not be correct; we cannot automatically assume that it is, but must assess the internal (and any other external) evidence for ourselves. And Gibert, having assessed it, concludes that *HippS* was the earlier play and *HippK* the later.[67]

That *HippK* – or, more specifically, the character of Phaedra in *HippK*[68] – did contain "objectionable impropriety" that was absent, or much less prominent, in *HippS*, is agreed by almost all critics. It is known from comedy[69] that contemporaries regarded Euripides' Phaedra, alongside his Stheneboea, as a prime example of his liking for creating women characters of exceptional wickedness (particularly in regard to sex); that the Phaedra of *HippK* deserved to be so categorized is evident enough from fr. C (430) in which she describes Eros as her "teacher of daring and audacity", implying that she is doing, or is about to do, something that she herself considers to be audacious. The Phaedra of *HippS*, on the other hand, is a woman who would rather starve herself to death than yield to her passion, and whose Nurse propositions Hippolytus on her behalf, against

---

[65] Similarly Sophocles' *Ajax* had the subtitle *Mastigophoros*, referring to Ajax's first scene, in which he apparently carried a whip to torment his supposed enemies (cf. *Ajax* 110).

[66] J.C. Gibert, *CQ* 47 (1997) 85–97, at 86.

[67] So now, bringing fresh arguments, does G.O. Hutchinson, *ZPE* 149 (2004) 15–28, at 24–25. Zwierlein (2004) 57 n.2, who knew of Hutchinson's work, accepts his and Gibert's conclusions *in toto*, and offers a further argument (see note 79 below).

[68] C.W. Müller, *Zur Datierung des sophokleischen Ödipus* (Wiesbaden, 1984) 23–24 suggested that the "objectionable impropriety" of *HippK* related as much to Theseus as to Phaedra; but he was writing before the papyrus Hypothesis revealed evidence indicating that in *HippK* Theseus was largely responsible for detecting Phaedra's crime. In any case it is on Phaedra's immorality that contemporaries remarked.

[69] Ar. *Thesm.* 497, 546–550; *Frogs* 1043–52.

her will and to her horror. Hanna Roisman's contention[70] that the Phaedra of *HippS* is to be seen as being no less wicked than her counterpart in *HippK*, but only cleverer in concealing her wickedness, is unconvincing.[71]

It still does not follow automatically, however, that *HippS* was the later of the two plays, the one produced in 428. We cannot *a priori* exclude the possibility that Euripides might have created an innovative, virtuous Phaedra first and reverted afterwards to a more traditional presentation of the story. It might seem surprising for it to have been the scandalous *HippK* rather than *HippS* that won first prize, but one can think of many possible explanations for that (e.g. an exceptionally brilliant performance, weak competition, or the quality or popularity of the other components of Euripides' four-play production). However, there are other considerations which between them make it highly likely that the ancient scholars were right to identify *HippS* as the later, successful play.

Aristotle, *Rhetoric* 1416a28–35 (= Eur. *test.* 59 Kovacs), discussing the rhetorical tactic of appealing to a judgement previously given, cites as an example a story about Euripides. Euripides, according to the story, was involved in an *antidosis* suit[72] against a man named Hygiaenon, and in the course of his speech Hygiaenon accused him of impiety, pointing to the verse in *HippS* (612) where Hippolytus, saying "My tongue has sworn, but

---

[70] H.M. Roisman, *Nothing is as it Seems: The Tragedy of the Implicit in Euripides' Hippolytus* (Lanham MD, 1999). A somewhat similar line has been taken by P. Oikonomopoulou, *Pathos in Euripides: Motivation and Characterization in Euripidean Love* (Diss. Nottingham 2005).

[71] See the review by L. Himmelhoch, *BMCR* (online) 1999.09.16; add that Artemis, who has every reason to want to condemn Phaedra as the killer of her protégé Hippolytus, in fact exonerates her, putting all the blame on Aphrodite and the Nurse (1300–6) and naming Phaedra as one of three victims of Aphrodite along with Hippolytus and Theseus (1404); she even speaks of Phaedra as having shown "in a manner of speaking, nobility" (1300–1).

[72] Such a suit would arise out of the allocation of compulsory public services ("liturgies"), such as the position of a *choregos* or a trierarch, to individual wealthy citizens. Anyone who had been allocated a liturgy had the right to challenge another person to perform the liturgy instead or alternatively to exchange all his property with the challenger; if the challengee refused both alternatives, the issue would be decided by a court, which, after hearing argument and evidence on both sides, would assign the liturgy to the person who the jury decided was the richer of the two (unless he could show that he was legally exempt from it). See D.M. MacDowell, *The Law in Classical Athens* (London, 1978) 162–4.

my mind is not under oath", appears to condone perjury,[73] Euripides retorted

> that he [Hygiaenon] was doing wrong to bring the judgements of the Dionysiac competition into the lawcourts; he [Euripides] had already rendered account for these words in the other place [i.e. the theatre], or would do so if he [Hygiaenon] wanted to make an accusation.

Since this story is presented by Aristotle as an instance of appealing to a judgement previously given, it only makes sense if Aristotle believed that *HippS* had in fact been successful in "the Dionysiac competition".[74] Moreover, the anecdote must either be true, or have been invented at some time between Euripides' day and Aristotle's (certainly not by Aristotle himself). If it is true, it proves that the play *was* indeed successful.[75] If it is an invention,[76] it proves that at the time when it was invented, the play was generally believed to have been successful – which is likely to take us back, at any rate, to a time when there were men living who remembered this relatively rare occasion when Euripides had been victorious. Unless, therefore, we are prepared to assume that *two* of Euripides' four lifetime victories were won with plays about Hippolytus and Phaedra, it must follow that *HippS* was the play that won first prize in 428.[77]

---

[73] Much quoted, and alluded to, in fifth-century comedy (Ar. *Thesm.* 275–6, *Frogs* 101–2, 1471) – always, as in Aristotle's story, out of context: not long afterwards (656–8) Hippolytus is speaking of his oath as binding, and in spite of strong temptation (1060–3) he keeps it even when breaking it would offer him his only chance of avoiding condemnation for an infamous crime of which he is innocent.

[74] Cf. P.D. Kovacs, *Euripides: Cyclops, Alcestis, Medea* (Cambridge MA, 1994) 18–19.

[75] Gibert (*CQ* 47 [1997] 90 n.20) claims that the story does not imply a first prize for *HippS*, but his only argument is that "if [Euripides] won with the play his opponent uses to mock him, a more obvious retort would be, 'The Athenians approved of my *Hippolytus*'". He does not explain how a statement by Euripides that he had "rendered account for these words" and undergone "the judgements of the Dionysiac competition" could serve to rebut Hygiaenon's charge, if this play had *not* been successful; and his claim that the phrase δεδωκέναι λόγον ("rendered account") "is not even applied specifically to *Hippolytus*" ignores the word αὐτῶν "for them" (i.e. for these words).

[76] This is, of course, possible; but would an anecdote-monger cast the otherwise completely unknown Hygiaenon in the role of Euripides' opponent?

[77] Wolfgang Luppe, who in *Philologus* 142 (1998) 173–5 had ingeniously suggested that the didascalic hypothesis of *HippS*, which states that the action of the play is set in Thebes [sic], was a blend of two hypotheses for two different plays (the other play, of course, being one that actually was set in Thebes), has now (*ZPE* 151 [2005] 11–14) suggested that the date 428 may belong not to *HippS* but to the other play; this, however, forces Luppe to abandon the plausible explanation he had previously been able to give of

It should also be noted that quite apart from the issue of Phaedra's character, there are several other features of *HippS* which look as though Euripides has gone out of his way, at the cost of some strain to plot or myth, to allude to his treatment in *HippK* or to avoid repeating what he had done in that play,[78] whereas it is hard to find anything in *HippK* which creates a similar impression in reverse.[79]

In metrical terms, both *HippK* and *HippS* are written in the "severe style" as defined by Cropp & Fick, but this only shows that neither is later than 428, which we knew anyway. The surviving fragments of *HippK* are not extensive enough to justify an attempt to pinpoint more precisely its position in the evolution of Euripides' metrical habits,[80] but as regards *HippS* it has been pointed out recently by Hutchinson[81] that if proper names are disregarded, *HippS* contains proportionally fewer resolutions in its iambic trimeters than any other Euripidean play,[82] which *prima facie* suggests that it might well belong to the 430s or even earlier. It is not clear, however, whether variations in resolution frequency within the "severe style" period can be regarded as significant, or whether it is right, for purposes of chronological interpretation, to disregard proper names.[83] And

how the blend came about (a slip of the eye from the archon-date ἐπ''Αμυνίου [423/2 – which would be the date of the other play] to ἐπ' <Ἐπ>αμείνονος [429/8]).

[78] See p. 259 above, on the idea of Hippolytus seizing the throne; p. 261, on the timing of Theseus' curse; pp. 262–3, on the "three wishes"; and pp. 265–6 n.60, on the relationship between Hippolytus and Artemis.

[79] Zwierlein (2004) 66, 83–90, suggests that the treatment of Theseus in *HippK*, particularly his testing of Phaedra, can be seen as designed to "correct" the portrayal of a naively credulous Theseus in *HippS* (contrast the argument of Müller discussed in note 68 above). However, it is not at all obvious that the Theseus of *HippK* was presented as significantly less naïve or less credulous than his counterpart in *HippS*. He becomes sceptical only after he has already cursed his son (i.e. too late), and perhaps only when prompted by a slave (cf. fr. K [440]); and unlike the Theseus of *HippS*, he does not have the fact of Phaedra's suicide to mislead him into believing that something traumatic must have happened to her to motivate it.

[80] We possess 32 iambic lines, which contain, in all, two resolutions, both directly following a third-foot caesura.

[81] G.O. Hutchinson, *ZPE* 149 (2004) 24–25.

[82] With proper names included, *HippS* is still the most resolution-free of the surviving plays, but by a much smaller margin.

[83] On the first point: the frequency of resolution in Euripidean trimeters does not increase by a steady progression; there are some notable jumps, including a very striking one in the early to mid 420s before *Andromache*, while at the end of Euripides' life the trend is reversed, with a sharp decrease in the frequency between *Orestes* and *Bacchae*, and some periods of near-stasis. On the second point: Hutchinson (*op. cit.* 25) censures Cropp & Fick for using the argument that the poet might have reduced his rate of resolution in words

HippS does not stand out as being exceptionally conservative in the *types* of resolution it employs, compared with other "severe style" plays.[84] On the evidence available it remains best to agree with the ancient scholars that *HippS* was the play that won first prize in 428, and that *HippK* was produced at an earlier date.

How much earlier? Euripides staged his first production in 455, but he did not win his first victory until 441, and it is reasonable to suppose that it was only then that he became a person of public note. It is therefore, on balance, likely that a play which acquired instant notoriety, as *HippK* evidently did, was produced in 441 or later.

Between 441 and 428 there are two fixed dates, 438 and 431, when we know that Euripides put on productions, and we know, furthermore, having the full list of four plays for each of these productions, that *HippK* did not figure in either of them. Several further dates can be ruled out if we accept the principle proposed by C.W. Müller[85] that tragic dramatists normally did not put on productions at Athens in successive years; this principle cannot in fact be maintained for the later part of Euripides' career,[86] but it is reasonable to apply it to his earlier years when his

---

other than proper names in order to compensate for the need to use proper names in which resolutions were unavoidable; yet he uses the very same argument himself, in his next paragraph, to explain the very low rate of fourth-foot resolutions in Euripides' *Suppliants*! Cropp and Fick have now responded magisterially to Hutchinson, making very much the same points as we do, in *ZPE* 154 (2005) 43–45.

[84] Of the types of resolution analysed by Cropp & Fick 27–57, there are five which occur in at least eleven of the thirteen Euripidean tragedies later than 428 but in only one of the four "severe style" plays. Of these five (let us call them "unique presences"), two (Cropp & Fick's types 2.1bD and 2.1cD) occur only in *HippS* (both, admittedly, only in proper names) while three (2.2aD, 10.1, and 1.1a) occur only in the prosatyric *Alcestis*. There are also five types of resolution ("unique absences") that occur in at least eleven of the thirteen later plays and in three of the four early ones; of these, two are absent only in *Alcestis*, produced in 438 and usually regarded as the earliest of the four (6.1e and 8.1fS), one is absent only in *Medea* (8.1fL), and two are absent only in *HippS* (4.1cS, and 1.1b in words other than proper names). If we score one point for each unique presence and deduct one for each unique absence, *Alcestis* scores +1, *Medea* –1, while *Heracleidae* and *HippS* both score zero – so that by this reckoning *Medea*, despite its relatively high overall resolution rate, comes out as on balance the most conservative of the four.

[85] *Zur Datierung des sophokleischen Ödipus* (Wiesbaden, 1984) 60–77.

[86] The metrical evidence points very strongly to the conclusion that he must have produced four suites of plays (i.e. twelve tragedies) between 414 and 407 inclusive; he is known to have put on productions in 415 (the "Trojan trilogy"), 412 (schol. Ar. *Frogs* 53), and 408 (schol. Eur. *Or.* 371), and there is no way in which two further productions can be fitted into the period 414–408 without breaking Müller's rule. The twelve tragedies concerned are the extant *Ion, Iphigeneia in Tauris, Helen, Phoenissae* and *Orestes*, and the

production rate is known to have been significantly lower.[87] If so, and if we assume (see p. 269 above) that the production which included *HippK* did not win first prize (which rules out 441), it will follow that *HippK* is datable to the period 436–433 inclusive.[88]

(c) Seneca's Phaedra

The last ancient dramatic treatment of the Phaedra-Hippolytus story that we have is by Seneca.[89] His *Phaedra*,[90] set in Athens (not Troezen), opens with Hippolytus preparing to go hunting in the company of Diana, to whom he is devoted. He departs, and Phaedra appears. We learn from her that Theseus is absent, aiding the attempt by his friend Pirithous to abduct Proserpina from the underworld (this idea, as we shall see, is taken from Sophocles); she, meanwhile, is hopelessly in love, and as in *HippS* has a craving to engage herself in Hippolytus' favourite pastime.[91] Her Nurse urges her to "suppress the flames of impious love", but Phaedra's *furor* (178, 184) is too strong for her *ratio*, and when she eventually yields (or professes to yield) to the Nurse's desperate supplication, it is only to declare that she will maintain her virtue by ending her life – which, as she evidently expected and intended,[92] brings the Nurse round at once, to agree, and indeed offer, to approach Hippolytus on her mistress's behalf.

---

fragmentary *Andromeda, Antigone, Auge, Hypsipyle, Meleager, Oedipus* and *Polyidus* (we exclude *Archelaus, Temenus* and *Temenidae*, since in Euripides' lifetime these *may* have been produced only in Macedonia). For the metrical evidence, see Cropp & Fick 69–92.

[87] The maximum number of Euripidean plays (other than satyr-dramas) likely to have been produced before 425 BC is 35 (to judge from the evidence summarized in Cropp & Fick 69–92), including the prosatyric *Alcestis*; if we assume that the remaining 34 included one other prosatyric play, we are left with eleven productions between 455 and 426. (We exclude *Andromache*, since according to schol. *Andr.* 445 this play was not produced in Athens at all.) One might then, in conformity both with Müller's principle and with the reasonable supposition that Euripides was awarded a chorus more frequently after 441 than before, posit five productions between 455 and 441 (inclusive) and six between 438 and 426.

[88] Since each of the eight other years in this period (440–437 inclusive, and 432–429 inclusive) was either the year of, or the year after, or the year before, another known Euripidean production.

[89] We do know that the early Hellenistic poet Lycophron wrote a *Hippolytus* (Suda λ827 = Lycophron test. 3 Snell), but nothing of it is extant.

[90] One of the two branches of the manuscript tradition gives the play the title *Hippolytus*; but it was known to Priscian (*Gramm.Lat.* 2.253.7), in the sixth century AD, as *Phaedra*.

[91] *Phaedra* 110–1, cf. *HippS* 215–231.

[92] Cf. Zwierlein (2004) 109.

She does so by indirect means, advising him in general terms to lead a less strictly disciplined life and give freer rein to his pleasures, and is getting nowhere when an impatient Phaedra bursts on the scene, falls suddenly in a dead faint (585–6) – and so finds herself being lifted up in the arms of Hippolytus (588).

Phaedra promptly takes full advantage of this opportunity, but she goes about doing so in a surprising way.[93] She begins, not by offering Hippolytus her love, but by offering him the throne (617–621) and begging him to "have mercy on a widow" (623). Hippolytus, while refusing to supplant his father (or, for that matter, Phaedra's children), readily agrees to protect her until Theseus' hoped-for return; increasingly plain indications of her passion fall on uncomprehending ears until at last she falls at Hippolytus' feet and says, this time, "have mercy on one that loves you" (671). Hippolytus is aghast, thrusts her away, and when she tries again to rush into his arms he grabs her by the hair and draws his sword as if to kill her (706–9) – but then, rage giving place to mere disgust, he throws her off, throws down the sword, and flees. For this turn to violence, however brief, on Hippolytus' part there is no known precedent; but it serves to suggest that Hippolytus too can have his *ratio* fatally overborne by *furor*. This concern with the power of passion recurs throughout the play, and in Theseus, too, we will see *ratio* and *furor* contending.

Uniquely, it is then not Phaedra (she has fainted again) but the Nurse who takes steps to set up the false rape allegation; the sword, the fact of Hippolytus' flight, and Phaedra's dishevelled hair, will be useful items of "evidence".[94]

Theseus returns, having been rescued from the underworld by Hercules, but marked and exhausted by his experiences. He hears sounds of grief. Upon his inquiry the Nurse tells him that Phaedra is determined on suicide. Theseus wants to know why, and calls Phaedra to him. Phaedra at first refuses to tell him anything, but he breaks her obstinacy by threatening to

---

[93] It is striking that Hippolytus is not put on oath; Phaedra only asks that they talk with no third party present (599–600). As in Diodorus, an oath is unnecessary to the plot, since Seneca does not allow Hippolytus and Theseus to meet.

[94] Zwierlein (2004) 92–94 argues that the motif of the Nurse contriving faked or misleading evidence was derived by Seneca from Sophocles; if so, Seneca must have moved it to an earlier stage of the action than it originally occupied, since the concoction of evidence to deceive Theseus is pointless when Theseus is still believed to be dead. Cf. note 119 below.

have the Nurse tortured. Phaedra then (evidently well coached by the Nurse) tells him that she has been raped by the owner of the sword which she shows him. Theseus, recognizing the sword as that of Hippolytus (898–900), believes the accusation unquestioningly and, knowing Hippolytus may flee to the ends of the earth, makes use of his one sure means of vengeance. His father Neptune has sworn to him that he will be granted three prayers without fail; this is the last of the three, which "I would never have used up, unless pressed by a great evil" (949–950); let Hippolytus not see another day (946).

A messenger soon arrives and narrates in detail how Hippolytus, fleeing in his chariot, was thrown and killed, and his body broken in pieces, when Neptune's bull made his horses panic. Theseus cannot help grieving for his death as a parent, even though he desired and caused that death (1114–22, cf. *HippS* 1257–60).

Phaedra reappears, remorseful and distressed, laments over the broken corpse, and cuts off a lock of her hair (1181–2), which she lays on the body[95] while confessing her own crime, finally putting herself to the sword.[96] The hair-offering is an obvious precedent for the cult of Hippolytus prescribed by Artemis in *HippS* 1423–7, and since it is virtually meaningless to anyone who does not know of this cult, Seneca probably took the action directly from a Greek source. If so, it is likely that this source is Sophocles:[97] in *HippS* Phaedra is already dead, in *HippK* the truth was extracted from her only by a trick. Sophocles may well thus also be the source for Phaedra's remorseful confession as the means of revealing the truth.

Theseus too begs for death and a return to the underworld he has so lately left; he in his turn laments over the corpse and then "assembles the

---

[95] Seneca, writing for the recitation-room rather than the theatre, has forgotten, or chosen to forget, that the body is not yet on stage (it is brought on between 1247 and 1249); cf. Zwierlein (2004) 121.

[96]On stage (as often in Seneca). Since "one cannot hang oneself on the stage, even Seneca's pseudo-stage" (Barrett [1964] 44 n.2) we cannot tell from this evidence whether the Phaedra of Sophocles (or even of *HippK*) committed suicide by hanging (as tragic women most often do) or by the sword (like the Sophoclean Deianeira and Eurydice). Zwierlein (2004) 95, 117, 128–9, however, notes some other wisps of evidence favouring a death by the sword in Sophocles' play; in particular, Phaedra would need a sharp instrument to cut a lock for the offering (cf. *Ajax* 1179, Eur. *Bacch.* 493).

[97]Cf. Barrett (1964) 43–44, Zwierlein (2004) 94. Kiso (1973) 31–32, on the other hand, argues that the confession in Seneca is based on *HippK*.

fragments ... in a grisly jigsaw" (Barrett [1964] 44),[98] only to find the body is still not complete. The play ends with Theseus ordering the preparation of a royal funeral pyre, the (apparently dishonourable) burial of Phaedra, and a search in the countryside for the body parts still missing.

In some cases, as we have seen (and there are others), there are grounds for tracing one or another passage or feature of Seneca's play to a particular Greek original; but basically the plot is his own creation, and it would be risky to rely on the uncorroborated evidence of Seneca to support any conclusions about *HippK* or about Sophocles' play.

(d) Sophocles' Phaedra

Phaedra takes place in Athens. The fragments give no direct clue, but Athens is the scene of the denunciation and curse in Seneca, in Diodorus, and in two of the three Ovidian treatments (see pp. 251–2 above); since we now know that *HippK* as well as *HippS* was set in Trozen, it becomes extremely likely that Sophocles was the source for an Athenian setting.[99]

A more important difference between *Phaedra* and both the Euripidean plays is the nature of Theseus' absence. In *HippS* (792, 807) he has gone on a brief visit to a sanctuary or oracle; in *HippK* he is in Thessaly with Peirithous; in *Phaedra*, he has gone down to Hades (frr. H, J [687, 687a]) – an idea used later by Seneca – and, crucially, is believed to be dead (fr. G [686]). It follows that Phaedra's passion for Hippolytus,[100] whatever else may be said of it, is not intentionally adulterous – though it may still be seen as disloyal to her husband's memory, if it should jeopardize the heirship and safety of his legitimate children, and of course also as a failure in Phaedra's own maternal duty towards them.

Whether or not Phaedra may at first have attempted to resist her passion (before the action begins, or in its early stages), the first we hear of it (fr. B [680]) indicates that she has decided she cannot or will not do so: she recognizes that she is about to act in a "shameful" way, but argues that no mortal "against whom Zeus unleashes evil" can avoid bearing such "god-

---

[98] If horror has not already tipped over into unintentional self-parody, it surely does so at 1267–8: "I'm not sure what part of you this is, but it *is* a part of you; put it here, here – it's not the right place, but it does need filling."

[99] Cf. Zwierlein (2004) 91.

[100] Casanova (forthcoming) not implausibly suggests, on the basis of Seneca (*Ph.* 646–666) and Heliodorus (*Aethiopica* 1.10.2; on the latter cf. R. Merkelbach, *RhM* 100 [1957] 99–100), that the Sophoclean Phaedra was attracted to Hippolytus because of his resemblance to the young Theseus (whom she would have seen when he was in Crete).

sent afflictions" – an argument not dissimilar to that deployed by the Nurse in *HippS* (437–477, esp. 476–7). The "shameful" action can only be an approach to Hippolytus, which, even though not adulterous, is clearly to be regarded as improper (seeing that she herself so regards it), because of its possible implications for her own children and/or because it was in any case not proper for a free woman, even a widow, to bestow herself on a man, whether in marriage or otherwise.[101]

These lines, being addressed to the chorus, are almost certainly spoken by Phaedra, not the Nurse, who would be more likely to speak directly to her mistress. The presence of the chorus also shows that the passage does not come from the prologue but (at earliest) from the first episode. It is possible that fr. A (688), which is lyric, may come from the chorus's *parodos*; the "storm-swift voices" (or rumours) which they have apparently heard might well relate to what one would expect to be the main subject of popular discussion in Athens, the fate of Theseus.[102]

It may now seem as though the action may develop much as it does in *HippK* (assuming for the time being that *HippK* is the earlier play – a matter to which we will return). But it does not. Fr. C (693a) – five lines from *Phaedra* that somehow found their way into the text of *Electra*[103] – gives the final exchange in a quarrel between a woman (A) and another person (B). A has been giving B advice which B has rejected – advice, apparently, to embark on some joint enterprise – and now A says she is going (into the *skene*, as line 3 shows), "since you can't bring yourself to

---

[101]In classical Athens, a widow with children under age could either return to her natal family (whose head would then be responsible for finding her a new husband), leaving her children in the care of the guardian or guardians appointed by their father or by the *archon*; or she could stay with the children under the protection of their guardian(s) (who then had the right to give her in marriage, according to the most natural interpretation of the law cited in [Dem.] 46.18 – cf. A.R.W. Harrison, *The Law of Athens* i [Oxford, 1968] 8, 19–20); or her husband might himself before his death, or by will, have arranged a new marriage for her (sometimes, as in the case of the mother of the orator Demosthenes, to one of the appointed guardians). See D.M. MacDowell, *The Law in Classical Athens* (London, 1978) 88–89; S.B. Pomeroy, *Families in Classical and Hellenistic Greece* (Oxford, 1997) 168–172, 185–9. Phaedra's position in this play is exceptional because Theseus has "died" without making any provision for the upbringing of his legitimate children, and has no relative in a position to step in and take charge; and there is the further complicating factor (emphasized by Casanova, forthcoming) that the city has been left without a ruler.

[102] In *HippS* the chorus have likewise been drawn to the scene by rumours – in that case, about Phaedra's self-starvation (*HippS* 121–140). Cf. also Soph. *Aj.* 137–152, 173–4, *Trach.* 103–111.

[103] See the Commentary on this fragment.

approve my words, and I can't bring myself to approve your behaviour"; B retorts that (s)he will never follow A, however much A may wish it, "since it is utter folly to hunt the unattainable".

Since B's language is quite unsuitable for Hippolytus (who would certainly have much harsher things to say than this about Phaedra's proposal, whether made to him directly or indirectly), the argument, if these lines do come from *Phaedra*, was almost certainly between Phaedra and her Nurse. Which is which? Phaedra, as we know from fr. B (680), has decided to take the path of "shame". She must therefore have asked the Nurse to cooperate with her – no doubt by approaching Hippolytus on her behalf – and it must be the Nurse who refuses and says her mistress is "hunt[ing] the unattainable". Hence A is Phaedra (and the "behaviour" that she cannot approve of is her slave's insubordination), B is the Nurse, and Phaedra goes inside after speaking, the Nurse addressing lines 3–5 to her departing back. She objects to Phaedra's proposal not because it is immoral but because it is impracticable, presumably being certain that there is no prospect of persuading Hippolytus. In *HippS* the Nurse for equally pragmatic reasons takes a diametrically opposite line, almost bullying a reluctant Phaedra into authorizing an approach to Hippolytus because, disregarding any question of duty to husband or children, she sees this as the only way to save Phaedra's life.

Phaedra, however, desperately wants to convince the Nurse to assist her; and we know that in the end an approach *was* made to Hippolytus. It is unlikely that Phaedra made the approach in person, which would have been a mere repetition of *HippK*.[104] Her only alternative would be to make a renewed attempt to persuade the Nurse to do so, despite her first failure. In Seneca, as we have seen, she does precisely this: her new attempt takes the form of a threat of suicide. Could this have happened in Sophocles too? We know that Sophocles' Phaedra does in the end commit suicide, and we know too, from fr. K (685), that she had seriously considered this as an option at some earlier stage. But that stage, as we shall see,[105] is likely to have been *after* Hippolytus' rejection of her; she will hardly have been driven to the ultimate extreme of despair by the obstinacy of a mere slave.

---

[104] Or, if *Phaedra* is considered the earlier of the two plays (on the question of relative date, see pp. 287–9 below), would imply that Euripides in the most controversial scene of *HippK* was merely imitating Sophocles. Either way, if *both* dramatists had made Phaedra approach Hippolytus directly, it would be surprising that one of them incurred savage criticism and the other apparently none.

[105] On the placement of fr. K (685), see the Commentary.

Any threat now, therefore, would have to be (as in Seneca) no more than a ploy to override this obstinacy – a ploy which can be relied on to appeal, either to the Nurse's affection for the mistress whom she has tended from babyhood, or to her awareness that with Phaedra dead she herself will have lost her role and status in the household. Just as in *HippS*, then, the Nurse will in the end be approaching Hippolytus in order to save Phaedra's life, and just as in *HippS* there is deception involved – but here it is Phaedra who is the deceiver.

How this part of the action was realized dramatically is not entirely clear. One would certainly want the threat of suicide, and the breakdown of the Nurse's resistance, to occur on stage, and yet fr. C (693a) implies that Phaedra goes inside with the Nurse still refusing to assist her. Possibly she came out again (after a choral song, with the Nurse having remained on stage?) declaring herself resolved to end her life; this would be a neat reversal of what Sophocles does in *Ajax* when Ajax, having shut himself up in his hut refusing to listen to the advice and pleas of Tecmessa and the chorus (583–595), comes out again (after a choral song) deceptively (though ambiguously) declaring himself resolved *not* to end his life (646ff).

At some point Phaedra appealed to the chorus, as fellow-women, to keep her "shame" a secret (fr. D [679]). She may have done this either when she first revealed her passion, or when she had gained the Nurse's agreement to take the action she desired, or even (as in *HippS*) after Hippolytus' rejection of her. In any case, the chorus's pledge of silence will be crucial to the plot, since they will consider themselves bound by it even when Phaedra makes her false accusation against Hippolytus; it is therefore quite likely that, as in *HippS* (713–4), the dramatist made them fortify their pledge by an oath.[106]

The next major event will have been the meeting of the Nurse and Hippolytus. Did this take place onstage? Two surviving fragments, E (684) and F (677), suggest that it did.[107] The former extols the power of Eros,

---

[106] In *HippS* they do this even though Phaedra had not actually requested so solemn an undertaking (cf. p. 265 and n.58 above); it may be significant that fr. D (679), like *HippS* 710–2, requests only that the chorus keep silent, not that they swear to do so.

[107] We see no reason to adopt Casanova's suggestion (cf. already T.B.L. Webster, *BICS* Suppl. 20 [1967] 151), based on Roman artistic evidence, that Phaedra sent the Nurse to Hippolytus with a *letter*. Why should she send a written message to a man in the same house, when she was in a position to send an oral one? A. Schober, *WSt* 47 (1929) 162, discussing the Roman evidence, says cogently that "there is no need to suppose a ... separate literary source, such as Ovid ... , since the motif of the letter could have been

who attacks "not only ... men, or women for that matter ... [but] even stirs up the souls of the gods in heaven",[108] the fact that men are mentioned first suggests, as Barrett (1964) 23 notes, that the addressee is male. The latter says that "a noble man" ought to reject any pleasure which is "wrongful"; these are most easily taken as the words of a "noble man" who has been offered what he sees as a wrongful pleasure[109] – and perhaps implicitly comparing himself with the woman, also noble in birth if (in his eyes) ignoble in character, who, through her agent, is offering it. An onstage approach to Hippolytus by the Nurse sets this play in contrast both with *HippK* (onstage approach by Phaedra) and with *HippS* (approach by the Nurse, initially offstage – with Phaedra eavesdropping – but then coming onstage as the disgusted Hippolytus bursts out of the house). At any rate, in the expressive words of someone later in the play referring to this episode (fr. N [678]), Hippolytus "spat out" the Nurse's proposal.

Hippolytus leaves and goes off driving.[110] Perhaps as he goes, he says he wants to "enjoy the spring weather by the seashore", as Zopyrus says (ap. Stobaeus 4.20.75), and let its pure air and water wash away the filth that has invaded his ears (cf. *HippS* 653–4). If he mentions either driving or the seashore in his exit speech, we will easily guess that we will not be seeing him alive again. One effect of having Hippolytus go off in this way is that there will be no need for Theseus to sentence him to exile, as he does in *HippS* and apparently did in *HippK* also (cf. *HippK* fr. Q [432]); some such device was essential for Euripides if he was to have, in accordance with his almost invariable practice,[111] a formal debate (*agōn*)

---

invented by the visual arts, as a convenient device for expressing [the idea of a rejected proposal], independently of any literary influence".

[108] The Nurse uses a rather similar argument – but to Phaedra – in *HippS* 443–458.

[109] Why wrongful? Only because the offer has come, indirectly, from Phaedra herself (cf. p. 276?) Or is Hippolytus refusing to accept that Theseus is dead (cf. Seneca, *Ph.* 623–9), and therefore regarding the Nurse's proposal as adulterous?

[110] There is no absolutely decisive evidence that in Sophocles (as in Seneca) Hippolytus made what proved to be his final exit before Theseus' arrival; but for any dramatist not committed in advance to creating a confrontation and debate between father and son, this arrangement has considerable advantages (no need for Hippolytus to swear secrecy; no need for the curse to be supplemented by a sentence of exile; no need to contrive for Hippolytus a defence speech which must fail to sway Theseus). If, moreover, Euripides had already produced at least one of his two *Hippolytus* plays, Sophocles would have an added incentive to adopt a distinctive treatment of this part of the story. Zwierlein (2004) 97–98 is thus right to suspect that the absence of an *agōn* in Seneca's play may well be a Sophoclean feature.

[111] See M. Lloyd, *The Agon in Euripides* (Oxford, 1992).

between Hippolytus and Theseus – Sophocles was not concerned about this. The early departure of Hippolytus has other significant structural consequences as well, as we shall see in a moment.

There is no need to suppose that Hippolytus in *Phaedra* had been sworn to secrecy. Looking at the matter from within the fictive situation, everyone – with the possible exception of Hippolytus himself (see note 109) – believes Theseus to be dead; hence, for one thing, Phaedra's passion while still "shameful" is not obviously criminal, and for another, there is no obvious person to whom it might be feared that Hippolytus would reveal it.[112] Looking at it from the dramatist's point of view, he does not need an oath for his plot because he has taken care to remove Hippolytus from the scene before Theseus arrives, so that they never meet.[113] On the other hand, he can use the *absence* of an oath to add to Phaedra's motivation for accusing Hippolytus: once Theseus has unexpectedly returned, there is every chance that Hippolytus will inform him; Phaedra must at all costs forestall this, and her desperate determination to do so will be heightened by the sudden transformation of her situation from almost total security to terrible danger.

It is possible that after Hippolytus' departure we see the Nurse telling Phaedra of his rejection of her proposals, and Phaedra's distraught reaction to the news, but it is not necessary to assume this: the scene could have ended with the Nurse going *inside* to tell Phaedra what has happened, and this has some advantage in avoiding a scene which could hardly be said to advance the action.

Now, without warning, Theseus returns. He is greeted by someone who expresses surprise that he is not after all dead (fr. G [686]): this might be a servant or (perhaps more likely) the chorus-leader.[114] Theseus is doubtless

---

[112] Had this play been set in Trozen, thoughts might have turned to the aged Pittheus (as did those of whoever inserted the interpolated verse 691 into *HippS*); but, as we have seen, it was almost certainly set in Athens.

[113] Phaedra probably never meets Hippolytus either in this play. In *HippS* it is the third of the three logically possible onstage pairings within this trio – that of Phaedra and Theseus – that never happens; Phaedra and Hippolytus are present together in one vital scene (601–668) but never exchange a word (indeed Hippolytus is probably not even aware of Phaedra's presence). In four of Sophocles' seven extant plays, he contrives to ensure that a pair of major characters who are closely connected by kinship, love or marriage never meet onstage: *Trachiniae* (Deianeira-Heracles), *Ajax* (Ajax-Teucer), *Antigone* (Antigone-Haemon), and *Electra* (Orestes-Clytaemestra).

[114] On the view followed here, Hippolytus has already departed. It is possible that a servant comes out to greet the new arrival, but there is no need to posit this additional

asked how he managed to escape from Hades, and he responds with an extended narrative, of which two lines survive, both of which, as it happens, probably refer to the hound Cerberus (frr. H, J [687, 687a]). The latter may possibly be part of a description of the death of Peirithous, who according to several sources was eaten by Cerberus,[115] that "eater of raw flesh" (Hes. *Thg.* 311) who fawns on those who arrive in the abode of his master Hades and devours those who would depart thence (*ibid.* 770–3). There are significant dramatic possibilities in the creation of a Theseus who has been narrowly rescued from death himself, has just lost his closest friend,[116] and is shortly to lose his wife and his son also.[117]

The return of Theseus will throw Phaedra into panic and desperation. She thinks of suicide, but rejects it for the sake of her children (fr. K [685]). But when Hippolytus returns from his drive, he will surely denounce her to his father, and she may then be put to death anyway. She thus has no alternative but to get her own stroke in first – a stroke that she hopes will silence Hippolytus for ever.[118] She is still committing murder

---

character (who would have nothing else to do, so far as we can tell), and there is no positive evidence supporting the suggestion by Casanova (forthcoming) that the first speaker is Phaedra herself. Sophocles often allows quite extended dialogue between a character and the chorus-leader (*Trach.* 663–733; *Aj.* 719–747, 977–1046; *Ant.* 162–222, 1091–1114, 1155–79; *OT* 512–530; *El.* 251–327), sometimes even when another speaking character is present (*OC* 457–492).

[115] Plut. *Thes.* 31.5 (a rationalizing version, apparently from Philochorus [*FGrH* 328 F 18], but presupposing an earlier mythical account), Tzetzes on Ar. *Frogs* 142. More usually Peirithous either simply remains bound in Hades for ever (as is implied by *Odyssey* 11.631, an interpolation but an early one, cf. Hereas *FGrH* 486 F 1) or is rescued together with Theseus (as apparently in the *Peirithous* of Euripides or Critias: see the Hypothesis by Johannes Logothetes [ed. H. Rabe, *RhM* 63 (1908) 144–5; *TrGF* i 171–2]).

[116] It is ironic, too, and will probably be thought-provoking, that Theseus furiously condemns Hippolytus, and causes his death, because Hippolytus has allegedly raped Theseus' wife, when he has just himself, with Peirithous, been attempting to abduct the wife of a god!

[117] On frr. H and J (687 and 687a), see further T.H. Talboy in *Shards* 233–240.

[118] Logically, of course, Phaedra (in *any* version of the story) could never be sure that her accusation, even if believed, would lead to Hippolytus' death; but the audience, who knew that this was in fact its result, would be very ready to assume (tacitly and fallaciously) that Phaedra too took such a result for granted. This assumption would be encouraged if Phaedra was made to use words that clearly indicated (to those in the know) that she had Hippolytus' death in mind. This is done in *HippS* 719–721, where Phaedra says that she does not intend to be disgraced before Theseus, or to disgrace her family, "for the sake of one life"; ostensibly she is referring to her own life, but the audience know (and the chorus seem to suspect; cf. Barrett [1964] on 722) that she actually means the life of Hippolytus.

(as, indeed, she does even in *HippS*), but she has at least one motive that can arouse not only understanding but sympathy, the desire to continue to be the mother her children need.

Thus Phaedra goes to Theseus and makes her accusation, before Hippolytus can return. Nothing survives that can be definitely assigned to her speech, though fr. L (690) may come from its opening, assuring Theseus that her words are not fraudulent; certainly of all the characters in the play, Phaedra at this moment is the one who will most strongly feel the need to give such an assurance. One would expect her to bolster her accusation in some way rather than leaving it to depend on her bare word.[119] Possibly, as in *HippK*, she added a political charge. Fr. M (683) shows that someone was accused in the play of taking, or seeking, power in the city through glib, dishonest speech; this could well be Hippolytus.[120] Such an accusation would be credible because Theseus' long absence, and the tender age of Phaedra's sons, had left a power vacuum which an adult bastard might very plausibly try to fill, and would be particularly likely to kindle Theseus' anger because success would have meant the disinheritance of his legitimate descent line.[121]

Theseus must now curse his son. In Diodorus, to be sure, he sends for Hippolytus with a view to questioning him, but Diodorus has no curse and no monstrous bull. Sophocles surely did have both, and he can hardly have

---

[119] In *HippS* she provides no evidence at all, but the credibility of her accusation is greatly increased by her suicide (958–965, 1077), and we are doubtless meant to assume she expected it to be. [Apoll.] *Epit.* 1.18 speaks of her fabricating physical evidence, as she does in Seneca; since the papyrus Hypothesis makes it difficult to find room for this in *HippK*, it may possibly derive from *Phaedra* (cf. Zwierlein [2004] 92–94 and note 94 above).

[120] Barrett (1964) 25 n.2, and more recently Gelli (2004) 197–8, think of Menestheus (leader of the Athenian contingent in the *Iliad*), who in Plutarch (*Thes.* 32.1, 33.1, 35.5), and perhaps already in the *Theseis*, had carved out a position of political power in Theseus' absence, and forced him to abdicate and leave Athens not long after his return. Possibly Phaedra's story cast Hippolytus in the same role, or perhaps she accused him of making common cause with Menestheus. Barrett says that the language of the fragment "is hardly suited to an attempt on Theseus' own throne", but apparently forgets that that throne had been believed to be vacant. It may also be noted that the phrase κηδεύει πόλιν, which can be taken to mean "wed himself to the city", may indicate (see Comm.) that Hippolytus was accused of trying to use a (coerced?) marriage with Phaedra as a stepping-stone to rulership, like (e.g.) the suitors of Penelope in the *Odyssey*.

[121] It does not necessarily follow that fr. M (683) is spoken by Phaedra (as suggested by Gelli [2004] 197–8); it is at least as likely to be Theseus' reaction to the allegation. A shrewd Phaedra might not think it wise to sound as though she were teaching her husband the principles of politics, particularly when he was an experienced political leader himself.

made Theseus decide *first* to give Hippolytus a hearing and *then* to curse him unheard.[122] Rather, his anger explodes and he prays to Poseidon for his son's immediate death.[123]

Presently – but probably after a choral song – a messenger reports the fulfilment of the curse; nothing survives that seems at all likely to have come from his speech. Theseus may perhaps, as in Seneca (*Ph.* 1114–22), have been torn between satisfaction at having obtained what he wished, and grief at having lost (and himself become the killer of) his son. He has still to learn the truth. How was it revealed? Was the body of Hippolytus brought back? What else of significance, if anything, did the ending of the play contain?

We have already, in our discussion of Seneca's play, found some reason to believe that the distinctive feature of his treatment – a remorseful confession by Phaedra over the body of Hippolytus, including the offering of a lock of her hair as a precedent for later cult practice – may derive from Sophocles. If this is correct, the final scenes may have run rather as follows.

After the messenger's report, the chorus grieve over Hippolytus' death,[124] and continue to do so when his mangled[125] body is brought back. Theseus may have mourned in a more restrained fashion, or he may have remained silent – or we may have been prevented from learning what he would have done by the sudden appearance of Phaedra.

Phaedra, like Theseus, has caused the death of one whom she had loved; but her guilt is the greater, since Theseus' action was itself caused

---

[122] Unless indeed (a possibility which cannot be excluded) his initial decision was based on the rape allegation alone, and Phaedra, desperate to ensure that Hippolytus was not allowed to present his side of the case, then brought forward the political allegation as a second barrel.

[123] The question whether the prayer is the first or last of Theseus' three, and the question whether it is to be regarded as revocable or irrevocable, may well not arise; we know Hippolytus is already driving on the seashore, and we will assume that the prayer is fulfilled as soon as made.

[124] In *HippS* (1102–50) they in effect mourn for Hippolytus while he still lives; it is true that their mourning is for his exile rather than for his impending death – since at this stage, like Theseus, they seem to have forgotten about the curse – but if it were not for a few explicit references to exile (1125, 1140, 1148–50) it would be hard to know this from the text of the ode itself.

[125] Though hardly, as in Seneca, dismembered – which is an extremely implausible (though not literally impossible) outcome of an accidental chariot-wreck; Pentheus in Euripides' *Bacchae*, whom Seneca doubtless had in mind, was deliberately torn apart by maenads endowed by Dionysus with superhuman strength.

by her deception. She confesses the deception and the truth about her passion (two words, fr. N [678], survive from a retrospective narrative, describing Hippolytus' rejection of the proposals made to him on Phaedra's behalf); cuts a lock of her hair as a mourning-offering,[126] and goes inside with words that make it clear that we shall not see her alive again.

This would be the appropriate point for a *kommos* in which Theseus and the chorus join in grieving over Hippolytus; perhaps in the midst of this, as happens in *Antigone* (1278–1316), he receives word from within that his wife is dead too. It is not clear whether her body is brought out to join that of Hippolytus, but the one-word dochmiac fragment O (693), which seems to speak of a woman lying "limp", might suggest that it is. Two other surviving fragments also seem, as Casanova (forthcoming) notes, to come from very near the end of the play. In fr. P (682), which apparently concludes a speech by summarizing its gist, the speaker says that no man can have anything worse than a bad wife or anything better than a virtuous one: each individual, he says, speaks about this from his own experience. Now most men have *either* a good *or* a bad wife; few have experienced both, and fewer still have experienced both in the same individual, as Theseus has. According to the argument of these lines, only these few will be able to speak authoritatively both about good and about bad wives; it is therefore highly likely that they are spoken by Theseus, when he is ready to reflect rationally on what has befallen him. Fr. Q (681), a commonplace reflection on the misery of the human condition, may perhaps be spoken by the chorus-leader,[127] but is more likely to be part of this same speech by Theseus (see Commentary on this fragment). It would not be surprising if Theseus, like his counterpart in *HippS* (836–7, 1325) or Creon in *Antigone* (1308–9, 1329–32), wished for death; it is perhaps significant that in the connected accounts of his career, his visit to Hades is his last exploit and is soon followed by his departure from Athens for Scyros where he meets his end.[128]

---

[126] Cf. *Aj.* 1171–9, Aesch. *Cho.* 7 (with Garvie's note). It is possible (Zwierlein [2004] 94) that the Sophoclean Phaedra did this *before* the arrival of Hippolytus' corpse, and laid her hair-offering not on the body itself (for which cf. *Iliad* 23.152–3) but on the stage-altar; this has the advantage that it reduces the similarity, and therefore repetitiousness, between the lament of Phaedra and that of Theseus.

[127] Cf. *Ant.* 1338, *OC* 1722–3; Eur. *HippS* 207.

[128] Cf. [Apoll.] *Epit.* 1.24; Plut. *Thes.* 35 (where the visit to Hades has been euhemerized into a visit to Aidoneus king of Molossia). Diodorus (4.62.4) places Theseus' exile and

Three one-word fragments can hardly be located in the play, even tentatively. Fr. R (689) consists of the word *agos,* which normally means "something that causes pollution", used in the sense of "something that expiates pollution, a purificatory offering",[129] it is conceivable that Phaedra's hair-offering was described in this way, either by her or by a *deus ex machina* (see below). Fr. S (691), referring to a treasonable desertion to an enemy, most likely refers to the alleged activities of Hippolytus in Theseus' absence[130] – if, that is, it comes from *Phaedra* at all.[131] It will not fit into a tragic iambic trimeter, and one would not expect to find either Theseus or the chorus denouncing Hippolytus in song – not Theseus, because individual characters in tragedy do not normally use lyric for denunciatory invective; not the chorus, because they know (though they cannot say) that Hippolytus is innocent. Possibly, though, the word appeared in the lamentations near the end of the play, referring bitterly to an allegation now known to be false. Fr. T (692) could belong almost anywhere.

One other question arises with regard to the end of *Phaedra.* Sophocles is known to have had a keen interest in the cult of the healing hero/god Asclepius,[132] which was officially introduced to Athens in 421–420, though the exact nature of his connection with this event is disputed; in one of his *Phineus* plays (fr. 710) Asclepius was represented as restoring Phineus' sight, and in *Philoctetes* (1437–8) Sophocles seems to go out of his way to give Asclepius the credit for healing Philoctetes' ten-year-old wound. Now we have many stories[133] in which Asclepius raises a man from the dead, for which he is generally punished with death himself through the thunderbolt of Zeus; and while at least eight different individuals are named as having returned to life through his intervention, the one named most often, from an early date, is Hippolytus.[134] Hippolytus

---

death directly after the Phaedra-Hippolytus episode, reserving the Hades story for separate treatment out of sequence (4.63).

[129] Cf. Griffith on *Ant.* 775.

[130] The enemy, in that case, might well be Menestheus (cf. note 120 above).

[131] See Commentary on this fragment.

[132] Sophocles test. 67–73, 174 Radt; *PMG* 737. See recently A. Connolly, *JHS* 118 (1998) 1–21; A.H. Sommerstein, *Aristophanes: Wealth* (Warminster, 2001) 11–12; E.M. Craik in *Shards* 45–48; F. De Martino in *Shards* 458–464; and, on this play, Gelli (2004) 201–8.

[133] Collected by E.J. and L. Edelstein, *Asclepius* (Baltimore, 1945) i 37–56 (test. 66–115).

[134] *Carmen Naupactium* fr. 10 West; Cinesias *PMG* 774; Telestes *PMG* 807; Staphylus *FGrH* 269 F 3; Callimachus fr. 190; Apollodorus *FGrH* 244 F 139; schol. Pind. *Pyth.* 3.96;

and Asclepius, too, were neighbours: from the point of the coastline nearest to Trozen it is some 20 km across the bay to Epidaurus, home of Asclepius' greatest sanctuary, and there was no place of any significance between them.[135] Although there is no direct evidence whatever, it is very tempting to suppose that a poet who cherished Asclepius made use of an already existing story about the greatest of Asclepius' miracles to end the tragedy of Hippolytus and Phaedra on a note that offered some degree of consolation.[136] This would require the use of a *deus ex machina*, possibly Asclepius' father Apollo;[137] this convention is rarer in Sophocles than in Euripides, but he does use it from time to time,[138] and the god could also have ordained the cult of Hippolytus[139] and possibly told Theseus of his future fate.

The only *dramatis personae* of whose existence we can be confident are Phaedra, her Nurse, Hippolytus, Theseus, a Messenger, and a chorus of women (plus a *deus ex machina*, if the speculation above about Asclepius is correct); but it is a plausible supposition that, as in the case of Eurydice in *Antigone*, there was also an *exangelos* to report the offstage death of Phaedra, and there may have been other minor characters.

By his crucial innovation of linking the Phaedra-Hippolytus story with Theseus' absence in Hades, Sophocles has created a tragedy of a

---

Virgil, *Aen.* 7.765–773; Ovid, *Met.* 15.531–546, *Fasti* 6.746–762; Hyginus *Fab.* 49; Lactantius, *Inst.Div.* 1.17.15; Libanius, *Or.* 13.42.

[135] Barrett (1964) 5 and Gelli (2004) 205 also point out that at Trozen there was a (probably fourth-century) sanctuary of Asclepius within the precinct of Hippolytus, and that the city Asclepieion at Athens (founded in 420) was close to the Hippolytus precinct there.

[136] The resurrection story, being intimately connected with the story of Asclepius' punishment by Zeus, requires that he be viewed as a hero, not a god; Asclepius the god can work wonderful cures, but he never raises the dead. This suggests (*contra* Gelli [2004] 208) that the play predates the introduction to Athens in 421–420 of the cult of Asclepius as a god: this is consistent with the tentative date range of 435–429 proposed below for *Phaedra*. The earliest passage in tragedy that clearly treats Asclepius as a god is *Philoctetes* 1437–8 (produced in 409; a mortal Asclepius would not have been able to come to Troy to heal Philoctetes).

[137] Not Asclepius himself, for when Asclepius is portrayed as raising the dead, he is always a mortal hero, not a god (cf. previous note).

[138] Compare *Philoctetes* among the extant plays, and *Syndeipnoi* and *Tereus* in this volume.

[139] Presumably giving instructions for him to be buried at Trozen, not Athens; cf. (a more extreme case) Eur. *Andr.* 1239–42 where, after the body of Neoptolemus has been brought back from Delphi to Phthia, Thetis instructs that it be taken back and buried at Delphi.

completely different kind from either of Euripides' two plays. Ironies and reversals abound: an improper, but not mortally perilous, initiative by Phaedra is turned into utter catastrophe by what in any ordinary circumstances would be a happy event, the unexpected return of Theseus after he had been supposed dead; Hippolytus, so loyal a son that he had apparently (cf. note 109) refused to believe that his father had perished when everyone else was certain he had, is condemned and cursed for betraying him; Theseus, who had just taken part in the attempted forcible violation of Persephone and been narrowly saved from death, condemns his son to death in the mistaken belief that he is guilty of the forcible violation of Phaedra – and then perhaps hears from divine lips that his victim will be restored to life and that he himself has not much longer to live. Phaedra herself, despite giving her name to the play, is perhaps a less interesting character, having neither the depth of villainy of the Phaedra of *HippK* nor the intense concern for honour and reputation that marks the Phaedra of *HippS*. She seems to have been dominated by rapidly-changing emotions – erotic passion, maternal love, fear, guilt, grief. In the final analysis, she is ruined by a single mistake – her decision to send her Nurse to proposition Hippolytus; she had been warned not to do this,[140] but she at least, unlike either of the other Phaedras, had the excuse that she believed herself to be a widow who lacked, and needed, a male protector.[141] To some extent, all three major characters brought their fate on themselves (even Hippolytus, whose angry response to the Nurse apparently convinced Phaedra that she could not risk letting him meet his father lest he denounce her); but all three were also victims, and the average spectator, placed in their circumstances, could very well have done as they did.

There is virtually no evidence for the dating of *Phaedra* except what may be furnished by a comparison with the two Euripidean *Hippolytus* plays. Perhaps the most significant evidence is the setting of the action at Athens. Hippolytus' fatal accident seems always (where its location is specified at all) to take place on the seashore not far from Trozen, and Trozen is the principal site of his cult; it is therefore the most obvious setting for a drama that depicts his death, and the first dramatizer of the story would be expected to site it there. This raises a presumption, though

---

[140] A. Lardinois in *Shards* 41–42 discusses fr. C (693a) as an instance of the phenomenon he calls the "adviser figure" in Sophoclean tragedy.

[141] Even more so if, as is quite possible, the action took place against a background of political agitation against the dynasty by a figure like Menestheus (see note 120 above).

only a presumption, that *HippK* was earlier than *Phaedra* and therefore was the first of the three plays. We can then see Sophocles as changing a major assumption of the story (by having Theseus absent *in Hades*) and thereby radically altering its dynamics. It is (even) more difficult to date *Phaedra* relative to *HippS*. The two plays have a number of parallels and contrasts, some of which have been noted above, but there is nothing in *HippS* of which one can confidently say either that it was written for an audience that had seen *Phaedra*, or that it was written for an audience that had not.[142] It is curious how careless Euripides is in *HippS* about explaining the absence of Theseus or even making clear that he *is* absent,[143] and this might suggest that he is not particularly concerned to distinguish his new play from that of Sophocles,[144] but he may just be seeking to mystify and even mislead his audience.[145] Almost all one can say is that it is more likely that Sophocles would have taken an early opportunity to try his hand at a story tackled controversially, and unsuccessfully, by Euripides than that he would have chosen to do so after Euripides had scored one of his rare successes with it,[146] and so, if not entirely for the same reasons, one finds oneself in the end agreeing with Barrett (1964) 29–30 that the sequence is most likely to have been *HippK*-

---

[142] There is one possible exception. At *HippS* 110–2 Hippolytus says that after having a meal he will yoke his horses to his chariot and give them appropriate exercise; this *might* be a Euripidean red herring, designed to arouse the expectation that he may meet his death on that drive (rather than on his way into exile, as in *HippK* – and as will turn out to be the case in *HippS* too). And we have suggested that the Sophoclean Hippolytus likewise went on his final drive of his own free will – though he did so as a result of an unexpected and upsetting event, not, as he apparently intends to do in *HippS*, as a matter of daily routine. Perhaps, therefore, Euripides is exploiting his audience's knowledge of Sophocles' play to create a false expectation about how the action will develop.

[143] From the prologue (especially 34–37) we might well gather that he is in fact in Trozen at the time of the action, particularly when we presently hear the chorus wondering whether Phaedra's illness (which is only in its third day, 135–7) is due to his keeping a mistress "in the house" (151–4); it is not till 281 that we (and the chorus) learn, for the first time, that he has gone abroad, and not till 792 that we learn (indirectly and vaguely) the nature of his journey.

[144] Whereas he does distinguish it carefully from *HippK* by having Aphrodite say that Phaedra will die "with a good reputation" (47).

[145] He certainly takes some pains, in this prologue, to mislead them in other respects; see A.H. Sommerstein, *Prometheus* 23 (1997) 195–6.

[146] A point made by M. Coffey and R.G. Mayer, *Seneca: Phaedra* (Cambridge, 1990) 9. Casanova (forthcoming), contrariwise, argues (to us less convincingly) that Euripides would be more eager to "correct himself" than Sophocles would be to "polemicize" against him.

Phaedra-HippS, while adding (as he does) that an earlier or later placement for Sophocles' play cannot be excluded. If *Phaedra* was indeed the middle play of the three, then in view of what has been said above (pp.[206–7]) about *HippK*, it would have to have been produced between 435 and 429 inclusive; in any case, for reasons given on p. 286 n.136 above, it is unlikely to be later than 421.

ΦΑΙΔΡΑ

Α (688)

ἀελλάδες φωναί

Α (688) *Etymologicum Magnum* 19.53 | ἀελλάδες V : ἄελλαι cett.

Β (680)

αἴσχη μέν, ὦ γυναῖκες, οὐδ' ἂν εἷς φύγοι
βροτῶν ποθ', ᾧ καὶ Ζεὺς ἐφορμήσῃ κακά·
νόσους δ' ἀνάγκη τὰς θεηλάτους φέρειν

Β (680) Stobaeus 4.44.50 | 1 ἃ χρὴ Holzner ‖ 2 ᾧ καὶ SMA: ᾧ κε Tr: ᾧ γε
Brunck: ᾧπερ Dobree: οἷσι Hermann | ἐφορμήσῃ SM: ἐφορμήσοι Α

C (693a Lloyd-Jones)

<ΦΑΙΔΡΑ>
    ἄπειμι τοίνυν· οὔτε γὰρ σὺ τἄμ' ἔπη
    τολμᾷς ἐπαινεῖν οὔτ' ἐγὼ τοὺς σοὺς τρόπους.
<ΤΡΟΦΟΣ>
    ἀλλ' εἴσιθ'· οὔ σοι μὴ μεθέψομαί ποτε,
    οὐδ' ἢν σφόδρ' ἱμείρουσα τυγχάνῃς· ἐπεὶ
    πολλῆς ἀνοίας καὶ τὸ θηρᾶσθαι κενά.

C (693a) Sophocles, *Electra* 1050–4 | 1–2 cited, and ascribed to *Phaedra*,
by Stobaeus 3.2.29: 1–5 ascribed to *Phaedra* by Lloyd-Jones ‖ 4 ἢν ...
τυγχάνῃς **Lpa** (-εις L^s): εἰ ... τυγχάνεις **rp**Xrt

PHAEDRA

A (688)

storm-swift voices

A lyric phrase, perhaps from the chorus's entrance-song; possibly referring to rumours that have brought them to the palace.

B (680)

Women, there could never be a mortal who could avoid shame, if Zeus unleashes evil against him; it is necessary to endure god-sent afflictions.

Phaedra to the Chorus, excusing her passion.

C (693a Lloyd-Jones)

\<PHAEDRA\>:

I'm going, then, since you can't bring yourself to approve my words, and I can't bring myself to approve your behaviour.

\<NURSE\>:

Go inside, then! I will never join with you, no matter how ardently you may desire it, since it is utter folly to hunt the unattainable.

Parting lines, evidently after the Nurse has rejected Phaedra's request to approach Hippolytus on her behalf.

D (679)

σύγγνωτε κἀνάσχεσθε σιγῶσαι· τὸ γὰρ
γυναιξὶν αἰσχρὸν σὺν γυναῖκα χρὴ στέγειν.

D (679) Stobaeus 4.23.16 | 1 σιγῶσαν (better σιγώσῃ?) Headlam ap.
Pearson ‖ 2 σὺν γυναῖκα Meineke: σὺν γυναικὶ A: ἐν γυναικὶ SM: ἐν
γυναιξὶ Grotius: συγγυναῖκα P. Schröder | χρὴ (χρῆ) M: δεῖ SA

E (684) (= Eur. fr. 431 Nauck)

Ἔρως γὰρ ἄνδρας οὐ μόνους ἐπέρχεται
οὐδ᾿ αὖ γυναῖκας, ἀλλὰ καὶ θεῶν ἄνω
ψυχὰς ταράσσει κἀπὶ πόντον ἔρχεται·
καὶ τόνδ᾿ ἀπείργειν οὐδ᾿ ὁ παγκρατὴς σθένει
Ζεύς, ἀλλ᾿ ὑπείκει καὶ θέλων ἐγκλίνεται

E (684) Stobaeus 4.20.24; (1–3) Clement of Alexandria, *Stromateis*
6.2.14.8 (ascribing the lines to Euripides) | 1 μόνον Clement ‖ 3 χαράσσει
Stobaeus | πόντων Stobaeus[M] ‖ 5 κοὐ θέλων van Herwerden

F (677)

οὐ γὰρ δίκαιον ἄνδρα γενναῖον φρένας
τέρπειν, ὅπου γε μὴ δίκαια τέρψεται.

F (677) Stobaeus 3.17.2; Orion, *Florilegium* 6.7 | 2 γε μὴ Schneidewin: γε
Orion: μὴ καὶ Stobaeus | τέρψεται Stobaeus: τέρπεται Orion

D (679)

Have sympathy and maintain silence! For a woman ought to join in concealing what is shameful for women.

Phaedra addressing the women of the Chorus.

E (684)

For Eros does not only attack men, or women for that matter; no, he even stirs up the souls of the gods in heaven, and moves over the sea; not even all-powerful Zeus is strong enough to repel him – he yields and gives way willingly.

Perhaps the Nurse trying to persuade Hippolytus.

F (677)

For it is not right for a noble-born man to pleasure his heart when the pleasures he is going to take are wrongful.

Probably Hippolytus to the Nurse, rejecting Phaedra's offer.

G (686)

<A>		ἕζης ἄρ', οὐδὲ γῆς ἔνερθ' ᾤχου θανών;

<ΘΗΣΕΥΣ>

	οὐ γὰρ πρὸ μοίρας ἡ τύχη βιάζεται.

G (686) Stobaeus 1.5.13

H (687)

	ἔσαινεν οὐρᾷ μ' ὦτα κυλλαίνων κάτω

H (687) Hesychius κ 4513 | ἔσαινεν Salmasius (ἔσαινε δ' Heinsius, ἔσαινε τ' e.g. Barrett): ἔσταιεπ' cod.: ἔσαινέ μ' Blaydes | οὐρᾷ μ' Hiller (οὐρᾷ Hemsterhuis): οὔραν cod. (οὐρὰν Salmasius) | οὐρᾷ μ' ἔσαινε(ν) Blaydes | ὦτα Salmasius: ὦτι cod.: ὦτε Nauck: τῶτα Hemsterhuis: τῶτε van Herwerden | κυλλαίνων κάτω Salmasius : κυαλάννων καὶ τὸ cod.

J (687a) (= 1016 Nauck, 886 Pearson)

	γλώσσης ἀπαυστὶ στάζε μυξώδης ἀφρός

J (687a) Photius α2288 Theodoridis (cf. Σ^R Aristophanes, *Lysistrata* 1257, and Suda α2946) | στάζε Tsantsanoglou: στάζει codd.

K (685)

	ἀλλ' εἰσὶ μητρὶ παῖδες ἄγκυραι βίου

K (685) Bekker, *Anecdota* i 338.15; Bachmann, *Anecdota* i 23.27; Photius α191Theodoridis; cf. Hesychius α578 and Suda χ9

G (686)

<?>:   So you were alive all the time, not dead and gone beneath
                 the earth?

THESEUS:

                 Chance cannot impose her will by force before the time set by
                 Destiny.

Someone (the chorus-leader?) expressing surprise at the unexpected return of Theseus.

H (687)

He fawned upon me with his tail, letting his ears droop down.

A description, from a narrative by Theseus, of Cerberus greeting him on his arrival in Hades.

J (687a)

A frothy saliva continuously dribbled from his tongue.

Theseus describing Cerberus again, this time his behaviour towards those who try to leave Hades.

K (685)

But to a mother, children are the anchors of her life.

Phaedra explaining (doubtless to the Chorus) why she is rejecting suicide (and instead falsely accusing Hippolytus).

L (690)

ἄκλεπτοι

L (690) Hesychius α2437

M (683)

οὐ γὰρ ποτ᾽ ἂν γένοιτ᾽ ἂν ἀσφαλὴς πόλις
ἐν ᾗ τὰ μὲν δίκαια καὶ τὰ σώφρονα
λάγδην πατεῖται, κωτίλος δ᾽ ἀνὴρ λαβὼν
πανοῦργα χερσὶ κέντρα κηδεύει πόλιν

M (683) Stobaeus 4.1.5; Σ Lucian, *Lexiphanes* 10 (199.19–25 Rabe) | **1** γένοιτ᾽ ἂν Σ Luc., Stobaeus^M: γένοιντ᾽ ἂν Stobaeus^S: γένοιτο Stobaeus^A | ἀσφαλεῖς Stobaeus^{S ac} | πόλεις Stobaeus^M || **4** χερσὶ cited by Brunck from "cod. Regius" of Stobaeus: χερσὶν Σ Luc.: χεροῖν Stobaeus^{SMA} | κέντρα Stobaeus: ἔργα Σ Luc. | κηδεύοι Σ^{ΕΥΦΩ} Luc.

N (678)

ἀπέπτυσεν λόγους

N (678) Hesychius α5993 | ἀπέπτυσεν Nauck: ἀπέπτυσε cod.

O (693)

μεμωλυσμένα

O (693) Hesychius μ2044 | μεμωλυσμένα Talboy: μεμωλυσμένη cod.: μῶλυς (from Hesychius' lemma) Pearson

L (690)

not dishonest

Perhaps Phaedra, assuring Theseus that she speaks the truth in her accusation against Hippolytus.

M (683)

For no city can ever be safe in which justice and virtue are trampled underfoot, and a smooth-tongued speaker villainously takes the goad in his hands and husbands the city.

Theseus denouncing Hippolytus' supposed treachery.

N (678)

He spat out the proposal.

From a retrospective narrative (perhaps by a remorseful Phaedra) referring to Hippolytus' reaction to the Nurse's overtures.

O (693)

having gone limp

Apparently said of a woman; the Chorus speaking of the dead Phaedra?

P (682)

οὕτω γυναικὸς οὐδὲν ἂν μεῖζον κακὸν
κακῆς ἀνὴρ κτήσαιτ' ἂν οὐδὲ σώφρονος
κρεῖσσον· παθὼν δ' ἕκαστος ὧν τύχῃ λέγει

P (682) Stobaeus 4.22.80 | **2** λήσαιτ' Nauck (cf. Hes. Works 702, Semonides fr. 6) ‖ **3** S^{ac} adds μεῖζον before κρεῖσσον

Q (681)

τὸν δ' εὐτυχοῦντα πάντ' ἀριθμήσας βροτῶν
οὐκ ἔστιν ὄντως ὄντιν' εὑρήσεις ἕνα

Q (681) Stobaeus 4.41.40 | **1** τὸν δ' Grotius: τὸ δ' AM: τὸν Papageorgiou | εὐτυχοῦντα M: εὐτυχοῦν A | ἀριθμήσας Grotius: ἀριθμῆσαι AM ‖ **2** ὄντως Gesner: οὗτος AM.

R (689)

ἄγος

R (689) Hesychius α734; cf. Bekker *Anecdota* i 330.31, Bachmann *Anecdota* i 15.1

P (682)

So there is no greater evil that a man can acquire than a wicked wife, nor anything better than a virtuous one; but each man speaks about them from his own particular experience.

Probably Theseus reflecting on Phaedra, whom he had thought the best of wives and who has proved to be the worst.

Q (681)

If you number every mortal on earth, you will still not find a single one who is truly fortunate.

A comment on the catastrophic outcome of the action, probably by Theseus or the chorus-leader.

R (689)

an offering to expiate pollution

Perhaps referring to an offering of hair by Phaedra as a mourning tribute to Hippolytus.

S (691)

αὐτομόλως

S (691) Hesychius α8445; Bekker, *Anecdota* i 466.7; Bachmann, Anecdota i 166.26; Photius α3235 Theodoridis; Suda α4510 | Nauck, followed by Latte (who cited the evidence of mss. of Cyril's *Glossary*), suggested that the attribution to *Phaedra* really belonged to Hesychius 8449 (αὐτόπαιδα = Soph. fr. 1029)

T (692)

ἀψεφές

T (692) Hesychius α8952; cf. Bekker *Anecdota* i 476.1, Bachmann *Anecdota* i 177.7

S (691)

like a deserter

If the ms. of Hesychius is right to ascribe this word to **Phaedra**, *it must come from a lyric (or anapaestic) passage, probably referring to the false allegation of treason against Hippolytus; but the ascription may really apply to another word,* own son, *which might have been used in reference either to Hippolytus' supposed offences against his father or to Theseus' responsibility for Hippolytus' death.*

T (692)

heedless

PHAEDRA

A (688)

For the swift movement of rumour or report cf. *Ajax* 137–8, Eur. *IA* 425–6, *Odyssey* 24.413; for comparison of speed of movement to that of a wind-squall (*aella*), *Iliad* 11.297–8, 13.795–8. The compression of such a comparison into the single adjective *aellas* (*OT* 466, Eur. *Ba.* 873) or *aellaios* (*OC* 1081) "storm-swift" is found only in tragic lyrics, and it is therefore almost certain that our fragment is lyric too, though in theory the two words could be the last word of one iambic trimeter and the first of the next. The metre is probably aeolic, with the two words separated by a colon boundary, as in *OT* 466–7 where both cola are telesilleans (×–∪∪–∪–). In *Ajax* (loc.cit., cf. 141–152, 173–4) and *Trachiniae* (103–111), and also in *HippS* (121–140), the chorus in their *parodos* say that rumours (in each case, about troubles besetting a person with whom they sympathize) have drawn them to the scene of the action.

B (680)

The notion that being in love is a "god-sent affliction" against which it is futile and even impious to fight is found in both Euripides' *Hippolytus* plays (*HippK* fr. S [444]; *HippS* 438, 443–6, 473–7); cf. also *Trach.* 441–6, and fr. E (684) below. In *HippS* it is exploited by the Nurse in her attempt to break down Phaedra's resistance to her passion; our fragment, however, as **Women** shows, is addressed to the chorus, and the speaker is therefore probably Phaedra herself.

1 **shame** (cf. fr. D [679] 2) may denote the disgrace Phaedra will incur if she is discovered to have committed adultery, and/or the consciousness of having done wrong that may afflict her in any case and may lead to discovery (cf. *HippS* 413–8), and/or the disgrace-incurring acts themselves (for this sense of the plural *aiskhē* cf. *Odyssey* 1.229, referring to the outrageous behaviour of the suitors in Odysseus' palace); see D.L. Cairns, *Aidos* (Oxford, 1993). It was an important concept in *HippK* (cf. fr. H [436]) and is emphatically so in *HippS* (see Cairns *op.cit.* 314–340, much his longest discussion of any single tragedy). In *HippS* Phaedra is desperate to avoid disgrace and to preserve her (and thus her children's) reputation (321, 329, 331, 385–7,

403–430, 488–9, 498–9, 505–6, 687–692, 717–721); here she can see
(or professes she can see) no way to avoid it.

2 Zeus here, as often, means little more than "divine power"; cf. *Aj.* 137,
Ant. 2.

3 god-sent: this adjective (Greek *theēlatos*) appears in a similar context
in *HippK* fr. S (444).

3 afflictions: Greek *nosoi*, lit. "diseases", a term applied to Phaedra's
passion in *HippS* 40, 394, 405, 477, 766, 1306, and often to erotic
passion elsewhere, e.g. *Trach.* 445, 544, Soph. fr. 149.

C (693a)

These five lines are transmitted in all the medieval mss. as part of the text
of *Electra* (lines 1050–4); if they are at home there, the first two lines will
belong to Chrysothemis and the last three to Electra. Stobaeus, however,
cites the first two lines as from *Phaedra*. It is not possible to separate the
two speeches from each other – Electra can hardly say to Chrysothemis
"go inside, but I won't follow you" when Chrysothemis has not indicated
any intention to go inside – so we must choose between two alternatives:

(a) Stobaeus has made a misattribution (perhaps influenced by the
similarity of meaning between the names Electra "shining" and Phaedra
"bright"), and the passage rightly belongs in *Electra* (though it may of
course be corrupt, lacunose, wholly or partly misplaced, etc.)

(b) Stobaeus has attributed the first two lines correctly, and the whole
five lines are actually part of *Phaedra* and found their way into the text of
Electra either as an actors' elaboration in a fourth-century production (see
D.L. Page, *Actors' Interpolations in Greek Tragedy* [Oxford, 1934];
Barrett 46) or through having been written in by a reader in the margins of
a copy, as a parallel passage, and subsequently mistaken for part of the
text; in the latter case, the parallel may have been suggested by the phrase
"you can't bring yourself to *approve my words*", which echoes an
expression used by Chrysothemis in *El.* 1044 and 1057.

We must first consider whether the five lines, as they stand, work
satisfactorily as part of the script of *Electra*. Believing Orestes to be dead,
Electra has been trying to persuade her sister Chrysothemis to join her in a
not very clearly conceived plan to kill Aegisthus (she does not mention
Clytaemestra) and thereby liberate both themselves and the whole city.
Chrysothemis rejects this as absurd and impossible, whereupon Electra
says that in that case she will do it on her own (1019–20), calls
Chrysothemis a coward (1027), and sarcastically bids her go inside and

inform on Electra to "your mother" (1031, 1033). Chrysothemis, believing that Electra is pointlessly throwing her life away, tries desperately to persuade her to desist, but to no avail; in the last exchange of their *stichomythia*, Chrysothemis says "You seem to be taking no notice of anything I say" and Electra replies "My mind has been made up about this for a long time, not just lately" (1048–9). Then follow the five disputed lines, after which Chrysothemis says "Well, if *you* think your attitude has any intelligence in it, be intelligent your way; when you find yourself mired in trouble, then you'll approve my words" (1055–7) and goes inside (not to be seen again).

The fundamental problem with these five lines, as part of *Electra*, is that 1052–4, except for the first two words, make no sense in Electra's mouth. It is Electra, not Chrysothemis, who, in pursuit of an aim which she "ardently ... desire[s]", has asked her sister to join her in an enterprise, and been rejected; it is Chrysothemis, not Electra, who thinks the other is committing the "utter folly [of] hunt[ing] the unattainable". The passage can only be retained in *Electra* if these three lines can somehow be transferred to Chrysothemis; and yet that too is unsatisfactory, since it is Electra, not Chrysothemis, who remains on stage, and therefore it should be Chrysothemis who says "I'm going" (1050) and Electra who says "Yes, go" (1052). It follows that if we reject the evidence of Stobaeus we must either delete all of 1052–7, making 1050–1 Chrysothemis' exit-lines (Morstadt), or adopt some more complex solution such as that of R.D. Dawe, who in his second Teubner edition of *Electra* (Stuttgart/Leipzig, 1996), refining an earlier suggestion, (i) made lines 1047 and 1049 change places (so that the *stichomythia* could end with an insulting remark by Electra), (ii) posited a lacuna between 1052 and 1053, including the end of Electra's speech and the beginning of that of Chrysothemis), and (iii) dropped the change of speaker indicated by the mss. at 1055, so that Chrysothemis spoke the whole of 1053–7. Neither solution is appealing. Morstadt has to sacrifice the blameless lines 1055–7, which make a good ending to the scene. Dawe posits at least two separate major corruptions, fails nevertheless to remove all the difficulties (the second half of 1052 is hardly more suited to Electra than are 1053–4) – and also creates a new one. Normal technique would make 1050–1 an exit-speech, and 1052–4 a Parthian shot "cast at a departing back" (O.P. Taplin, *The Stagecraft of Aeschylus* [Oxford, 1977] 221–2); with Dawe's changes, these two speeches will be followed by a further speech of at least six lines (since 1053 cannot be the opening line of a speech) by the departing character. It is far simpler, with Lloyd-Jones (so already, more cautiously, H. Lloyd-

Jones and N.G. Wilson, *Sophoclea* [Oxford, 1990] 62), to accept Stobaeus' attribution of 1050–1 and extend it to cover 1052–4 also, thus leaving 1055–7 as Chrysothemis' final answer to Electra's final statement (1049) of her determination. The five lines 1050–4, then, will be treated here as a fragment of *Phaedra*, and will hereinafter be numbered 1–5. In the Introduction (p. 277) it has been shown that Phaedra is the first speaker and her Nurse (or other female confidant) the second. Phaedra will go into the *skene* as soon as she has finished speaking; the Nurse will remain on stage.

1–2   you can't bring yourself to approve is presumably sarcastic: as a slave, it was not the Nurse's business to pass judgement on her mistress's wishes, but simply to carry them out. Cf. Men. *Epitr.* 1062–75 (Smikrines to his daughter's nurse) "Devil take me, Sophrone, if I don't break your head! Are *you* going to admonish me? I'm being precipitate in taking my daughter away, am I, you sacrilegious old hag? … You'll really howl if you say another word. Am I to be judged by Sophrone? … Did you see that pond we passed? I'm going to duck you in it all night, till you're dead – that'll teach you to agree with me and not to quarrel!"

1–2   my words … your behaviour: the former presumably refers to a request by Phaedra to the Nurse to approach Hippolytus on her behalf, the latter to the Nurse's refusal to obey her mistress's orders.

4   ardently … desire: the verb *hīmeirein*, in the active voice, is more common in Sophocles (×5) than in all other fifth-century tragedy combined (×4).

D (679)

A woman (evidently Phaedra) asks other women (evidently the chorus) to keep a "shameful" secret of hers. The secret is probably that of her passion for Hippolytus; the fragment is less likely to belong to the later stage at which she makes her false accusation against him, since "shameful for women" applies better to improper behaviour in the sexual sphere (a far more serious matter for a woman than for a man) than to an attempt at murder. Phaedra makes a similar plea to the chorus and/or the Nurse in *HippS* 311–2 (cf. 685–6) and 710–2; cf. also *El.* 468–471, Eur. *Med.* 259–263, *Ion* 666–7, and (with a similar appeal to feminine solidarity) *IT* 1056–64. On the possibility that the chorus reply by *swearing* to keep Phaedra's secret, even though they have not been asked to do so, see Introduction, p. 278 n.106.

1 have sympathy: Greek *syngignōskein* implies not only compassion but also condonation, and therefore draws attention to the fact that by concealing Phaedra's adulterous intentions the chorus are in effect making themselves her accomplices in wrongdoing. This kind of issue does not arise in *HippS*, where Phaedra never has adulterous intentions, and where the chorus do not understand until too late that she is planning to cause the death of Hippolytus; it does, however, in *Medea*, where the chorus agree to keep silence about Medea's plans on the explicit grounds that she will be punishing her husband justly (*Med.* 267–8), even though they already have good reason to expect that her revenge will be murderous (cf. *Med.* 171–2, 195–8, 265–6).

1 maintain silence: lit. "endure being silent", very likely alluding to the belief (of men) that women were incorrigible babblers (cf. Ar. *Thesm.* 393).

2 a woman ought to join in concealing: adopting Meineke's reading, and treating *syn* "together, jointly with others" as adverbial (cf. T.G. Tucker, *CR* 18 [1904] 246). Schröder's conjecture, giving the sense "a fellow-woman ought to conceal", is ingenious; but **syngynē* "fellow-woman" is neither itself attested, nor supported by the parallels he cites. In particular, the most frequent of these parallels, *syndoulos* "fellow-slave", invariably in classical Greek, as Pollux (3.82) rightly claims, denotes a slave *owned by the same person* as the other slave or slaves on whom interest is currently centred (cf. Eur. *Med.* 65, *Andr.* 64, *Hec.* 204, *Ion* 1109; Ar. *Peace* 745; Hdt. 1.110.1, 2.134.3; Theopompus com. fr. 33.7; Arist. *EN* 1148b26; Men. *Perinthia* 5; the word for one of two or more slaves who have only their slave status itself in common is *homodoulos*, as in Eur. *Hec.* 60 (Hecuba and the other Trojan women have been, or will be, allotted individually to different masters; contrast *ibid.* 204 where Polyxene is lamenting the now lost prospect of enduring slavery *in company with* her mother, to their mutual consolation). Hence we would expect **syngynē* to mean, if anything, "fellow-wife" (of the same man, in a polygamous household), which is certainly not the meaning required here.

E (684)

These lines are ascribed by Stobaeus to Sophocles' *Phaedra*, by Clement of Alexandria to Euripides (without naming a play). Pearson and all subsequent editors have accepted Stobaeus' attribution: it is the more specific of the two, and Clement may have confused this passage with a very similar, though longer, one in *HippS* (443–458), or simply have assumed that it was Euripidean because of Euripides' reputation as a dramatist of love (so Casanova). Other passages in the *Hippolytus* plays emphasizing the universal power of Eros (or Aphrodite) include *HippK* frr. C (430) and F (428) and *HippS* 1–6, 525–564, 966–9, 1268–82; cf. also Aesch. *Supp.* 998–1005, 1034–42, Aesch. fr. 44, Soph. *Trach.* 441–4, 497–506, Eur. *Tro.* 948–950, Ar. *Clouds* 1079–82. In the Introduction (pp. 278–9) it has been argued that this passage is part of the Nurse's unsuccessful appeal to Hippolytus on behalf of Phaedra; the Nurse uses much the same arguments in *HippS* 443–458, where she is addressing Phaedra.

2–3 stirs up the souls of the gods: the same verb (*tarassein*) is used in *HippS* 969 of the effect of Aphrodite on the minds of young men. Stobaeus' *kharassei* ("whets, stimulates") might be acceptable (cf. Eur. *Med.* 157), but elsewhere this verb and its synonym *thēgein* are normally applied to the passion of anger rather than to that of love, and the corruption would have been easy given that the previous syllable also begins with *kha-*. Tales of the influence of Eros on gods are of course legion; in *HippS* the Nurse (451–8) refers to the passion of Zeus for Semele (so too the chorus, *ibid.* 555–564) and of Eos for Cephalus.

3 moves over the sea: cf. *HippS* 447–8, 1272–3. The point here, as in these two passages (and as in Lucretius 1.6–9), is that Eros/Aphrodite reigns over earth ("men … women"), sea, and sky ("the gods in heaven"), i.e. over the whole universe (or at least the whole *living* universe).

5 he yields and gives way willingly: i.e. he is so sure he will be overcome by Eros that he does not even attempt to fight him. Van Herwerden's conjecture gives the superficially simpler sense "unwillingly", but it is very hard to picture the Zeus of myth as a reluctant lover!

F (677)

As "for" (Greek *gar*) shows, this is a generalization introduced to justify a specific statement or decision, most likely (see Introduction, p. 279) Hippolytus' rejection of Phaedra's approach to him made through the Nurse. The tone seems much more measured and less extreme than that of Hippolytus' speech in *HippS* (601–668); that Hippolytus finds the proposal filthy and disgusting (601–6, 614, 653–5), this one simply finds it contrary to his ideas of right and wrong and to what is proper for a man of high birth and character (see below).

1 noble: this adjective (Greek *gennaios*), and in particular the idea that a man who claims to be *gennaios* ought to aspire to high ethical standards, are favourites with Sophocles; cf. *OT* 1469, 1510, *Phil.* 51, 475, 799, 801, 1068, 1402, *OC* 76, 569, 1636.

G (686)

These two lines probably come from a stichomythic dialogue. The first speaker expresses surprise that the other is alive when (as the imperfect tense shows) he had been supposed dead for a considerable time; the latter replies, in effect, that the destined time for him to die had evidently not yet come. The second speaker can only be Theseus, returned from his time in Hades (as in Seneca's *Phaedra*). Hartung thought it might be Hippolytus (returning alive from his chariot-wreck, as in *HippS*), but this will not do: not only is the interval since his supposed death much too brief, but line 2 is hardly fitting on the lips of a man who, though alive, is mortally injured. On the identity of the first speaker, see Introduction, p. 280 and note 114.

2 before the time set by Destiny: lit. "before Destiny". The idea is that Destiny (*moira* – in Homer often *aisa*) determines when a person shall die, and nothing (sometimes not even the gods) can change it; cf. Aesch. *Cho.* 612, and see R. Janko, *The Iliad: A Commentary Vol. IV* (Cambridge, 1992) 4–6. Antigone says she is being taken below the earth "before reaching the *moira* of my life" (*Ant.* 895–6) – but she is not necessarily correct in believing so.

H (687)

This line is transmitted in a very corrupt form, but Hesychius' lemma
(*kul<l>ainōn katō* "letting droop down"), his explanation ("casting down
his ears"), and his citation as a parallel of *Odyssey* 17.302 (the dying dog
Argus wagging his tail and drooping his ears on seeing his master after
many years), make it fairly easy to restore the text, except for one
uncertainty (about whether, and where, the line included the pronoun *m(e)*
"me") which makes little difference to the sense. Nor can there be much
doubt that the line refers to Theseus' meeting with Cerberus in the
underworld, since it reflects Hesiod's description (*Thg.* 770–1) of
Cerberus' behaviour towards new arrivals there, on whom "he fawns at
once with his tail and with both his ears", and, as Barrett (1964) 24 says,
"it is hard to believe that the fawning of another dog could have merited
description".

J (687a)

This line, cited from Sophocles by Photius (α2288) in illustration of the
adverb *apausti* "continuously", was not known to come from *Phaedra*
until the Zavorda ms. of Photius came to light in 1959. It must come from
an extended narrative, as is proved by the unaugmented imperfect *staze*
(Tsantsanoglou's necessary emendation of the unmetrical ms. reading
stazei); on unaugmented past tenses in extended narratives (not necessarily
"messenger-speeches") in tragedy see L.S. Fotheringham in L. Hardwick
et al. ed. *Theatre: Ancient and Modern* (Milton Keynes, 2000) 225–231.
Phaedra is likely to have contained at least two extended narratives, one
by Theseus telling of his time in the underworld (and including fr. H
[687]) and one, probably by an anonymous messenger, telling of
Hippolytus' fatal chariot-wreck: as Fotheringham's data show, our
fragment could, in principle, come from either of these. If it came from an
account of the chariot-wreck, the beast foaming at the mouth would
doubtless be the monstrous bull (so Lloyd-Jones 329) – which is associated
with foam, if in a different way, in *HippS* (1210–1). But no other bull in
Greek literature is described as foaming at the mouth; the animals that *are*
so described (correctly, of course) are rabid dogs (Galen, *de temperamentis*
3 [i 664.13–17 Kühn]). This makes it likely, as Tsantsanoglou thought,
that the reference is again to Cerberus, who may fawn on new *arrivals* in
Hades but is savage towards any who attempt to *depart* (Hes. *Thg.* 772–3).
Theseus may be narrating an attempted getaway by himself and Peirithous,

prior to the rescue by Heracles, perhaps ending in the devouring of Peirithous by the infernal hound (see Introduction, p.[281]). For a fuller version of the above argument, see T.H. Talboy in *Shards* 233–240.

K (685)

The sentiment expressed here is identified well by Barrett (1964) 24: "The anchor keeps the ship from drifting to disaster." He sees two possible interpretations of the metaphor: either (i) "the children secure [the mother] in her progress through life, are the stay of her fortunes" (cf. Eur. *Hec.* 80, Callim. fr. 191.47, *IG* xii[7] 123.2) or (ii) "they secure her existence, are a tie to keep her alive". In (i) the point would be that if any harm were to come to Phaedra's children it would be disastrous to her, and the line would probably have been uttered in the context of some perceived threat to the children. In (ii) the point would be almost the reverse: Phaedra (if, as is likely, she is the speaker) would be saying that it is the thought of her children that motivates her to continue living, with the implication that *her* death would be disastrous to *them* (the same argument that the Nurse uses in *HippS* 304–310 to deter Phaedra from suicide). The key to a choice between these interpretations is the word *alla* "but", which indicates that the point being made, whatever it is, is being made as a *counter-argument* to some course of action that would otherwise be tempting. In interpretation (i) it is hard to see what that course of action might be; in interpretation (ii) it is clear – Phaedra has been contemplating suicide, and has decided against it for the sake of her children. In *HippS*, as we have seen, this same argument is used in *the Nurse's* attempt to save Phaedra's life; Phaedra herself later makes very different use of arguments from the interests of her children, first of all to justify her refusal to yield to her passion even at the cost of her life (418–430) and later to justify her action in falsely accusing Hippolytus (716–7).

In Seneca's *Phaedra* (254–273) Phaedra threatens suicide in order to overcome the Nurse's refusal to condone her passion and aid her approach to Hippolytus; and she may have done likewise in Sophocles' play (see Introduction, pp. 277–8). Our fragment, however, which is an argument for *rejecting* suicide, cannot have come from a scene of that kind; it is more likely to belong to a later part of the play, when the return of Theseus has put Phaedra in danger of exposure and irrevocable disgrace (see Introduction, p. 281). With suicide ruled out, she will then see an accusation against Hippolytus as the only alternative option.

The issue of Phaedra's suicide may thus have arisen no less than three times in this play: once before the approach to Hippolytus, a second time after Theseus' return, and a third time when the suicide actually happens.

L (690)

Hesychius, citing the adjective *akleptoi* from *Phaedra*, glosses it as *ou paralogizomenoi* ("not fraudulent") or *alētheis* ("true"). The word occurs nowhere else. In two Sophoclean passages (*Ajax* 188 and *Electra* 56) the verb *kleptein* "steal, deceive, do underhandedly" is applied to verbal falsehoods, in the former passage having *mūthous* "words" as its object, and it is a plausible supposition that in the passage from which Hesychius' citation comes the noun with which *akleptoi* agrees was *mūthoi* or its synonym *logoi*. Speakers do not normally take the trouble to state specifically that their words are true, or are not fraudulent. When they do so, indeed, it is sometimes an indication that they are in fact lying; thus in Aesch. *Ag.* 1584 Aegisthus' phrase "to speak plainly" introduces an account of the quarrel between Thyestes (Aegisthus' father) and Atreus which entirely omits what Cassandra (*ibid.* 1191–3) had regarded as its originating cause, the adultery of Thyestes with Atreus' wife, and treats the quarrel as having arisen purely from a political dispute. It is thus an attractive supposition that the word may come from the speech in which Phaedra makes her false accusation against Hippolytus.

M (683)

This is a political statement about the danger that is posed to a community when a demagogue (to use a word that may or may not, by a margin of a few years, be anachronistic) gains control of its affairs through his skill in oratorical persuasion. In *Phaedra* this is most likely to have referred to actual or alleged attempts, with Theseus supposedly dead, to usurp the power that should have been inherited by his legitimate children. In *HippK* (where, of course, Theseus was *not* believed dead) Phaedra first encouraged Hippolytus to make such an attempt, and then probably accused him of having done so on his own initiative (see Introduction, pp. 259–261); in *HippS* (1010–20) Hippolytus, in defending himself against Phaedra's posthumous accusation, takes some trouble to refute the suggestion (which no one has made) that he might have been trying to seize the throne. In *Phaedra*, with the throne believed to be vacant, a charge of attempted usurpation against Theseus' only adult son would be a very credible one, and Phaedra is very likely to have made it. On the speaker of these lines (probably Theseus rather than Phaedra), and on the possibility of a connection with the accounts that speak of political agitation and eventual usurpation by Menestheus, see Introduction, p. 282 n.120.

Casanova (forthcoming) thinks that the speaker is Hippolytus, rejecting an offer (by Phaedra) of political power because "to accept would make him a mere chatterbox"; but the attainment of political power by the kind of person described in these lines is being deprecated not because of its effect on him, but because of its effect on the city.

1 **no city can ever be safe:** verses of the same structure (a negative or interrogative + *an genoit' an* "can be" + an adjective + *polis* "city") are found in Eur. *Supp.* 447 (referring to tyranny) and (parodying that passage and/or this one) in Ar. *Birds* 829.

2–3 **justice and virtue are trampled underfoot:** cf. Aesch. *Ag.* 383, *Cho.* 643, *Eum.* 538–543.

3 **a smooth-tongued speaker:** Greek *kōtilos* "chattering, glib", applied to swallows in Anacreon *PMG* 453, Simonides *PMG* 606 and Strattis fr. 49.6, to a human chatterbox in Theognis 295; the cognate verb *kōtillein* means "to win a person round by ingratiating talk, to sweet-talk" (*Ant.* 756, Hes. *Works* 374, Solon fr. 34.3, Theognis 363, 852). Here it is evidently applied to a politician who wins popular support by professing his love of the people (for the idea cf. e.g. Ar. *Knights* 730ff, 1340–4); the word does not appear to be found in a political context again until Dionysius of Halicarnassus (*Ant. Rom.* 6.70.1) who likewise applies it to a populist agitator.

4 **villainously:** the Greek adjective *panourgos* is applied to demagogues in *Phil.* 448 (Thersites), Ar. *Knights* 45, 56, 247–250, 317, 331, 450, 684, 803, 823, 950, *Wasps* 1227, *Peace* 652 (all Cleon).

4 **takes the goad in his hands:** the city is figured as a team of chariot-horses, its political leader as their driver; cf. Solon fr. 36.20.

4 **husbands the city:** Greek *kēdeuein* has three meanings that could be relevant, "care for, tend, look after" (as in *OT* 1323, *OC* 750; of caring for a community, Eur. *IT* 1212), "marry" (*Trach.* 1227, [Aesch.] *Prom.* 890), and "make a marriage alliance with" (Eur. *Med.* 367, fr. 395). Here, if used in the first sense alone, the verb would have to be ironic, since the whole point of the passage is that the demagogue will do *harm* to the city; but by a play on all three senses it might make a very powerful point, if the idea is that Hippolytus hoped to gain power over the city by marrying its supposedly widowed queen (as Oedipus did,

and as the suitors of Penelope hoped to do), not in order to care for the city and promote its best interests but in order to exercise the kind of domination over the city (n.b. *polis* is feminine) that a husband exercises over his wife.

N (678)

There can be little doubt that this refers to Hippolytus' evidently contemptuous rejection of Phaedra's proposals. It is possible that the words were spoken by the Nurse reporting back to Phaedra on her interview with him, but this report may well not have been given onstage (see Introduction, p. 280), and it is more likely that the fragment belongs to a scene near the end of the play where the falsity of Phaedra's accusation was revealed (as in *HippS* 1307–8, where the speaker is Artemis). In the Introduction (pp. 274, 283–4) it is argued that the revelation was most probably made, as in Seneca, by Phaedra herself, in remorse, after Hippolytus' death. For *apoptuein* "spit out" in the sense "reject contemptuously", cf. *HippS* 614, Aesch. *Eum.* 303.

O (693)

Hesychius (µ2044) glosses the adjective *mōlus*, in the masculine gender (as is shown by the use of the masculine definite article *ho*), as *amathēs* "dull, stupid" (cf. *mōlux* "uneducated", cited *ib.* µ2041 from the dialect of Zacynthus), and then appends a note stating that Sophocles in *Phaedra* uses *memōlusmenē*, the feminine of the perfect passive participle of the verb derived from this adjective, in the sense of *pareimenē* "relaxed, weakened, limp". Pearson supposed that Hesychius' meaning was that Sophocles, unlike the (unknown) author cited in the main entry, had used *mōlus* as a *feminine* adjective in the sense of *memōlusmenē*; but had Hesychius meant that, he would have drawn attention explicitly to the difference of gender.

The participle, scanning $\cup - - \cup -$, cannot fit into any spoken metre and so must come from a lyric passage; it forms, in fact, a perfect dochmiac metron. Sophocles must therefore have written it with the "Doric" ending *–menā*, which Hesychius (or a later copyist) will have atticized (or assimilated to the ending of the following word, *pareimenē*).

The verb *mōluein* means literally "to half-boil", but various forms of it are glossed by Hesychius (µ2039) and Phrynichus (*PS* 89.15 de Borries) in the metaphorical senses "relax", "pull apart", "cause to wither" and, in the mediopassive, "grow old" (cf. also *mōlutikē* "terrifying", Hesychius μ2042) – senses which can be unified under the rubric of causing (active) or undergoing (mediopassive) a loss of firmness and/or solidity. The passive participle might thus be applied not only to a person who had grown old, but also to one whose body had gone limp through fainting (from terror or other cause), sleep, or death; and the Hesychian citation clearly indicates that the latter is the sense in which it was used in *Phaedra*. The word Hesychius uses to gloss it, *pareimenos*, is several times similarly applied in Euripides to those who are asleep (*HF* 1043, *Cycl.* 591, *Ba.* 683), dying (*Alc.* 204), or prostrated by sickness (*Or.* 210, 881); in the masculine and feminine genders it invariably, in tragedy, describes a person.

If the feminine participle *memōlusmenā* in our play likewise described a person, that person can hardly have been anyone but Phaedra. Now in each of Sophocles' surviving plays, except for the late *OC*, only one character, other than the chorus, is ever allowed to sing in dochmiacs, and that is always a character undergoing a high degree of tribulation (Heracles, Ajax, Creon [at the end of *Antigone*], Oedipus, Electra, Philoctetes). In our play, since Phaedra herself hardly comes into consideration as a possible speaker (or rather singer), the passage must thus have been sung either by the chorus or possibly by a shattered Theseus. If the singer is Theseus, then Phaedra must be dead; if the chorus, it is possible that the passage comes from an earlier scene in which Phaedra had fainted (e.g. from lovesickness, or as a ploy to induce the Nurse to help her), but it remains more likely that the words refer to Phaedra's limp body after she has been cut down from her noose (if she did indeed hang herself; on this, see Introduction, p. 274 n.96) and laid out. In all but one of the Euripidean passages cited above, the speaker who describes a person as *pareimenos* has seen that person with his/her own eyes, and our fragment therefore tends to indicate that Phaedra's corpse was brought out of the *skene* after her suicide, most probably on the *ekkyklema* (as it is in *HippS*, and as the bodies of Eurydice and Clytaemestra are brought out in other Sophoclean plays).

P (682)

This fragment is based on two famous passages of early archaic poetry about good and bad wives. Hesiod (*Works* 699–705) had advised men to be very careful in the choice of a wife, because "there is nothing better that a man can acquire than a good wife, and nothing more pernicious than a bad one" (702–3): the vices he had in mind were unchastity ("lest your marriage bring pleasure to your neighbours", 701) and gluttony/extravagance ("one who dines on the sly, roasts her man without fire ... and brings him to a premature old age", 704–5). Semonides (fr. 7), after enumerating ten types of wife (all but one of them evil), gloomily concludes that women are "the greatest evil that Zeus has made" (96) and that a man who thinks he has a good wife is deluded (103–111): "each of us," he continues, "praises his own wife when he mentions her, and criticizes the other man's – we don't realize that we're all in the same boat" (112–4). The first sentence of our fragment *paraphrases* the words of Hesiod, the second *modifies* those of Semonides to bring them into conformity with the Hesiodic passage: Semonides had said that most men believe (or profess to believe) that their own wife is one of the few who are virtuous, whereas the speaker in our fragment is saying rather, in the words of John Stuart Mill twenty-three centuries later, that "one can, to an almost laughable degree, infer what a man's wife is like, from his opinions about women in general" (Mill, *The Subjection of Women* [1869], in *Collected Works* xxi [ed. J.M. Robson, Toronto, 1984] 278).

The passage reads like the conclusion of an argument, at or near the end of a longish rhesis; this is particularly indicated by the opening word *houtō* "so, therefore" (cf. *Ant.* 677–8, Aesch. *Supp.* 771, *Ag.* 1610, *Eum.* 739). It is argued in the Introduction (p. 284) that the speaker is probably Theseus, reviewing, and generalizing from, his experience of Phaedra, who had been successively a "good" and a "bad" wife.

3 each man ... particular experience: this explains why most men do not recognize the truth of the preceding statement.

3 speaks ... from his own particular experience: lit. "speaks of whatever he happens to have experienced" or "having experienced (i.e. on the basis of his experience), speaks of whatever he has come across"; the former construction gives a simpler sense, the latter makes it easier to account for the Greek word-order.

Q (681)

That no mortal is truly happy was a commonplace; cf. *OT* 1186–95, *OC* 1722–3, *Iliad* 24.525–533, Theognis 167–8, Aesch. *Cho.* 1018–20, Eur. fr. 45, 273, 661.1, Hdt. 1.32. It is a particularly appropriate reflection in situations where a person whose good fortune had seemed secure has met with unexpected disaster, and it is thus plausible, though far from certain, that in *Phaedra* it was uttered, towards the end of the play, in reference to what had befallen Theseus. The connective particle *d'* in line 1 suggests that the fragment is not a self-contained two-line speech but is part (very likely the end) of a rhesis, and this tells in favour of identifying the speaker as Theseus himself rather than the chorus-leader. The fragment may thus be the conclusion of the same speech from which fr. P (682) also survives.

R (689)

Greek *agos* normally means "pollution", but somewhere in our play, according to Hesychius, it was used in the sense of "something that averts pollution; a purificatory or expiatory offering" in which it is found at *Ant.* 775 and possibly at Aesch. *Cho.* 155. R. Parker, *Miasma* (Oxford, 1983) 6 n.22, in an important discussion of *agos*, finds its use in this sense "puzzling ... on any view"; it may perhaps have originated in ambiguous prepositional phrases such as *pros agos*, given that *pros* with accusative can mean, among other things, both "in opposition to" and "for the purpose of".

There is no sure clue to the context in which this word, in this sense, may have been used in *Phaedra*. We have seen reason, however (see Introduction, pp. 274, 283–4), to suspect that the Phaedra of Sophocles, like the Phaedra of Seneca, may before her suicide have cut a lock of her hair as a mourning-tribute to Hippolytus, thus providing an aetiology for the Trozenian ritual also referred to in *HippS* (1423–30) and probably in *HippK* (fr. U [446]); if so, it is likely that either she or a *deus ex machina* made explicit mention of this future ritual practice, and possible that it was explained as an act of expiation by women for the pollution which the violent death of Hippolytus, caused by a woman, might otherwise have brought upon them.

S (691)

The adverb *automolōs* "in the manner of a deserter; traitorously" (the latter is Hesychius' gloss) is found nowhere else before Byzantine times. The word is a choriamb and therefore must come from a lyric or anapaestic passage. Once again there is no sure clue to the context, though reference to allegedly treasonable designs by Hippolytus against his father (cf. fr. M [683], and see Introduction, p. 282) is an obvious possibility; it would be particularly appropriate to speak of this as desertion (sc. to the enemy camp) if the accusation were one of plotting with the malcontent Menestheus (see Introduction, p. 282 n.120).

It was, however, suggested by Nauck that the attribution of this word to Sophocles' *Phaedra* was due to a textual displacement in Hesychius, and that *Phaedra* was really the source, not of *automolōs*, but of another word cited by Hesychius four entries later, *autopaida* "own son". In the Bekker and Bachmann *Anecdota* (i 467.15 and i 168.3 respectively) this word is ascribed to Sophocles without naming a play (Soph. fr. 1029); in Hesychius (α8449) no author is named. If it is indeed the case that *autopaida* rather than *automolōs* is the word that appeared in our play, it will most probably have referred either (once again) to Hippolytus' alleged plotting against his father, or to his alleged rape of his father's wife, or to his father's fatal curse against him, and by emphasizing the father-son relationship will have emphasized also the horror of whichever violation of it was being spoken of. The only other appearance of *autopais* in tragedy (or indeed in any ancient text) is at *Trach.* 826, referring to Heracles "the very son of Zeus", and it is thus also possible that in *Phaedra* the reference may have been to Theseus as son of Poseidon: in *HippS*, on learning that his curse has been fulfilled, Theseus exclaims "So, Poseidon, you really were my father!" (1169–70), implying that he would not have been sure of this had his prayer not been answered.

T (692)

The adjective *apsephēs* "heedless" is known only from this fragment, though Hesychius (α8953) also records a participial form of a verb *apsephein* "be unconcerned". This word-family is based on *psephas* or *psephos* "darkness" (used by Pindar, according to Galen xix 763.6 Kühn; cf. *psephaios* "dark" in *Troilus* fr. Q [624a] and *psephennos* "obscure" in Pind. *Nem.* 3.41) and on the verb *psephein*, originally no doubt "darken" but mostly used, it seems, in the metaphorical sense "darken the mind of; cause grief, fear or worry to" (cf. Hesychius ψ141); it must once have been familiar enough in Athens to generate the personal name Apsephion "Dauntless", which was borne (for example) by the archon of 469/8 BC (who presided over the City Dionysia at which Sophocles won his first victory: Plut. *Cim.* 8.7). We cannot tell in what context *apsephes*, the neuter form of the adjective, was used in *Phaedra*.